The Figure of the Migrant in Contemporary European Cinema

The Figure of the Migrant in Contemporary European Cinema

Temenuga Trifonova

BLOOMSBURY ACADEMIC
NEW YORK · LONDON · OXFORD · NEW DELHI · SYDNEY

BLOOMSBURY ACADEMIC
Bloomsbury Publishing Inc
1385 Broadway, New York, NY 10018, USA
29 Earlsfort Terrace, Dublin 2, Ireland

BLOOMSBURY, BLOOMSBURY ACADEMIC and the Diana logo are trademarks of
Bloomsbury Publishing Plc

First published in the United States of America 2020
This paperback edition published in 2022

Copyright © Temenuga Trifonova, 2020

For legal purposes the Acknowledgments on p. vi constitute an extension
of this copyright page.

Cover design: Eleanor Rose
Cover image © Temenuga Trifonova

All rights reserved. No part of this publication may be reproduced or transmitted
in any form or by any means, electronic or mechanical, including photocopying,
recording, or any information storage or retrieval system, without prior
permission in writing from the publishers.

Bloomsbury Publishing Inc does not have any control over, or responsibility for, any
third-party websites referred to or in this book. All internet addresses given in this
book were correct at the time of going to press. The author and publisher regret any
inconvenience caused if addresses have changed or sites have ceased to exist,
but can accept no responsibility for any such changes.

Library of Congress Cataloging-in-Publication Data
Names: Trifonova, Temenuga, author.
Title: The figure of the migrant in contemporary European cinema / Temenuga Trifonova.
Description: New York: Bloomsbury Academic, 2020. | Includes
bibliographical references, filmography, and index.
Identifiers: LCCN 2020003357 | ISBN 9781501362514 (hardback) |
ISBN 9781501362491 (pdf) | ISBN 9781501362507 (ebook)
Subjects: LCSH: Immigrants in motion pictures. | Emigration and immigration
in motion pictures. | Motion pictures–Europe–History–21st century. |
Group identity–Europe–History–21st century.
Classification: LCC PN1995.9.E44 T75 2020 | DDC 791.43/652691–dc23
LC record available at https://lccn.loc.gov/2020003357

ISBN: HB: 978-1-5013-6251-4
PB: 978-1-5013-9296-2
ePDF: 978-1-5013-6249-1
eBook: 978-1-5013-6250-7

Typeset by Deanta Global Publishing Services, Chennai, India

To find out more about our authors and books visit www.bloomsbury.com
and sign up for our newsletters.

CONTENTS

Acknowledgments vi

Introduction: The Figure of the Migrant as a Challenge to the Idea of "European Identity"   1

1   The Migrant as a Symbolic Figure   61

2   Rethinking European Identity and European Cinema in the Age of Mass Migration: Between Abjection and Impersonation   113

3   The Figure of the Migrant and Cinematic Ethics   173

4   Crossovers Between the Cinema of Migration and the Cinema of Precarity   231

Bibliography 265
Index 279

ACKNOWLEDGMENTS

I would like to thank Le Studium Center for Advanced Studies in Tours, France, where I spent one year as a Marie Curie Research Fellow. In particular, I want to thank Aurelien Montagu, Sophie Gabillet, Oriane Mousset, and Marie-Frédérique Pellerin for their wonderful hospitality and generous support. Thank you to all the participants in the conference I organized at Le Studium—On the Ruins and Margins of European Identity in Cinema: European Identity in the Era of Mass Migration—for their thoughtful contributions: Thomas Elsaesser, Daniela Berghahn, Elizabeth Ezra, Mary Harrod, Mariana Liz, James Harvey, Dorota Ostrowska, Sandra Ponzanesi, Camil Ungureanu, and Delphine Robic-Diaz. Their ideas about European cinema in relation to migration and the migrant crisis have been crucial to developing my own arguments here. Finally, I want to thank the editorial team at Bloomsbury, particularly Katie Gallof and Erin Duffy. This book is dedicated to my mother.

Introduction

The Figure of the Migrant as a Challenge to the Idea of "European Identity"

Today, even as "Europe" has become an institution, it is less and less an idea. This observation serves as the underlying premise of a number of recent studies, mostly French, that set out to recover the idea of "Europe" that many now perceive as a meaningless term used by cultural elites and populist parties spanning the political spectrum and transcending the old cleavages between the right and the left. In the unambiguously titled *La merveilleuse histoire de l'Europe* (2019), Jean-Louis de Valmigere hopes to re-enchant the idea of "Europe" while Philippe Demenet, in *Ils ont rêvé l'Europe* (2019), attempts to revive the dream of "Europe" by retelling the story of how some of the most prominent European philosophers and writers have engaged with the idea of "Europe," from Erasmus, Voltaire, Rousseau, Goethe, and Kant to Barthes, Camus, and Levinas. Others return to 1989 as they try to understand why the promise that historical moment held for Europe never came to be and what can be done about it now. To the current political and ethical crisis described so vividly by Marion Van Renterghem in *Mon Europe, je t'aime moi non plus: 1989-2019* (2019), there is, Dominique Moisi insists in *Leçons de lumières* (2019), only one possible response, "l'esprit des Lumières." The desire to re-enchant the "idea" of Europe is often presented in terms of emancipating Europe from the "Dark Ages" into which it has been plunged, this time by the "dark forces" of neoliberalism: thus, in *Libéron l'Europe* (2019) and *Sauver l'Europe* (2017), Bruno Odent and Hubert Vedrine, respectively, call on Europeans to "save" Europe by fighting ordoliberalism on several crucial fronts, including democracy, climate change, peace, immigration, and social justice. Others call for disobedience as the only strategy of resistance to neoliberalism, the latter increasingly seen as an illness of which Europe has to be cured (*Cette Europe malade du néolibéralisme: L'urgence de désobéir* [Attac and La Fondation Copernic, 2019]). More pragmatically minded theorists, like Arnaud Jean-Michel, call on Euro-skeptics to reconsider their view of European integration by pointing out the practical advantages, in terms of population growth, military power, foreign policy, and the economy, of controlling nationalism and populism (*L'Europe Utile*, 2019).

The present book is based on the premise that a compelling case can be made for reorienting the study of contemporary European cinema around the figure of the migrant viewed both as a symbolic figure representing "postnational" citizenship, urbanization, and the gap between ethics and justice and as a figure occupying an increasingly central place in European cinema in general rather than only in what is usually called "migrant and diasporic cinema." I hope to demonstrate that amid the recent resurgence of populism and ethno-nationalism across Europe, European cinema remains a *site of resistance* by reviving the paradoxical philosophical foundations of the idea of "European identity" in *skepticism*, a suspiciousness toward and questioning of any preconceived notions and established political, moral, and religious authorities that is as constitutive of Europe's Enlightenment legacy as is the belief in reason and rationality.[1] Recent attempts to rethink "European cinema" in terms of "mythopoetics" and "thought experiment" (see Chapter 2) inscribe themselves squarely in this philosophical tradition—sketched out below—which posits skepticism and self-critique as constitutive of the idea of "Europe."

The history of the idea of "European identity" is characterized, on the one hand, by a constant oscillation between two poles, one instrumental or pragmatic (the Europe of norms), the other affective (the Europe of values and feelings) and, on the other hand, by a persisting, unresolved conflict between the belief in some ineffable European "spirit" or "ethos" and the outright rejection of any sort of "European identity." The idea of "European identity" has proven surprisingly resilient, as evidenced by various philosophical analyses of a fleeting yet allegedly recognizable "European structure of feeling," "the structure of feeling of the Old World, characterized by smug complacency on the one hand and by unrecognized nostalgia on the other."[2] At the basis of this "structure of feeling" is Europe's refusal to recognize its own colonial guilt, which comes back to haunt it in the form of a self-indulgent, quasi-existential feeling of loss whose real historical causes remain occluded: for example, Antoine Compagnon "diagnoses" Europeans with a sense of morbid ennui or spleen, something he sees dramatized in a specifically European "masochism or guilt which is the other side of colonialism and which now leads us to take the blame for everything that went wrong with the world."[3] The idea of a "European identity," "spirit," or "sensibility," resurfaces, as well, in scholarship on European cinema, from analyses of a specifically European chronotope to stylistic discussions of European cinema distinguished, according to Wendy Everett, by its "*ironic gaze* [which] seeks to provoke, challenge and disturb"[4] and by its fascination with the past, memory, history and identity. For Luisa

Passerini, too, *irony* or *performativity* is constitutive of European identity: "To act one or more parts on a stage composed of concentric circles—the city, the country, Europe, the world—cannot be separated from an attitude that is ironic, at least in part, toward the performance and one's role within it."[5] As John Caughie puts it, what all Europeans share is a common *ironic sensibility*, "the ability to say there is no absolute truth, there is no final vocabulary, there is no real identity, and yet . . . where the 'and yet . . .' forms the occulted desire concealed with the ironic distance."[6] The construction of the self, the writing and rewriting of the self, remains for many theorists who see European cinema as exploring the very *conditions of possibility of identity*, and thus as inherently self-reflexive, an essentially European idea.

In 2004 Polish filmmaker Stanislaw Mucha and his crew set out on a quest, through Central and Eastern Europe, for "the center of Europe"—a quest that served as a pretext for an exploration of what "Europe" means to its various inhabitants, especially those on Europe's periphery—only to find out that the inhabitants of precisely those places that claim the honorable status of Europe's "center" feel themselves the most disenfranchised members of this "Europe" to which they supposedly belong, living in an almost separate temporal realm and in places increasingly abandoned and forgotten. The further east Mucha and his crew travel in the documentary *Die Mitte/The Center* (2004), the more nebulous and amorphous identities and borders become, testifying to the central role internal and external migration and emigration have historically played in the construction of "Europe" to the hybrid and movable nature of "European identity." Although the film explores internal migration and the repercussions of the EU's post-1989 eastward expansion, the questions it raises about the borders of Europe and the elusive nature of "European identity" have hardly gone away; indeed, they have reemerged even more forcefully following the 2008 economic crisis and the ongoing migrant and refugee crisis.

Ironically, many of the arguments for and against immigration sound structurally similar, the difference between them stemming from what aspect of the issue those making the argument choose to emphasize. For instance, while those in favor of open borders demand that Europe reflect on its own past, reminding us of the millions of Europeans who fled persecution and intolerance in the United States and Canada in the course of the twentieth century, anti-immigrationists point out that Europe's history has been generally one of emigration rather than immigration. Most of the debates around immigration to Europe revolve around several key issues, including the nature and importance of Europe's core Enlightenment values, the growing demographic, environmental, and economic challenges Europe is facing, the decline of solidarity within the EU, the gradual mainstreaming of populist and far right political movements and parties across the continent, the dangers of human trafficking, the perceived risks of radicalization, extremism and terrorism, and the role of the EU in an increasingly unstable, globalized world.

Those advocating hard borders and limits on integration and settlement initiatives argue that since welcoming refugees is "unpopular" with voters, letting them in would undermine European democracy. Although few, if any, of those opposing immigration base their arguments on explicitly racist beliefs, they all subscribe to a new form of cultural racism that construes non-European refugees and migrants as terrorists and sexual deviants, a threat to "wholesome Christian values," and a burden on the welfare state. Curbing the migrant "flow" is seen as the only, and absolutely necessary, way of bolstering Europe's security and identity and tackling the problem of the mafia's increasing involvement in large-scale migrant trafficking. Rather than acknowledge the right to immigrate as a basic human right, anti-immigrationists prefer to stress the basic right of every human collective—"the nation" being the exemplary case here—to defend itself against "invasion," whether in the form of soldiers or migrants, the latter two being apparently indistinguishable. This basic right to self-protection justifies the adoption of any type of immigration policy the nation-state deems necessary, including policies that explicitly discriminate against immigrants on the basis of religion, ethnicity, culture, or sexual identity. The assumption is that non-European—African and Middle Eastern—migrants and refugees are culturally, religiously and linguistically too different from Europeans and thus not only unable to integrate but actually posing a threat to the assumed internal coherence of the national body. For anti-immigrationists, the sheer number of refugees and migrants (which is negligible compared to Europe's total population) represents a burden on Europe's social services, health and educational systems, and housing departments, while the absence of any long-term agreements among EU members about sharing that burden places undue pressure on certain countries, thereby undermining solidarity within the EU. Anti-immigrationists continually draw attention to what they see as the failure of Europe's political elite to address the growing economic anxiety among low-skilled European workers who feel threatened and displaced by migrants. Finally, they point out that welcoming refugees who are fleeing war in their native land is, in the long run, not in their best interest since once they have settled down in Europe they will be less likely to return to their homeland and actively participate in the postwar reconstruction effort (this, of course, presumes that it is possible to project the end of the war in question). The solution proposed by the World Bank is to develop legal channels of migration based on the demands of the labor market, a solution premised on stricter border controls, detailed repatriation agreements, more intrusive measures against hiring "illegal" migrants, and a more reliable method for screening "genuine asylum seekers" from "merely economic migrants," whose claims are assumed to be, by definition, bogus.

The argument in favor of open borders is firmly rooted in the belief that we should uphold Europe's core values of tolerance, freedom, compassion, solidarity, and democracy. Welcoming refugees and migrants is not just a matter of respecting international laws, including the Geneva Convention and other international agreements, but an implied moral duty we Europeans share toward fellow human beings. Defending immigration as a basic human right is one way of curbing the spread of populist and xenophobic beliefs that have been taken over by center-right or centrist parties (e.g., in Sweden, the Netherlands, France, and Denmark). Closing the borders to refugees and migrants would not, in fact, "bolster" Europe's security—as is well-known, almost all terrorist attacks in Europe have been executed by European citizens or residents. Non-state actors, such as nongovernmental organizations, businesses, and city leaders all see the benefits of migration in terms of economic growth and diversity. In addition to being a powerful tool for fighting global poverty (migrants from poor countries earn higher wages compared to what they would have earned back home, which allows them to support their families) migration is one obvious way to deal with Europe's rapidly shrinking native population and declining workforce. As history has shown over and over again societies that welcome migrants from different religious, ethnic, linguistic, and cultural backgrounds are technologically, culturally, and intellectually more advanced.

The purpose of this Introduction is—following a brief survey of the historical, philosophical, religious, racial, and political foundations of the idea of "Europe"—to identify the ways in which globalized migration has challenged the idea of "European identity" before analyzing, in the following chapters, the role European cinema has played in rethinking "European identity" as a philosophical idea rather than an entity with objectively existing and clearly definable or "recoverable" historical *roots/origins*.

1 Historical and Philosophical Foundations of the Idea of "European Identity": Skepticism as "Proof" of the Existence of a "European Identity"

To grasp the profound ambiguity pervading attempts to define "European identity," including European identity in cinema, one need only juxtapose the traditional characteristics of "Europeanness" deriving from the continent's founding philosophical and religious traditions, including Christianity, Roman law, and the Enlightenment—here "Europeanness" is defined in relation to the concepts of the polis, citizenship, democracy, rationalism, universality, and cosmopolitanism—with the immense contradictions underlying the concept of "Europeanness" defined in relation to political and economic circumstances. Thus, while during the first half of the twentieth century, the two world wars and the processes of decolonization associated

"Europeanness" with self-destruction and decline as a world power, and European integration processes since the 1960s promoted an association of "Europeanness" with a shared *cultural* identity, with the start of the debt crisis in the Euro-zone the pendulum has swung from a celebration of a shared European identity to an economically based notion of "European" that denies "Europeanness" to those without euros.[7]

A recurring theme in historical and philosophical writings on Europe is the paradoxical idea that to be European is to doubt that there is something like "European identity." In his introduction to Max Beloff's *Europe and the Europeans: A Report Prepared at the Request of the Council of Europe* (1957), Denis de Rougemont underscores the *doubt* in the existence of a European identity expressed by all contributors to the report:

> Certainly there is nothing more European than these doubts and this skepticism—this habit of questioning things again, of retreating from platitudes and of insisting upon differences. [. . .] But did those who adopted [this attitude of mind] fully understand that they were thereby illustrating one of these major common characteristics which they were occupying themselves with calling into question? [. . .] Would not the European be in fact this strange man who manifests himself as a European precisely in the measure in which he doubts it?[8]

Ironically, to counter those who argue that "Europe" is only an idea or an "expression" rather than a reality, de Rougemont compares the difficulty of locating the "origins" of Europe to the difficulty of establishing the origin of a work of art, a *fiction*, thus offering the perfect demonstration of the skepticism he identifies as quintessentially European:

> Is [the work of art, or "Europe"] born on the day when its outline is sketched, when the order for it is received, or when its climate of feeling is first felt? Or is it the hour when its first page was written, the first stroke of the brush applied to the canvas, or the first harmony recorded? Would it not rather be the moment of a particular intuition several years before?[9]

The idea that the *critique* of the concept of identity is *constitutive* of European identity pops up in a wide range of theoretical discussions of Europe. Paul Gifford, for instance, describes European identity in terms of "a highly developed critical reflexivity, marked by relativism, representationalism and constructivism, motivated by some form of attachment to a decentered, pointillistic . . . form of sense-making; a set of attitudes often expressed as a horror of 'closure' or a mistrust of 'depth' and of organic roots."[10] Reviving Husserl's argument that the birth of "the European spirit" can be traced back to ancient Greece when the *theoretical* approach to life—

"reason" or "philosophy"—was born, Cornelius Castoriadis posits Greece (and implicitly Europe) as the origin of philosophy *as such*, the latter being nothing but the constant self-questioning of the very legitimacy of thought. For Castoriadis, the Greek polis and the creation of democracy embody a particularly European way of being in the world that he describes, once again, in terms of *skepticism*, the rejection of any ultimate foundation for anything, including knowledge, inasmuch as since Plato "it has been known that every demonstration presupposes something which is not demonstrable."[11] In a formulation reminiscent of de Rougemont's passage quoted earlier, Castoriadis proposes that it is only "Greco-Westerners" (Europeans) who, by developing rational arguments for rejecting the European tradition, "confirm *eo ipso* this tradition and that they belong to it."[12] Castoriadis's concept of "Europe" is informed by his metaphysical account of Being: he thinks Europe in the same terms he thinks Being, that is, in terms of chaos, abyss, and groundlessness understood positively as the infinite potential for change and reinvention.[13]

Michael Herzfeld offers a less utopian perspective on Europe's Greco-Roman roots when he reminds us of the core-periphery tensions in the definition of European identity embodied precisely by Greece, which is, at one and the same time, "the European's spiritual cradle and . . . the Orientalized 'bad child' of the EU," "the idealized central source and the contested border of Europe itself."[14] Challenging Castoriadis's celebration of Greek (European) thought and democracy Herzfeld points out the irony of European individualism as necessarily a *conformist* concept, grounded as it is in the relationship between property ownership and selfhood. In *Les Trois Europes* (1985), historian Jeno Szucs also draws attention to the core-periphery tension within definitions of "Europe," although for him it is Central East Europe (Poland, Hungary, and Bohemia) rather than Greece that constitutes the "core" in relationship to which the other two "Europes"—Western and Eastern—define themselves.[15] In *The Future of Nostalgia* (2002), Svetlana Boym historicizes this division of Europe, reminding us that while from antiquity to the Renaissance the division between North and South was the central one, during the Enlightenment the division of Europe into East and West became more prominent as Eastern Europe became increasingly excluded from the civilized world.

Philosopher Remi Braque takes an even more radical stance on the core-periphery tension underlying definitions of European identity, describing it as "ex-centric," lacking a core or a unique origin: "Europe's self-image has always pointed to something else that existed before it [e.g., the Judeo-Christian tradition, the Greco-Roman tradition]. From a religious point of view Christianity grew out of Judaism, and politically the Roman-republican tradition was inspired by the Greek democracy of the city-states."[16] In *Europe and the Europeans*, produced at the request of the Council of Europe for a historical rather than a merely geographical definition of

Europe, Beloff had already argued that a historical definition cannot afford to exclude parts like "the Iberian peninsula, despite its involvement in the Muslim world and its affinities with Africa, the parts of the former 'alien Ottoman Empire' (Romania, Albania, Bulgaria), Greece or the remainder of the Balkan peninsula, or Poland and Bohemia, or even nations outside of Europe that have been shaped by European civilization such as Israel";[17] even Russia should be considered part of "the European family." He inevitably runs into definitional difficulties for if the definition of "Europe" includes all nations that have been influenced by European civilization, the whole world would have to be called "European." Beloff addresses this challenge by identifying this openness of European civilization to outside influences as its most distinguishing mark. However, if "neither Europe's present nor its past can be understood in purely European terms"[18] Europe appears to have no identity of its own, always "transcending" itself: for example, capitalism and the Industrial Revolution, socialism and the welfare state, are all European inventions that have spread beyond Europe.[19] Ultimately, in place of a definition Beloff simply underscores Europe's "importance as a general repository of the achievements of humanity and of its records. [. . .] Europe could then be defined in part by its sense of its own history."[20] In this "meta-definition" Europe emerges as nothing less than *an archive of the world*, a self-reflexive consciousness of its own (and of the world's) past. Like Braque and Beloff, historian Anthony Pagden locates the origin of Europe *outside* it, in Asia, reminding us that while in the popular version of Europe's "origin story," Europe was the result of "divine appropriation" (the abduction of Europa by Zeus), in mythopoeic history "'divine appropriation' becomes transformed into "a hatred between two continents [Europa being an Asian woman], a hatred that would burn steadily down the centuries, as the Trojans were succeeded by the Phoenicians, the Phoenicians by the Ottoman Turks, and the Turks by Russians."[21]

Complementing such views of "Europe" as *ex-centric* are reflections on European identity as synonymous with exile, discussions of nostalgia as a specifically European experience, and arguments about the concept of "the Other" as a uniquely European one. Tracing poststructuralist theories of subjectivity as essentially incomplete, fragmented, and estranged from itself back to Jewish and Christian views of humanity, John Peters locates the origins of contemporary notions of exile, nomadism, and diaspora in the Hebrew Bible, ancient Greece, and Christianity, concluding that "exile is, perhaps, the central story told in European civilization: the human existence as exile from God, the garden of Eden, the homeland, the womb, or even oneself."[22] Arguably, this tendency to appropriate and rebrand a universal experience—such as exile—as "quintessentially European" is itself typically European. For instance, although in their introduction to *Europe and Love in Cinema* (2012) the editors profess a desire to challenge the Eurocentric idea of romantic love as a defining characteristic of European culture that makes it "superior" to other cultures, by describing the European idea of romantic love as a "refined kind of 'impossible love' characterized by absence and lack,"[23] they actually reaffirm a Eurocentric view of "absence" and "lack" as supposedly "European" concepts reflecting specifically "European" experiences.

While the idea of "the Other" is central to the construction of any identity some have argued that "the Other" is a specifically European concept. According to Stuart Hall, for instance, "otherness was from the beginning an invention of European ways of seeing and representing difference. [Europe] has been reinventing 'the Rest' ever since."[24] Although Hall's statement may sound like an acknowledgment of Eurocentrism, it actually disguises an even deeper Eurocentrism, which comes to the fore in Anthony Pagden's survey, in *The Idea of Europe* (2002), of the evolution of the concept of the "Other" in the construction of European identity from the Christian crusades against Moors and Ottomans to the more recent Islamophobic formulations in response to South to North migration. Discussing the eighteenth-century Venetian artist Giambattista Tiepolo's *Four Continents,* Pagden endorses Svetlana Alpers and Michael Baxandall's reading of the artist's work as a confirmation of the idea that "to look at Europe one should look from Europe" inasmuch as Tiepolo depicts Asia, Africa, and America only in their relation to Europe, "the rubric, the initial code."[25] Based on this reading of Tiepolo, Pagden proceeds to argue that "Europeans are unusual in sharing . . . a sense that it might be possible to belong to something larger than the family, the tribe, the community or the nation yet smaller and more culturally specific than 'humanity.'"[26] Pagden's reasoning reflects a neocolonial stance disguised as a postcolonial critique of Eurocentrism: if the peoples of Uganda or Congo are aware of belonging to a continent called "Africa," he claims, it is only as a result of European colonization and racism, which have created among them this self-awareness. In short, the *relational concept of identity*, according to Pagden, is *uniquely European.*

The veiled Eurocentrism in Paul Gifford's reading of the role of interperceptions in the construction of identity should, like Pagden's, give us pause. Gifford traces the origins of the idea of "the Other" back to the "father" of modern philosophy, reminding us that for Descartes, "our own identity is not . . . solid or monolithic; we contain a vast hidden shadow of otherness—an unconscious persona or shadow self conceived in Freudian terms, the negativities or knots of which are projected onto the fellow human being(s) opposite whom we then designate as strange and as 'strangers.'"[27] Drawing upon Ricoeur's theory of narrative identity, which posits "identity" as "a representational construct discovered or created at the point where the shared memory of a narrativized past helps to articulate a common project which is bonding and engages a common future,"[28] Gifford identifies the book of Genesis as the foundational text (in a formative and historico-genetic sense) of the European mind, and the story of Adam and Eve as containing the paradigmatic signifier of Otherness—sexual difference—which he reads as providing an anthropological definition of "identity" based on relationality rather than on singularity or essence. Like Pagden, Gifford presents the European idea of "Otherness" derived from the Bible as somehow more "enlightened" or "ethical" insofar as it recognizes *the relationality of identity*.

2 Religious Foundations of the Idea of "European Identity"

Two important books came out in 1957, both written by British historians, both downplaying the importance of the religious matrix of Europe's identity: Max Beloff's *Europe and the Europeans* and Denys Hay's *Europe: The Emergence of an Idea*. In opposition to earlier historians, notably Toynbee, Beloff considers the idea of Europe as a religious unity, for all intents and purposes, groundless: to say that Europe was held together by Catholic Christianity, he asserts, is to ignore both the significance for the Middle Ages of the Byzantine Empire, which, until the Fourth Crusade, was the main Christian State in the world, and the fact that far from being unified the medieval empire was actually a medley of kingdoms and city states.[29] Denys Hay largely agrees, observing that although the idea of "Christendom" had a particular advantage inasmuch as it provided something like a general language (Latin) and a common adversary (Islamic Asia and North Africa) as a way of compensating for the serious difficulties of establishing Europe's geographical borders, precisely because of its potentially universal nature "Christendom" was also weak as an inspiration. Taking to task other historians, notably Bernard Voyenne, for their sweeping, poetic generalizations about the past, Hay calls for a sober approach to the study of European identity, emphasizing the rational, secular, and internationalist strands of European inheritance. In his *Histoire de l'idée européene* (1964) Voyenne writes:

> L'idée de l'Europe ne doit pas être trop choisie par la géographie: ce serait plutôt par la géographie de son serviteur selon le temps et les circonstances. [. . .] L'Europe n'a pas de frontières, elle a un visage, et personne ne s'est trompée. Il ne faut pas craindre d'ajouter . . . quelle a une a ame. [. . .] L'idée n'était pas si elle s'était faite dans une réalité qu'elle transcende et ne fait pas, pourtant, elle ne peur pas se passer. Inversement, elle est immanente à ce moulin, elle s'est dégagée peu à peu comme le fruit de la graine.[30]

Dismissing this lyrical and naively optimistic image of Europe, Hay insists that if there is any way Europe could be considered an entity it would be found "in the severe realities of 20th century economic and military power, not in those transcendental legacies of Greece and Romania and Christendom often invoked by contemporary publicists."[31] Although he traces the origins of the different *emotional* content with which the continents had been invested since the seventh century back to chapters 9 and 10 of Genesis—Japheth's progeny are allocated to Europe, Ham's to Africa, and Shem's to the East—Hay emphasizes the development of a specifically *territorial*—rather than *religious* or *spiritual*—notion of Christianity. What held Europe together from the fourteenth century onward, with the church and the empire losing their power even as the area of Christendom extended to cover most of the continent, was not Christianity and the church but political and economic relations made possible by new types of cartography, particularly by the emergence of *portolani*, which, unlike older maps, indicated the political authority of different territories, marking the areas of Muslim domination with the Crescent of Islam to prevent traveling Christians from inadvertently entering Islamic territory.[32]

In the last several decades, however, scholars have begun to resensitize us to the persistent importance of Christianity to the idea of "European identity." In her reappraisal of Hay's seminal study Jane Pettegree faults Hay for overemphasizing the secular and rational definition of Europe, while underestimating the importance of religious and transnational ideologies in the period after the Middle Ages. "Christendom" came to be replaced by "Europe" as a territorial term, she claims, not because faith lost its importance but because "the over-emphatic application of the term to literal regional geography was gradually revealed to generate disunity rather than social cohesion."[33] At the same time, the role of Islam in Europe's cultural legacy is now increasingly recognized, although too often such recognition remains limited to an acknowledgment of Islam as a "carrier" civilization merely responsible for transmitting Greek and Roman values. Thus, although Wolfgang Huber declares that "anyone referring to Europe's Christian roots must consider its relationship to the antique legacy together with the Jewish and Islamic influences on the development of Europe,"[34] he still maintains that "Europe has Greece to thank for the spirit of philosophy, the awakening to science, the openness to the arts," a legacy merely "passed on" to us "by medieval Islam."[35] Gerard Delanty, however, explicitly acknowledges the constitutive role played by Islam in the construction of European identity, arguing that if there is one thing that remains unvarying in the discourse of Europe, it is not the unity of its history but its adversity to Islam, making Islam Europe's single most important "Other."[36]

Although it is widely assumed that we now live in a secular Europe, secularism is not the end of religion.[37] As Hent de Vries has shown, the sacralization of the principles of secularism is part of a larger process, triggered by globalization, of the decoupling of religion and territory, of religion and culture, the deterritorialization of religion, its transformation into something "abstract and formal, ethereal and virtual, everywhere and nowhere,"[38] with the result that "religiosity" (the manner in which the believer lives her relationship to religion) is now far more important than religion.[39] What brings together the diverse political formations affirming the idea of Islam's incompatibility with the West, according to Meyda Yegenoglu, is not the critique of Islam's failure to separate the religious from the political—which was, historically, essential to the construction of Islam as "the Other"—but rather the critique of Islam's *excessive religiosity* seen as an ostentatious intrusion into the "European way of life" so that the exclusion of Islam now takes place through "a process that registers religion as something more than religion and attests to religion's becoming cultural."[40] Underscoring the increased prominence of religion in the public and political sphere, Yegenoglu challenges the assumed hegemonic narrative of secularism and its alleged separation between the secular and the religious, proposing instead to supplement the idea of "the return of the religious," where "the religious" has been exclusively identified with Islam, with an analysis of the "return of Christianity," which is perhaps less visible since it is displaced onto the issue of cultural difference. Uncovering the unacknowledged theological roots of the concept of secularism demonstrates that it is not only the concept of the secular but the very distinction between the religious and the secular that is produced by the latter, demonstrating the impossibility of excluding the religious from the realm of ethics, morality, and nationality.

For Catherine Wheatley, too, the defining distinction between cultures today is one of faith and religion—we may be living in a secular Europe, but "it is nonetheless a Christian secular Europe."[41] Thus, although European cinema claims to be secular, it is suffused with Christian iconography and symbolism, invoking Christianity not through narrative but through what Paul Schrader calls a "transcendental style," and through the recurrence of questions of guilt, responsibility, and forgiveness. Peter O'Brien warns against the dangerous conflation of Christianity with liberalism and the Christian favoritism it has given rise to, as evidenced by former vice president of the European Parliament Mario Mauro's claim that "Europe will be Christian or it will not be at all."[42] With the need to "protect" Christianity from the messianic nature of "new Islamic terrorism" regularly presented as a need to protect liberal values, secular liberal values are intentionally conflated with Christianity on the assumption that modern universal liberal values, such as freedom and equality, "have been foreshadowed in a longer Judeo-Christian heritage involving such important notions as the equality of all persons before God."[43]

Recent intersectional studies of immigration, religion, and class confirm the central role religion plays in contemporary debates on Europe: political sociologists Frederic Gonthier and Pierre Brechon have shown that the most salient and most pronounced polarization between Europeans in terms of their values becomes evident when socioeconomic status is crisscrossed with religious identity.⁴⁴ Similarly, debates about references to a common Christian legacy in the draft of the European constitution reflect a renewed interest in the religious roots of European identity. Chiara Bottici and Benoit Challand's survey of a series of treaties from the beginning of the EU project to the present suggests that religious differences between Western Catholic/ Protestant and Eastern Orthodox traditions were never an issue when Romania and Bulgaria, both predominantly Orthodox, joined the EU, and none of the legal documents around Turkey's first requests to join the EEC (dating back to the 1950s) contain a single reference to "Islam" or "religion." Arguably, Europe's migrant crisis has contributed to the movement of what was before a peripheral issue to the center of heated public debate. The response of Christianity to the migrant crisis has been described in terms of two opposite theologies of "belonging" and "believing," the former stressing "belonging" (where defending Christian culture from "the Other" is more important than faith), the latter emphasizing "believing" (where faith, and thus care for "the Other," is more important than defending Christian culture). The first theology has given rise to the construction of Islam as "the Other" on the basis of an erroneous assumption that Christianity can be secular or that secularism can be Christian.⁴⁵ This controversial idea continues to inform the work of historians like Anthony Pagden, who not only insists on the supposedly seamless continuity between Europe's "Greco-Roman" and "Judeo-Christian" traditions but also on the Christian basis of Europe's Enlightenment legacy, arguing that the Enlightenment idea of modern pluralism, however secularized, "depends, as does any idea of the unity of European culture, upon a continuing Christian tradition."⁴⁶

3 Racial Foundations of the Idea of "European Identity"

Just as we don't live in a "post-secular" Europe we don't live in a "post-racial" Europe—tellingly, one critical response to the European migrant crisis was to invoke an analogy with the African American civil rights struggle by insisting that "Migrant Lives Matter." The term "European" has retained its association with whiteness "despite the fact that Europe's population has been 'hybridized,' 'creolized' and 'colored' by waves of non-white, non-Christian migrants throughout its history,"⁴⁷ while UN documents and World Bank demographic figures reveal the number of black Europeans to be close to 20 million.⁴⁸ Indeed, as Nicholas de Genova has argued, the question of Europe's borders is deeply imbricated in "a global (postcolonial) politics of race that redraws the proverbial color line and refortifies Europeanness as a racial formation of whiteness."⁴⁹ It is along the southeastern borders of Europe—the parts that were previously part of the Ottoman Empire and that have a substantial Muslim population—that cultural differences are implicitly converted into racial ones, so that "Europeanness" is conceived as a series of concentric circles starting from a white center and extending outward into a series of "'not-quite-white' borderland identities."[50]

One reason it has been difficult to raise the issue of race in the European context, according to Yegenoglu, is that when Europe asks itself, with reference to the Holocaust, "how did we manage to do it to people who are (pretty much) like us, to those who were among us, and indeed who are us?"[51] this formulation already suggests the possibility of doing it to people who are actually different; in fact, the only reason the condemnation of the Holocaust led to the irreversible rejection of genocide is because it affected "white" Europeans. To re-politicize the discussion of race it is necessary to uncover "the embeddedness of the idea of 'race' in the structures of the modern state, which has [so far] been masked by the dominant narrative of the Holocaust"[52] and by the displacement of the issue of race onto that of *cultural* difference, parallel to the displacement of the issue of religion onto that of culture. It is only in the last couple of decades that multiculturalism has become discredited as "an euphemism for colonialist and racialist categories,"[53] a form of "cultural essentialism," or an "inverted, self-referential form of racism, a racism with a distance."[54] "Immigration" has now become the most recent term for "race," and European citizens' attitudes toward immigrants represent a new form of racism described by Étienne Balibar and Immanuel Wallerstein as "benign, cultural or differentialist neo-racism"[55]—exemplified by anti-Semitism, Arabphobia,[56] or the systematic confusion of "Arabness" and "Islamicism"—which has displaced the older, more overt form of biological racism. On the other hand, the singling out of the migrant as a victim of racism fails to reflect the range of more implicit forms of racism prevalent in Europe, from the racism between Northerners and Southerners in Italy or Flemish and Walloons in Belgium to general racism against the Roma.[57]

Neo-racism represents one instance of Freud's notion of "the narcissism of minor differences" insofar as it is produced by, and reproduces itself as, a constant need for classifying and reclassifying, a relentless search for new and more precise criteria to tell "them" from "us." Tracing the origins of neo-racism back to anti-Semitism, which was already a culturalist racism rather than being based solely on pseudo-biological grounds,[58] Balibar underscores the class-based character of anti-immigrant racism,[59] which is predicated on a maximum identification between class and ethnic origin, an identification inherent in the proletariat's condition of constant mobility—interregional, international, and intercontinental—in search of employment. While the working class does not have a permanent identity but is constantly under construction in response to the changing availability and conditions of work and to the movement of capital, class-based racism creates the illusion of "the proletariat" as a concrete and permanent identity precisely so as to deny it social mobility. Neo-racism—including anti-immigrant racism—is thus a product of the contradictory logic of the accumulation of capital, whose goal is to destabilize permanently the conditions of production (the precarization of labor and the proletarization of workers) while, at the same time, creating the illusion of a "hereditary" class identity impossible to transcend. White intellectuals' response to neo-racism has too often been driven by the same white guilt—often indistinguishable from moral responsibility—underlying their response to the older type of biological racism. To address the problem of "white guilt," Stuart Hall has proposed redefining the concept of "race" by extending it beyond the idea of skin color to highlight the solidarity between ethnic groups with shared experiences of social marginalization and oppression: "Black is not a question of pigmentation. The Black I am talking about is a historical category, a political category, a cultural category. [. . .] We have to create an equivalence between how people look and what their histories are."[60] Most of the films I examine later in this book can be fruitfully discussed precisely through such an extended notion of "race," which lets us grasp the structural and affective similarities in the experiences of Europeans and nonEuropeans, migrants and non-migrants (Chapter 4).

4 Political Foundations of the Idea of "European Identity"

We can identify two main stages in the scholarship on the political idea of Europe: first, from the postwar period to the 1960s, and second, from the late 1980s to the present day. Influenced by the aftermath of the Second World War and the signing of the Treaty of Rome, the literature produced during the first period can be divided into historical and political approaches, depending on whether it discusses the idea of Europe as a continent with cultural significance (generally locating the origins of "Europe" in the values of the French Enlightenment, or in a combination of Greek-Latin, Jewish-Christian, and Byzantine components), or reflects on the significance of the EEC. The literature of the second stage has been shaped by discussions about the Maastricht Treaty and the growing importance of culture within the EEC.[61]

Heikki Mikkeli traces the political idea of Europe back to utopian novels of the Renaissance, which envisioned peace as the product of alliances between European nations.[62] Although some have argued that the very idea of "identity" and its cognate terms "individualization" and "individuation" derives from Europe's Christian heritage,[63] it was during the Enlightenment that the notion of "Europe" as a political and philosophical ideal, and of Europe as a civilization of peace, democracy, and rationality really gained currency, supplanting the idea of Christian universalism. Recently, the stereotypical notion of "European identity" as "individualist" has come under attack, with Michael Herzfeld exposing its basis in the "conventional self-view of Europeans as autonomous selves possessing discrete property and distinctive properties,"[64] a telling formulation betraying the colonialist roots of the European notion of "identity" understood in terms of property ownership (note the semantic shift from "possessing property" to "possessing a distinctive property," the property of "being European"). Ginette Verstraete has similarly drawn attention to the Eurocentric, colonialist undertones of the Enlightenment/cosmopolitan notion of "Europe." Starting with Kant the notion of Europe based on a trans-European capitalist expansion presupposed an idea of Europe as literally and figuratively "outside itself," with Europe defined "as a distance in time and place."[65] In fact, the ex-centricity constitutive of the idea of "Europe" simply disguises the inherently incomplete nature of the colonialist project that is "European civilization." Criticizing the usually celebratory take on Kant's *Perpetual Peace* (1795)—which, according to Anthony Pagden, has served as a regulative idea in political thought and action over the last several centuries, marking the transition from the idea of empire to federation—political scientist James Tully underscores the cultural imperialism inherent in the Kantian idea of free states and federation, which, far from being "culturally neutral . . . is [in fact] the bearer of processes of a homogenizing or assimilating European cultural identity."[66]

If the main topic of debate during the period 1830–80 were the theoretical and juridical grounds for a federalist Europe, at the turn of the century the focus shifted to the problem of combining the idea of freedom with the hierarchical structure of European administration, the challenge now being to decide at what level political decisions ought to be made (anticipating later debates around the EU's democratic deficit and the principle of subsidiarity in decision-making). The most important movement for a European union in the early twentieth century was the Pan-European movement led by Richard Coudenhove-Kalegri who proposed, in *Pan-Europe* (1923), that the only way to counter Europe's marginalization on the global scene was through the establishment of a European federation rooted in Europe's cultural and religious unity.[67] With the rise of National Socialism in Germany, however, the Pan-European movement faded into oblivion. The history of European integration since 1945 has been driven by two conflicting visions of Europe, a federalist one embodied in supranational institutions, and an inter-governmentalist one based on the desire to preserve national identity and sovereignty. By the end of the 1960s the various models of European integration shared a vision of Europe as a buffer zone between two superpowers (the United States and the Soviet Union) without, however, giving any precise definition of the EU's political objective.[68]

The scholarship on Europe emerging since the beginning of the new millennium has been mostly preoccupied with political and institutional, rather than cultural-historical, conceptions of Europe—for example, Étienne Balibar's *We, the People of Europe: Reflections on Transnational Citizenship* (2003), Mabel Berezin and Martin Schain's *Europe without Borders: Remapping Territory, Citizenship, and Identity in a Transnational Age* (2004), and Richard Hermann, Thomas Risse-Kappen, and Marilynn Brewer's *Transnational Identities: Becoming European in the EU* (2004) examine the notion of borders, territory, and citizenship—or with the role of myths and symbols in the construction of European identity [e.g., Luisa Passerini's *Images and Myths of Europe* (2003) and Michael Wintle's *The Image of Europe: Visualizing Europe in Cartography and Iconography throughout the Ages* (2009)]. There seems to be a shift from strictly historical to political, philosophical, ethical, and empirical approaches, with scholars becoming increasingly interested in reexamining the legacy of the Enlightenment, the affective cartography of Europe, the concepts of community/the common, the political idea of "Europe," and the place of religion in public life. In the last several decades there has been a strong tendency to conflate debates about "European identity" with debates about "European integration" and "the EU." The territorial recalibration following the establishment of the EU has led many scholars to declare the emergence of a "postnational" citizenship based on universal human rights rather than on the rights of persons as members of nation-states.[69] Others, however, have warned that "postnationalism," with its stress on personhood and human rights rather than citizenship rights, may actually threaten the legal rights of migrants and refugees and contribute to the decline of social solidarity by overemphasizing rights at the expense of responsibilities. From this point of view "transnational" is a more appropriate term than "postnational" insofar as one is "European," as defined by the EU, only if one is a member of a EU member state.

There is no shortage of studies decrying the *affectively neutral* nature of the EU[70] and of European integration often attributed to the end of the Cold War and the collapse of the Soviet Union, which "may have only left in place two ideologies in Europe: nationalism and the market."[71] Not only has the process of European integration produced new inequalities but, according to many, it has hardly resulted in a real form of solidarity, being instead just a reflection of "broader cultural and market flows and common circumstances," so that "the ways in which Europeans are most similar, and are growing more similar, are not specifically European."[72] In his study of the anthropology of the EU Marc Abeles shows that the very structure of the EU's governing bodies precludes the possibility for transparent political debate inasmuch as they are characterized by deterritorialization, nomadism, and multilingualism, which give rise to literal mistranslations and irreconcilable differences in the political rhetoric mobilized by different civil servants.[73] In reality, Abeles argues, the EU's governing bodies are involved not in the production of a European identity but in what he dismissively calls "Europe-building," which is nothing but "lobbying, bargaining and compromising" rather than meaningful political debate. Abeles does manage to tease out one positive aspect of this process of "building" or "tinkering with" Europe, observing that it forces people to reflect on their own conception of politics and identity; in short, one could perhaps argue that "Europe-building" fulfills a *(positive) deconstructionist purpose.*

Given that, as has become abundantly clear, the EU's bare form of instrumental legitimacy cannot provide the "glue" necessary for a shared European identity, Bottici and Challand have argued for a more complex form of legitimacy based on some form of common European identity that is, however, not merely cultural so as to avoid both the historicist fallacy, "which presents the future as always conforming to the past," and the culturalist fallacy, "which flattens the identity of a political body into its supposed cultural roots."[74] Cultural identity is not inherited passively but actively produced and open to change—as Habermas points out, "history can only propose as candidates certain experiences as signifiers of a common identity because, without a *conscious reappropriation of them*, historical events would never be able to generate identity."[75] Accordingly, Bottici and Challand opt for the term "identification," rather than "identity," reminding us that "there can be no identity without a process of self-identification through self-recognition."[76] It should be remembered, however, that such "self-recognitions" are necessarily shaped by national self-perception and historical memory: for instance, while the Second World War and coming to terms with the communist past remain the two most salient narratives for West Germans and East Germans, respectively, Britain's attitude toward European integration is shaped by Britain's colonial history and its anxiety over the loss of sovereignty and national identity.[77] The very idea of "Eurohistory" is differently inflected by the histories of individual nations: for example, the German idea of "Europeanness" and "Eurohistory" is based on a particularly German understanding of the "Other" as located not in another part of the world (as it is for France) but in Germany's own militaristic past and balance of power.[78] In short, the building of "Europe" is a process not just of harmonization and integration but also of constant legitimization as evidenced by the rewriting of national histories to incorporate the history of "the idea of Europe."

Recent studies of European identity are distinguished by a growing investment in the affective and symbolic, rather than institutional, aspects of European identity. Macro studies of European identity dealing with thousands of people and relying solely on data provided by Euro-barometer are increasingly replaced by analyses of Europeans' support for European integration rather than of their identification with the EU. Such analyses are frequently supplemented by direct ethnographic research and individual-based empirical analyses of intimacy, affect, and "forms of attachment" so as to do justice to the complexity of proliferating, intersecting, and overlapping types of identity (cultural, political, civic, national, ethnic, religious, etc.). This "affective turn" in studies of European identity is also reflected in recent attempts to theorize and explore transnational feelings of belonging via new vocabulary, including terms like "diasporic" or "cultural intimacy" (Svetlana Boym), "transnational saudade" (Jack Draper III), "nostalgia" as a more open type of "belonging without belonging" (Barbara Cassin), and "post-Fordist affect" (Lauren Berlant).

Michael Bruter's *Citizens of Europe? The Emergence of a Mass European Identity* (2005) and Laurent Berlant's *Cruel Optimism* (2011) are representative of the affective turn in, respectively, political and film scholarship on contemporary Europe.[79] Contrary to popular opinion, Bruter maintains that political identity is not affectively neutral but should be studied through bottom-up rather than top-down approaches. While top-bottom approaches seek to understand "who should be considered European . . . what unifies Europe and Europeans in terms of cultural heritage, values . . . and [what is the] presumed European common heritage,"[80] Bruter is interested in who *feels* European rather than who *is* European. Instead of "normative questions, and objective analyses of whether there is theoretically enough 'ground,' in objective terms, for a European common identity to have emerged,"[81] he examines individual citizens' affective relations to their individual political identities in order to demonstrate the double aspect of political identity (cultural and civic),[82] its affective dimension, and the dynamic nature of identity as an active process of identification rather than a passive act of recognition. By drawing a distinction between "the 'recognition' of a pre-existing identity and the 'active' identification of an individual with a new identity group,"[83] Bruter shifts the discussion of a shared European identity as an "objective reality" to a discussion of *subjective feelings of belonging*: "Thinking of identity as an identification [rather than a recognition] process . . . implies the necessity to consider identity formation as a purely mental phenomenon largely independent from any true category of actual shared characteristics it might relate to."[84]

Another sign of the affective turn in studies of European identity is a notable semantic and cognitive shift from talking about "European norms" to talking about "European values." According to sociologist Hans Joas, "to feel European is to feel committed without feeling constrained in our commitments"; thus, to understand what it means to be "European" we should not examine norms, which are "restrictive" but values, which are "attractive," "emotionally laden notions of what is desirable."[85] Joas identifies several "European" values, including "toleration of difference," "inwardness," "the affirmation of ordinary life," "freedom," and "a practical rationalism of world mastery. Tracing the roots of the first of these—toleration of difference—back to the clashes between followers of different religions in the Middle Ages, historian Michael Borgolte asserts that "the important thing about European culture is not just its key ideas but also the fact 'that all these ideas have their opposites.'"[86] The second value—inwardness—derives, according to Joas, from Christian thought.[87] Drawing on Charles Taylor's *Sources of the Self: The Making of Modern Identity* (1989) and Jan Assmann's *Monotheismus und Kosmotheismus* (1993), Kurt Flasch has shown how the value of introspection and self-reflection became part of European identity, as evidenced by the history of the diary, the emergence of conscience and an awareness of guilt, the history of lyric poetry, and the development of the division between private and public.[88] The third value, "the affirmation of ordinary life," finds expression in various genres of European art, for example, in Dutch still-life painting.

Debates around the concept of the value of "rationality" have also shifted from exploring rationality as a norm to approaching it as a value. Reminding us that the roots of the stereotypical distinction between a rational European "us" and a "prelogical" alien "them" can be found in the litigious practices of the ancient Athenian marketplace, where contestants called their own arguments literal and dismissed those of their opponents as "mere metaphor," Michael Herzfeld exposes the arrogance subtending the assumption that Europeans have "exclusive claims on rationality" or that European thought is literal while that of other peoples is "merely metaphorical."[89] Others have proposed rethinking the Enlightenment concept of "rationality" from a quality one is simply "endowed with" to a dynamic process of doubting and questioning,[90] a move that mirrors the semantic shift from the idea of "European identity" as a passively inherited quality to a process/project oriented toward the future.

For the majority of scholars, however, "freedom" remains the main value associated with Europe and European identity. Orlando Patterson traces the origins of freedom as a value back to the emergence of large-scale slavery in Athens at the end of the seventh century BCE, and the construction of the demos as free vis-à-vis the unfree aliens (and eventually all foreigners) sharing power over them.[91] For the Greeks, slavery was "a violation of nature, of what is most seemingly natural in the human condition—being a taken-for-granted part of the community in which one is born; owning, being in possession of, one's most intimate, carnal, social, and spiritual self."[92] Reminding us of the flip side of this celebration of freedom as quintessentially European, Mark Mazower has challenged the liberal approach to European history, which often downplays the role of totalitarianism, reducing it to a matter of "personal dictatorship" (e.g., Mussolini and Hitler).[93] Ewa Mazierska and Lars Kristensen have recently argued that the turn to the far right in Europe (and the United States) is not a sign of growing xenophobia among Europeans but "a natural consequence of the wholesale embracing of a neoliberal [neo-totalitarian] mindset,"[94] predicated precisely on the undue valorization of "freedom" to the exclusion of other values. French philosopher and journalist Abdennour Bidar makes a similar point in his latest book *Libéron-nous! Des chaînes du travail et de la consummation*

(2018) when he observes that over the last several decades France's national "motto"—liberté, égalité, fraternité—has unduly privileged the first value and ignored the last. As the following chapters will show, it is precisely this last value—fraternity/solidarity—dramatized most forcefully and with a sense of urgency by the figure of the migrant that is at stake in Europe's current political and ethical crisis.

5 Re-Politicizing the Idea of "European Identity" in the Age of Globalized Migration

Internal and external migration have thus profoundly challenged the notion of "European identity" outlined earlier by re-politicizing debates around globalization, borders, national identity, ethics, and the "Other," citizenship, and cosmopolitanism as a possible corrective to multiculturalism.

5.1 Globalization

Most studies of globalization emphasize its internally contradictory nature as "a deeply historical, uneven and even localizing process"[95] producing an asymmetry between "the extraterritorial nature of power and the continuing territoriality of the 'whole life.'"[96] Such analyses are implicitly indebted to Ferdinand Tönnies's view of modernity as a passage from *Gemeinschaft* (communal) to *Gesellschaft* (associational) societies signaling the decline of socially cohesive communities as a result of time and space compression, which has rendered all human relations previously organized close to the human body disembodied/alienated. Two of the main *human* consequences of globalization Zygmunt Bauman identifies are the eclipse of meaning(fullness) and the depoliticization of the public sphere. The effects of the vanishing of the idea of the "limit" on all levels—economic (the deregulation of the economy), political (economies becoming severed from, and unaccountable to, politics), existential ("co-presence," nomadism), and sociocultural (geographical and state borders becoming a function of the speed limit and the degree to which it can be overcome)—have been profound. If everything can be made present at the same time, nothing appears meaningful any more inasmuch as meaning is possible only in a world defined by temporal and spatial gaps or distances, a world of *difference(s)*. The eclipse of meaning(fullness) marks, as well, the (proverbial) end of politics. While the Cold War guaranteed that "everything in the world had a meaning and that meaning emanated from a split, yet single center—from the two enormous power blocs locked up, riveted and glued to each other in an all-out combat,"[97] the end of the Cold War marked the eclipse of that single center of meaning and its replacement with the disturbing impression of the increasingly "indeterminate, unruly and self-propelled character of world affairs, the absence of ... a controlling desk, of a board of directors."[98]

Attempts to provide a more nuanced account of globalization have taken their cue from Arjun Appadurai's analysis of diasporic public spheres and subversive micronarratives as evidence of the inevitable indigenization of chaotic and intangible global cultural flows that are best approached through new methodologies and vocabularies reflecting this very uncertainty. The new terms Appadurai has coined—*ethnoscape, mediascape, technoscape, financescape, and ideoscape*—to denote the building blocks of "imagined worlds," which, unlike Anderson's "imagined communities," are transnational or even post-national, point up the portability and indigenization of ethnicity, technology, finance, media, and ideology, reminding us that these are fluid, irregular landscapes rather than objectively given relations.

While Appadurai's account of globalization has been crucial to conceptualizing the transnational indigenization of processes of globalization, it has also been criticized for being overly optimistic, particularly with respect to the amount of agency it attributes to new transnational/post-national diasporic public spheres to contest the nation state. In his later book *Fear of Small Numbers* (2006), Appadurai revised some of his earlier ideas precisely to foreground the new system of inequalities and hierarchies brought about by globalization. Whatever the drawbacks of his earlier analysis of globalization, however, its primary importance lies in alerting us to the danger of positing globalization as some kind of "natural" phenomenon that renders agency or resistance unthinkable. Accordingly, over the last couple of decades scholars working in different disciplines, from sociology and anthropology, through philosophy and political theory, to cinema and media studies, have sought to re-politicize the discussion of globalization and, as we shall see, of European identity, with debates around migration playing a central role in this project of re-politicizing the public sphere. We can point, for example, to (1) Appadurai's own reconceptualization of the relationship between politics and imagination/fantasy; (2) Jacques Rancière's rethinking of the politics of aesthetics and the aesthetics of politics; (3) the European leftist intelligentsia's renewed interest in the legacy of colonialism and imperialism; and (4) new theories of neoliberalism, which demonstrate that in extending an economic logic to all spheres of life neoliberalism has come up against its own limits, making possible the "re-enchantment of politics" (William Davies).

For Appadurai, migration, in tandem with electronic media, is inherently emancipatory inasmuch as it transforms the work of the imagination into a collective, social practice with the result that fewer and fewer people see their lives "as mere outcomes of the givenness of things."[99] While Appadurai invites us to rethink the imagination as a political rather than a merely cultural fact, Rancière addresses the supposed disappearance of politics from public life by reminding us that aesthetics does not simply refer to the study of art, beauty, or taste but extends beyond the realm of art, encompassing everything that presents itself to sense experience, for "sense perception and experience are not subjective domains but highly political matters."[100] Drawing on Edward Said's rethinking of the historical experience of empire as a common one, "pertaining [in equal part] to Indians and Britishers, Algerians and French,"[101] and on Dipesh Chakrabarty's notion of "the denial of coevalness" in historical accounts of "Europe," the majority of which limit the developments of capitalism, modernity, and the Enlightenment to the geographic territory of Europe,[102] leftist intellectuals like Alain Badiou and Marcel Gauchet have urged us to examine the relationship between globalization and imperialism, with Gauchet describing globalization as a sign of the de-imperialization of the world and Badiou countering that globalization constitutes a return to the normal, imperial form of capitalism, the only difference now being that countries are no longer simply administered (as in classic imperialism) but bought "piece by piece, sector by sector."[103] Whatever their disagreements, both Badiou and Gauchet insist on the importance of reexamining the relationship between democracy and imperialism, rather than solely that between capitalism and imperialism. Finally, political economists, notably William Davies, have begun to excavate the intangible values underlying neoliberalism's supposedly purely rational logic. Indeed, for Davies neoliberalism is ultimately not primarily about economic profit but about simplifying life by removing all ambiguity from it, and neoliberalism's defining characteristic is "its hostility to the ambiguity of political discourse, and a commitment to the explicitness and transparency of quantitative, economic indicators, of which the market price system is the model."[104] Neoliberalism's agenda—to eliminate all normative judgment from public life—is, in fact, an implicitly moral one, relying on critical and normative presuppositions. In the context of Davies's critique, what Rancière and Badiou have called "the ethical turn" in the humanities and social sciences—in the form of an immeasurable debt to the "Other"—might be seen as a response to, or a manifestation of, the destabilization of neoliberalism's economic logic of rationalization, which assumes everything in life is measurable. Indeed, we can identify numerous instances of the return of "the immeasurable" in contemporary theory: Rancière's distinction between "politics" and "police," Balibar's between "justice" and "procedural or normative justice" ("the justice gap"),[105] and Derrida's notion of "community" as those who cannot say "we" are all attempts to leave room for "the incalculable."[106]

Over the last several decades, the historical, philosophical, religious, and political foundations of the idea of "European identity" outlined in the Introduction have been shaken up by various processes of globalization, notably by the globalization of migration. Migration both within and from outside Europe is, of course, not a new phenomenon. The recent migrant crisis might appear less dramatic if we recall the thousands of refugees seeking asylum from religious persecution from the late fifteenth century onward, or the mass migration from Europe to the New World in the early twentieth century and in the postwar years when several million refugees fled fascism and communism and over thirty million people were displaced.[107] The questions raised by the migrant crisis should thus be seen in the context of older histories of migration and the production of difference, from Jews' and Muslims' experience of the Reconquista and Inquisition campaigns to the struggle of indigenous people against the European Conquista.[108] The question of European identity is inseparable from that of migration, the latter serving merely "as a proxy for an ever-deferred confrontation with the European Question as a problem of race and postcoloniality."[109]

Yet there is something qualitatively new about migration in the twenty-first century, Catherine Wihtol de Wenden argues in *La Question migratoire au XXIe siècle: Migrants, réfugiés et relations internationales* (2013), pointing to the ways in which global migration has undermined the two pillars of the international political system, sovereignty and citizenship. By challenging the principles of the Westphalian state—through its transgression of frontiers and its appeal to supranational norms imposed on the nation state—migration contributes to the deconstruction and re-composition of international space. At the same time, as a result of global migration, citizenship, originally a political category unrelated to nationality that became synonymous with nationality in the nineteenth century, has become, once again, increasingly dissociated from nationality. The "globalization" of migration refers to the arrival of foreigners in countries with which they don't have historical connections; the effacement of borders between country of departure, transit country, and host country, with many countries functioning as all three (e.g., Turkey, Morocco); the blurring of the distinction between temporary and settled migrants; the decline in "classical" long-term migration[110] and the rise in short term and "circulatory migration"[111] post-1989, with a growing number of Europeans living in "permanent mobility" and "co-presence"[112] as distinguished from "the double absence" theorized by Abdelmalek Sayad;[113] the emergence of new forms of migration that do not follow the traditional center-periphery paradigm (e.g., "*ex-centric*" migrations from the Maghreb to Spain, Italy, or the Netherlands rather than to France, and "diverging migration" from France to Africa);[114] and, starting in the 1990s, the erosion of the distinction between "economic migrants" and "refugees," with asylum seekers no longer corresponding to the stereotype of "the dissident from the East," the ideal example of the "refugee" in the Geneva Convention. The status of "refugee" now refers primarily to the endangerment of human rights rather than to "persecution by the State," and while some have argued that asylum should be granted only to those facing political persecution,[115] it is undeniable that political persecution, economic inequalities, the abuse of human rights, and environmental factors are interconnected.[116]

An important aspect of the current discourse on migration in Europe is the lesser importance attributed to the East-West axis that split Europe into two parts in the second half of the twentieth century. One reason for this is that irregular migration is driven by the labor market: studies of the European Commission's policy briefs reveal immigration policy to be a function of labor shortage and/or surplus within the EU.[117] Referring to recent statistics, according to which migration within Europe and the EU is larger than migration from outside Europe—with two-thirds of immigrants in an EU state originating from another European country, either a EU or a non-EU one—Leen Engelen and Kris Van Heuckelom conclude that former political or ideological distinctions have given way to socioeconomic ones, the East-West axis now replaced by another split "dividing the Continent into a 'northern A-zone' and a 'southern B-zone.'"[118] For Philipp Ther, too, the East-West political axis has all but been supplanted by a North-South economic one: for example, the "poor" and "backward" countries that make up PIGS (Portugal, Italy, Greece, and Spain) are considered as one large homogenous block similar to how the Eastern bloc was seen previously, while many of the privatization and liberalization reforms imposed on them recall the neoliberal cuts in post-communist Europe as pre-conditions for their entry in the EU.[119] Conversely, observing that the region of the former Eastern bloc has become a makeshift buffer zone or B-zone, "the zone of the abject, that which reminds of economic instability and degraded working conditions on the periphery of the privileged [A] zone,"[120] Helga Druxes persuasively argues in favor of preserving the East-West axis precisely *because* of the overlapping of current economic with former political divisions within Europe.

Recent scholarship on Europe and migration is distinguished by a deep-seated uncertainty as to the most appropriate disciplinary and methodological approach to the subject at hand. In their introductions to a wide range of academic texts dealing with Europe in the age of globalized migration, scholars repeatedly wonder whether anthropology, sociology, psychology, ethnography, or political philosophy might offer the most appropriate perspective through which to approach the idea of "European identity." This disciplinary and methodological uncertainty manifests in a growing preoccupation with the concept of "legitimacy": consider, for instance, Appadurai's notion of "the narcissism of minor differences" as a reason for the questioning of claims of legitimacy made by "small numbers" (minorities); Balibar's preoccupation with the legitimacy of law in enforcing justice (and thereby betraying it, insofar as justice is the opposite of power/force); Rancière's distinction between "police" and "politics" rooted in the questionable legitimacy of the police order; numerous studies concerned with the legitimacy of the EU and its "affective deficit"; the concept of "legitimate European identity" (understood in terms of "credentials"); the continually contested legitimacy of Europe's borders; the criminalization of refugees as illegitimate (illegal) migrants; the proliferation of new nations claiming to be recognized as legitimate; or the legitimacy of the mass media coverage of the migrant crisis as a humanitarian disaster. The term "legitimacy" has several related meanings—"lawfully begotten," "having full filial rights and obligations by birth," "being exactly as purposed, neither spurious nor false," and "being in accordance with law or established legal forms and requirements"[121]—all of which are mobilized in the present *crisis of legitimacy*. At the same time, however, "legitimacy" is also understood not only as having to do with the law or "lawfulness" but as inherently suspect: it is in this sense that Rancière's distinction between "police" and "politics" demands a rethinking of "politics" as a contestation of the assumption of legitimacy *as such*, while Balibar's distinction between "distributive" and "substantial" justice calls for a rethinking of "ethics" as being in excess of law and thus "in excess" of what is considered "legitimate."

Given that "illegal"[122] migration had been taking place for a long time prior to the 2015 migrant crisis, why did it suddenly become such a major talking point, some have asked. In the opinion of American journalist Christopher Deliso the migrant crisis was *not* a *legitimate* humanitarian disaster; although it was represented as such by the media,[123] politicians, and various international organizations the crisis had more to do with the logistics of EU bureaucracy and the UN's foreign policy agenda than with ethics. To account for this *logistical crisis* Deliso offers a cynical, absurdly macabre, account of the origins of European integration and the "secret agenda" behind it. Weaving together a darkly paranoid discourse of a "shadow government," "the migration deep state," and "the secretive globalist cabal" he points his finger at a wide range of guilty parties, from "global business, the military-industrial complex [and the humanitarian-development complex]" to "the technology sector, big pharma, the development sector, philanthropy and more."[124] His unflattering, at times frightening, picture of the EU as a "shadow network" of "hard core left and right wing federalism, funded by the old European aristocracy, globalist financial interests and ... the American intelligence apparatus"[125] attributes the lack of a coherent European identity to the loss of the political center, the decline, across Europe, of a traditional system of two major parties as a result of new players on the left and right margins diluting the vote.

In contrast to Deliso's paranoid account of the migrant crisis, which fails to distinguish between different types of mobilities, most recent scholarship on migration is characterized by a heightened attention to migration-related terminology, to sorting and ranking different types of mobilities, evidence that the migrant crisis is not only a humanitarian and geopolitical crisis but also an *epistemic* one: as migration is increasingly seen as a discursive category rather than a "fact," "Europe," too, is viewed as a discursive entity whose borders are epistemic rather than only, or primarily, geographic or geopolitical. To underscore the meaning of "migration" as a discursive category—and a strategy—Nicholas de Genova reminds us that were it not for borders there would be no migration, only mobility: "Even to designate this elementary and elemental fact and primacy of human mobility as 'migration' ... is already to risk colluding in the naturalization of borders ... [and in] constructing the very profoundly consequential difference between the presumably proper subjects of a state's authority and those mobile human beings variously branded as 'aliens,' 'foreigners' and indeed 'migrants.'"[126]

In short, the very term "migration" belongs to a discourse of power and control inasmuch as it represents an attempt to manage and control human mobility that is understood as primary and autonomous. For instance, Cagla E. Aykac draws attention to the discrepancy between different EU countries' conventions of naming and categorizing migrants as "immigrant," "ethnic migrant," "third-country national," "foreigner," "non- national," "non-Western," "alien," "asylum-seeker," "refugee," "ethnic minority from non-Western countries" or "third country immigrant" as a result of their different histories of migration and different integration policies.[127] In some European countries, Italy for instance, migration terminology is especially confusing: the term "extracomunitari"—the common euphemistic term used to describe immigrants, literally meaning "non-European Community citizens"—is, in fact, used only for visibly nonwhite immigrants.[128] The term "refugee" is equally controversial. While some insist on a narrow definition of the term, others believe the status of "refugee" should also be granted to "illegal migrants" who exist "outside the law in a status of non-jurisdiction that excludes them from the most basic human rights, a status in which committing a crime would actually improve their legal position."[129] Senadin Musabegovic, however, has proposed extending the term "refugee" to anyone deprived of human rights, even if they have not been displaced from their homeland.[130] Other distinctions, such as that between "people-trafficking" and "people-smuggling"—which erroneously assumes the former is forced and the latter voluntary—are also the subject of ongoing debate.[131]

5.2 Borders

The very practice of bordering, some have argued, is essentially European inasmuch as Europe was conceived as overwhelmingly urban, a fact reflected in our entire political and social vocabulary: "'Politics' and 'polity' have their roots in the Greek term 'polis.' Similarly, 'civil,' 'civility' and 'civilization' have their root in the Latin word 'civitas,' which describes the same spatial, political and cultural entity."[132] The "polis" has always signified a bounded space, with barbarians and savages relegated to "a state of nature" outside it. The practice of bordering is exemplified by the concept of "Europe" itself, which has migrated—both geographically and historically—West, while "the lands to which the term 'Europa' originally applied (Thrace, Macedonia, Illyria, modern Bulgaria, Albania, and Serbia) have been expelled beyond the conceptual borders of 'Europe,' being considered only marginally European."[133] While borders might be a European invention, however, thanks to European colonialism they have become a global phenomenon.[134]

Recent debates about borders tend to focus on the relative importance attributed to their material, symbolic, or social aspects. At one extreme are poststructuralists like Kenichi Ohmae, for whom globalization, especially the transfer of power from states toward corporations, has produced a "super-territorial" global economic system that makes the idea of territorial borders meaningless. Randall Halle's *The Europeanization of Cinema: Interzones and Imaginative Communities* (2014), which approaches Europe as an ideational—rather than cartographic—space, not bound by geographical or political borders, is also representative of this line of reasoning. To demonstrate that borders are first ideational before being spatial-geographical, Halle points to the fact that the lifting of state borders in the EU has resulted in the proliferation of mental borders based on class, region, ethnicity, religion, and so forth. Extending the argument to European cinema he claims that the best way to understand recent European cinema is by exploring what he calls "the interzone," "an experience *not limited to geographic cartographic proximity* but rather an *ideational space*, a sense of being somewhere that unites two places, if even only transitionally or temporarily."[135] In line with the rethinking of European identity from an entity with a supposedly objectively existing past that can be "excavated," to a shared political project (see the Introduction), Halle's notion of Europe as an ideational space, and of European cinema as consisting of "interzones," redefines European cinema from an *ontological entity* into a *dynamic process*: "The question . . . of apparatus and interzone is not a question of the 'being' of film . . . but rather a question of activity: What does a film *do*?"[136]

Even as he sets himself apart from such "ontologically minimalist" theories, John Williams also challenges the ontological status of territorial borders by questioning the idea of borders as material or natural and viewing them instead as "social practice,"[137] reminding us that political structures, for example territorial borders, are the product of human agency and thus of the mutual imbrication of politics and ethics. In the absence of a common framework of ethical values, such as that provided by Christianity during the Middle Ages and into the Reformation and counter-Reformations, Williams asserts, contemporary problems like humanitarian intervention, used to justify various neo-imperialist policies, and transnational terrorism cannot be dealt with by a concept of international politics rooted in exclusively territorial notions of identity and political authority. Along similar lines Ginette Verstraette has argued that, to the extent that information and surveillance technologies have become essential to disseminating borders between selves and others and legitimizing practices of inclusion and exclusion, they have also become constitutive of European identity. Thus, the notion of "imagined mobility" has become more essential to conceptualizing European identity than Benedict Anderson's "imagined community," which is still territorial in nature. To her credit, Verstraette later questions this neoliberal notion of "shared belonging through shared mobility," which pertains to only one subject—the white, male, Northern European, Christian, EU citizen, described by Verstraette in terms that recall the nineteenth-century flâneur: "The ideal European citizen is someone with a thin connection to any single place—a rootless, flexible, highly educated, and well-travelled cosmopolitan, capable of maintaining long-distance and virtual relations without looking to the nation-state for protection."[138] Surprisingly, despite acknowledging the power imbalances concealed by such an idealized view of European-identity-as-unlimited-mobility through a homogenous economic space—which has given rise to the present distinction between *mobility* (positively understood) and *migration* (the "vulgar" version of mobility, negatively understood as involuntary or forced), and between *travel* (associated with a cultivated aesthetic sensibility like that of the eighteenth-century traveling elite) and *tourism* as its "vulgar" version—in the rest of her study Verstraette privileges the role *cultural tourism*—predicated precisely on the idea of unlimited mobility—has played historically in the construction of the idea of "Europe" and "European identity," from the seventeenth- and eighteenth-century "grand tour" and its association of the idea of "Europe" with "the romantic picturesque."

In contrast to such pronouncements about the deterritorialization and virtualization of borders, Michael Heffernan's project of a "historical geography" of Europe seeks to reclaim the continued importance of territoriality and rootedness in the "post-national" age. What we encounter throughout the history of the idea of "Europe," Heffernan avers, is "a tenacious territoriality, an enduring European conviction that human existence can only be fulfilling and meaningful if it is rooted in a particular place, a specific and bounded geographical area . . . which has bestowed upon it, usually as a result of a violent struggle, the mystique of a 'homeland.'"[139] The main challenge Europe faces today is a direct result of this tenacious territoriality, exemplified as much by the old nation states as by the EU, both of which rest on common territorial assumptions. In cinema studies, the importance of Hamid Naficy's *An Accented Cinema: Exilic and Diasporic Filmmaking* (2001) for recuperating the tenacious territoriality most scholarship on globalization dismisses cannot be overstated. Skeptical of the "over-celebration of the extra-national and extraterritorial cyber communities created by computer connectivity, interactivity, and bandwidth,"[140] Naficy posits territoriality, rootedness, and geography as the defining characteristics of what he calls "accented cinema." It is *because* accented films are deterritorialized that they are deeply concerned with territory and territoriality, with representations of "the homeland" emphasizing boundlessness and timelessness and those of life in exile and diaspora stressing claustrophobia and bounded temporality.

Indeed, that borders are becoming more complex and differentiated, existing simultaneously on various spatial scales, signals not a deterritorialization but a "reterritorialization of political power that includes a selective reduction of the barrier role of state borders for specific categories of flows."[141] The emergence of new types of borders and borderings extending beyond national boundaries and often beyond physical space—"from tax heavens and offshore trading centers to . . . offshore migrant detention facilities"[142]—is indicative of a new regime of "securitized freedom," in which the responsibility for surveillance and policing is extended beyond specialized institutions to society at large.[143] Rather than disappearing, borders have simply become more invisible and part of everyday life, with external borders increasingly brought within the EU and integrated deeply into the state's administrative apparatus through surveillance, monitoring, and biodata-based security checks.[144]

The growing interest in borderland studies, which emphasize the border's paradoxical nature, could be seen as the silver lining to this seemingly inexorable process of refortifying Europe's external and internal borders in response to globalized migration. Borders and walls divide as much as they bind for the "mere existence of the wall embeds . . . the awareness of the existing 'other side' of the wall line."[145] Thus, the proliferation of new types of borderings—for example, the creation of "countries of transit" on the external frontiers of the EU[146]—has been accompanied by the emergence of bilateral struggles and the convergence of struggles between collectives of illegalized migrants, and by the establishment of worldwide migration forums and networks, such as the Forum of Migrants and Justice without Borders for Migrants.[147]

5.3 National Identity

What becomes of national identity in this context of increasingly complex, plural and often invisible, borders and processes of bordering? Are we now living in a "post-national" Europe? Not quite. Over the last couple of decades Europe has seen a trend of populist right-wing parties riding on the wave of multicultural backlash across Europe and gaining widespread support. The extreme right has moved away from overt neofascist discourse, gaining wider electoral support with xenophobic slogans purporting to save ethnonationalist culture from the threat of immigrants: "Keep Sweden Swedish" (Sweden Democrats), "Give us Denmark back" (Danish People's Party), "Greece belongs to the Greeks" (Golden Dawn), "Stop the foreigners" (Austrian Freedom Party), "Masters in our own house" (Northern League).

Right-wing populist rhetoric uses asylum seekers, the unemployed, and those on social welfare as convenient scapegoats, diverting the public's attention from the financial and economic crisis, the recession, political corruption, class struggle etc. As French journalist Natalie Nougayrede provocatively puts it, "Europe isn't confronted with a refugee and migrant crisis. It's the refugees and migrants who are confronted with a crisis of Europe."[148]

A notable aspect of recent scholarship on nationalism are the surprisingly similar psychological or quasi-psychoanalytic explanations offered by film scholars like Thomas Elsaesser (Chapter 2), political philosophers like Michael Sandel and Ian S. Lustic,[149] sociocultural anthropologists like Appadurai, and political economists like William Davies. Appadurai and Davies, for instance, offer analogous explanations for the resurgence of nationalism and ethnic violence on one hand, and for the limits of neoliberalism on the other: while Davies views neoliberalism itself as a *defense mechanism* against the ambiguity inherent in political discourse, Appadurai considers the resurgence of nationalism a *defense mechanism* against the blurring of identity categories in a post-national context of ephemerality, volatility, and contingence, in which people seek firmer markers of identity.

Globalized migration has exacerbated the long-standing tension between the political and cultural concepts of the nation: the former, emerging in post-Revolutionary France, conceives the nation as constituted by free and equal citizens brought together by a common goal rather than by a common language or culture, while the latter, originating in German idealism, emphasizes the importance of language, culture, a shared religion, and a shared past as embodying "the spirit of the people."[150] The globalization of migration has had two major consequences: the re-ethnicization of national identity ("neo-tribalism") and "long-distance nationalism" exemplified by migrant-driven extremist nationalism.[151] On the positive side, the crisis of the nation state has resulted in a new emphasis on the affective dimension of identity and a rethinking of citizenship as a concept of human, rather than strictly national, rights. This is not to say that the "crisis of the nation state" has been uniformly accepted as a fait accompli; on the contrary, there is an ongoing debate across disciplines about the continued authority and relevance of the nation state. In *Modernity at Large* (1996), Appadurai declared the nation state on its deathbed, arguing that we have entered a "post-national" age, the age of "post-blurring" (the blurring of ethnic, cultural, and state borders brought about by globalization). What were previously assumed to be primordial markers of the nation-state—ethnicity and religion—have now become as deterritorialized and globalized as finance and markets. The "death" of the nation-state, exemplified most clearly by former Yugoslavia, follows logically from the deterritorialization of both ethnicity, "insofar as [ethnic] groups are no longer tightly territorialized, spatially bounded, historically unselfconscious, or culturally homogenous"[152] and religion, which "in the past was resolutely national [but] now pursues global missions and diasporic clienteles."[153] The nation state has grown obsolete because primordial affinities have become globalized.

For Michael Herzfield, too, the "nation" is an obsolete concept, though for different reasons. Distinguishing "national identity" as it is conceived by European elites from "national identity" as ordinary citizens experience it, Herzfield warns against the dangers of an essentializing discourse that ignores "the ways in which ordinary people recast [or translate] what their leaders tell them about their national identity."[154] A more appropriate model, he believes, is Anthony Cohen's notion of "personal nationalism," which bypasses the sociocentrism of Durkheimian anthropology. While dismissing Appadurai's celebration of the death of the nation-state as premature, Randall Halle agrees that Anderson's idea of the nation as an "imagined community" is no longer relevant in the wake of new imagined communities formed outside and across national borders, which tend to develop "not as meta-communities but as subcultures, micropolitical associations, ethnic migrant identities, midlevel economic partnering, sexual communities and other 'lower order' distinctive societies"[155]—in short, "interzones," in the construction of which cinema plays a major role.

The November–December 2018 issue of the French magazine *Diplomatie*, featuring a special dossier on the specific inflections of nationalism in different European countries, testifies to the continued relevance of the nation state as a source of identity in Europe.[156] Indeed, the importance of "primordial" aspects of national identity—ethnicity, language, and territory—is often hidden in plain sight, as Robert Stam and Ella Shohat make clear in their analysis of the French Constitution, which not only identifies French as the language of the Republic but is also written "as if 'the French people' were an ethnic group that has always existed ... is unified and ... speaks the French language."[157] For Mabel Berezin, too, the nation-state has not lost any of its relevance or authority. Challenging the increasingly dominant constructivist view of national identity, Berezin insists that national identity is profoundly affective, rather than merely territorial, and thus the object of political struggle.[158] To illustrate the virility of the nation state, she points to minorities, for example, the Roma, refugees and asylum seekers, who live on others' territory and are thus deprived of legal rights since, regardless of the supposed dissolution of borders under globalization, modern citizenship still embeds both identity and legal rights in the territorial nation-state. Rather than fall back on a primordialist argument, however, Berezin offers a rational explanation for the continued importance of blood ties in our supposedly "post-national" age, citing William James's 1956 essay "The Sentiment of Rationality," in which James states that the "feeling of rationality and the feeling of familiarity are one and the same thing."[159] National identity is experienced as a "familiar habit" and the national space as "a comfortable place"[160] because the expectation of continuity is rational, that is, emotionally satisfying, whereas novelty is a "mental irritant."

For Riva Kastotyano, as for Berezin, the nation state remains the basic political unit in Europe in terms of citizenship and legal rights. This was made explicit, argues Kastotyano, by the transnational Forum of Migrants, which, by excluding non-European migrants, reinforced the nationalist sentiments of the EU original members and created an ambiguity in the definition of European identity.[161] Those celebrating post-nationalism as fostering international norms referring to the person or residence instead of legal citizenship fail to recognize that EU citizenship is still national rather than post-national: according to the Maastricht Treaty, a citizen of the EU is someone who holds the nationality of one of the member states. Another strong argument illustrating the authority of the nation state comes from studies of border control surveillance systems, like that by Dennis Broeders, who has shown that data collected for one specific purpose [migration policies] are made available for other purposes, thereby enlarging the powers of the state over citizens.[162] Similarly, Verstraette has demonstrated, again in the context of migration, that although national geopolitical conflicts within the EU seem to have disappeared, they have reappeared in another form in relation to Europe's TCNs (Third Country Nationals). The introduction of the Schengen Information System (SIS), which allows for the denial of an asylum claim in one country to be applied automatically to the rest, provides evidence that "by extending national orders to Europe's external frontiers the powers of the nation state are increased."[163]

Neither professing the "death" of the nation state nor insisting on its unassailability, Christian Karner defines national identity as the product of collective *(re)interpretations* of a common past. Drawing upon Stuart Hall's concept of identities as *routes* rather than static *roots*, on Michael Billig's *Banal Nationalism* (1995), and on Pierre Bourdieu's *Outline of a Theory of Practice* (1977), Karner stresses the importance of studying the processes through which "previously non-reflexive national habitus and doxa" are transformed into "discourses articulated for the purposes of identity politics."[164] The relative well-being of the nation state is also the object of analysis in *The Limits of Neoliberalism*, in which Davies "diagnoses" the nation state as still alive though existing in a contingent, "zombie-like" state largely due to an underlying tension within neoliberalism between universalism (with its roots in Enlightenment ideas about the presumed universal rationality of individual and collective subjects) and various forms of particularism (political, cultural, national). If during its heyday, 1989–2008, neoliberalism could be described as "the disenchantment of politics by economics," then the last decade has seen the "re-enchantment of politics" by images of nationhood, race, and religion, a "re-enchantment" Davies attributes to the waning of the Enlightenment idea of "rational human subjectivity as a stable epistemological and moral basis from which to reorganize society" and its replacement with various forms of authority with an unevenly distributed power, lacking "a grammar of justification or evaluation"[165] and based on a politics of difference rather than on the assumption of common/shared humanity. Opposing the widely held view of neoliberalism as driven by a "liberal" logic that transcends geographical and national borders, Davies proposes that the resurgence of nationalism, borders, and ethnic violence over the last decade illustrates "the state-centric nature of neoliberalism as an anti-political mode of politics."[166]

Like Davies, Quin Slobodian questions the established narrative of neoliberalism by arguing that neoliberalism's real focus "is not on the market per se but on redesigning states, laws and other institutions to protect the market."[167] In his alternative intellectual history of the neoliberal movement as told by social scientists rather than by historians, Slobodian focuses not on the well-known Chicago School but on the Geneva school of ordoliberalism, whose main preoccupation was statecraft and law rather than economics.[168] Slobodian provides a much needed corrective to the common (mis)understanding of markets as presumably natural, self-regulating entities, reminding us that markets "cannot reproduce themselves without political effort."[169] Furthermore, the argument that neoliberalism has weakened the nation state ignores one form of nationalism that is biopolitical in nature and that fuels and feeds upon systemic violence against racial and immigrant Others—viewed this way, far from becoming "unbound," nations are, in fact, "becoming re-bound in resistance to growing racial and ethnic diversity."[170]

5.4 Ethics, Justice and the "Other"

All forms of anti-immigrant nationalism are predicated on the exclusion of (ethnic/racial/cultural/national) "Others" and on the promotion of an illusory idea of Europe as a homogenous space and of its history as a linear narrative.[171] The history of these exclusions is also the process by which the "Other" is constructed as an independent entity. However, while in *Beyond Anthropology: Society and the Other* (1990) Bernard McGrance suggested that during the Renaissance the non-European other was experienced on the horizon of Christianity, during the Enlightenment on the horizon of reason, and in the twentieth century on the horizon of culture, I would argue that the figure of the non-European Other in the age of globalized migration contains aspects of all three.

The construction of national "Others" mirrors that of the non-European Other. Laia Soto Bermant provides a succinct analysis of this process in her discussion of the way in which, beginning in the late eighteenth century, and in opposition to a series of "Others"—from the Moors to the Jews, heretics, Protestants, Lutherans, gypsies, and Africans—a notion of a Spanish national identity, tied to Catholicism, gradually emerged.[172] It was through its disavowal of its African heritage that Spain's "Europeanness" was eventually recognized, making way for Spain's incorporation in the EEC. Tellingly, Vetri Nathan's analysis of the process through which Italy's "Europeanness" was eventually acknowledged echoes Bermant's: "Italy sees itself as ... being the quintessential internal Other in Western Europe. [...] This permanent crisis—the contradiction of being both European and ... yet not quite—has caused a situation of what I term as 'chronic ambivalence' with regard to its national identity."[173] On the other hand, numerous critics have theorized the Balkans—rather than Spain or Italy—as playing the role of "the internal Other" in the construction of European identity. Norman Davies summarizes the vast scholarship on the subject when he states that "all of Europe's historic 'fault-lines' (political, religious, ethnic, linguistic and cultural) responsible for all the continent's historic upheavals, run preferentially through ... the Balkans."[174] In her seminal study of the Balkans,[175] Milica Bakić-Hayden has shown Balkanism to be a version of Orientalism, which renders the Balkans both a part of Europe and outside Europe "proper" because of their long history of Ottoman/Oriental rule, an in-between status they continued to "enjoy" even after the end of the Cold War when they "were chosen as a little piece of Cold War Eastern Europe to be retained as the model of otherness."[176]

The fact that such a diverse range of countries and/or regions—Spain, Italy, the Balkans, Eastern Europe—have been identified as "Europe's quintessential internal 'Other'" reveals the multiple and intersecting processes of "Othering" in Europe, both along the North-South axis (e.g., Southern versus Northern Italians, Italy versus Northwestern Europe) and the East-West axis (e.g., Romania versus Italy) so that the same country, for example Italy, can be viewed as occupying the core of Europe *and* its periphery. What this phenomenon of "nesting Orientalisms" (Bakić-Hayden)[177] reveals is not only the relative meaning of "core" and "periphery" but also the superimposition of cultural, political, ethnic, racial, and technological processes of Othering, each with its own distinctive logic: for example, geographically Italy might occupy the periphery of Europe but politically it belongs to the West and thus to the "core" of Europe as it is imagined from the periphery (e.g., by East European, ex-communist countries). While recognizing the work of scholars like Dina Iordanova and Maria Todorova on the different mechanisms of Othering in Europe, Leen Engelen and Kris Van Heuckelom, nevertheless, warn that it would be a mistake to "perceive the emergence of these modern discourses as a unidirectional process—the West constructing the East as its antithetic Other—while neglecting the interactional and dialectical nature of such practices [e.g., strategies like 'occidentalization' or 'self-orientalization']."[178] Paul Gifford and Tessa Hauswedell's anthology *Europe and Its Others: Essays on Interperception and Identity* (2010) offers a corrective to established views about the process of identity construction by demonstrating that as much as Europe has constructed a series of religious, sexual, and ethnic Others, these

"Others" have, in turn, constructed the idea of "Europe."[179] Furthermore, while the delineation of boundaries between in- and out-groups is common to all identity politics, Christian Karner reminds us that there is "*ideological variation* in how the relationship between self and other is understood."[180] Drawing upon Gerd Baumann's and Andre Gingrich's notion of three "grammars of identity" (ways of conceptualizing self-other relationships)—an Orientalizing grammar, a grammar of segmentation, and a grammar of encompassment—Karner proposes that while the dominant grammar of identity in Europe has been the grammar of encompassment, recently a new type of grammar has emerged, an *instrumentalist* discourse of self-other relation based on arguments about the economic desirability of immigrant Others.

Over the last couple of decades "the Muslim" has emerged as Europe's preeminent "Other." Patricia Ehrkamp has shown how public discourses in Germany and Switzerland presenting Muslim migrants as disrespectful of law and order, unenlightened, and anti-democratic have been used to justify restrictive legislation and increased surveillance of Muslim migrants and to introduce an imbalance in the expectation of German citizens and Muslim migrants to practice active citizenship and affirm democratic values.[181] Rinella Cere has drawn attention to the material effects of the construction of the Muslim migrant as "Other" in the Italian media and the public discourse of the Lega Nord, Forza Italia, and Allianza Nazionale. The criminalization of the Muslim migrant as "Other," she claims, presupposes and reconfirms the problematic conflation of Italian identity with Catholic identity.[182] The instrumental role the Paris attacks of November 2015 played in the transformation of "the Muslim" into Europe's chief "Other"—despite the fact that all of the alleged culprits in the attacks were racialized minority Europeans—confirms that the controversies surrounding migration are better understood as reflecting deep-seated intra-European tensions rather than tensions between "a pre-existing, presumably largely unified [Western] Europe and a recently settling (invading) non-European 'Other' ('Islam')."[183]

That migration has put into question the idea of the nation state as the traditional "container" of justice is evidenced by the growing role of European and international law in individual nations' legal orders. At the same time, discussions of what an ethical relationship to the Other might look like have become central to rethinking European identity along ethical and humanitarian lines, with scholars remaining deeply divided in their views of "the ethical turn," some arguing that the only justifiable concept of European identity is one based on hospitality to the Other and others remaining suspicious of the hidden agenda behind "the ethical/humanitarian turn." According to advocates of Levinasian ethics—which has emerged as the dominant theoretical paradigm in current theorizations of European identity in ethical terms—the only way to combat Western philosophy's preoccupation with ontology, which rests on the elimination of relationality and thus of ethics, is through Levinas's notion of "hospitality," which challenges the dominant notion of the subject in terms of self-identity. The Levinasian turn in philosophy has infiltrated other fields, from political philosophy and sociology through anthropology to cinema studies, via the figure of the migrant, who has become more or less synonymous with Levinas's notion of the "Other," as well as via the concept of "hospitality." Starting from the assumption that "hospitality has a bearing on the very way in which subjectivity is defined,"[184] Yegenoglu has drawn a parallel between the ways in which the Levinasian notion of the Other interrupts the European concept of subjectivity and, on the other hand, "the ways in which the sovereignty of the European self or the self-founding European subject is established, maintained, as well as destabilized or compromised in its encounter with the migrant other."[185] Although the debate about human rights, "rebooted" by the migrant crisis, appears to be about the proper "distribution of rights" between citizens and noncitizens, the real question is what constitutes a right in the first place. The notion of "rights" is meaningless when thought of in relation only to a singular subject: it is only in relation to Others that I have rights, and it is only in relation to me that Others have rights. From this point of view, the concept of "rights" can have two different meanings depending on whether one locates rights in the realm of ethics or in that of politics. Yegenoglu's critique of Kant's notion of "hospitality" is premised on this distinction between a moral or religious realm of responsibility (the notion of "unconditional hospitality" endorsed by Levinas and Derrida) and a politico-legal realm of responsibility (embodied by Kant's "conditional hospitality").

The problem of the *political* application of "unconditional hospitality" is dramatized in the growing skepticism toward humanitarianism or what some have called "humanitarian ideology." As Ruben Andersson has demonstrated, humanitarian initiatives by coast guards, the Red Cross, the International Organization of Migration (IOM) and UNHCR accompany, rather than contradict, strict migration controls, pointing to the intermixing of care with coercion in migratory reception.[186] In *No Path Home: Humanitarian Camps and the Grief of Displacement* Elizabeth Dunn posits humanitarianism as one of the new ordering principles of the international system since the end of the Cold War, dividing society into donors and receivers. Far from being a sentiment, humanitarianism has become "an ideology, a system of categorization, a massive industry"[187] and, for many, a way of life. "Humanitarian ideology" refers not only to the discourse of pity produced by humanitarian aid agencies but also to these agencies' hidden agenda, which, far from protecting displaced people, consists of "protecting donor countries from the displaced."[188] Ipek Celik, too, questions the discursive shift in contemporary representations of ethnic and racial Otherness "toward a dialectic of *humanitarianism*, in which racialized bodies function as affective objects [to be feared or pitied] rather than as political subjects,"[189] while Sonia Tascon warns that the "humanitarian gaze" prevalent in human rights film festivals reproduces unequal geopolitical relationships by depriving migrants/refugees of agency.[190]

Bulent Diken and Carsten Bagge Lausten's *The Culture of Exception: Sociology Facing the Camp* (2005) is exemplary of the ways in which the migrant crisis and "the ethical turn" have challenged traditional disciplines like sociology. After a quick detour through Kantian ethics, Diken and Lausten arrive quickly to the period "after the camp" in order to pose a question one would not have expected from a couple of sociologists: Can there be a "truly universal ethics . . . [that] testifies to the nakedness of *homo sacer*, a nakedness that is . . . shared by all?"[191] Unsurprisingly, given their theoretical reliance on Lyotard and Agamben, they frame their discussion with references to "Absolute Evil" (the Holocaust), testimony, and the incommunicable (Lyotard), and insist on the absolute necessity to infinitely bear witness without allowing our testimony to find a specific object, which, they believe, would be tantamount to attributing meaning to the Holocaust and thus justifying it. It is precisely this analogy between the Holocaust and the migrant crisis, between the figure of the Muselmann and that of the migrant/refugee, both viewed as instances of Agamben's "homo sacer," that critics of "the ethical turn," notably Badiou and Rancière, have called into question.

In many ways Badiou's and Rancière's critique of "the ethical turn," which they view as an "ethical ideology," was already prefigured in Pascal Bruckner's merciless critique of the notion of "the Other" as an embodiment of white man's guilt in *The Tears of the White Man: Compassion as Contempt* (1986). For Bruckner, "white man's guilt," which forces the white man endlessly to atone for his "sins," is just an inverse form of the very Eurocentrism he is supposedly atoning for, inasmuch as his infinite guilt (his assumption of responsibility for *everything*) is just another way of restoring his power. From this point of view, the ethical turn is just the latest expression of postcolonial guilt, which depends on upholding the ideas of "infinite guilt," "man in the abstract," "universal human suffering," and "universal human rights." Bruckner is equally critical of the other side of white man's guilt, pity, which reduces "Others" to subhuman victims, denying them the status of proper political subjects. Bruckner's critique of the concept of the Third World as a homogenous mass of "indigenous/indigent" people (Arabs, Orientals, and Africans) calls to mind numerous television and cinematic examples of suffering anonymous migrants and refugees whose only purpose is to awaken our moral indignation, arousing nothing more than mild sympathy accompanied by indifference.

In the conclusion to his book, however, Bruckner declares Eurocentrism as not only unavoidable but also fundamental for an ethical relationship to the Other. In a section titled "In Defense of Eurocentrism," he proposes that the only way for Europeans to free themselves from bad faith/infinite guilt is through a compromise between Eurocentrism and Euro-hatred: "Both the anti-European Inquisition and aggressive Eurocentrism *must be affirmed together*. Because it is impossible to avoid choices that by themselves could tear us apart, to be legitimate we must practice both skepticism and allegiance."[192] Challenging the discourse of moral universalism predicated on the idea of a universal subject and universal human rights, Bruckner avers that ethics cannot be a matter of dispensing justice in a disinterested, dispassionate manner àla Kant; on the contrary, the only genuine ethics is one sustained by "emotional particularism" and a certain exoticism—even eroticism—in our relationship to the Other:

> My sense of moral responsibility can be sustained only by an admiring fascination for the other. Neither generosity nor duty is enough to establish strong ties, and the dictates of conscience are not what usually motivate people. [. . .] Nobody would leave his borders if the far-off were not, above all, *seductive*. . . . A foreigner inspires me [enchants me] before he fills me with pity or astonishment.[193]

In *Ethics: An Essay on the Understanding of Evil*, Badiou condemns the "ethical turn" with its appeals to "humanism" and "human rights" as based on a meaningless notion of universal ethics—for Badiou (as for Bruckner), "there can be no ethics in general . . . only an ethics of singular truths, and thus an ethics relative to a particular situation."[194] Reclaiming the anti-humanist idea of "the death of man," Badiou rejects the abstract doctrine of "natural man" and of "the rights of natural man" ("human rights") as a possible basis for ethics, arguing that this "ethical doctrine" is predicated on the splitting of the human subject into a "a passive, pathetic or reflexive subject—he who suffers"[195] and "the active, determining subject of judgment—he who in identifying suffering knows that it must be stopped by all available means. [. . .] Who cannot see that this ethics ... hides, behind its victim-Man, the good-Man, the white-Man?"[196] Such an understanding of ethics reduces politics to nothing more than "the sympathetic and indignant judgment of the [privileged, Western, white] spectator of [suffering]."[197] Ostensibly rooted in Levinasian ethics, "ethical ideology" actually perverts Levinas's notion of "the Other" to "the recognition of the other." While in Levinasian ethics the Other embodies a principle of alterity that transcends finite experience—the principle of the "Altogether-Other" (God)—ethical ideology strips Levinasian ethics of its religious dimension so that all we are left with is "a pious discourse without piety."[198]

For his part, Rancière views "the ethical turn" as resulting from a misunderstanding of the notions of "community," "the common," and "dissensus," which has perverted our understanding of politics, political subjectivization, and the rights of the subject. "What lies behind the strange shift from Man to Humanity and from Humanity to the Humanitarian?"[199] he asks. His answer is that the discourse of human rights rests on the victimization of displaced people and on the idea of "humanitarian interference," which is used to justify various types of military campaigns and the struggle against "Radical Evil." Rancière blames the shift from "the rights of Man" to "Human Rights" on Arendt's and Agamben's radical suspension of politics in the exception of bare life and their (mis) understanding of rights as "merely the predicates of a non-existing being."[200] Rights do not "belong" to certain subjects that are located within a given "sphere" ("the sphere of politics"): just as the subjects that belong to a political community cannot be counted (counting is the logic of "the police" whereas "politics" is the name given to the count of the uncounted) so rights cannot be "apportioned" among members of a preexisting (political) community. There is thus no "Man" of "the Rights of Man," and there is no need for one: the only meaning the notion of a "right" could have is "in the back-and-forth movement between the initial inscription of the right and the dissensual stage on which it is put to the test."[201]

Rancière holds Lyotard (among others) responsible for the perversion of "rights" into "Human Rights" In his article "The Rights of the Other" (1993) Lyotard claims that renewed outbreaks of religious and racial violence are "not so much the specific effects of perverse ideologies and 'outlaw regimes' as the manifestations of an infinite wrong, one that could not be accounted for in terms of the opposition between democracy and anti-democracy . . . but which appears as an absolute evil—an unthinkable and irredeemable evil."[202] What Rancière finds particularly pernicious about this claim is that Lyotard's introduction of a positive notion of "the Inhuman" (identified with "the Other" or "the Law of the Other"), the betrayal of which is the other Inhuman (Radical Evil), reduces ethics (and aesthetics) to a witnessing of "unpresentable catastrophe," which is "nothing but the endless work of mourning"[203] easily perverted into a justification for "infinite justice" under the pretense of humanitarianism.

The anthology *The Borders of Justice* (2012), edited by Étienne Balibar, is representative of "the ethical ideology" targeted by Badiou and Rancière. All essays in this volume are heavily indebted to Lyotard's concept of "the differend" and to Derrida's notion of "the structural excess of justice with respect to every historically given regime of justice administration."[204] Challenging a purely normative or distributive theory of justice, which views justice as simply a response to what is perceived as injustice, contributors to the volume explore the "justice gap"—the gap between claims for justice and governmental (including legal and juridical) regimes of justice— dramatized particularly well by the phenomenon of migration. One of the contributors even suggests that references to justice—to moral or legal definitions of justice—are, more often than not, used to depoliticize political conflicts.[205] On the contrary, Rancière urges us to think justice not only in the ethical-normative sense but also in the political sense, and this means, as Francisco Naishtat observes, recuperating the notion of a hermeneutic pre-comprehension of justice: "When we talk about the injustice of a particular social order it is because we have already understood the corresponding social order as a contingent historical product that can be disrupted by political action."[206]

5.5 Citizenship

As the preceding discussion of ethics and justice suggests, Western political culture based on liberal values has been in decline for some time now, demanding a rethinking of liberal values. While much of the scholarship on Europe has been shaken up by the ethical turn and the affective turn (see the Introduction and Chapter 4), the increasingly central role occupied by citizenship in debates about European identity is evidence of another, *normative turn* in European studies.[207] The "normative turn" finds expression in the proliferation of comparative analyses of different political theories of citizenship, from liberal (emphasizing the equality of rights) and communitarian (prioritizing duties and responsibilities owed to the community over individual rights) to republican (stressing participation in public affairs as the foundation for the promotion of the civic good) and multicultural (challenging universal theories of citizenship while being themselves criticized as a dangerous retreat from universalism). Political subjects who are unauthorized yet recognized—"illegal" migrants and refugees—play a central role in redefining the borders of citizenship. Arguably, the most important transformation of our understanding of citizenship has been that from "a conception of rights attached to persons to a discussion of rules of inclusion, relational processes and rights attached to groups,"[208] that is, a shift from a notion of citizenship as a personal right to that of citizenship as a group right articulated in the form of "claims." Conversely, some locate the main challenge of defining citizenship today in the difficulty of "finely calibrating ... the infinite reserve of potentiality held in the materiality of labor-power"[209] inasmuch as it is precisely labor-power that is at stake in contemporary struggles over citizenship.

The traditional state-centric model of citizenship is increasingly seen as obsolete in our globalized world, in which rights are more often than not tied to residency rather than nationality, something Michael Lister and Emily Pia see as evidence of the emergence of a post-national and cosmopolitan citizenship, whose meaning is not stable but varies depending on whether one defines citizenship as a legal status, a system of rights, a form of political activity, or a form of identity.[210] Even as nation states continue to regulate the distribution of citizenship and the process of naturalization, they increasingly face the demands of international jurisprudence and can be held accountable for violating human rights in denying citizenship to certain "aliens." This has resulted in the growing liberalization impact of international law on citizenship in Europe (e.g., the legalization of dual citizenship) leading some to argue that the nation state is becoming "a territorial administrative unit of a supranational legal and political order based on human rights";[211] conversely, others believe the liberalization of citizenship has led to its re-ethnicization inasmuch as dual nationality allows people to maintain ties to the nation despite their physical distance from it.[212]

Far from being self-evident, the term "citizenship" has been reformulated multiple times, with scholars distinguishing between legal/juridical and cultural/affective citizenship, and between the notion of global citizenship (referring to global citizens' lack of political loyalty to a state) and the idea of corporations as global citizens. The proliferation of different meanings of "citizenship" has led to a "flexibilization of citizenship," as the traditional nation state logic of political identity gives way to a "market-oriented" notion of citizenship as a commodity to which particular subjects with particular skills have preferential access.[213] The main challenge to this market model, which subordinates national and civic attachments to the forces of the global market, has been Habermas's model of civic citizenship, according to which the idea of a European "fatherland" must be replaced by that of a European public space, a non-national political community, a "multitude" freed from the idea of "ethnos," a community without essentialized subjects. However, as Chantal Mouffe notes, Habermas's "constitutional patriotism"—the idea that "the law of a concrete legal community must, if it is to be legitimate, at least be compatible with moral standards that claim universal validity beyond the legal community"—fails to take into account "the power relations and antagonisms that constitute the political completely," and, instead, searches in vain "for a view point above politics [in universal rationality] from which one could guarantee the superiority of democracy."[214]

The idea of a "postnational citizenship" remains a matter of debate, breeding enthusiasm and skepticism in equal measure. On one hand, "cosmopolitanism" has become one of the "buzzwords" in recent attempts to reinvigorate classic liberalism with the understanding that the politics of recognition, on which cosmopolitanism is based, "entails a positive recognition of difference"[215] rather than being merely about plurality (multiculturalism). The unbundling of nationality and territoriality, seen as one of the defining features of cosmopolitanism, has been promoted as somehow more ethical than other theories of political identity, such as communitarianism, for instance: if communitarianism defends "the right of a specific political community, often a territorially bounded and idealized nation, to a substantial degree of ethical closure," cosmopolitanism "argues in favor of a universal ethical schema."[216] However, cosmopolitanism's alleged ethical superiority rests on the valorization of mobility, travel, nomadism, and hybridity, terms that may describe certain European subjects (mostly those living in the wealthier parts of Europe) dismissing nonmobile subjects whose lives cannot be written into "cosmopolitan scripts."[217]

In *Strangers in Our Midst: The Political Philosophy of Immigration* (2016), David Miller makes explicit the significant challenge migration represents for political philosophy, which has traditionally concerned itself almost exclusively with the internal relationship between the state and its citizens. Classic texts of political philosophy such as John Stuart Mill's *Considerations on Representative Government* (1861) and Hegel's *Philosophy of Right* (1820) do not mention immigration, and although some point to Kant's "Perpetual Peace" (1795)—in which Kant speaks of the principle of "cosmopolitan right"—as anticipating contemporary discussions of cosmopolitanism, Kant saw this right as having a limited scope, limited to the foreigner's right to try to establish a relationship with the inhabitants of the country, mostly for business purposes.[218] John Rawls's *Theory of Justice* (1971) does not consider immigration either, since he assumes that the principles of justice apply to a society whose membership is already fixed. With his book Miller proposes to fill this gap in political philosophy by discussing institutions and policies he believes should be adopted with respect to immigration (that is, he is *not* concerned with the *ethics* of immigration). Ironically, having criticized the limited scope of Kant's notion of "cosmopolitan right," Miller ultimately defends a "weak" version of moral cosmopolitanism grounded in a very narrow definition of "refugee," according to which refugees are "people whose human rights cannot be protected except by moving across a border, whether the reason is state persecution, state incapacity or prolonged natural disasters."[219] Throughout the discussion Miller adopts the substantive definition of self-determination as "national" rather than understanding it as citizens' self-determination without reference to the national identities of the people making up the citizen body. His "weak version of moral cosmopolitanism" ultimately amounts to nothing more than a hypocritical affirmation of the need to respect migrants' human rights despite the absence of a basic human right to immigrate, an absence that Miller uses to justify his conclusion that there are "considerable reasons" to keep borders closed.

Those who remain skeptical of the idea of a "postnational" citizenship, argue that the construction of a postnational European citizenship weakens the political dimension of citizenship replacing it with social and economic claims, thereby obstructing the establishment of a European public sphere. Michael Heffernan is in agreement: describing "postnational Europe" in terms of "the new Medievalism" (inasmuch as the emergence of autonomous regions, like Lombardy and Baden-Wurttemberg, can be seen as a throwback to the medieval city regions and the older trading alliances that existed under the Hanseatic League), he reminds us that the "unbundling" of the concept of territoriality from its traditional "container," the state, functions mostly in the wealthier parts of Europe.

6 Floppy Concepts

What, then, remains of the idea of "European identity" today? On one hand, despite pronouncements of the disappearance of specifically European "lieux de mémoire"[220] and despite the discrediting of human rights and the desire for peace (which have now become globalized) as uniquely "European,"[221] it is still possible to find traces of a certain nostalgic notion of "European identity" as, for example, when media scholar William Uricchio urges us to excavate what he describes, in quasi-psychoanalytic terms, as a *latent Europeanness*:

> Probing beneath the surface of the present, one can find the densely patterned tracings of vaguely remembered borders, old trade routes, language areas, ideological, economic and religious zones, and former ethnic enclaves. Any and all of these are in principle subject to activation... and therefore, manipulation, particularly in a setting where a contrastive logic reigns, as it does in Europe.[222]

Employing a poetic language reminiscent of Voyenne, Rob Kroes declares that to battle "the pernicious presentism of people's ideas about Europe" we need to turn European space into "one, big memory space, a lieu de mémoire, the sort of space as it emerges from W. G. Sebald's journeys across time and space, stumbling upon triggers of memory, bringing back voices long gone silent, shimmering faces emerging from mists before being enveloped by them once again."[223]

An increasing number of scholars, however, acknowledge that the question "What is European identity?" is not properly formulated since it fails to take into account *both* the retrospective and prospective aspects of identity, and that this has inevitably led to a fragilization and fragmentation of the discourse of European identity. According to Peter O'Brien, contemporary discourse on Europe is characterized by "normative messiness," which differs from "mere discord between distinct normative camps" arising instead "through imprecise and incomplete application of normative theories that obfuscates their critical differences."[224] Faced with the problem of conceptualizing an increasingly "liquid" world, politicians, policy makers, and scholars have had to resort to "fuzzy concepts" or "normative bricolage": what we find in European politics today are not various political theories applied wholesale and systematically but "mere fragments of these larger normative outlooks that have become unmoored... from their theoretical homes."[225] Rather than seeing normative messiness as a problem, however, O'Brien welcomes it as allowing a more nuanced reading of Europe, renouncing the search for an overarching consensus.

Dismissing the common-sense notion of identity as "sameness and constancy over time," Peter Wagner asserts that the question "What is European identity?" is, first and foremost, a political question: Europe does not "have" an identity but can "acquire" one through collective interpretations of shared experiences, which are thus kept alive in people's minds. Significantly, the shared European experiences Wagner identifies are all predicated on discord and conflict rather than on unity and harmony: (1) the Reformation and the wars of religion; 2) revolution and nation; 3) the public and private sphere; 4) capitalism and class struggle.[226] By translating these four "schisms" into "questions" Wagner is able—"with a bit of effort" as he himself acknowledges—to read the often violent divisions of Europe in a *positive* way.[227] In this reading "European identity" refers to collective interpretations of historical schisms, that is, what Europeans share are not so much the events/schisms themselves but the similar ways in which they have interpreted them. In short, *the shared interpretations of what divides us (schisms) make us European*, a definition that calls to mind Geoffrey Barraclough's statement that "the history of Europe is not a sequence of *happenings* but a series of *problems*."[228]

For Chiara Bottici and Benoit Challand even a *divided* memory, like that of Europe, can be a powerful reservoir of *significance* so that Europeans' *shared divided history* can serve as the basis for an *affective attachment* in the construction of a *common identity*. Bottici and Challand emphasize the significance of political *myths* over political *narratives*, pointing out that, "while the concept of political narrative entails that of series of events organized in a more or less coherent plot, the concept of myth entails that of a surplus, of an emotional attachment that motivates political action."[229] If narratives provide *meaning*, myths are narratives "that coagulate and reproduce *significance*."[230] Like Wagner, Bottici and Challand underscore the *constitutive* nature of political myths and their *dynamic* aspect (unlike cultural myths, political myths are oriented toward action/the future).

Philosopher Simo Knuuttila also regards discord or *the conflict of values* as a positive aspect of European identity, an argument that will be taken up by Thomas Elsaesser in his discussion of contemporary European cinema's philosophical potential (Chapter 2). According to Knuuttila,

> Europeans have, in the course of their brief history, generated common values that have simply accumulated without ever being ordered to form a harmonious synthesis. The dilemma of European sense and sensibility lies in precisely this mass of values not ordered to form any balanced entirety. The European mind is not, therefore, very reliable, having a ready tendency to assimilate various fashions, ideals and values.[231]

Heikki Mikkeli finds the silver lining in this conceptual and normative messiness, reassuring us that precisely "the diversity and even contradiction of the idealistic subconscious prevents very biased ideologies from gaining ascendancy for very long."[232]

Arguing that the concept of "identity" is useless in conceptualizing the individual's relation to the collective, Paul Jones and Michal Krzyzanowski opt for the term "belonging," whose conceptual ambiguity they welcome as a possible strength. Unlike "identity," which is "hermetically sealed and internally consistent," "belonging" "is not necessarily based on a distinction from a clearly defined 'other,' as is the case to a greater degree with collective identities: on the contrary, individuals often express a sense of belonging with an 'other,' while remaining outside the bounds of the group."[233] In addition to being inclusive the term "belonging" also "does not necessarily need to be based on 'objective' external sameness but can be posited on a more fleeting solidarity"[234] that acknowledges the internally fluid nature of attachments. "Belonging" captures better than "identity" the transiency, weakness, fluidity, and ambiguity of a self's relationship to others.

One of the major effects of globalized migration and of the migration and mediation of images of mobility has been the declining importance of "primordial markers of identity" (inherited and thus taken for granted) and the increased rationalization of identity (viewing identity as a matter of conscious choice). In contrast to older studies of the "idea of Europe," which tirelessly tried to locate the historical roots of "European identity," recent scholarship tends to deny the usefulness or relevance of the very concept of "European identity." Bo Strath expresses this view most strongly when he claims that "the concept of European identity is of limited value today. Like the classification of human beings according to ethnicity and 'race' it has reached its limits. It should be seen as a historical concept, which played a crucial role during a difficult phase of European integration between the 1970s and the 1990s. The twenty-first century requires a new conceptual topography, less Eurocentric and narcissistic and more global."[235]

According to Strath, European society has been mistakenly theorized either through a neoliberal rhetoric, with a focus on the market concept, or through a rhetoric of human rights, democracy, and ethnicity, both of which are inscribed in an American rather than a European historical context. Invoking the familiar distinction between American individualism and the European tradition of social solidarity, Strath suggests that "an urgent task in a European reconceptualization would be to integrate the individual in a social context."[236] This specifically "European" reconceptualization of identity would abandon the search for the "essence" of European identity, preferring instead to work with "identity" as a "floppy concept" that is intentionally more vague, discursively shaped, open to ambivalences and paradoxes, and understood in terms of a shared political project rather than a common cultural identity, that is, oriented toward the future rather than the past. This shift from a historical/archaeological to a political understanding of European identity, from talking about European "identity" to talking about "belonging" and "solidarity," signals the growing importance attributed to the affective rather than merely rational aspect of belonging. And here cinema has an important role to play.

Notes

1. For an analysis of the traces of skepticism within the Enlightenment project see Anton Matytsin, *The Specter of Skepticism in the Age of Enlightenment* (Baltimore, MD: Johns Hopkins UP, 2016).
2. Ien Ang, "Hegemony-in-Trouble: Nostalgia and the Ideology of the Impossible in European Cinema," *Screening Europe: Imaging and Identity in Contemporary European Cinema*, ed. Duncan Petrie (London: BFI, 1992), 21.
3. Antoine Compagnon, "Appendix 2: Mapping the European Mind," *Screening Europe: Imaging and Identity in Contemporary European Cinema*, ed. Duncan Petrie (London: BFI, 1992), 111.
4. Wendy Everett, "Introduction: European Film and the Quest for Identity," *European Identity in Cinema*, ed. Wendy Everett (London: Intellect, 2005), 10.
5. Luisa Passerini, "From the Ironies of Identity to the Identities of Irony," *The Idea of Europe: From Antiquity to the European Union*, ed. Anthony Pagden (Cambridge: Cambridge UP, 2002), 208.
6. John Caughie, "Becoming European: Art Cinema, Irony and Identity," *Screening Europe: Imaging and Identity in Contemporary European Cinema*, ed. Duncan Petrie (London: BFI, 1992), 37.
7. Mary Harrod, Mariana Liz, and Alissa Timoshkina, "The Europeanness of European Cinema: An Overview," *The Europeanness of European Cinema: Identity, Meaning and Globalization*, ed. Mary Harrod, Mariana Liz, and Alissa Timoshkina (London: I.B. Tauris), 1–13.
8. Denis de Rougemont, "Introduction," *Europe and the Europeans: An International Discussion. A Report Prepared at the Request of the Council of Europe*, ed. Max Beloff (London: Chatto and Windus, 1957), x–xi.
9. Ibid., xv. Ruben Östlund's *The Square* (2017) also frames the question of "Europe" in aesthetic terms by drawing a parallel between the challenge to essentialist notions of "European identity" and Dada-like provocations to established ideas about the nature of art.
10. Paul Gifford, "Defining 'Others,': How Interperceptions Shape Identities" *Europe and Its Others: Essays on Interperception and Identity*, ed. Paul Gifford and Tessa Hauswedell (Bern: Peter Lang, 2010), 21.
11. Cornelius Castoriadis, "The Greek Polis and the Creation of Democracy," *The Castoriadis Reader*, ed. David Ames Curtis (Oxford: Blackwell Publishers Ltd., 1997), 271.
12. Ibid., 272.
13. Cornelius Castoriadis, "Culture in a Democratic Society," *The Castoriadis Reader*, ed. David Ames Curtis (Oxford: Blackwell Publishers Ltd., 1997), 338–49.
14. Michael Herzfield, "The European Self: Rethinking an Attitude," *The Idea of Europe*, 147.

15 On the long historical heritage of the process of Europe finding its image through its relationship to, and transformation of, other "Europes," see Sobrina Edwards, "Enlargement and Beyond: Moving Boundaries and (Re)Constituting Identities in Post-Wall Europe," *Globalization, Migration, and the Future of Europe: Insiders and Outsiders*, ed. Leila Simona Talani (London: Routledge, 2012), 127–54.

16 Quoted in Peter Wagner, "Does Europe Have a Cultural Identity?" *The Cultural Values of Europe*, ed. Hans Joas and Klaus Wiegandt (Liverpool: Liverpool UP, 2008), 361.

17 Max Beloff, *Europe and the Europeans: An International Discussion. A Report Prepared at the Request of the Council of Europe* (London: Chatto and Windus, 1957), 5–6.

18 Ibid., 18.

19 Inocencia Mata, "On the Periphery of the Universal and the Splendor of Eurocentrism," *Europe in Black and White: Immigration, Race and Identity in the "Old Continent"*, ed. Manuela Sanches, Fernando Clara, and João Ferreira Duarte (London: Intellect Books, 2011), 91–100.

20 Beloff, *Europe*, 18.

21 Anthony Pagden, "Europe: Conceptualizing a Continent," *The Idea of Europe*, 34.

22 John Durham Peters, "Exile, Nomadism, and Diaspora: the Stakes of Mobility in the Western Canon," *Home, Exile, Homeland: Film, Media, and the Politics of Place*, ed. Hamid Naficy (New York: Routledge, 1999), 17.

23 Luisa Passerini, Jo Labanyi, and Karen Diehl, "Introduction," *Europe and Love in Cinema*, ed. Luisa Passerini, Jo Labanyi, and Karen Diehl (Bristol: Intellect, 2012), 10.

24 qtd in Mariana Liz, *Euro-Visions: Europe in Contemporary Cinema* (London: Bloomsbury, 2016), 15.

25 qtd in Pagden, "Europe," 51.

26 Ibid., 53.

27 Gifford, "Defining 'Others,'" 26.

28 Ibid., 15.

29 Beloff, *Europe*, 36.

30 The idea of Europe should not be overdetermined by geographical considerations: rather, its geographical determination is determined by time and circumstances. [. . .] Europe has no frontiers; it has a face, and an unmistakable one. One should not be afraid to add that . . . it has a soul. [. . .] The idea [of Europe] emerges from a reality that it also transcends, is not afraid to transcend. At the same time, the idea emerges gradually, like a seed coming to fruition (my translation). Quoted in Denys Hay, *Europe: The Emergence of an Idea* (Edinburgh: Edinburgh UP, 1968), xviii.

31 Hay, *Europe*, xix.

32 Ibid., 116–17.

33 Jane Pettegree, "Writing Christendom in the English Renaissance: A Reappraisal of Denys Hay's View of the Emergence of 'Europe,'" *Europe and Its Others*, 42.

34 Wolfgang Huber, "The Judeo-Christian Tradition," *The Cultural Values of Europe*, ed. Hans Joas and Klaus Wiegandt (Liverpool: Liverpool UP, 2008), 44.

35 Ibid., 43.

36 Gerard Delanty, *Inventing Europe: Idea, Identity, Reality* (London: Palgrave Macmillan, 1995).

37 Max Weber suggested as much when he argued that the processes of rationalization and disenchantment were produced by a tendency within Christianity (Protestantism).

38 qtd in Meyda Yegenoglu, *Islam, Migrancy and Hospitality in Europe* (New York: Palgrave Macmillan, 2012), 11.

39 Roy qtd in Yegenoglu, *Islam, Migrancy*, 122.

40 Yegenoglu, *Islam, Migrancy*, 25. To demonstrate the asymmetry between the terms "Europe" and "Islam" Yegenoglu cites Bernard Lewis's *The Emergence of Modern Turkey* (1961), which reaffirms an Orientalist notion of Islam as something that cannot be confined to mere faith, belief, or worship system but is identical with Muslim culture.

41 Catherine Wheatley, "Christianity and European Film," *The Europeanness of European Cinema*, ed, Mary Harrod, Mariana Liz, and Alissa Timoshkina (London: I.B. Tauris, 2015), 89.

42 qtd in Peter O'Brien, *The Muslim Question in Europe: Political Controversies and Public Philosophies* (Philadelphia: Temple UP, 2016), 177.

43 Delanty, *Inventing Europe*, 178. Elsewhere Delanty attributes this idea to Karl Lowith's *Meaning in History: The Theological Implications of a Theology of History* (1949), in which Lowith claims that liberal values are derived from the Christian belief that all people are equal in the eyes of God, "God" being eventually replaced by "Law." See Gerard Delanty, "Dilemmas of Secularism: Europe, Religion and the Problem of Pluralism," *Identity, Belonging and Migration*, ed. Gerard Delanty, Ruth Wodak, and Paul Jones (Liverpool: Liverpool UP, 2008), 78–97.

44 See Frederic Gonthier and Pierre Brechon, "Systèmes de valeurs et classes sociales en Europe," *Les valeurs des Européens: évolutions et clivages*, ed. Pierre Brechon et Frédéric Gonthier (Paris: Armand Colin, 2014), 205–20.

45 On the role of religion in the refugee crisis, see *Religion in the European Refugee Crisis*, ed. Ulrich Schmiedel and Graeme Smith (London: Palgrave Macmillan, 2018).

46 Pagden, "Europe," 12.

47 Yosefa Loshitzky, *Screening Strangers: Migration and Diaspora in Contemporary European Cinema* (Bloomington, IN: Indiana UP, 2010), 4.

48 Uli Linke, "Technologies of Othering: Black Masculinities in the Carceral Zones of European Whiteness," *Europe in Black and White*, 126.

49 Nicholas de Genova, "The Borders of 'Europe,'" *The Borders of "Europe,"* ed. Nicholas de Genova (Durham, NC: Duke UP, 2017), 21.
50 Ibid., 20. Vron Ware has explored the other side of this issue, that is, the resentment felt by white working-class members toward what they perceive as "privileged" treatment of racial others. See Vron Ware, "White Resentment – The Other Side of Belonging," *Europe in Black and White*, 157–72.
51 Yegenoglu, *Islam, Migrancy*, 149.
52 Alana Lentin, "Racism, Anti-Racism and the Western State," *Identity, Belonging and Migration*, ed. Gerard Delanty, Ruth Wodak, and Paul Jones (Liverpool: Liverpool UP, 2008), 118.
53 Isolina Ballesteros, *Immigration Cinema in the New Europe* (Bristol: Intellect, 2015), 5.
54 Žižek qtd in Ipek A. Celik, *In Permanent Crisis: Ethnicity in Contemporary European Media and Cinema* (Ann Arbor, MI: University of Michigan Press, 2015), 10.
55 The vanishing of race from neo-racism is paralleled, in Balibar's analysis, by a similar vanishing of class.
56 On the ethnicization of the Islamic diaspora, see Bassam Tibi, "The Return of Ethnicity to Europe via Islamic Migration? The Ethnicization of the Islamic Diaspora," *Ethnic Europe: Mobility, Identity, and Conflict in a Globalized World*, ed. Roland Hus (Stanford, CA: Stanford UP, 2010), 127–56.
57 Cagla E. Aykac, "What Space for Migrant Voices in European Anti-Racism?" *Identity, Belonging and Migration*, ed. Gerard Delanty, Ruth Wodak and Paul Jones (Liverpool: Liverpool UP, 2008), 120–33.
58 See Étienne Balibar, "Y a-t-il un 'neo-racisme'?" *Race, nation, classe, classe: les identités ambiguës*, ed. Balibar, Étienne, and Immanuel Wallerstein (Paris: La decoverte/Poche, 1997), 27–41.
59 See Balibar, "La racism de classe," *Race, nation, classe*, 272–308.
60 Stuart Hall, "Old and New Identities, Old and New Ethnicities," *Culture, Globalization and the World-system: Contemporary Conditions for the Representation of Identity*, ed. Anthony D. King (Minneapolis: University of Minnesota Press, 1997), 53.
61 Hartmut Kaelble, *A Social History of Europe, 1945–2000: Recovery and Transformation after Two World Wars* (New York: Berghahn Books, 2013).
62 Heikki Mikkeli, *Europe as an Idea and an Identity* (New York: St. Martin's Press, Inc., 1998).
63 Wilfried Nippel, "Homo Politicus and Homo Oeconomicus: The European Citizen According to Max Weber," *The Idea of Europe*.
64 Herzfeld, "The European Self," 139.
65 Ginette Verstraette, *Tracking Europe: Mobility, Diaspora, and the Politics of Location* (Durham, NC: Duke UP, 2010), 25.
66 James Tully, "The Kantian Idea of Europe: Critical and Cosmopolitan Perspectives," *The Idea of Europe*, 339.

67 Mikkeli, *Europe as an Idea*, 97.
68 Philip Ruttley, "The Long Road to Unity: The Contribution of Law to the Process of European Integration since 1945," *The Idea of Europe*, 228–59.
69 Mabel Berezin, "Territory, Emotion and Identity: Spatial Recalibration in a New Europe," *Europe without Borders: Remapping Territory, Citizenship and Identity in a Transnational Age*, ed. Mabel Berezin and Martin Schain (Baltimore, MD: The Johns Hopkins UP, 2003), 1–30.
70 Anthony D. Smith, "Towards a Global Culture?" *Theory, Culture and Society* 7, no. 2–3 (June 1990): 171–91.
71 Richard Robyn, "Introduction: National versus Supranational Identity in Europe," *The Changing Face of European Identity*, ed. Richard Robyn (London: Routledge, 2005), 2.
72 Craig Calhoun, "The Democratic Integration of Europe: Interests, Identity and the Public Sphere," *Europe without Borders*, 246.
73 Marc Abeles, "Virtual Europe," *An Anthropology of the European Union: Building, Imagining, and Experiencing the New Europe*, ed. Irene Belier and Thomas M. Wilson (Oxford: Berg, 2000), 31–52.
74 Chiara Bottici and Benoit Challand, *Imagining Europe: Myth, Memory and Identity* (London: Cambridge UP, 2013), 21.
75 qtd in Boticci and Challand, *Imagining Europe*, 31. See Jürgen Habermas, *The Postnational Constellation: Political Essays* (Cambridge, MA: MIT Press, 2001).
76 Bottici and Challand, *Imagining Europe*, 37.
77 Diez-Medrano, "Ways of Seeing European Integration: Germany, Great Britain and Spain," *Europe without Borders*, 169–96.
78 See Thomas Risse and Daniela Engelmann-Martin, "Identity Politics and European Integration: The Case of Germany," *The Idea of Europe*, 287–316.
79 On the affective turn in political studies, see *Politics and the Emotions: The Affective Turn in Contemporary Political Studies*, ed. Paul Hoggett and Simon Thompson (London: Bloomsbury, 2012), and Peter Sloterdijk, *Rage and Time: A Psychopolitical Investigation* (New York: Columbia UP, 2012).
80 Michael Bruter, *Citizens of Europe? The Emergence of a Mass European Identity* (New York: Palgrave Macmillan, 2005), 5.
81 Ibid., 7.
82 Political identity has two aspects, cultural and civic: the former, developed by German thinkers like Fichte and Herder, locates the legitimacy of political communities in a corresponding "nation" defined by a common culture and a common language; the latter, derived from the French Enlightenment and the 1789 Revolution, locates it in political institutions implicitly accepted by society through a social contract (Bruter, *Citizens of Europe?* 11). The problem is that in Europe the two identities do not match.
83 Ibid., 13.
84 Ibid., 14.

85 Hans Joas, "Introduction," *The Cultural Values of Europe* (Liverpool: Liverpool UP, 2008), 4. On the power-laden nature of the very concept of "values," see Gudrun Kramer, "The Contest of Values: Notes on Contemporary Islamic Discourse," *The Cultural Values of Europe*, ed. Hans Joas and Klaus Wiegandt (Liverpool: Liverpool UP, 2008), 338–56.

86 Michael Borgolte, "How Europe Became Diverse: On the Medieval Roots of the Plurality of Values," *The Cultural Values of Europe*, ed. Hans Joas and Klaus Wiegandt (Liverpool: Liverpool UP, 2008), 86.

87 The prime example of "inwardness" comes from the Gospel of Luke, the passage on sisters Martha and Mary who give shelter to Jesus.

88 Kurt Flasch, "The Value of Introspection," *The Cultural Values of Europe*, ed. Hans Joas and Klaus Wiegandt (Liverpool: Liverpool UP, 2008), 152–65.

89 Herzfeld, "The European Self," 148.

90 See Reinhart Koselleck, "The Status of the Enlightenment in German History," *The Cultural Values of Europe*, 253–64.

91 See Orlando Patterson, "Freedom, Slavery, and the Modern Construction of Rights," *The Cultural Values of Europe*, 115–51.

92 Patterson, "Freedom, Slavery, and the Modern Construction of Rights," 151.

93 See Mark Mazower, "The Dark Continent – Europe and Totalitarianism," *The Cultural Values of Europe*, ed. Hans Joas and Klaus Wiegandt (Liverpool: Liverpool UP, 2008), 265–76.

94 Ewa Mazierska, Lars Kristensen, and Eva Näripea, "Introduction," *Postcolonial Approaches to Eastern European Cinema: Portraying Neighbors on Screen*, ed. Ewa Maziersak, Lars Kristensen, and Eva Näripea (London: I.B. Tauris, 2014), 3–4.

95 Arjun Appadurai, *Modernity at Large: Cultural Dimensions of Globalization* (Minneapolis: University of Minnesota Press, 1996), 17.

96 Zygmunt Bauman, *Globalization: The Human Consequences* (Cambridge: Polity Press, 1998), 9.

97 Ibid., 58.

98 Ibid., 59.

99 Appadurai, *Modernity at Large*, 54.

100 Jacques Rancière, *The Politics of Aesthetics* (London: Bloomsbury, 2006), 20.

101 Edward Said, *Culture and Imperialism* (London: Chatto and Windus, 1993), xxi–xxii.

102 See Dipesh Chakrabarty, *Provincializing Europe: Postcolonial Thought and Historical Difference* (Princeton: Princeton UP, 2000).

103 Alain Badiou and Marcel Gauchet, *What Is To Be Done? A Dialogue on Communism, Capitalism, and the Future of Democracy* (Cambridge: Polity Press, 2016), 90.

104 William Davies, *The Limits of Neoliberalism: Authority, Sovereignty and the Logic of Competition* (London: SAGE Publications, 2017), 6.

105 While Rancière construes "politics" as a structural excess within the "police order," Balibar relies on Samaddar's definition of justice as "in excess over law" which "demands always something more than legal changes or settlements" (14). See Étienne Balibar, "Justice and Equality: A Political Dilemma? Pascal, Plato, Marx," *The Borders of Justice*, ed. Étienne Balibar, Sandro Mezzadra, and Ranabir Samaddar (Philadelphia: Temple UP, 2012), 9–33.

106 Derrida attributes his aversion to the term "community" to its connotations of fusion and identification, since what is proper to a culture is not to be identical to itself. See Jacques Derrida, *The Other Heading: Reflections on Today's Europe* (Bloomington, IN: Indiana UP, 1992).

107 See Christina Boswell and Andrew Geddes, *Migration and Mobility in the EU* (London: Palgrave Macmillan, 2011).

108 Robert Stam and Ella Shohat, "The Culture Wars in Translation," *Europe in Black and White: Immigration, Race, and Identity in the "Old Continent,"* ed. Manuela Sanches, Fernando Clara, and João Ferreira Duarte (London: Intellect, 2011), 20.

109 de Genova, "The Borders of 'Europe,'" 23–24.

110 Catherine Wihtol de Wenden, *La question migratoire au XXIe siècle: Migrants, refugies et relations internationals* (Paris: Science Po Presses, 2013), 13–73.

111 Thomas G. Deveny, *Migration in Contemporary Hispanic Cinema* (Toronto: The Scarecrow Press, 2012), x.

112 See Dana Diminescu, "Le migrant connecté: pour un manifeste épistémologique," *Migrations Société* 17, no. 102 (2005): 275–92.

113 See Abdelmalek Sayad, *La Double Absence. Des illusions de l'émigré aux souffrances de l'immigré* (Paris: Seuil, 1999).

114 See Hakim Abderrezak, *Ex-Centric Migrations: Europe and the Maghreb in Mediterranean Cinema, Literature, and Music* (Bloomington, IN: Indiana UP, 2016).

115 See Matthew Price, *Rethinking Asylum: History, Purpose and Limits* (Cambridge: Cambridge UP, 2009).

116 Some situations leading to forced migration are not covered by the Geneva Convention. See Greg Philo, Emma Briant, and Pauline Donald, *Bad News for Refugees* (London: Pluto Press, 2013).

117 Laia Soto Bermant, "The Mediterranean Question: Europe and Its Predicament in the Southern Peripheries," *The Borders of "Europe": Autonomy of Migration, Tactics of Bordering*, ed. Nicholas de Genova (Durham, NC: Duke UP, 2017), 137.

118 Leen Engelen and Kris van Heuckelom, "Introduction: From the East to the West and Back: Screening Mobility in Post-1989 European Cinema," *European Cinema after the Wall: Screening East-West Mobility*, ed. Leen Engelen and Kris van Heuckelom (Lanham, MD: Rowman & Littlefield, 2014), xviii.

119 See Philipp Ther, *Europe since 1989: A History* (Princeton: Princeton UP, 2014).

120 qtd in Agnes Kakasi, "Transcending the 'Poor Relative' Metaphor: The Representation of Eastern European Migrants in Recent Irish Films," *European Cinema after the Wall: Screening East-West Mobility*, ed. Leen Engelen and Kris van Heuckelom (Lanham, MD: Rowman & Littlefield, 2014), 26.

121 https://www.merriam-webster.com/dictionary/legitimate, accessed August 3, 2019.

122 The term "illegal migration" is problematic though still widely used. Hakim Abderrezak has proposed replacing "illegal" with "clandestine," a term inviting us to see "illegal" immigration in human terms rather than from the point of view of the nation state.

123 Orban Wallace's documentary *Another News Story* (2017) explores how the media coverage framed the 2015 crisis.

124 Christopher Deliso, *Migration, Terrorism, and the Future of a Divided Europe: A Continent Transformed* (Santa Barbara, CA: Praeger Security International, 2017), 198.

125 Ibid., 41.

126 de Genova, "The Borders of 'Europe,'" 6.

127 See Cagla E. Aykac, "What Space for Migrant Voices in European Anti-Racism?" *Identity, Belonging and Migration*, ed. Gerard Delanty, Ruth Wodak, and Paul Jones (Liverpool: Liverpool UP, 2008), 120–33.

128 See Vetri Nathan, *Marvelous Bodies: Italy's New Migrant Cinema* (West Lafayette, IN: Purdue UP, 2017).

129 Steffen Kohn, *Mediating Mobility: Visual Anthropology in the Age of Migration* (London: Intellect, 2016), 35.

130 qtd in Bo Strath, "Belonging and European Identity," *Identity, Belonging and Migration*, ed. Gerard Delanty, Ruth Wodak, and Paul Jones (Liverpool: Liverpool UP, 2008), 28.

131 What distinguishes people-trafficking since 2000 from earlier cases of smuggling is the increasing professionalization and global nature of smuggling networks and their intertwining with criminal organizations.

132 Pagden, "Europe," 40.

133 Pocock qtd in Pagden, "Europe," 60.

134 See Gabriel Popescu, *Bordering and Ordering the Twenty-First Century: Understanding Borders* (Lanham, MD: Rowman and Littlefield Publishers, 2012).

135 Randall Halle, *The Europeanization of Cinema: Interzones and Imaginative Communities* (Champaign, IL: University of Illinois Press, 2014), 4.

136 Ibid., 44.

137 John Williams, *The Ethics of Territorial Borders: Drawing Lines in the Shifting Sand* (London: Palgrave Macmillan, 2006), 6.

138 Verstraette, *Tracking Europe*, 8.

139 Michael Heffernan, *The Meaning of Europe: Geography and Geopolitics* (London: Arnold, 1998), 239.

140 Hamid Naficy, *An Accented Cinema: Exilic and Diasporic Filmmaking* (Princeton: Princeton UP, 2001), 5.

141 Popescu, *Bordering and Ordering the Twenty-First Century*, 25. For a critique of different variants of poststructuralist and post-humanist thinking such as "flat ontology," "assemblage thinking," and "the new materialism," which consider "scale" an obsolete concept, see Jouni Hakli, "Afterword: Transcending Scale?" *Scaling Identities: Nationalism and Territoriality*, ed. Guntram H. Herb and David H. Kaplan (Lanham, MD: Rowman and Littlefield, 2018), 271–82.

142 Bermant, "The Mediterranean Question," 137.

143 See Dace Dzenovska, "'We Want to Hear from You': Reporting as Bordering in the Political Space of Europe," *The Borders of "Europe,"* 284–98. On the mutual entanglement of migration, integration, and security, see Huub Dijstelbloem, Albert Meijer, and Michiel Besters, "The Migration Machine," *Migration and the New Technological Borders of Europe*, ed. Huub Dijstelbloem and Albert Meijer (London: Palgrave Macmillan, 2011), 1–22.

144 See Evelien Brouwer, "Legal Boundaries and the Use of Migration Technology," *Migration and the New Technological Borders of Europe*, 134–69.

145 Daniela Vicherat Mattar, "Did Walls Really Come Down? Contemporary Bordering Walls in Europe," *Walls, Borders, Boundaries: Spatial and Cultural Practices in Europe*, ed. Marc Silberman, Kren Till, and Janet Ward (London: Berghahn Books, 2012), 90. See also Fabrice Schurmans, "The Representation of the Illegal Migrant in Contemporary Cinema: Border Scenarios and Effects," *RCCS Annual Review* [Online], 7/2015 for a discussion of the border as a kind of *heterotopia* inviting comparisons with the heuristic potential of the utopian subjectivity with which many American historians invest the US Western frontier.

146 See Sandro Mezzadra and Brett Neilson, *Border as Method, or, the Multiplication of Labor* (Durham, NC: Duke UP, 2013).

147 See Clara Lecadet, "Europe Confronted by Its Expelled Migrants: The Politics of Expelled Migrants' Associations in Africa," *The Borders of "Europe,"* 141–64.

148 https://www.theguardian.com/commentisfree/2016/oct/31/refugees-problem-europe-identity-crisis-migration, accessed August 5, 2019.

149 Ian S. Lustic and Roy J. Eidelson argue that increased level of cultural mixing under globalization produces more parochialization among native identities, with the need to belong to a well-defined community functioning as a defense mechanism against the anxieties produced by globalization. See Ian S. Lustic and Roy J. Eidelson, "National Identity Repertoires, Territory, and Globalization," *Europe without Borders*, 89–117.

150 Mikkeli, *Europe as an Idea*, 74.

151 Loshitzky, *Screening Strangers*, 7.
152 Appadurai, *Modernity a Large*, 48.
153 Ibid., 22.
154 Herzfield, "The European Self," 143.
155 Halle, *The Europeanization of Cinema*, 185.
156 According to the contributors to the dossier, British nationalism is actually English nationalism, Belgian nationalism is actually Flanders nationalism, Italian nationalism is driven by Italy's desire to reclaim its former status as an economic power, Poland's and Hungary's nationalism is overdetermined by their different relations to their communist past and to Russia, German nationalism reflects the unresolved problem of German national identity (the question of *Leitkultur*), the Cold War division, and the country's reunification, while Scandinavian nationalism is "a nationalism of prosperity."
157 Stam and Shohat, "The Culture Wars in Translation," 21–22.
158 Mabel Berezin, "Introduction: Territory, Emotion and Identity," *Europe without Borders*, 1–30.
159 Williams qtd in Berezin, "Introduction," 9–10.
160 Berezin, "Introduction," 10.
161 See Riva Kastotyano, "Transnational Networks and Political Participation: The Place of Immigrants in the European Union," *Europe without Borders*, 64–85.
162 See Dennis Broeders, "A European 'Border' Surveillance System Under Construction," *Migration and the New Technological Borders*, 40–67.
163 Verstraette, *Tracking Europe*, 99.
164 Christian Karner, *Negotiating National Identities: Between Globalization, the Past, and the 'Other'* (Farnham: Ashgate, 2011), 86.
165 William Davies, *The Limits of Neoliberalism: Authority, Sovereignty and the Logic of Competition* (London: SAGE Publications, 2017), 189.
166 Ibid., 192.
167 Quinn Slobodian, *Globalists: The End of Empire and the Birth of Neoliberalism* (Cambridge, MA: Harvard University Press, 2018), 6.
168 For a summary of the main points of Geneva School neoliberalism (ordoliberalism), see Slobodian, *Globalists*, 271–72.
169 Ibid., 95.
170 John D. Marquez, "Nations Re-bound: Race and Biopolitics at EU and US Borders," *Europe in Black and White*, 39.
171 Talal Asad, "Muslims and European Identity: Can Europe Represent Islam?" *The Idea of Europe*, 216.
172 Laia Soto Bermant, "The Mediterranean Question: Europe and Its Predicament in the Southern Peripheries," *The Borders of "Europe*," 133.
173 Ibid., 5.

174 Davies qtd in Boris Previsic, "Europe's Blind Spot on Violence: the Fall of Yugoslavia and references to World War II," *Europe and Its Others*, 201.
175 On the differences between Balkanism and Orientalism, see Maria Todorova, *Imagining the Balkans* (New York: Oxford UP, 1997).
176 Hammond qtd in Elzbieta Ostrowska, "Postcolonial Fantasies: Imagining the Balkans: The Polish Popular Cinema of Wladyslaw Pasikowski," *Postcolonial Approaches to Eastern European Cinema*, 178.
177 "Nested Orientalisms" refers to the tendency of each Yugoslav region to view the cultures and religions to its South and East as more primitive.
178 Engelen and van Heuckelom, "Introduction," xii.
179 Tessa Hauswedell, "Introduction," In *Europe and Its Others*, 1–13.
180 Karner, *Negotiating National Identities*, 176.
181 See Patricia Ehrkamp, "Migrants, Mosques, and Minarets: Reworking the Boundaries of Liberal Democracy in Switzerland and Germany," *Walls, Borders, Boundaries: Spatial and Cultural Practices in Europe*, ed. Marc Silberman, Kren Till, and Janet Ward (London: Berghahn Books, 2012), 153–72.
182 See Rinella Cere, "Globalization vs. Localization: Anti-immigrant and Hate Discourses in Italy," *Beyond Monopoly: Globalization and Contemporary Italian Media*, ed. Michela Ardizzoni and Chiara Ferrari (Lanham, MD: Lexington Books, 2010), 225–44.
183 O'Brien, *The Muslim Question*, 2.
184 Yegenoglu, *Islam, Migrancy*, 15.
185 Ibid., 29.
186 See Ruben Andersson, "Rescued and Caught: The Humanitarian-Security Nexus at Europe's Frontiers," *The Borders of Europe*, 64–94.
187 Elizabeth Dunn, *No Path Home: Humanitarian Camps and the Grief of Displacement* (Ithaca, NY: Cornell UP, 2017), 9.
188 Ibid., 207.
189 Celik, *In Permanent Crisis*, 133. See also Ipek Celik-Rappas, "Refugees as Innocent Bodies, Directors as Political Activists: Humanitarianism and Compassion in European Cinema," *Revista Latinoamericana de Estudios sobre Cuerpos, Emociones y Sociedad*, no. 9 (2017): 81–89.
190 See Sonia Tascon, "'The Humanitarian Gaze,' Human Rights Films, and Glocalised Social Work," *Social Work in a Glocalised World*, ed. Mona Livholts and Lia Bryant (New York: Routledge, 2017), 71–86.
191 Bulent Diken and Carsten Bagge Lausten, *The Culture of Exception: Sociology Facing the Camp* (New York: Routledge, 2005), 177.
192 Pascal Bruckner, *The Tears of the White Man: Compassion as Contempt*, trans. William R. Beer (London: The Free Press, 1986), 149, my emphasis.
193 Ibid., 153–54.
194 Alain Badiou, *Ethics: An Essay on the Understanding of Evil*, trans. Peter Hallward (London: Verso, 2001), lvi.

195 Ibid., 9.
196 Ibid., 12–13.
197 Ibid., 9.
198 Ibid., 23.
199 Jacques Rancière, *Dissensus: On Politics and Aesthetics* (London: Bloomsbury, 2015), 63.
200 Ibid., 78. For Agamben, "the fact that must constitute the point of departure for any discourse on ethics is that there is no essence, no historical or spiritual vocation, no biological destiny that humans must enact or realize" (42).
201 Rancière, *Dissensus*, 71.
202 Lyotard qtd in Rancière, *Dissensus*, 73.
203 Rancière, *Dissensus*, 200.
204 Balibar, Mezzadra and Samaddar, "Introduction," *The Borders of Justice*, 2.
205 Emmanuel Renault, "Struggles for Justice: Political Discourses, Experiences, and Claims," *The Borders of Justice*, 99–122.
206 Francisco Naishtat, "Global Justice and Politics: On the Transition from the Normative to the Political Level," *The Borders of Justice*, 38.
207 On the normative turn, see Michael Lister and Emily Pia, *Citizenship in Contemporary Europe* (Edinburgh: Edinburgh UP, 2008).
208 Berezin, "Introduction," 12.
209 Mezzadra and Neilson, *Border as Method*, 199.
210 Lister and Pia, *Citizenship*, 59.
211 Jacobson qtd in O'Brien, *The Muslim Question*, 69–70.
212 O'Brien, *The Muslim Question*, 75.
213 See J. Nicholas Entrikin, "Political Community, Identity and Cosmopolitan Place," *Europe without Borders*, 51–63.
214 qtd in Lister and Pia, *Citizenship*, 175.
215 Gerard Delanty, Paul Jones, and Ruth Wodak, "Introduction: Migration, Discrimination and Belonging in Europe," *Identity, Belonging and Migration*, ed. Gerard Delanty, Ruth Wodak, and Paul Jones (Liverpool: Liverpool UP, 2008), 6.
216 Williams, *The Ethics of Territorial Borders*, 36.
217 Yegenoglu, *Islam, Migrancy*, 79.
218 Miller, *Strangers in Our Midst*, 14.
219 Ibid., 83.
220 Rene Sigrist and Stella Ghervas, "La mémoire européenne a l'heure du 'paradigme victimaire,'" *Lieux d'Europe: Mythes et limites*. Sous la direction de Stella Ghervas et François Rosset (Paris: Editions de la Maison des sciences de l'homme, 2008), 215–43. Examining exemplary images of Europe in art, Paul Dethurens has argued that after the Second World War, Europe

ceased to serve as a "lieu de mémoire," appearing instead "in ruins," a non-place (un non-lieu) not in a juridical but in an ontological sense, as evidenced by Max Ernst's *L'Europe après la pluie II* (1940–1942). See Paul Dethurens, "Europe, lieu-fantasme: Le mythe d'Europe dans l'histoire de l'art," *Lieux d'Europe: Mythes et limites*. Sous la direction de Stella Ghervas et François Rosset (Paris: Editions de la Maison des sciences de l'homme, 2008), 1–21.

221 Gerard Bossuat, "La quete de l'identité européenne," *La culture slave et l'Europe: du rêve européen aux réalités*, ed. Antoine Mares (Paris: Institut d'etudes slaves, 2005), 19–44. For a discussion of one attempt to create such a "lieu de mémoire" for Europe, see Elie Barnavi, "Un musée de l'Europe pour les Européens," *La culture slave et l'Europe: du rêve européen aux réalités*, ed. Antoine Mares (Paris: Institut d'etudes slaves, 2005), 53–64.

222 William Uricchio, "We Europeans?" Media, Representations, Identities," *We Europeans? Media, Representations, Identities*, ed. William Uricchio (Bristol: Intellect Books, 2008), 14.

223 Rob Kroes, "Imaginary Americas in Europe's Public Space," *We Europeans? Media, Representations, Identities*, ed. William Uricchio (Bristol: Intellect Books, 2008), 29.

224 O'Brien, *The Muslim Question*, 12.

225 Ibid., 13.

226 Wagner, "Does Europe," 364.

227 Ibid., 365.

228 qtd in Beloff, *Europe*, 10.

229 Bottici and Challand, *Imagining Europe*, 4.

230 Ibid., 4.

231 qtd in Mikkeli, *Europe as an Idea*, 210.

232 Mikkeli, *Europe as an Idea*, 210.

233 Paul Jones and Michal Krzyzanowski, "Identity, Belonging and Migration: Beyond Constructing 'Others,'" *Identity, Belonging and Migration*, ed. Gerard Delanty, Ruth Wodak, and Paul Jones (Liverpool: Liverpool UP, 2008), 45.

234 Ibid., 46.

235 Strath, "Belonging and European Identity," 33.

236 Ibid., 33.

1

The Migrant as a Symbolic Figure

The two principal approaches in contemporary scholarship on audiovisual representations of migration have been phenomenological approaches and autonomy-of-migration (AoM) approaches. While some of the films discussed in the present study underscore the autonomy and agency of the migrant, while others dramatize the frequently intangible ways in which migrant bodies are "governed" and "blocked," both approaches share an awareness of the iconic nature of migration, acknowledging the central role cinema and television have played in shaping the public perception of migrants.

Phenomenological studies of migration highlight the various institutional practices and administrative mechanisms that continue to govern and regulate migrants and refugees beyond the physical border of the camp by drawing attention to the ways in which migrant bodies are "contained" or "blocked" not only in space but also psychologically and emotionally. In contrast to AoM's emancipatory notion of "mobile subjects", phenomenological approaches view migrants as "governed subjects" inasmuch as the government of freedom of movement does not only operate through sheer blockage—incarceration, detention, or encampment—but works, as well, "through mechanisms of spatial and temporal suspension of people's lives beyond the regime of visibility sanctioned by such institutional technologies' lifespans."[1] Underscoring the subjective and existential dimension of migration, which remains largely unexplored, Fiorenza Picozza employs the term "decelerated circulation" to describe the temporal and spatial regulation of migration through various practices of detention (including waiting, hiding, unexpected diversion) that profoundly affect migrants' experience of time and of their own bodies.[2] With their trajectories of movement continually disrupted and fragmented migrants experience their own self as a "self-in-transit," always imagining their life elsewhere and elsewhen. Borrowing a term from R. D. Laing, Picozza describes the migrants' sense of being doubly absent (physically from their home country and mentally and emotionally from the country they currently find themselves in), and of their lives as being forever postponed as "a schizoid experience of unembodiment."[3]

Ipek Celik approaches the link between temporality and migration from a slightly different perspective. Instead of studying migration as a specific temporal experience constituted by absence, transitoriness, and unbelonging, and in contrast to earlier work on the spatial cartography of Otherness in European cinema and media, she analyzes the temporality assigned to migrants by the media, a temporality "of violent events followed by periods of incurable social crisis pregnant with the threat of impending rupture."[4] Citing numerous examples of media depictions of migrants and refugees in relation to emergency situations, Celik seeks to understand "how and why violence and temporality of crisis have become central to the articulation of ethnic and racial difference in today's Europe."[5] More often than not, she claims, migrants are denied what Johannes Fabian, in *Time and the Other* (1983), calls "coevalness" by being represented either through "'untimely' acts such as 'honor' crimes that seem to emerge from a distant temporality, instead of being placed within the more general framework of domestic violence,"[6] or by being assigned a catastrophic temporality of crisis.

Dismissing traditional, realist forms of representation as no longer capable of accounting for today's "traveling cultures" (Clifford) and "global ethnoscapes" (Appadurai), visual anthropologist Steffen Kohn also calls for a phenomenological approach to the study of migration. According to Kohn, the increased mobility and interconnectedness of people, things, and places poses an epistemological problem for anthropology, which has traditionally been based on an obsolete "sedentarist metaphysics" that has allowed the anthropologist to "segregate himself and his world from the static, fixed and timeless world of the (primitive) cultural world he studied."[7] Not only would a phenomenological approach reveal "how global relations are necessarily inscribed in local lifeworlds"[8] and analyze migration as a temporal experience (through Husserl's theory of time-consciousness), but a more sensuous approach to ethnography would benefit the social analysis of power relations. Cinema offers an invaluable opportunity for the study of migration thanks to its phenomenological qualities "which inherit an important *ethical* potential[9] as they bring us into an empathetic position toward the other and make abstract political processes become understandable in their effects on individuals and their lifeworld."[10] Drawing on Sobchack's phenomenological theory of film, Kohn argues that certain cinematic techniques, specifically montage, are better suited to convey the complex spatial and temporal aspect of migration (e.g., by disorienting viewers so they can feel the sense of dislocation and deterritorialization experienced by migrants) thus helping us rethink contemporary culture from the perspective of mobility, movement, and interconnectedness rather than singularity, situatedness, belonging, and home. Insofar as transnational subjects like migrants, refugees, and travellers "experience global processes foremost in the form of absences,"[11] cinema, which also works through absences, gaps, and ellipses, can transcend "the limitations of the micro perspective of situated observers and their subject-centered vision."[12]

At the opposite end of the spectrum from phenomenological approaches are AoM approaches to migration. Emerging in reaction to the traditional view of migration as a mere response to socioeconomic factors and to the discourse of human rights with its patronizing conception of migrants as passive victims of globalization, AoM approaches (Nicholas de Genova, Catherine Wihtol de Wenden, Thomas Nail, Souad Osseiran, Stephan Scheel, Ranabir Samaddar) seek to restore agency to migrants by rethinking migration as a dynamic and autonomous way of reimagining/re-bordering Europe. Osseiran's study of the ways in which Syrian refugees in Istanbul imagine migration into and within Europe is exemplary here. According to Osseiran, "Syrian refugees/migrants configure Europe and the EU not in terms of core and periphery, or centers and margins, but rather in more fragmentary ways that draw attention to some spaces and overlook others."[13] As they plan their migration route into and within Europe migrants bypass certain countries, where they do not want to, or cannot, stay permanently, viewing them merely as transit zones on the way to other countries. By "re-bordering" Europe via their discrepant and unpredictable movements migrants are "producing their own imagined 'Europe,'" which, Osseiran insists, should be seen as a political act by political subjects or "mobile actors" with specific "mobility projects."[14] In a similar vein, examining the ways in which aspiring migrants "appropriate mobility to Europe via Schengen visas in the context of biometric border controls,"[15] Stephan Scheel believes that the term "appropriation" "is better equipped than the inherently reactive concept of 'resistance' to account for the *constitutive* role that practices of subversion and dissent by the governed play in the transformation of regimes of government."[16] Adding to the critique of the dominant tendency to see refugees as mere objects of Western pity, Nicholas de Genova reminds us that "refugees never cease to also have aspirations and . . . they remain subjects who make more or less calculated strategic and tactical choices about how to reconfigure their lives and advance their life projects."[17] He urges us to see the migrant crisis as something positively exciting, "a remarkable site of unprecedented experimentation and improvisation, a transnational and intercontinental laboratory for the regimentation and subordination of human powers and freedoms in relation to the space of the planet."[18]

Along similar lines, and distancing herself from studies that associate migration primarily with suffering, injustice, and death, Catherine Wihtol de Wenden credits migration with putting the individual back on the scene as an "agent" that influences international relations and defies the power of the State by appealing to supranational and non-state powers, especially through the appeal to human rights. This time, however, the individual dominating international relations is neither the individual embodying the State (the monarch), nor the individual representing the state (the national hero), but rather the ordinary person whose strength lies not in his power but in his number.[19] Rejecting the pessimistic conclusions critics like Fukuyama and Bauman draw from neoliberalism's commodification of citizenship and its celebration of individual over communal interests, de Wenden celebrates the migrant as anticipating a utopian world, in which the nation state will no longer be the principal actor, and which will be governed by new values, for example, the value of "vivre-ensemble."[20] It is thanks to the migrant, she believes, that a new human right—the right to migrate—has begun to constitute itself, finally correcting the asymmetry between the right to leave a country, including one's own (guaranteed by the 1948 Universal Declaration of the Rights of Man) and the right to enter another country, not yet established as a right (a situation that is the inverse of that in the nineteenth century, when it was difficult to leave one's country but relatively easy to enter another country).

In de Wenden's analysis, the seemingly most powerless—refugees and minorities—emerge, paradoxically, as the most powerful in opposing the state by appealing to transnational non-state actors (e.g., human rights treaties and organizations). Rather than enumerate the seemingly infinite number of obstacles to mobility migrants/refugees face every day, de Wenden prefers to view such obstacles as motivating migrants to develop new, creative strategies of adaptation and multiple overlapping identities: for example, the same migrants can, in the course of their life, occupy a plurality of statuses, from *sans-papiers*, student, tourist, salaried worker, asylum seeker, family reunification applicant to qualified elite, a plurality of identities unthinkable in the past when the Soviet dissident was the main model of the "refugee." The emphasis on the plurality of identities represented by the figure of the migrant is indicative of a tendency in recent scholarship to valorize, rather than bemoan, the migrant's precarious (transitory, multiple and uncertain) status: here we might refer to Giorgia Ceriani-Sebregondi's notion of "capital mobilitaire,"[21] which construes mobility as "a strategy of adaptation"; Mehdi Alioua's description of the transit migration of Subsaharrians in Morocco as an "adventure" through which migrants fashion themselves into "'entrepreneurs' 'working on their mobility projects;'"[22] Marie-Therese Tetu's romantic description, in *Clandestins au pays des papiers* (2009), of the everyday life of *sans-papiers* as a modern "odyssey"; or even Laurent Berlant's "cruel optimism," which she also defines as "a strategy of adaptation," though she does acknowledge that "strategy" to be ultimately self-destructive.

Heavily indebted to Paul Patton's and Stephen Muecke's adaptation of Deleuze and Guattari's theories of nomadology—the idea of nomadic groups using "nomadic strategies" (mobility) in their political struggles[23]—Thomas Nail's *The Figure of the Migrant* (2015) uses the migrant to rethink political philosophy along the lines of what he calls "kinopolitics," profiting from the double connotation of "kino" (referring both to movement/migration and cinema). There are unmistakable similarities between Nail's conceptualization of "kinopolitics" as an analysis of "social *flows*" and Appadurai's rethinking of Anderson's (static and nation-based) "imagined communities" in terms of five types of "*scapes*," though Appadurai's concepts are derived from botany while Nail draws upon the fluid sciences (aerodynamics and hydrodynamics) and statistics. Nail's central argument is that insofar as "flows" (of which migration is one instance) cannot be blocked or controlled but only slowed down or redirected, the migrant is always on the move; even when he is deported or deprived of social status his absence still shapes the society from which he has been expelled. In short, the migrant is never a passive victim but an active force to describe which Nail coins a new term—"kinopower"—that invests movement with agency in opposition to the prevalent tendency to associate movement with powerlessness. Drawing on Bergson's philosophy and on various strands of poststructuralism to reclaim the value of movement over stasis and recuperate displacement from a lack to "a positive capacity or trajectory,"[24] Nail rewrites history from the point of view of what used to be seen as marginalized figures—nomads, barbarians, vagabonds, the proletariat, and migrants—who, far from being passive victims of social expulsion, are celebrated as the primary driving force of social and political history.

Nail's reframing of migration in terms of autonomy is typical of AoM approaches, which, in seeking to correct the (pre)conception of migrants as victims, tend to swing to the opposite extreme of over-valorizing and/or misrepresenting what is often involuntary, even forced, movement as "voluntary" and "free." But does changing the vocabulary we use to talk about migration—replacing "migration" with "mobility project" or "aspirations," or "migrant/refugee" with "mobile actor"—endow migrants/refugees with real agency? The rhetoric of "excess" frequently employed by AoM approaches to underscore migration's supposed autonomy and unpredictability—"escape, creativity, stubbornness, potentiality, uncontrollability, supplement, independence, surplus"[25]—runs the risk of idealizing and romanticizing migration, as evidenced by the return of an old sociological figure—the flâneur—in migration scholarship.

One way to gauge the growing influence of AoM approaches is to consider the wide range of symbolic meanings with which the figure of the migrant has been endowed over the last couple of decades. Ironically, while on one hand migrants and refugees have become, in Rey Chow's words, "the new 'primitives' of Europe, replacing the 'classical Others' of Europe (the Jews and the Roma)," on the other hand, the figure of the migrant has also been seen (and celebrated) as a model for the mobile subject of globalization, a symbol of "postnational" citizenship, nomadic excess, the "structural excess" constitutive of law and morality, or even postmodern subjectivity: thus, Salman Rushdie declares migrants "the outriders of the emerging postnational society [and] a metaphor for all 'humanity,'"[26] while Francesco Cattani advocates the Roma—the quintessential migrant community in Europe—as a model for a transnational European identity.[27] The migrant has come to symbolize, as well, the nomadic identity championed by radical thinkers like Rosi Braidotti, who sees the migrant as "a figuration for the kind of subject who has relinquished all idea, desire, or nostalgia for fixity... an identity made of transitions, successive shifts, and coordinated changes, without and against an essential unity."[28] On the other hand, those more cynically inclined have suggested that by appropriating the figure of migrant and applying a "quick semiotic fix" to replace the obsolete, primordial, and static notion of identity with the more attractive vocabulary of "hyphenation," "hybridity," "syncretization," and "creolization," *multiculturalism*—newly "clothed in a human rights discourse"[29]—has made a comeback.

The human rights discourse has recast the migrant from a *peripheral* into *a utopian figure*, which, by undermining "from the bottom upwards" the nation-state and pointing to "a third way" between nationalism and imperialism, promises to transform the very idea of citizenship and identity. Nail's *The Figure of the Migrant*, which the author himself introduces as "a philosophical history of *the political subject we have become today: the migrant*,"[30] celebrates the figure of the migrant as the preeminent symbol of radical autonomy and of the political *as such*. Nail's study is representative of ontologically minimalist theories of migration, which seek to de-emphasize the material aspects and effects of migration and borders, underscoring instead their symbolic power or value. For instance, Nail denies the possibility of a general ontology of migration: for him, the emigrant and the immigrant are two sides of the same "coin" (the migrant) depending on whether you are looking at them from the point of view of the host country or from that of the source country. In the absence of a notion of a "center," from which migrants are expelled or into which they are assimilated, there are no migrants *as such*—there is only a continuous, random movement between two poles, a movement that occasionally becomes "embodied" in specific figures of the migrant.

The migrant has also been discussed as a figure metaphorically representing our *universal, existential* condition of *exile*, an argument predicated on a broader notion of exile than that associated with spatial and temporal displacement alone. Already in 1999 Hamid Naficy emphasized the virtualization of the concept of "exile": "There was a time when exile explicitly and implicitly involved a present or absent home, or a homeland, as referent. However, the referent is now in ruins or in perpetual manipulation, and the concept of 'exile,' once stabilized because of its link to the homeland, is now freed from the chains of its referent."[31] More recently, media historian John Durham Peters has analyzed the transformation of the term "nomadism" from a description of a particular group of people into a poststructuralist concept of identity partly as a result of the transformation of the territorial idea of home (the patria) into the virtual/temporal idea of home ("located" in the past). For poststructuralists, nomadic identity is not the result of a particular historical trauma but "part of the characteristic motion of subjectivity through signs, otherness and time"[32]—hence Braidotti's concept of nomadism as defined by "*the subversion of set conventions . . . not [by] the literal act of traveling.*"[33]

Positioning his project closer to Simmel's than to Durkheim's—the former interested in the existential or psychological experience of displacement, the latter in migration as a socioeconomic phenomenon)—in *La condition de l'exile: penser les migrations contemporaine* (2015) Alexis Nouss also approaches migration and exile as an existential condition rather than a historical and sociopolitical experience. In an attempt to articulate an ethical approach to the migrant crisis Nouss describes those who perished in the Mediterranean as "exiles" rather than "migrants," the term "migrant" being, in his view, an "empty socioeconomic category" that keeps us within a purely objective/objectifying description grounded in juridical criteria, as opposed to the term "exile," which restores to those people their individuality and dignity while bringing into focus their shared experience for the purpose of a political analysis. Distancing himself from studies of "migration" in terms of "numbers" or "tendencies," Nouss draws on Ricoeur's theory of narrative identity, placing the exile's *recit* at the center of his study. The recit is essential to the exile's attempt to maintain a sense of self, because what the exile suffers from is not the loss of a particular place (the homeland) but the loss of a sense of place (the loss of a sense of identity). Recalling de Wenden's analysis of the asymmetry between the right to leave one's country and the right to enter another, Nouss insists on "a right to exile," which he grounds in Levinas's notion of "exceedance" to the need/right to leave one's own self. As with other studies that purport to render justice to migrants' individual experiences, however, Nouss's ethically inspired choice of "exile" over "migrant" ends up sacrificing the very particularity he supposedly seeks to reclaim: "exile" becomes reduced to a symbol that can be used to describe *any*, and *anyone's*, experience. Ironically, having underscored the centrality of the *recit* to his approach, Nouss fails to offer any specific examples of exile; instead of delving into the political analysis he promised his readers, he veers into philosophical reflections that obscure, rather than bear witness to, migrants' singular experiences. Eventually he dismisses even the term "exile," which still has some basis in the real world, proposing in its place "post-exile," a term describing the experience of ontological foreignness "detached from empirical conditions."[34]

Like Nouss, Wendy Everett and Peter Wagstaff believe that "it is not enough to think of exile exclusively in terms of the spatial and temporal estrangement of individuals forced to abandon their place—and time—of origin. So pervasive is the *trope of exile* that it has come to be seen as a potent *metaphor* for a range of phenomena concerned with the distinctive, the disjunctive and the alienated."[35] This broad, vague definition allows them to discuss under the same rubric of "exile" phenomena as divergent as the inaccessibility of the past (which they regard as an instance of "temporal exile" rather than simply as nostalgia) and the "formal or visual exile" in Chantal Akerman's work. One consequence of this conflation of several different concepts—identity, migration, exile, nostalgia—is that when they ask, later on, whether we might consider the new European cinema of migration a variation on the American road movie, all they can do is repeat the familiar analysis of the latter as an embodiment of the frontier myth while failing to suggest what is *different* about the symbolic meaning of the road/exile/identity in European cinema of migration. Furthermore, their analysis of exile and displacement in contemporary European cinema rests on a problematic conflation of the *historical* with the *philosophical* figure of the migrant, which leads them to treat twentieth- and twenty-first-century migratory experiences as constitutive *both* of contemporary European identity and of the universal metaphysical sense of homelessness we call "the modern condition."[36] Finally, in her recent meditation on the idea of "home"—*Nostalgia: When Are We Ever at Home?*—that aims to recuperate nostalgia as a potentially progressive emotion, Barbara Cassin redefines nostalgia as "a much broader and welcoming way of thinking, a vision of the world freed of all belonging."[37] The lesson of Homer's *Odyssey*, she concludes, is "that we cannot stay 'there' i.e., we 'are' never 'there,' never at home. Rather than cultivating roots, [she] would cultivate the elsewhere, a world that does not close itself off, full of the 'likes' of us, all different—like us, not like us."[38]

Even postcolonial theory is not entirely free of such triumphant readings of the migrant as the ultimate figure of deconstruction. Ella Shohat privileges the migrant/exile as the quintessential and supposedly omnipotent figure of hybridity, "the destabilizer of fixed centers" over the preeminent figure of colonial discourse, the explorer, "as the dynamic center of the text/discourse who teleologically settles on the range."[39] Another instance of the blind spot in the cultural elite's triumphal appraisal of the migrant as a symbol of intellectual freedom is Edward Said's *Culture and Imperialism* (1993), which posits the migrant as an emancipatory figure embodying nothing less than "liberation as an intellectual mission," a figure of

> resistance and opposition to the confinements and ravages of imperialism [which] has now shifted from the settled, established, and domesticated dynamics of culture to its unhoused, decentered and exilic energies, whose incarnation today is the migrant, and whose consciousness is that of the intellectual and artist in exile, the political figure between domains, between forms, between homes and between languages.[40]

Zygmunt Bauman provides a much needed corrective to such celebratory accounts of migrancy, exile, and nomadism when he reminds us that nomadism is a privilege rather than a right granted automatically to everyone and that theories of hybridization and anti-essentialism are, in fact, class-based.

The important symbolic function attributed to the migrant by political philosophers, sociologists, and anthropologists, has not been lost on cinema studies. Following up on David Harvey's argument that the movement of people is more important than the movement and accumulation of capital in shaping urbanization, Gareth Millington has analyzed the migrant as the principal *symbolic figure* through which films represent urbanization on a planetary scale. In his view, it is through the figure of the migrant that cinema foregrounds the ambivalent nature of neoliberal globalization, gentrification, and urbanization inasmuch as the migrant "experiences expulsion and displacement but they are also shown as active, traversal 'citizens' independent of whether they possess any legal form of citizenship."[41] Paradoxically, the migrant as a symbolic figure embodies two opposite processes, the (welcome) de-coupling of the global city from nation and region, but also the dissolution of the city concomitant with the death of the social (the global city as made up of "non-places," lacking a center/an "agora" and thus depriving migrants of the ability to claim citizenship rights). This ambivalence marks Millington's entire study: for example, while he suggests that migrant cinema's distinguishing qualities are its affinities with melodrama (which is similarly structured around the passive suffering of the victim-protagonist) and its ethical claim (which constitutes it as a "cinema of witness" or, in Sarita Malik's derogatory terms, a "cinema of duty"), he also underscores the active role the migrant plays in planetary urbanization, thus inscribing himself within AoM approaches.

One could perhaps argue that Jacques Rancière's influential definition of a "political subject" describes nothing other than the symbolic figure of the migrant. In *The Politics of Aesthetics* Rancière explains that

> a political subject is neither a political lobby nor an individual who seeks adequate representation for his or her interests and ideas. It is an empty operator that produces cases of political dispute by challenging the established framework of identification and classification. Through the process of subjectivization political subjects bring politics proper into existence and confront the police order with the heterology of emancipation.[42]

According to this "definition," a migrant/refugee seeking rights or citizenship cannot be a political subject while, at the same time, a political subject is indistinguishable from a migrant/refugee inasmuch as "the manifestation of politics occurs only via specific acts of implementation and political subjects [such as migrants/refugees] forever remain precarious figures that hesitate at the borders of silence maintained by the police."[43] Rancière's reluctance to provide a more concrete definition of "political subject" is very much in line with his general aversion to substantive definitions: for example, he "defines" political subjects as *processes* irreducible to a particular anthropological or biological essence; rights (for example, citizenship) as *events/actions* rather than substances/predicates; and democracy as the regime of politics *as such* rather than one political regime among many. Thus, rather than being a particular process, politics is only a "crack" or a "fissure" within a specific regime of the sensible, while the "political subject"—which, I think, we can replace with "the migrant" without sacrificing Rancière's intended meaning—is nothing but this fissure, "the inadmissible" of which nothing else or nothing more can be said because if subjectivization "is the process by which a political subject extracts itself from the dominant categories of identification and classification," then "the very act of identifying these political subjects necessarily has recourse to misnomers i.e. names that inadequately refer to the anonymous multitude that has no title in the police order."[44]

For Badiou, too, nothing can be said of the political subject since it is not an attribute or an entity but rather an event/process, which "splits open and overturns the stagnant order of the world by opening new possibilities of life, thought and action."[45] Just as Rancière argues that the political subject emerges only in specific moments, rather than being an entity endowed with preexisting properties, for Badiou "the subject"

> denotes not a permanent property of the actor ... but a stage which s/he reaches in specific situations ... "[S]ubject" applies not to a constitutive attribute of what we are but to an experience that people can have under certain conditions. ... We are subjects at well defined moments, and we are so when a universal is involved in our situation.[46]

If Rancière emphasizes the *dissensual aspect* of political subjectivization, Badiou foregrounds its *collective aspect*, thinking the political subject as "someone who breaks free from self-centered demands and obeys transindividual imperatives."[47] For both, however, the political subject remains an *empty operator* or, put differently, a symbolic figure since, as Rancière puts it, politics is not "tied to a determined historical project [e.g., the French Revolution] ... [but] exists when the figure of a specific subject is constituted, a supernumerary subject in relation to the calculated number of groups, places, and functions in a society."[48] Here one is tempted to ask: Who is this "supernumerary subject" if not the migrant/refugee? But also: Are all films about migrants/refugees inherently political inasmuch as the migrant/refugee embodies most closely the notions of "dissensus" and "politics"? And if we follow Rancière wouldn't we have to say that a film in which a migrant or refugee is struggling to gain rights (e.g., citizenship) is *not* political because the film treats citizenship as a good to be obtained rather than a presupposition that makes thinking politics possible in the first place? I will return to these questions in Chapter 2 when I consider Thomas Elsaesser's and Nico Baumbach's work on the relationship between cinema and politics.

The rethinking of the migrant as a symbolic rather than historical figure has been accompanied by a parallel rethinking of the (refugee) "camp" as a *symbol* or *nomos* of modernity. In his history of the camp, Olaf Briese establishes a continuity between the various transit camps, reception camps, detention camps, transfer camps, and distribution camps set up post–Second World War to organize the flow of the twelve million people displaced in Europe (with many former concentration camps being reused for these new purposes) and the numerous detention centers and refugee camps set up in Europe, North Africa, and the Middle East to deal with the migrant crisis.[49] Like Briese's book, the majority of recent "camp studies," usually indebted to Agamben, are premised on a loosely metaphorical or euphemistic definition of the camp that is ultimately meaningless. This is the case, for instance, with Bulent Diken and Carsten Lausten's *The Culture of Exception: Sociology Facing the Camp* (2005), which opens with the following sweeping generalization: "We live in an increasingly fragmented society in which distinctions between culture and nature, biology and politics, law and transgression, mobility and immobility, reality and representation, immanence and transcendence, inside and outside . . . tend to disappear in a 'zone of indistinction.' The camp, the prototypical zone of indistinction, is the hidden logic behind this process."[50] Here "the camp" is equated with "the hidden logic" that explains a bewildering array of phenomena, despite the fact that the "indistinction" (another euphemism for "the camp") the authors see between the phenomena enumerated above functions very differently in each case. The authors base their examination of the camp as the "hidden logic" of contemporary society on the belief that sociology (like anthropology and political philosophy) has had to re-examine its disciplinary assumptions in the face of the migrant crisis. Diken and Lausten's Agambenian argument is that while the concentration camp embodied a space of exception, a space in which the citizen was reduced to "bare life,"[51] "the production of bare life is today extended beyond the walls of the concentration camp. That is, today the logic of the camp is generalized: the exception is normalized. Hence it is no longer the city [conceived as a space of meeting and sharing] but the camp that is the paradigm of social life."[52] Whereas sociology used to construe the camp as an anomaly and social relations as the norm, the camp, with its logic of exclusion and unbonding, has now become the norm rather than the exception. The authors' pessimistic account sees the contemporary city as dominated by urban structures (gated communities, shopping centers, theme parks, holiday resorts, university campuses, war camps, ghettos) whose very organization replicates that of the camp. One wonders, however, whether it is really necessary to invoke Agamben's notion of "the camp" in order to theorize what numerous critics have already described as the fragmentation of society, the dissolution of social ties, and the proliferation of transitory, any-space-whatever(s) under globalization. Not only do Diken and Lausten reify the notion of "the camp" into a convenient but ultimately meaningless metaphor, taking advantage of its repeated and sanctified use in academic scholarship and of its diffuse meanings, but they proceed to do the same with Agamben's other fashionable term, viewing the asylum seeker as the latest (metaphorical) incarnation of "homo sacer."

Given the multiple symbolic uses to which the figure of the migrant has been put, it is perhaps not surprising that recent scholarship on mobility and migration in Europe has seen the return of a familiar sociological figure—the flâneur. In *The Europeanization of Cinema*, for instance, Randal Halle describes the ideational nature of both Europe and European cinema through a new term he coins, the "interzone," which he defines as "at once a space but also slang for a walk, to bum about, the actions perhaps of a flâneur."[53] Given that flânerie has long been part of the discourse of the modern city, invoking the figure of the flâneur in a discussion of contemporary Europe and European cinema presupposes that one can extend the idea of the modern metropolis to contemporary Europe as an ideational space, that is, that the current idea of Europe has more in common with the idea of the city than with the idea of a supranational space. While this might be an argument worth pursuing Halle does not offer any evidence in support of it. Marianna Liz fills in the gap when she argues that the flâneur has been instrumental to defining the "Europeanness" of European cinema inasmuch as "contemporary European cinema uses cities [which are walked, hence the importance of flânerie] as defining elements of its Europeanness."[54] This is true not only of films set in a single city and functioning as "cinematic postcards" but also of those set in several cities, which present cosmopolitanism as a particular feature of Europe. In opposition to such affirmative visions of Europe, which put forward "a middlebrow idea of Europeanness,"[55] other films paint a picture of Europe as a space of "unfair globalization" rather than "happy cosmopolitanism."[56] One could perhaps argue, then, that if the flâneur is essential to defining a *middlebrow sense* of "Europeanness," the migrant is essential to articulating an *ethical sense* of "Europeanness."

Seeking to address the prevailing myopia regarding the place of empire in histories of European modernity and in the scholarship on globalization, in *From Empire to the World: Migrant London and Paris in the Cinema* (2015) Malini Guha also calls for a reconsideration of "the prominent position the mobilities of the flâneur have come to occupy within early scholarship on the cinematic city,"[57] drawing attention to the continuity between the figure of the migrant and Benjamin's—rather than Simmel's and Kracauer's—flâneur. Insisting on the Benjaminian legacy is important because Benjamin understands the flâneur not only as an emblematic figure of modernity but, at the same time, as representing a resistance to modernity's emphasis on speed, rationalization, progress, and efficiency—it is this unresolved, contradictory nature of the flâneur that "returns" in the contemporary figure of the migrant. While Guha is right to bring attention to the ambivalence underlying Benjamin's understanding of the flâneur, her subsequent comparison of the migrant to the flâneur overemphasizes the superficial similarities between them and ignores the important differences in their political and socioeconomic status. Although both the flâneur and the migrant are outsiders, the flâneur's purposeless wanderings are ultimately the source of a specific, aesthetic type of pleasure that functions, at the same time, as a kind of "'walking cure' against the prevailing melancholy in capitalist modernity—the melancholy to which the modern subject is subjected in his periods of waiting, transit, and transition, certainly, but also the melancholy that is the very condition of modern life."[58] One can hardly describe the migrant's disposition as an aesthetic response to, and a cure for, the melancholy experienced by the inhabitants of the modern metropolis. The idle pleasures of flânerie are a matter of luxury while the frustrated wanderings of migrants bring mostly suffering or death rather than enjoyment.[59]

The gradual consolidation of "the migrant" as a symbolic figure of globalization, the growing popularity of "the camp" as a sort of symbolic shorthand for the aporia constitutive of "law," and the reification of "exile"—disconnected from its real referent—into a metaphor for the human condition, are reflected, as well, in the tendency of many European films to treat migration/exile/homelessness and the loss of identity associated with it as primarily symbolic rather than historical experiences. Consider, for instance, two otherwise very different films, Theo Angelopoulos's *Eternity and a Day* (1998) and Iva Radivojevic's essayistic documentary *Evaporating Borders* (2014), in both of which the experience of migration becomes an occasion for a broader philosophical reflection on the human condition as groundless and thus mirroring the condition of the migrant. In *Eternity and a Day* the subject of migration—in this case from Greek-speaking Albania to Greece—offers Angelopoulos the opportunity to indulge his predilection for Proustian narratives and philosophical musings on the nature of time, mortality, and regret. The story follows an old writer (Alexander) as he reminisces nostalgically about his happy childhood while slowly dying from an unnamed disease, full of regrets for never finishing the work he started—a translation of the poetry of a famous Italian poet of Greek origin—and for not having loved enough his (now deceased) wife. Feeling like a relic from another time, Alexander does not feel "at home" among the fancy apartment buildings of modern Athens, a world that fails to nourish his imagination the way his nostalgically remembered past does. One day he follows a truck of traffickers to an abandoned building on the outskirts of town where he witnesses the "sale" of Albanian children (illegal immigrants) to rich Greek families who cannot legally adopt them. Alexander saves one of the boys and takes him to the Albanian border where the boy confesses that he has no family waiting for him in Albania. Alexander and the boy then flee the border control authorities and return to Athens. It is only now that Alexander, who has apparently spent his life in the protective cocoon of his private thoughts and memories, learns—from a few men he meets randomly on the road—that there has been an influx of Albanian illegal immigrants in Greece.

But what does this jaded, self-obsessed, world-weary European intellectual have to do with a little Albanian boy roaming the streets of Athens with dozens of others like him and washing passing cars for some spare change? What happens when an established "auteur" introduces the topical issue of illegal migration into the rarified world of the European art film? In *Eternity and a Day* the subject of migration is not treated as a subject in its own right but rather as a sort of *generic variation of the art film*, which expands the latter's familiar generic palette—Time, Death, Mortality, Identity, Memory, and now, Migration. Angelopoulos is not really interested in the little Albanian boy; rather, he uses the figure of the migrant as a starting point for a series of reflections on the essentially nomadic/exilic human condition, the irreversibility of time, and the fluid nature of identity. The boy, who remains unnamed—identified simply as "the Child" in the film's credits—is little more than cinematic fodder for the grand philosophical machine Angelopoulos sets in motion, with a nod to Bergman's *Wild Strawberries*, Proust's *Remembrance of Time Lost*, and Fellini's *8 ½*.

As Alexander and the boy drive around through a landscape that remains suspended on the border between the real and the fictional/the metaphorical, Alexander recounts the story of a great Greek poet of the nineteenth century who lived in Italy but when one day he heard that the Greeks, who were living as slaves under the Ottomans, had taken up arms to fight them, decided to return to his native Greece. As the poet travelled back, overwhelmed by memories of his forgotten homeland and his childhood, he dreamed of his mother, all dressed in white and summoning him to return. The story of the poet, who can be seen as Alexander's surrogate since this is the poet to the translation of whose work Alexander has devoted his entire life, is central to Angelopolous's exploration of nostalgia that, paradoxically, conflates homesickness—in the restorative, nationalistic sense of nostalgia and of national identity as something that has been lying dormant within the poet's bosom and is now reawakened—with nostalgia in the broader, philosophical or "reflective" (to use Svetlana Boym's term) sense of nostalgia (the inevitable regret over the passing and irreversibility of time, the nostalgia for one's childhood). In a series of symbolically heightened images the boundaries between the image of the motherland and the image of the mother, between the nation and the private self, become blurred so that the poet is, at one and the same time, summoned by his motherland to return to his native land and fight for the liberation of the nation from its oppressors (the Ottomans), *and* summoned by his mother, dreaming of his happy childhood to which he can never return. It is not accidental that the protagonist of the story is a *national poet*: after all, for the national poet the most intimate memories—the memory of one's childhood, of one's mother—are inseparable from the memory and love of one's country/nation, the nation inscribed deep within the poet's private self. For him—and it is always a "him"—the public and the private, the nation and the self, remain mutually imbricated. As Alexander recounts the poet's story, the camera pans to the right and, bringing past and present together with one fluid camera movement, we see the poet walking back into his hometown, finding again the familiar faces, colors, and smells of his childhood. Wanting to sing for the revolution, but having forgotten his mother's language, the poet wanders through the countryside, buying words from people (significantly, only from farmers and peasants, who enjoy a privileged, "organic" connection to the land) to compose the Hymn to Liberty. Ultimately, the poet's story, which reaffirms an expressly patriotic, restorative, organic notion of the nation as an "authentic" community, in which membership is established through ethnicity, religion, language, customs, and culture, remains in stark contrast with the appeal to hospitality to the Other conveyed by the subplot of Alexander's relationship with the Albanian boy.

In *Evaporating Borders* (2014), a documentary depicting the plight of migrants and refugees in Cyprus, Iva Radivojevic traces the origins of xenophobia through interviews with asylum seekers and various government officials, interspersed with personal mediations on the meaning of identity, home, and belonging. Throughout the film Radivojevic, herself an immigrant to Cyprus from former Yugoslavia, uses visual and narrative techniques to deliberately blur the borders separating her native and host countries, challenging the idea of a single, "authentic" homeland. The film opens with beautiful sweeping shots of Dubrovnic, Croatia's tourist hot spot, and of the Mediterranean sea, accompanied by the director's voice recounting, in sharp contrast to the beautiful visuals, stories about migrants from Syria and Tunisia drowning in the Mediterranean while trying to reach the Italian or Greek coast. Radivojevic includes images of her native Yugoslavia, which no longer exists and which has become "a distant land strangely familiar." It is noteworthy that she uses the same expression, "strangely familiar," to describe her relationship both to her home, former Yugoslavia, and to her host country, Cyprus, deliberately blurring the borders separating the two and challenging the idea of a single, "authentic" home. The film draws out the similarities between the two countries: there are visually similar shots of daily life in both countries, similar shots of streets, churches, and mosques (reflecting the religious diversity of both countries), old men sitting at cafés, etc. The implication is that in a certain sense Cyprus, like former Yugoslavia, does not exist: they are both imagined communities that can disintegrate at any moment (as Yugoslavia, in fact, did).

Ironically, having challenged the conservatively nostalgic concept of "nation," "national identity," and "borders," Radivojevic ends her film with a nostalgic poem about the loss of home written by an Iraqi asylum seeker and poet living in Belgium. Radivojevic herself reads the poem, entitled "Sea Sickness"—a metaphor for nostalgia for the homeland—over beautiful shots of ruins, clouds, the sea, and the sky: "We will never recover from this sea sickness no matter where we land and we will always vomit our dreams and memories of those we left behind until we spit the last piece of home and die." The idea of "home," Radivojevic suggests, is a fiction, a figment of the imagination we will never give up because we cannot live without it, and insofar as we all share the same existential homelessness we are *all* migrants or refugees. Thus, the postscript dissolves the film's political argument into a broad lyrical-philosophical reflection on the human condition.

While it is true that many European films tend to conflate the historical, political, spiritual, existential, and philosophical meanings of "migration," as my two examples above have demonstrated, one could also argue that it is precisely this semantic confusion, this proliferation of the symbolic meanings of migration [which calls to mind the notion of "floppy" or "fuzzy" concepts discussion in the Introduction], that has made the figure of the migrant central to the project of rethinking the "Europeanness" of European cinema and the idea of "European identity." It is now widely acknowledged that the traditional categories through which "the Europeanness of European cinema" used to be thought—"national cinema," "auteurism," and "art cinema"—have been gradually losing their discursive value. As debates around the meaning of "European" and of "Europeanness" are superseded by discussions of "global cosmopolitanism," European cinema is increasingly discussed in transnational terms, addressing "the long legacy of colonialism, the ongoing process of European integration, the geopolitical repercussions of the collapse of communism, continuing intra-European mobility, and the influx of migrants and refugees from across the world."[60] The scholarship exploring the prominent place of migration in European cinema is growing, with already established transnational and postcolonial approaches being now supplemented by new, interdisciplinary approaches drawing on sociology, Continental philosophy, political philosophy, ethics, feminist criticism, historiography, performance theory, and museum studies. Sandra Ponzanesi and Daniela Merolla's *Migrant Cartographies: New Cultural and Literary Spaces in Post-Colonial Europe* (2005), Guido Rings's *The Other in Contemporary Migrant Cinema: Imagining a New Europe* (2016), James Harvey's *Nationalism in Contemporary Western European Cinema* (2018), and the edited volume *Moving People, Moving Images: Cinema and Trafficking in the New Europe* (2010) all attest to the integral role migration has come to play in the construction of "European identity," while Ewa Mazierska and Laura Rascaroli's *Crossing New Europe: Postmodern Travel and the European Road Movie* (2006) focuses on the ways in which one particular genre, the European road movie, dramatizes the paradoxes and ambiguities of globalized migration. Distancing herself from Berghahn and Sternberg's "utopian" assumption of a "postnational" "New Europe," in *Screening Strangers: Migration and Diaspora in Contemporary European Cinema* (2010) Yosefa Loshitzky explores the ways in which migrants and refugees are perceived as a threat to Europe and European identity in the wake of the London Underground bombings and the Paris banlieues riots. In *Mythopoetic Cinema: On the Ruins of European Identity* (2017), Kris Ravetto-Biagioli analyzes European films that resist the comforting idea of a "new Europe" emerging after the fall of communism and, instead, reveal Europe's ethical failure to respond to the resurgence of nationalism and ethnocentrism, while Anca Parvulescu's *The Traffic in Women's Work: East European Migration and the Making of Europe* (2014) challenges the optimistic reading of cross-border mobility and the idea of an East-West "kinship" that the fall of the Berlin Wall seemed to promise by revisiting Lévi-Strauss's concept of kinship through the critical lens of second-wave feminism, reminding us that kinship has traditionally been anchored in the traffic in women or, in the case of the supposedly "new" Europe, East European migrant women.

As postcolonial and postcommunist studies of European cinema have shown, the present preoccupation with the migrant Other is inscribed within the legacy of both the colonial and the communist past. Michael Got and Todd Herzog's *East, West and Centre: Reframing Post-1989 European Cinema* (2014) and Leen Engelen and Kris van Heuckelom's *European Cinema after the Wall: Screening East-West Mobility* (2014) consider the ways in which notions such as "East" and "West," "national" and "transnational," "central" and "marginal" are rethought in European cinema through an increasing preoccupation with the subjects of migration, the economic crisis, and sociopolitical debates about Europe's identity, while Sandra Ponzanesi and Bolette B. Blaagaard's *Deconstructing Europe: Postcolonial Perspectives* (2011) explores the role of Europe's colonialist and imperialist past in the construction of European identity, which is contested both internally (by the proliferation of ethnic, religious, and regional "Others") and externally (by the dissolution of particular borders and the simultaneous erection of new ones).[61] While Third Cinema is often identified as a precursor of postcolonial cinema, the latter is less explicitly polemical than the former, engaging "with society and the 'real' more obliquely, often problematizing the cinematic tools, media technologies and distribution networks through which we receive images and information."[62] Haunting and spectrality, in particular, are central to postcolonial European films' disabling of imperial and colonial paradigms.[63]

Ponzanesi and Blaagard's study is especially concerned with making visible historical legacies that have been forgotten or silenced, for example, Nordic, Austrian, Spanish, and Italian colonialisms. Other recent contributions to this project of "making visible" colonial histories that have remained occluded include Clara Guillen Marin's *Migrants in Contemporary Spanish Film* (2017), which analyzes the contested exchanges between marginal voices and mainstream Spanish society by focusing on the representation of migrants in twenty-first-century Spanish films, and Aine O'Healy's *Migrant Anxieties: Italian Cinema in a Transnational Frame* (2019), which traces the phenomenology of anxiety running through Italian films exploring migrant labor, Italian whiteness, and Italy's disavowed colonial legacy. Sabine Schrader and Daniel Winkler's survey of the history of migration cinema in Italy presents migrants as "the new subalterns," the successors of neorealism's favorite figures, fishermen and peasants,[64] but for Vetri Nathan there is something qualitatively "new" about migrant cinema in Italy, prompting him to coin a new term: *Italy's New Migrant Cinema*. In Nathan's view, while all Italian migrant films made between 1990 and 2010, regardless of genre, are influenced by past Italian traditions, especially neorealism, the commedia all'italiana, and the auteur film, Italy's New Migrant Cinema has moved beyond its neorealist roots, no longer considering immigration as a social issue but, instead, using the figure of the migrant as a prism through which to examine the Italian nation itself.

Ipek A. Celik's *In Permanent Crisis: Ethnicity in Contemporary European Media and Cinema* (2015) draws attention to mass media and cinematic depictions of ethnic and racial Others in terms of "crisis" and "catastrophe," the main two ways in which they become visible in public discourse only to be criminalized or reduced to objects of pity. Although in *Affect and Belonging in Contemporary Spanish Fiction and Film: Crossroads Visions* (2018) Jesse Barker focuses on Spanish cinema, she does so in order to make a more general claim about the importance of *affective attachments* and *belonging*—rather than (national) *identity*—in European cinema, while at the same time problematizing the ahistoricity of ideals of cultural nomadism and affective immersion. Nilgun Bayraktar's *Mobility and Migration in Film and Moving Image Art: Cinema Beyond Europe* (2017) goes one step further by opening up the discussion of representations of migration and mobility in Europe beyond cinema to consider new, counter-hegemonic visions of Europe in the work of video essayists and installation artists.

Although national cinema approaches to European cinema continue to be popular, as are studies analyzing individual national cinemas in terms of a particular theme or subject deemed historically significant to that cinema—for example, the Nazi past in German cinema (Axel Bangert's *The Nazi Past in Contemporary German Film: Viewing Experiences of Intimacy and Immersion* (2014)); terrorism and political violence in Italian cinema (Alan O'Leary's *Tragedia all'italiana: Italian Cinema and Italian Terrorisms, 1970-*

2010 (2011)); Catholicism in Spanish cinema (Elisabeth Scarlett's *Religion and Spanish Film: Luis Buñuel, the Franco Era, and Contemporary Directors* (2014)); or the integration of Maghrebi immigrants in French cinema (Sylvie Durmelat and Vinay Swamy's *Screening Integration: Recasting Maghrebi Immigration in Contemporary France* (2012))—a growing number of studies re-examine individual national cinemas, or specific genres and styles, by placing them in dialogue with transnational and global cinemas. Thus, Marco Abel and Jaimey Fisher's *Berlin School and Its Global Contexts: A Transnational Art Cinema* (2019) approaches the Berlin School as an instance of transnational art cinema; Verena Berger and Miya Komori's *Polyglot Cinema: Migration and Transcultural Narration in France, Italy, Portugal, and Spain* (2010) considers plurilingual migrant narratives in contemporary European cinema through theories of translation and language use, focusing on issues of locality, globality, and postcolonialism; Anna Batori's *Space in Romanian and Hungarian Cinema* (2019) employs a transnational approach to cinematic space to demonstrate the similar structuring of space as an imprint of the socialist past on the postcommunist present in two ex-communist national cinemas; finally, in *Post-communist Film – Russia, Eastern Europe and World Culture: Moving Images of Post-communism* (2013) Lars Kristensen theorizes "a postcommunist condition"—which has arisen after the fall of the Berlin Wall and of the Soviet Empire from the loss of a bipolar world order and the absence of Cold War counter-narratives aimed at "destabilizing either capitalist or socialist hegemonies"[65]—as a shared geopolitical experience unlimited by national and cultural borders (accordingly, his analysis ranges from Russian blockbusters and Chinese independent films to Serbian city films and revolutionary Mozambique films). Like the postcolonial condition, which continues to shape the lives of *both* colonizer and colonized, the "postcommunist condition" is cross-cultural and global—some of its consequences include human trafficking, economic migration, nostalgia for a lost community, and increased tensions with the "Other"—rather than affecting only the former communist Eastern bloc.

Although the last couple of decades have seen a proliferation of terms—"transnational," "migrant and diasporic," "accented," 'postcolonial," "post-communist," "hybrid," "multilingual," and "plurilingual"—to describe the transformation of European cinema in response to decolonization, globalization, and the increased internal and external mobility in Europe, some object to what they see as the undue privileging of "transnationalism" and the "postnational" in film scholarship. Encarnacion Rodriguez believes the concept of "transculturation," developed by Cuban theorist Fernando Otiz, is better suited than the concept of "transnationalism" to address "the question of the colonial, imperialist and economic links between Europe and other parts of the world by focusing on the impact of these histories on everyday culture."[66] Conversely, Randall Halle urges us to excavate the "prenational" (rather than the transnational or the post-national), and through it "the imperial," which is often dismissed on account of its association with colonialism.

Not only do terms like "transnational," "migrant and diasporic," and "postcolonial" overlap but in some cases they seem to have become unmoored from their original meaning, becoming increasingly vague. For instance, Berghahn and Sternberg try to circumvent the "biographical fallacy" by including in their category of "migrant and diasporic cinema" films by non-migrant and nondiasporic directors who draw on a prosthetic memory: "It is not the filmmaker's nationality or ethnicity that determines the classification of a production as migrant and diasporic . . . *migrant and diasporic cinema is demarcated by subject matter in the broadest sense rather than by a combination of biographical and representational factors*."[67] Instead of defining migrant and diasporic cinema as a transnational cinema, which "implies processes of standardization and mass production,"[68] they align it with Elsaesser's cinema of double occupancy, Croft's sub-state cinema, and Will Higbee's cinema of transvergence, all of which, they believe, "can be subsumed under the broad notion of '*post-national cinema.*'"[69] In contrast to Berghahn and Sternberg's tendency to efface the distinctions between categories like "migrant and diasporic," "transnational," "postnational," and "postcolonial," in their introduction to a special issue of *Transnational Cinemas* Sandra Ponzanesi and Verena Berger insist that, although often used interchangeably, "migrant cinema" and "postcolonial cinema" retain important differences, the second term having "a wider theoretical and aesthetic resonance."[70] On one hand, as Ponzanesi herself has shown, the themes of migration, Otherness, and Europeanness are treated not only by migrant filmmakers but also by non-migrant ones;[71] on the other hand, "postcolonial cinema" "not only addresses the question of mobility and uprooting, but also wider issues of visual hegemony and aesthetic counter-discourses. The "postcolonial" in postcolonial cinema refers to a specific "aesthetic language that foregrounds notions of multilingualism, non-places and hapticness, as well as interstitial modes of production and alternative distribution channels that best make it possible to rethink Europe from different viewpoints."[72] "Postcolonial cinema," in the sense Ponzanesi and Berger use it, is a more encompassing term than "migrant cinema" and refers to *any kind of oppositional or anti-national cinema*, which does not necessarily have to deal with migration/mobility, nor does it have to be made by one of the three types of filmmakers grouped under Naficy's category of "accented cinema." Indeed, as we shall see in the next chapters, a growing number of European films escape the "migrant cinema" ghetto—to which films dealing with some aspect of migration and globalization used to be confined—by drawing upon genres and styles typically not associated with the subject of migration.

To question the notion of cinema as a socio-historical collective imaginary—as the term "transnational" does—is to point to the growing difficulty of nations to imagine themselves as singular, internally cohesive entities with a stable collective identity. Used as an explicit conceptual framework, Tim Bergfelder argues, "transnational cinema" has shifted the focus "towards the formation of interstitial forms of existential experience (exile, diaspora, migration, mobility), marginal or decentralized modes of production, the study of circulatory hubs and fluid exhibition networks, as well as questions of affect."[73] Transnational approaches to European cinema purport to make evident the growing obsolescence not only of physical and cultural-geographic boundaries but also of "deep" historical time conceived as a collective experience. And yet, Bergfelder's own study of European audiences' film preferences since the 1990s suggests that the flattening of historical time supposedly registered by the transnational turn has not weakened but, on the contrary, strengthened the nostalgic/cinephilic tendencies in European cinema. The fact that, according to Bergfelder's empirical study, the most popular European films since the 1990s have been comedies (especially genre parodies and/or pastiche like the *OSS117* films), prestige literary adaptations (*Oliver Twist, Pride and Prejudice, Atonement, Perfume*), WW1 and WW2 films (*A Very Long Engagement, Downfall*), live action adaptations of classic comic books, or films targeting the family market and youth audiences, points to a strong *nostalgic* and *cinephilic* tendency in European cinema, as well as a strong *transnational* tendency, exemplified by what Bergfelder calls *middlebrow cinema*, a term he proposes as a way of overcoming the opposition between "art house" and "mainstream cinema." Middlebrow films—for example, *The Sea Inside* (2004), *The Lives of Others (2006), The King's Speech* (2010)—are both popular and critically acclaimed, and, more importantly, have more in common with each other than with their respective national cinemas. According to Bergfelder, this transnational middlebrow cinema, which has generally been more likely to be financed by the major European financing bodies and which, like heritage cinema, is engaged in "creating hierarchies of value and maintaining regimes of taste,"[74] can be seen as "more European."[75]

In Bergfelder's account, then, the transnational dimension of European cinema appears to be not so much the result of the opening of borders and the creation of a transnational socio-historical collective imaginary; rather, it is the *nostalgia* permeating European national cinemas and the *cinephilic turn* which this nostalgia has given rise to, on one hand, and the importance of hierarchies of value and taste (artistic taste being something that transcends the limits of national cinema) on the other, that together produce the *transnational* dimension—the "Europeanness"—of European cinema.

If Bergfelder approaches transnational European cinema from the perspective of reception studies, Anne Jäckel has analyzed the transnational nature of European cinema from an industry perspective, arguing that co-productions, funding mechanisms, and film awards are constitutive of "the Europeanness of European cinema."[76] Today most European countries have co-production agreements with each other and with partners outside Europe, but if in the postwar period co-productions were one of the main strategies for rebuilding national film industries, they have also played an increasingly important role in shaping and promoting a certain idea of Europe. The "Europeanization" of European cinema has been an ongoing project supported by the EU and finding expression in a range of initiatives, from special programs supporting European cinema like *Eurimages*[77] and the European Cinema Night organized by the MEDIA program, to special prizes awarded to European films dealing with the challenges facing "the New Europe." In the case of the LUX prize, for instance, established in 2007 to promote a sense of a shared European identity, the final selection of the winning film is made not by cinema experts but by Members of the European Parliament whose main criterion is the subject of the film and the "European" values projected in it rather than the film's cinematic achievements.[78]

Bergfelder's and Jäckel's studies suggest that the "Europeanness" of contemporary European cinema should be located not in the collapse of geo-cultural borders but either in European cinema's nostalgic/cinephilic tendencies (Bergfelder) or in the various bureaucratic bodies financing European cinema, including the European Union, the Council of Europe and their various Europeanizing initiatives (Jäckel). Sharing Jäckel's skepticism toward the mutual imbrication of funding mechanisms and a certain idea of "Europe" promoted by Brussels technocrats, Randall Halle regards co-productions funded by *Eurimages*, especially films about the hardships of immigration and integration and meant to promote a certain idea of "Europeanness," not that different from "Euro-puddings." While Halle remains reluctant to call "transnational" European co-productions that have been made simply to satisfy preexisting criteria of "Europeanness," Mariana Liz has sought to rethink the Euro-pudding in a more positive light by examining the changes in the use of the term. Conceding that older Euro-puddings like *Auberge espagnole* (2002) offer only "amorphous representations of Europe,"[79] Liz sees co-productions like *Joyeux Noël* (2005) and *The Edge of Heaven* (2007) as signaling the emergence of a "more organic flavor of Euro-puddings" that "tackle the growing interconnectivity of European society."[80] In particular, she endorses *Joyeux Noël*'s rewriting of Europe's traumatic past (the First World War) by replacing nationalism with humanism and "depicting the war not as a moment of conflict but as an opportunity for concord [thus legitimizing] the European integration process widely challenged in the year of the film's release after the rejection of the EU constitution."[81] Liz's suggestion that European co-productions can transcend the status of Euro-puddings and claim a truly transnational character by replacing *nationalism* with *humanism* is predicated on rethinking "humanism" as synonymous with "European integration" or "Europeanization." To sum up, if Bergfelder locates the transnationalism/Europeanness of European cinema in its nostalgic and cinephilic tendencies, and Jäckel in its preoccupation with human rights, for Liz the transnationalism of European cinema—which she presents as a criterion for distinguishing (bad) Euro-puddings from (good) "natural/ organic" European co-productions—lies in a specific narrative theme or worldview—humanism—rather than in a particular film aesthetic.[82] If a film naively celebrates Europe's cultural diversity, as *Auberge espagnole* does, it is disparaged, but if a film is critical, that is, "anti-European," like *The Edge of Heaven* (2007), for example—a LUX prize winner widely praised for deconstructing Europe's "imperialist outlook"—it is considered a humanist film, that is, a "good" transnational film that addresses the audience as "good Europeans." From this point of view, the Europeanness of European cinema lies not (or not only) in its nostalgic, cinephilic or humanitarian aspect, but mainly in its "capacity" for self-flagellation, that is, in its "anti-Europeanism" (unmasking the ideology or rhetoric of "the new Europe"). As we shall see in the next chapter this emphasis on masochistic self-critique/ anti-Europeanism is central to Thomas Elsaesser's rethinking of European cinema as a "thought experiment."

While the term "transnational" has become a buzz-word in the scholarship on Western European cinema, it has not been as prominent in studies of East European and East Central European cinema, suggesting that the overemphasis on the transnational dimension of European cinema obscures previously concealed processes of internal Othering that postcommunist countries are still coming to terms with (e.g., the GDR's anti-Semitic tendencies or the Othering of former GDR citizens as a "minority group" within a reunited Germany). Dina Iordanova has been among the most vocal advocates of a postcolonial—rather than transnational— approach to postcommunist cinemas, on the grounds that "the prevailing economic and political discourse of progressive transition from centrally controlled state socialism to free market capitalism"[83] does not correspond to the postcolonial reality in which postcommunist societies in Europe find themselves. For other critics, however, approaching postcommunist cinema through a postcolonial lens does not address the specificities of different postcommunist countries' experiences of the transition from communism to capitalism, and fails to account for the different conceptions of "otherness" (ethnic, racial or political) that have shaped different national cinemas in their search for a "lost national identity." Robert Stam and Ella Shohat criticize the term "postcolonial" for obfuscating or neutralizing power hierarchies and failing to indicate the specific perspective from which the shared colonial experience is approached—for example, in the case of French cinema, the (ex)colonizer (French), the (ex)colonized (Algerian), the ex-colonial settlers (pied noir), or the displaced immigrant in the metropolis (Algerians in France).[84] Petra Hanakova has analyzed another instance of this "indigenization" of supposedly neutral terms like "transnational cinema," namely the articulation of a Czech metaphor of the nation as "a little but well-tended garden, fenced from its surroundings."[85] The fact that this notion, which pictures the nation in idyllic domestic terms, was dominant not only during the Czech National Revival but was also promoted by the communist regime (which condemned international travel as morally suspicious) and continues to dominate postcommunist Czech cinema (which often links international travel to organized crime), suggests that the dramatic political changes of the last several decades have not overthrown Czech cinema's "stubborn parochialism" and "cultural isolationism." The reluctance, or refusal, to "become transnational" is also evident in postcommunist Hungarian films, which remain mostly concerned with political and historical issues specific to the Hungarian nation, for example, unresolved questions pertaining to the 1956 revolution, the Holocaust, Hungary's ethnic minorities, and anti-Roma racism.[86]

In her study of East Central European (ECE) cinema, Aga Skrodzka argues convincingly that a significant part of post-1989 ECE cinema has consciously resisted globalization/transnationalism by moving in the direction of magic realism. Invoking Hakim Abderrezak's discussion of the disproportionate speeds and levels of globalization, Skrodzka posits ECE magic realist cinema as a resistance to the triumphant narrative of globalization, affirming instead non-synchronic or ancient values "often related to marginalized peasant traditions and the silenced (neo-) pagan folk beliefs and practices,"[87] and emphasizing "acts of embodiment and emplacement"[88] rather than displacement and deterritorialization. Extending Hanakova's analysis of Czech postcommunist cinema, Skrodzka claims that a version of the "small fatherland" discourse—"the idea of home as located in one's nostalgically embellished backyard"[89]—existed in all ECE countries, representing their analogous attempts to reimagine the nation in opposition to the communist doctrine of internationalism. Importantly, the small fatherland discourse did not disappear after 1989 but continued to provide people with a sense of comfort and belonging; indeed, Skrodzka regards it as an escape not only from communist ideology but "from all ideologies and history into a transgressive, often stylistically excessive, private microcosm."[90] As we shall see in Chapter 2, Elsaesser's conception of what he calls the "abjection" of recent European cinema bears striking similarities to Skrodzka's description of ECE magic realist cinema's deliberate embracing of marginality, though Skrodzka limits her argument to ECE cinema while Elsaesser's argument extends to all of European cinema (although his examples are drawn mostly from Western European cinema).

It is not only ECE cinema that has resisted the expectation to become transnational. According to Massimo Locatelli and Francesco Pitassio, despite the increasing number of studies of Italian migration cinema, which often position films about migrants as continuing the legacy of neorealism, Italian cinema has generally remained isolated from the globalizing discourse that has reshaped, to a greater degree, French and German cinema. That Italian film producers remain ignorant about, and uninterested in, transnational discourse can be gauged from their persistent tendency to swap the national identity of actors and the characters they are supposed to portray, so that a Polish actor can embody a Russian, a Slovak can turn into a Croatian, while Roma and Romanians are regularly treated as identical.[91] The continued relevance of *la questione meridionale* and the dominant position occupied by canonical movements like neorealism have been identified as important reasons for the dearth of scholarly literature on cinema made by non-Italians living in Italy.[92] Alberto Zambenedetti, too, paints an unflattering picture of the representation of migration and diaspora in "the New Italian Cinema," unmasking the racist undertones of Italian "multiculturalism"—he identifies two trends in Italian migration cinema, films about dark-skinned immigrants ("negri" and "marocchini") and films about light-skinned immigrants ("slavi" and "Albanese")—in opposition to the ideal of "the transnational."[93] There is, however, reason to be hopeful, given the recent appearance of a number of films, mostly Sicilian, that remap the Italian national imaginary by featuring characters from the North moving South rather than the other way around.[94]

The skepticism toward postcolonial studies of European cinema, particularly of East European and East Central European cinema, has not completely discredited postcolonial approaches, however, as evidenced by a number of recent studies approaching postcommunist European identity as postcolonial and foregrounding the *rhetorical-discursive* functions of "the neighbor" (rather than "the stranger") in the construction of national identity. Mazierska, Kristensen, and Naripea's *Postcolonial Approaches to Eastern European Cinema* (2014) is representative of this focus on the representation of "neighbors," "people living in a neighboring country, ethnic minorities inhabiting the same country but regarded as ethnically and culturally different as well as those located further away but exerting significant political, cultural or economic influence on the examined group."[95]

Arguably, the debates about the most appropriate methodological approach to contemporary European cinema—should it be called "transnational," "postcolonial," "postcommunist," or something else altogether—emerged in response to the growing number of European films that, starting in the late 1980s/early 1990s, began exploring themes of mobility and migration. From the late 1980s up until the early 2000s one of the most prevalent storylines in films featuring migrant characters involved a culture clash between Europeans and first- or second-generation immigrants, or a generational clash within an immigrant community: for example, *40 m² Deutschland* (Tevfik Baser, 1986) [a Turkish woman marries a migrant worker and moves to Germany with him, where she spends her days locked in his apartment], *Yasemin* (Hark Bohm, 1988) [the love story of a Turkish girl and her German boyfriend trying to navigate the cultural differences threatening their romance], *Yara* (Yilmaz Arslan, 1998) [a Turkish-German girl is torn between two cultures], *April Children* (Yüksel Yavuz, 1998) [the disillusionment experienced by second-generation Turkish-Germans, alienated both from their home country and from their adopted country], *Brothers and Sisters* (Thomas Arlsan, 1997)[set in Kreuzberg and sketching the lives "between two cultures" of three Turkish-German teenaged siblings], *Short Sharp Shock* (Fatih Akin, 1998) [three friends living in Germany, a Turk, a Serb and a Greek, fall into a life of petty crime], *Banlieue Nord* (Balbara Albert, 1999) [set against the backdrop of the Bosnian conflict and following five young people from different ethnic backgrounds whose lives intersect in working-class north Vienna], *Salut cousin!* (Merzak Allouache, 1996) [the misadventures of two Algerian cousins in Paris], *Café au lait* (Mathieu Kassovitz, 1992) [a love triangle between a white girl, a black Muslim, and a Jew], *East Is East* (Damien O'Donnell, 1999) [the traditional role of a Pakistani patriarch of a 1970s mixed-ethnicity British household is challenged by his Anglicized children], *Ghettokids* (Christian Wagner, 2002) [the struggle of two Greek brothers living in Munich's poorest neighborhood to start a new life in their adopted land], *Le grand voyage* (Ismaël Ferroukhi, 2004) [a generational clash story, in which a young Frenchman is forced to take his aging Moroccan father on a cross-European trip to Mecca], and others.

While many of these films were clearly invested in what came to be known as a "politics of recognition,"[96] other films were already beginning to question multiculturalism's privileging of cultural over other types of identity. The assumption that Europeans display different types of allegiances, depending on the appropriate context—what Anthony D. Smith refers to as "concentric circles of loyalty and belonging"—was becoming increasingly hard to sustain, as evidenced by a growing number of films in which these "concentric circles of belonging," moving out from the regional to the national to the supranational/European, turned out to be complicated by class, race, gender, and generational allegiances often overriding regional or national loyalties. In *The Promise* (Jean-Pierre Dardenne and Luc Dardenne, 1996), for example, power relations between characters are not structured along national or regional lines, but rather along class lines: migrants from Burkina Faso, Belgium's ex-colony, migrants from the former communist empire, and Belgian nationals from the rural, underdeveloped parts of the country, share the same subordinate position in the film. The same is true of Jean, the French farm lad in *Code Unknown* (Michael Haneke, 2000) and of second-generation Arab and African immigrants in both *Code Unknown* and *Caché* (2005). Jean is a white French citizen but his marginal socioeconomic status places him on the periphery of the post-industrial, global order represented by the Parisian metropolis and thus closer to the various (legal or illegal) immigrants in France, who occupy a similar position of homelessness, albeit a double homelessness (existing on the periphery of the capitalist order *and* having lost their homeland) than to French middle-class nationals.

Indeed, what is notable about many European films, beginning in the 1990s, is a reluctance to represent "migrant" identities (e.g., legal or illegal immigrants, various subcultures within such migrant communities, etc.) *as* marginalized: rather than being merely "recognized" as "different" such identities are often represented as *differing from themselves* and producing their own "underothers," against which they define themselves.[97] Rather than focusing on the most obvious or "visible" conflicts between the center and the periphery, between nationals and foreigners, films like *Bhaji on the Beach* (Gurinder Chadha, 1993), *Gadjo Dilo* (Tony Gatlif, 1997), *Lola and Billy the Kid* (E. Kutlug Ataman, 1999), *Flowers from Another World* (Icíar Bollaín, 1999), *Inch' Allah Dimanche* (Yamina Benguigui 2001), *Dirty Pretty Things* (Stephen Frears, 2002), *Head-On* (Fatih Akin, 2004), *Up and Down* (Jan Hrebejk, 2004), *Yella* (Christian Petzold, 2007), *The Edge of Heaven* (2007), *35 Shots of Rum* (Claire Denis, 2008), and others replace the question of national and cultural *identity* with explorations of ambivalent, transitory, fluctuating feelings of *belonging* and *solidarity* drawn along intersecting class, political, gender, race, legal, ethical or generational lines, thus challenging Smith's notion of "concentric circles of belonging."[98]

Head-On, a substantial departure from such obvious predecessors as Fassbinder's *Katzelmacher* (1969) and *Ali: Fear Eats the Soul* (1973), is a case in point. Rather than emphasize Sibel's difference or marginality as a Turkish-German woman, the film contrasts Sibel's polycentric or hybrid identity—which, precisely because of that, is figured as "authentic"—with the unproblematized identity of her workaholic cousin, a successful business woman still living in Turkey. Sibel does not identify with the traditional image of a Turkish woman her own family seeks to impose on her, and neither does she identify with her cousin's Western work ethic: she refuses to be either a Turkish woman living in Germany or a westernized Turk living in Turkey. Similarly, in *Inch' Allah Dimanche*, the story of Zouina who leaves Algeria along with her children and her mother-in-law to join her husband in France, the main conflict is not that between Algerian immigrants and the French but that between Zouina and other Algerian women (her mother-in-law and another female Algerian immigrant). Furthermore, the queering of Sibel's identity in Istanbul is echoed in Zouina's sexual liberation and gender emancipation so that becoming French is implicitly equated with becoming an independent woman, while being stuck in one's old ways is associated with self-imposed gender marginalization and martyrdom. *Bhaji on the Beach*, which explores a day in the life of a group of Indian women living in Birmingham, also depicts the conflict between nationals and nonnationals as an instance of the patriarchal exploitation of women, exploring racism and intolerance within the community of immigrants as well as in the interactions between two groups of immigrants (Indian and Jamaican), while scenes that supposedly dramatize the exclusion of Indian women from the "Nation" construct nationalism in terms of patriarchy rather than nationality.[99]

In an early scene of *Gadjo Dilo*, the French protagonist (Stéphane) wakes up in Izidor's house after a night of heavy drinking. The Roma note his torn shoes and language and conclude scornfully that he is a bum, "a crazy stranger." Thus, even before Stéphane, and the viewer, has had the time to identify *them* as "crazy strangers," the Roma "steal" this "Othering" gesture. Recalling some of the strategies of postcolonial cinema (particularly the tropicalist phase of Cinema Novo characterized by a carnivalesque inversion of established hierarchies, as in Nelson Pereira dos Santos' 1971 *How Tasty Was My Little Frenchman*), *Gadjo Dilo* has its Roma protagonist Izidor adopting a paternalistic stance toward the Frenchman, referring to him as "my Frenchman" and defending Stéphane's rights before the Romanian villagers who, in another gesture of inversion of center and margins, suspect the Frenchman of stealing their chickens and determine to drive him out of their village. The film thus draws an analogy between the exclusionary politics that operates both at the level of the EU and its margins, and *within* the margins: the central conflict here is not that between the Roma and the Frenchman, but between the Roma, regarded as the quintessential marginalized group in Europe, and the Romanians, another nation considered "marginally European."[100]

In *Dirty Pretty Things,* which figures immigrants as the new European proletariat, the invisible labor force that drives the West European market economy, the main conflict is, once again, not that between British and non-British but that between social classes and, within the underclass of non-nationals, between legal and illegal immigrants, the former occupying the privileged status of white West-Europeans and employing the same strategies of exploitation to affirm their privileged status over the *sans-papiers*. Similarly, the Czech comedy *Up and Down* does not examine the border/conflict between nationals and nonnationals, but situates this border within a political context, juxtaposing the nationalistic ideology of communism (which tends to remain hidden, the most common and incorrect assumption about communism being that it constructs, and enforces, a shared identity along class rather than national lines) with the liberalist, free-market ideology of postcommunism where "anything goes" (babies are sold, like black-market cellphones, from the back of a video store).

In the same vein as the films discussed above, although on the surface *Lola and Billy the Kid* appears to be about the conflict between Turkish immigrants and Germans, the deeper issue is the homophobia shared by both Germans *and* Turkish-Germans. Thus, the Germans' racist attacks are couched in homophobic terms: for them all Turks are perverted homosexuals, and vice versa. When the German gang attempts to initiate its youngest member into their cleansing project, he goes along with it not because he hates Turks but because he is afraid to admit his own homosexual leanings. Like *Head-On* and *Gadjo Dilo*, Ataman's film exposes the logic of exclusion *within* the margins by focusing on a subculture (transvestites, homosexuals) within the margins (Turkish immigrants), locating intolerance and prejudice both within the "center" and the "margins." *A Little Bit of Freedom* (2003) by Kurdish director Yüksel Yavuz, and *Fratricide* (2005) by Turkish-German director Yilmaz Arlsan, also explore ethnic strife and violence *within* marginalized immigrant communities in Germany. Yavuz's film traces the interracial relationship between Chernor, an openly gay African illegal immigrant trying to survive in Hamburg's St. Pauli neighborhood by dealing drugs, and Baran, a Kurdish illegal immigrant working as a bicycle delivery boy in a relative's kebab restaurant, whose parents were killed by the Turkish militia. The film explores conflicts between Kurds and Turks, Africans and Kurds, legal and illegal Kurdish immigrants, Kurds who supported the rebels, and those who betrayed them, rather than conflicts between Germans and immigrants. *Fratricide* is similarly concerned with the Kurdish-Turkish conflict, tracing the tragic consequences of an accidental encounter between two young Kurdish refugees newly arrived in Germany and two second-generation Turks (brothers). However, *Fratricide* falls into the trap of self-exoticization by depicting the Kurdish-Turkish conflict as one that supposedly transcends time and constitutes "Turkishness" and "Kurdishness," thus nourishing the neo-tribalist trend in cinema that feeds off stories about "clan wars" and "honor killings" (e.g., Feo Aladag's *When We Leave* (2010)). Like *Fratricide* and *A Little Bit of Freedom*, *Fraulein* (2006) by Andrea Staka, a Swiss of Bosnian and Croatian heritage, remains within the world of three generations of immigrants from former Yugoslavia living in Switzerland instead of depicting conflicts between Swiss and ex-Yugoslavians. Similarly, instead of focusing on the single story of an illegal Cuban immigrant who marries a Spanish farmer in order to acquire legal status in Spain, *Flowers from Another World* juxtaposes three parallel stories (involving two Cuban women and one Spanish woman) to trace the mutual imbrication of multiple lines of belonging/non-belonging along geographical (city/country), generational, and gender lines.

Petzold's *Yella* is structured around a "false" flashback (since the protagonist to whom it is attributed is dead), a technique widely used in Hollywood psychological thrillers, though the fantasy aspect of the false flashback also has a precedent in German post-1989 cinema, notably in *Good Bye Lenin!* (Wolfgang Becker, 2003), which imagines the communist past as coexisting with the capitalist present. *Yella* conflates Yella's past (her ex-East German identity) and her present (a successful corporate accountant) by making her East German ex-husband and her West German lover/"teacher" doppelgängers. Thus, a dominant theme in German cinema—negotiating the past—is given a new twist: instead of returning to the past (usually the Nazi past) to uncover things that have been long buried/repressed, the film works through the trope of "haunting" with its ambivalent temporality: Is it the past that haunts the present (the memory of a politically divided Germany haunting the reunified nation), or is it the present that haunts the past (the capitalist present retrospectively revealing the increasingly obsolete political divisions of the past)? (see the discussion of Petzold's *Transit* (2018), which also relies on the trope of "haunting," in Chapter 3). Underscoring the increasing obsoleteness of the political distinctions that defined the past in the face of the impersonal allegiances demanded by the global capitalist order, the film relegates historical/national conflicts to the background, focusing instead on the effects of cut-throat capitalism and globalization on personal relationships. *Yella* uses the traces of division within German national identity to dramatize another, more important division between the national as such (the pre-global order of the past, in which the political division between East and West Germany still made sense) and the seemingly post-political global order of the present.

In *The Edge of Heaven*, Akin continues to decouple nationality from the idea of home (Heimat)—as he already did in *Head-On*—by having the fate of every character mirrored in the fate of another character in a series of reflections, substitutions, and symmetries. At the end of a series of symbolic exchanges of national identity and family bonds, every loss is symbolically recuperated: when one mother is lost, another one (of a different nationality) occupies her place, and when one daughter lost, another one (of a different nationality) occupies her place, along the lines of Elsaesser's notion of an "always-already" state of semantic occupation: following Lotte's death, Susanne becomes Ayten's surrogate mother and Ayten becomes Susanne's surrogate daughter. Within this structure of symbolic exchanges, generational/family bonds outweigh in importance political, social, cultural, or national identities.

35 Shots of Rum (Claire Denis, 2008) is an intimate family drama about the inevitable separation between parent (Lionel, a train conductor of African descent) and child (his daughter Joséphine, a university student) following years of intimacy and codependence. This is not a film about the painful process of immigration or about the nostalgic attempt to reclaim a common past, a shared history, a lost homeland. Denis refrains from overtly addressing questions of race and colonialism, suggesting that history—the history of colonialism, immigration, integration—is no longer something to be excavated, reclaimed, or rewritten but simply part of the backstory of every European.

The protagonists' backstory, revealed through their trip to Germany, where Joséphine's mother is from, is figured as always already transnational. The perennialist concept of national identity, defined in terms of ethnoscapes or ethnomemory, is no longer relevant here: instead of a distant homeland, the film depicts a return to another, geographically and culturally close West European country, Germany, thus rendering the past close and familiar, with migration an always already constitutive element of it. In *35 Shots of*

Rum, the changed face of Europe as a multiethnic, multicultural society is presented as a fait accompli rather than as something still in the making: Joséphine's German ancestry positions her as unquestionably European precisely by virtue of her transnational identity (African–German–French).

We could perhaps see films made in the late 1980s/early 1990s as having a *pedagogical* function. By dramatizing conflicts within the margins of "Europe" rather than conflicts between European nationals and foreigners, by exploring how migrants (or other marginalized "Others") produce their own "underothers" against which they define themselves, these films signaled their investment in *making visible* (to the European viewer) the logic of exclusion through which the notion of the Other is constructed in the first place. As we enter the 2000s, the multiculturalist concern with the recognition of hybrid identities—which is still predicated on an obsolete "sedentarist metaphysics" of "home" and "host" country, of "origins" and "destinations," and on the "classical" notion of long-term migration—begins to give way to the awareness of the globalization of migration and the emergence of new forms of migration, for example, circulatory migration and "ex-centric" migration. These transformations are reflected in recent films, which deconstruct the organic notion of identity as territorially bound, privilege fluid identities and transitory relationships, underscore the recursiveness or inconclusiveness of migrant journeys and the foreclosure or the stilling of movement (waiting in limbo), conflate departure and return journeys (often reversing the dominant East-West axis of mobility), and dramatize the phenomenological aspects of living "in transit."

To appreciate these changes it is instructive to consider an earlier migrant film like Xavier Koller's *Journey of Hope* (1990), the story of a poor Turkish family trying to immigrate illegally to Switzerland.[101] The film's extended opening sequence, set in a poor Turkish village where the protagonist, Haydar, and his family live, paints an idyllic picture of a tightly knit agrarian community bound together by a set of rituals and customs dating back to time immemorial and organically linked to the land/the nation. These shots of an earthly paradise are contrasted with the postcard image of another, "fake" paradise—a postcard of the Swiss Alps Haydar receives from a relative abroad. Despite the disapproval of his father—who views the city/foreign land/Europe as sources of material, that is, "inauthentic" well-being—Haydar decides to immigrate illegally to Switzerland, where he hopes to join his brother Cemal already working in a factory there. When Haydar sells his land and animals to pay his smuggler and buy Swiss chocolate bars, a Swiss knife, and silver earrings for his wife, he is reminded by his father that "once you've sold everything you're worth less than this grass. You will be without roots, a nothing." Haydar's "sin," for which he is severely punished—during the difficult winter crossing of the Italian-Swiss border his son dies from hypothermia—is to sell that which is not for sale, his home and thus his identity.

Journey of Hope suggests that leaving the native land demands too big of a sacrifice and ultimately leads to death, both literal and spiritual. Although Michael Winterbottom's *In This World* (2002) resembles *Journey of Hope* in that it also faithfully traces the clandestine journey of its protagonists, the Afghan Jamal and his cousin Enayat, from Pakistan to London, there is one major difference: Jamal and Enayat are not leaving "home" (as Haydar's family did) in search of a better life; rather, they are leaving a refugee camp in which they have been living for years. If there is one thing that defines all refugees, it is the desire to leave, not to stay—thus, there is no talk here of the "danger" of losing one's identity or one's roots. The film presents the first part of the boys' journey as an improvised, adventurous, and exciting road trip until they get to Iran where the authorities, suspecting they are Afghans, deport them back to Pakistan—the boys must start all over again and pay an even higher fee to their smugglers. They finally make it to Turkey, but during the crossing from Istanbul to Trieste, Enayat dies from asphyxiation and Jamal runs away. We see him two weeks later in Trieste, selling cheap necklaces in the street. He eventually makes it to the Sangatte refugee camp, where another refugee helps him cross the English border and reach London, where he gets a job working in a restaurant. Paradoxically, by the end of the film the refugee camp in Pakistan acquires the familiar appeal of "home" rather than a place of exile—however, "home" not in the national/territorial sense of the term but in the sense of a community of homeless residents, who have nothing in common except their shared exile, to which the inhospitable European city, through which Jamal now wanders alone, stands opposed.

Like Winterbottom's film, Mostefa Djadjam's *Borders* (2001) traces with documentary realism the clandestine journey of a group of African migrants trying to reach Spain, where the few of them that survive the grueling journey are "saved" by the Coast Guard and reassured they will soon be "back home," to which the group's marabout responds, "Home? You tell me where my home is! My home is everywhere," once again positing the migrant's "homeland" as a purely hypothetical, virtual, indeed fictional place, the journey to which begins over and over again, without ever arriving at a final destination. *La Pirogue* (Moussa Toure, 2012), the sea-version of the land-journey depicted in *Borders*, follows a dozen clandestine African migrants as they cross the Atlantic from Senegal to Spain, tracking the breakdown of solidarity between migrants while foregrounding the recursiveness of their journey—as soon as they reach their destination they are sent back home. The film focuses on Baye Laye, a family man and fisherman forced by economic pressures (the fish that once supplied his livelihood have grown scarce) to "captain" the boat, whose passengers come from a diverse array of ethnic and religious backgrounds. In a scene foreshadowing the migrants' tragic destiny, they come upon another pirogue whose engine has broken down but their smuggler Lansana (a money-driven, smooth-talking, Westernized entrepreneur, who regularly cheats his customers, speaks the language of the colonizer, and is unable to distinguish the different ethnic and religious groups to which his "clients" belong, constantly requiring someone to translate for him) forbids them from helping the people on the other boat. Eventually their own engine breaks down during a storm and they start drifting, and dying, until a few remaining survivors, including Laye, are rescued/caught by the Spanish Coast Guard and immediately deported to Senegal, where they are generously given a free EU sandwich and faced with the prospect of repeating the journey.

If the abovementioned three films borrow some of the conventions of the road movie—without, however, exploring in depth the emotional and psychological effects of the journey on the protagonists—Tony Gatlif's *Djam* (2017) is a full-blown road movie that destabilizes the privileged trajectory of most migrant journeys (East-West, South-North) by following a "side" journey (Lesbos to Istanbul, and back) while underscoring, once again, its circularity. A young Greek woman (Djam) living on Lesbos is sent to Istanbul by her stepfather Kakourgos to find a rare engine part for their broken boat. In Istanbul she meets Avril, a French girl who has come to Turkey to work as a humanitarian volunteer with Syrian refugees but has found herself homeless after her boyfriend stole her money and all her possessions. Having nothing else to do and no place to go, Avril follows Djam on her return trip to Greece. Throughout the film the refugee crisis remains in the background: in the graffiti scribbled in Arabic on the walls of train stations in Greece, in all the talk about exile, in the fact that the two girls' road trip follows the overland route most commonly used by Syrian refugees, and in the fact that there is a general transport strike, which causes their journey to be constantly interrupted. It is only toward the end of the film, when Avril takes a walk on the beach in Lesbos, that we finally see the refugees' deflated boats and piles of safety vests. The trip takes the girls through peripheral, unrecognizable, mostly abandoned landscapes dotted by dilapidated houses and inhabited by desperate men drowning their sorrow in ouzo. Like all of Gatlif's films this one, too, celebrates, rather than bemoaning, the experience of exile, depicting migration as an occasion for singing and dancing—after all, without exile and loss the music would not be so heart-wrenching. Thus, the exploration of Europe's most pressing issues remains an excuse to celebrate a particular type of music, the traditional, life-affirming Greek song form "rebetiko." Greece's financial crisis (Djam's uncle's house and restaurant are repossessed after he fails to pay his taxes), the refugee crisis, the wandering life of the gypsies, and exile in general are all treated as instances of the same vague, bitter-sweet sense of homelessness, which is sometimes represented as the greatest tragedy that can befall a man, but more often as the greatest form of freedom worthy of a song.

In *Fidelio: Alice's Journey* (Lucie Borleteau, 2014) also, the refugee crisis remains in the background, subordinated to Alice's personal journey of self-discovery. The film follows Alice, a mechanic on the freighter Fidelio, torn between her romantic and sexual desires for two men, Felix, her faithful Norwegian boyfriend, and Gael, her ex-lover, the freighter's captain. The subject of the refugee crisis comes up only once during a relaxed conversation between members of the ship's international crew when an inexperienced cadet asks Alice if she has ever seen illegal aliens. She tells him they usually try to hide among the dockers, but are generally easy to spot because they wear anoraks and hats. When the cadet asks what he is supposed to do if he ever comes across them, the captain instructs him to lock them up in the prison cabin, making sure to get their names first, because one time he ended up with a "Johnny Walker" and a "Jack Daniels" and went all over Europe looking for the country they belonged to, and since no European country wanted them he ended up returning them to Africa. Another crewmember advises the cadet to tie up "the aliens" because they tend to beat each other up and then blame crewmembers in order to get asylum. This entire conversation is played straight, making it difficult to determine whether the captain and the rest of the crew are really instructing the cadet not to follow the law of the sea or they are being sarcastic. The topic of refugees is never picked up again, nor does it intersect in any meaningful way with the film's main storyline, which explores the notion of personal fidelity through Alice's amorous journey. By vaguely suggesting a parallel between the experience of migration, of not belonging, being constantly on the move and, on the other hand, Alice's uninhibited exploration of sexuality and desire, her unwillingness to be with only one man, the film reduces the refugee crisis to a convenient metaphor supposed to illuminate the emotional problems experienced by white Europeans like Alice (arguably the refugee crisis fulfills a similar function in films like *Welcome, Happy End,* and *The House by the Sea*).

Abderrahmane Sissako's *Waiting for Happiness* (2002), set in a Mauritanian coastal town serving as a transit point (in Mali such transit places are called "heremakono," which means "waiting for happiness"), focuses on the seventeen-year-old Abdallah passing through town on a visit to his mother before leaving for Europe. Like Sissako's other films, *Waiting for Happiness* is a loosely structured episodic narrative of everyday moments—observed from a distance by the estranged protagonist, who speaks mostly French—in the lives of a socially diverse group of rootless characters (played by nonprofessional actors), including West African migrants on their way to Europe, a group of Bidhan women, a Chinese immigrant, a prostitute, an old handyman and his child apprentice, and an orphan. While the films analyzed so far draw attention to the recursiveness of migrant journeys, *Waiting for Happiness* approaches exile as an experience that precedes the journey itself inasmuch as, in Sissako's own words, "those who are about to leave have in a sense already left." Rather than depicting this state of in-betweenness or non-belonging as a depressing experience, however, Sissako underscores the serenity of living in limbo, although it is also possible to read the film not so much as a celebration of nomadic identity and non-belonging but as a veiled expression of the disappointment, despair, and, often, death that come with actually arriving at one's destination.

Unlike earlier migrant films, which tend to focus on the practical difficulties of the journey to Europe, marking clearly the journey's departure and arrival points, *L'Afrance* (Alain Gomis, 2001) and *Wilaya* (Pedro Perez Rosado, 2012) explore the experience of "co-presence" and the multidirectionality and recursiveness/circularity of the migrant journey, particularly in the case of better-off African immigrants who are neither political refugees nor asylum seekers. In *L'Afrance,* El Hadj Diop, a Senegalese student living in Paris, about to graduate, is torn between returning to Senegal to marry his fiancée and remaining in Paris. The choice between his two identities—Senegalese and French—is framed as a personal one, that is, the source of his sense of belonging is not a nation/"homeland" but romantic love (he becomes romantically involved with a French woman, which leads him to question his plans to return to Senegal). Like *Waiting for Happiness, Wilaya* is a film about living in limbo. As the opening title cards explain, Wilaya is a refugee settlement of displaced people (Spanish-speaking Sahrawi, a stateless mixed ethnic population) who, following the Spanish decolonization of Mauritania and Morocco, settled in large numbers in the Western Saharan desert. Insofar as it centers on a character (Fatimetu) born in a refugee camp (like *In This World*) and returning years later to the camp, the film does away with any conventional notion of "home" or "homeland." Although Fatimetu, like El Hadj Diop, is torn between family ties in the camp and her new life in Spain, she has no home to return to: her homelessness *is* her home. The film's narrative structure reflects this as well: although at first Fatimetu appears to want to return to Spain she lingers on in the camp, because of inertia rather than driven by a strong sense of family duty, the dramatic stakes (if there were any to begin with) becoming increasingly irrelevant and Fatimetu's decision (to stay or go) being perpetually postponed. Although she remains in the camp longer than she originally intended, the film does not present this as an active choice on her part; rather, she stays on simply to escape her personal problems back in Spain (her Spanish boyfriend has broken up with her), her camp family proving a welcome distraction.

Problemski Hotel (Manu Riche, 2015) continues Sissako's poetic meditation on exile and living in limbo as providing a perverse sense of home/belonging as homelessness/non-belonging. A stylized adaptation of Dimitri Verhulst's 2005 novel about residents of an asylum-seeking center in Arendonk, Flanders, written from the point of view of one of the center's long-term residents (Bipul Masli), the film zooms in on several refugees, including a few Russians, a girl from Kazakhstan (Lidya), a couple of Turks, a few African men, and a couple from the Middle East. There is a romantic subplot involving Bipul and Lidya, and another subplot involving

Lidia's pregnant girlfriend Martina, who, having been raped by members of Russia's *Nashi*, plans on giving birth and paying another resident to kill the baby so that she and Lidya can immigrate to London. Nothing much happens: as in Sissako's film, the residents spend their time in limbo, waiting for a letter from the immigration authorities, which usually denies them legal status in Belgium. Legal citations from Belgian immigration law are interwoven with Bipul's reflections on time, identity, home, exile, freedom, and desire. Inasmuch as nothing specific is known about Bipul he comes to represent "the figure of the migrant"—he himself is ignorant, or feigns ignorance, about his past, nor does he want to remember it, resisting others' attempts to attribute an identity to him or understand him. He thinks of himself and speaks of himself as a "nobody"—not only in the trivial sense of being unimportant but in the existential sense of "being no one" = "not being." When Lidya asks him to come to London with her, he tells her he doesn't have an ID and when she tells him to get one he seems genuinely surprised: Who is he to get an ID?! After all, he is no one. How can a "no one," someone who "is not," have an identity? We can assume that like the other asylum seekers he has been the victim of atrocities in his home country, but in his case the trauma extends beyond a particular past experience: the destruction of identity has become a choice, Bipul embracing it, rather than suffering from it. Inasmuch as he has been stripped of an identity he has also been stripped of any desires or wishes, so when Lidya invites him to join her in London, Bipul does not even give her a negative answer but keeps not answering, a nonresponse reminiscent of Melville's Bartleby the Scrivener's "I prefer not to" (see Elsaesser's invocation of Bartleby in his discussion of "abjection" in Chapter 2).

It is tempting to read Bipul's lack of desire to immigrate to London as a symptom of depression or despair. And yet, regardless of how he feels about his own fate, Bipul is constantly helping others achieve their goals, whether it is by testing a Russian young man's knowledge of French, testing another resident's strategy for finding a Belgian woman to marry in order to get legal status, or helping Lidya and Martina financially when their plans fall through. He functions as a translator (translating conversations between residents, as well as between residents and various Belgian authorities), legal aid (his knowledge of Belgian immigration law is impressive, evidence of the long amount of time he has spent at the center), judge or even executioner (he reads out the official letters sent by the immigration authorities in response to residents' asylum applications, letters that generally "sentence" the residents to deportation). In short, inasmuch as he acts as a liaison between asylum seekers and Belgian authorities and performs the duties of a translator, Bipul functions symbolically like the mythical figure of the ferryman Charon, in Greek mythology, in charge of transporting the dead (in this case, asylum seekers) from the limbo of the asylum center to "Hades," that is, the state of "nonbeing" equivalent to "being illegal."[102]

Like *In This World* and *La Pirogue*, which dramatize the recursive, meaningless nature of the migrant journey—a macabre variation on Harold Ramis's classic *Groundhog Day* (1993)—films like *Spare Parts* (Damjan Kozole, 2003), *Daha* (Onur Saylak, 2017) (Chapter 3), and *Ohthes/ Riverbanks* (Panos Karkanevatos, 2015), which adopt the point of view of the smugglers rather than the migrants, either depict a circular movement, crossing from one side of the border to the other, only to return and repeat the same movement over and over again (Kozole) or focus on the middle/ in-between part of the refugees' journey, as they wait, imprisoned, for the next leg of the journey (Saylak). *Djam* traces a return journey that only superficially appears as a homecoming, being undercut at the end by the expropriation of the uncle's house and café, forcing him and his whole family to board the boat and leave their home with no destination in sight. In fact, the whole purpose of Djam's trip to Istanbul, we understand in retrospect, is to procure the mechanical device that would make the boat operational again, allowing them to leave their homeland, that is, the journey of homecoming appears to have been exactly a preparation for leaving, not returning. *Waiting for Happiness, Djam,* and *Problemski Hotel* extend further the reflection on the recursiveness and foreclosure of movement by conflating the return home with the leaving home journey (*Djam*), by focusing on the waiting rather than on the journey (*Waiting for Happiness*), and, in the most extreme case, by presenting the negation of the will to movement as the logical conclusion of the constant frustration of movement (Bipul's chosen immobility in *Problemski Hotel*).

I will end this chapter by considering two films with identical titles made twenty years apart—Manuel Poirier's *Western* (1997) and Valeska Grisebach's *Western* (2017)—both engaging with the question of personal, national, and European identity through the conventions of a quintessentially American genre, the western, a genre whose investment in mobility (the western hero is essentially a nomadic character) and in the idea of "the Promised Land" invites comparisons with the centrality of migration and the idea of "Europe" as yet another "Promised Land" in contemporary European cinema.

Poirier's *Western* is that rare thing, a European road movie/relationship western about two outsiders, a Spanish shoe salesman (Paco) and a Russian-Italian car thief (Nino), as they walk and/or drive across the French countryside (specifically Brittany) in search of love. We don't really know how long Paco and Nino have been living in France, whether they intend to settle down in France or plan on returning to their respective countries of origin. Their journey is amusing rather than eventful since Poirier is more interested in exploring the idea of belonging through (romantic) love rather than through official membership in a particular nation. It is by no means accidental that the two protagonists are not of French descent, and neither is a third character they encounter later, Baptiste, an African immigrant from the Ivory Coast now living in Brittany (Poirier himself is French-Peruvian). The irrelevance of national identity is made blatant in the film, which is structured around several displacements: not only are the two protagonists foreigners in France, but they are also outsiders in their home countries (Paco is Catalan and Nino is Italian-Russian), and they travel through a part of France (Brittany) distinguished by its self-conscious difference from the French nation. The notion of belonging as something subjective and rooted in feelings—romantic love and camaraderie—rather than an objective, primordial marker of identity, is introduced as well on the level of plot. When Paco asks Nino why he came to France, Nino explains that ever since his French fiancée left him (he had moved to France to marry her), he had lost any desire for stability, implying that the sense of belonging/home is a subjective/emotional experience rather than a stamp in one's passport. This idea is developed further when Paco comes up with the plan to do a poll (a Nouvelle Vague-like strategy offering a cross-section of French attitudes to foreigners) among local women to determine their image of the ideal man, all with a view to finding Nino a girlfriend. Nino and Paco's encounter with Baptiste also underscores the film's ludic approach to identity. Baptiste introduces the duo to a game he invented (a game through which he met his girlfriend) called "Bonjour, la France!" which involves sitting in a café and taking turns saying "bonjour" to people passing by—whoever gets a response to their "bonjour" wins a point. Far from subscribing to an organic, territorially bound notion of national and personal identity, *Western* constructs a utopian image of a multicultural and multiracial France, conceiving identity as affective/subjective—its main source being romantic love and friendship—rather than collective and bound to a national territory. The decision to set the story in Brittany, the westernmost corner of France, and the western frontier of Europe, is not accidental in a film featuring a Spaniard, a Russian, an African, and many Britons, and exploring the concept of borders and identities. While the title refers to the geographical setting of the story it also explicitly references the western genre, presumably to rewrite its conventions within a European context.

What are the primary conventions of the genre that has provided America with its founding myth, and how do these conventions help illuminate the notion of European identity? A simple definition of the western would be a film set on the American frontier and dealing with the archetypal problem of law and order through a series of dichotomies such as virtue versus evil, man versus nature, settlers versus Native Americans (often portrayed as savages), civilization versus wilderness/lawlessness, lawman/sheriff versus gunslinger, law and order versus anarchy, rugged individualism versus community, settler versus nomad, farmers versus industrialists, and so on. The iconography of the western includes gun fights, horses, trains, bank robberies, runaway stagecoaches, shoot-outs, outlaws and sheriffs, cattle drivers, stampedes, barroom brawls, open vistas, etc. Poirier's film has none of that. Indeed, it resembles a classic road movie more than it does a western. And this is precisely the point, for if the western is foundational in its construction of a territorially bound, organic sense of (American) national identity, the road movie is its deconstruction. In Poirier's film Brittany does not fulfill the highly symbolic function of the frontier in the American western: the Spaniard, Italian-Russian, and African protagonists are not trying to "settle" (on) the supposedly wild frontier of Europe (Brittany); on the contrary, they are wandering aimlessly along the frontier, searching for personally meaningful, romantic connections rather than for a way to legitimize their identity (e.g., by becoming naturalized French citizens), while their doubly destabilized identities—a Catalan and an Italian-Russian in Brittany—point up further the irrelevance of national identity to the forging of a meaningful sense of belonging based on friendship, love, and socioeconomic solidarity.

Like Paco and Nino, the protagonist of Grisebach's *Western* (2017), the middle-aged German construction worker Meinhard, is looking for a sense of belonging/home rather than for ways to bolster up his German identity. If anything, Meinhard identifies much more with the foreigners (Bulgarians) on whose land he has been recruited to work than with his fellow Germans. Grisebach's Euro-Western is concerned with a symbolic rather than a literal journey—the Eastern expansion of the EU and the "integration" of Europe's eastern periphery into the concept of "Europe." The story centers on German construction workers Meinhard and Vincent, migrant contract workers working on a hydroelectric plant in the remote Bulgarian countryside near the Greek border. Unlike the aggressive foreman Vincent, Meinhard is a loner, a man of few words. Vincent perceives their presence in this little country on the periphery of the EU/Europe not only as legitimate but also as something the locals ought to be grateful for: early on in the film he raises a German flag over the work camp, dismissing Meinhard's criticism that this flagrant display of nationalism is out of place on foreign territory, while in another scene Meinhard playfully throws the German flag in the river, an act Vincent perceives as desecrating. In the very same scene, Vincent acts aggressively toward a trio of local women (including Vyara), over whom he believes he has certain "rights" as a man, a German (Western European), and a representative of the EU (which is funding the construction of the plant in the EU's poorest member state).

While Vincent and the rest of the German crew keep their distance from the locals, Meinhard slowly gets to know them during his frequent walks down to the village, where he is first greeted with animosity that soon gives way to hospitality. Meinhard befriends one of the locals, Adrian, an Albanian-Bulgarian who invites him into his extended family. Soon enough, one of the local youths is teaching Meinhard how to ride a horse, and Meinhard is invited to local gatherings and parties. On one hand, the language barrier preserves Meinhard's liminal position as a foreigner; at the same time, the absence of any visual markers of his "Germanness" makes him a slippery figure that effortlessly crosses the border between locals and foreigners, without belonging to either. In the second part of the film, as his brotherly bond with Adrian grows deeper (the two men share personal secrets, Meinhard confiding in Adrian about a personal tragedy, the death of his brother, and Adrian sharing with Meinhard how lonely he feels, his children having immigrated abroad), and as he becomes romantically involved with Vyara, a local woman who has spent some time in Germany, Meinhard seems to consider the possibility of settling down in Bulgaria (he asks whether there are any houses for sale in the area) since there is nothing keeping him in Germany. One evening, as Meinhard sits with Vyara by the road, looking at the silhouette of the mountains and a little church in the distance, Vyara tells him how much she loves this village and how homesick she gets when she is away. When she asks him if he ever feels homesick, he does not respond; instead, the camera cuts to the same view of the mountains, suggesting that perhaps this could be Meinhard's home as well. Even if the decoupling of home from national identity does not result in the idealization of Bulgaria as "the authentic" home Meinhard has been looking for—for example, although Meinhard is welcomed by Adrian and his family he also manages to create some enemies among the locals—the film does distinguish "identity" from "belonging"/"identification," contrasting Vincent's brand of aggressive nationalism with Meinhard's much more tenuous/fragile relationship with the local villagers and his personal connection to this supposedly foreign land, in which he feels much more at home than in his native Germany.

But why is the film called *Western*? In his classical study *Sixguns and Society: A Structural Study of the Western* (1977) Will Wright argues that the western (1) dramatizes the conflict between law and morality, "between the ethic of work and the ethic of leisure";[103] (2) represents "a legitimation of violence in a context of Puritan control over feelings";[104] (3) "affirms the necessity of society" by presenting and resolving "the conflict between key American values like progress and success and the lost virtues of individual honor, heroism and natural freedom";[105] and (4) "opposes Wilderness to Civilization in the contrasting images of the Garden and the Desert."[106] Wright distinguishes four periods in the genre's evolution: (1) the classical plot (1930 to 1955), in which a lone gunfighter saves the town from the villains (gamblers or ranchers); (2) the vengeance variation (1955 to 1960), in which the hero, failing to adjust to society, seeks vengeance; (3) the transitional phase (early 1950s), in which the hero defends justice but is ultimately rejected by society; (4) the professional plot (1958 to 1970), in which the hero is replaced by a group of professional gunfighters who "defend" society in exchange for money rather than out of love for, or commitment to, any ideals of law and justice.[107] The evolution of the genre reflects the major shift in American institutions between the 1930s and the 1970s, "from a competitive market society to a planned corporate economy."[108] In the classical plot, the conflict between individualism and conformity is developed through the different uses of the land: the homesteaders want the land to build churches, schools, and businesses, while the villains (the ranchers) want it for personal gain. The classical Western represents "an aristocratic tendency with a democratic bias":[109] initially society grants the hero a special status but once he has saved them from the villains he is expected to surrender his special status and become equal with the other members of society.[110] By the 1950s westerns had become more critical of the settled frontier community whose conformism, selfishness, and complacency paralleled too closely the qualities of the "lonely crowd," the affluent, conformist middle-class American society of the 1950s.

What does Wright's analysis have to say about Grisebach's European take on the genre? First of all, *Western* flips the geography of the American genre by setting the story not on the Western border of Europe but on its eastern periphery, which arguably occupies the same symbolic space the western frontier occupies in the American imagination: if Europe's western border has always been well defined (the Atlantic Ocean), its eastern border has been historically a constant source of anxiety, imagined as an abject space governed by unruly, instinctive, and dangerous forces of lawlessness and eroticism (remember *Dracula*?). While for a long time the classical Others of Europe—the Jews and the Roma—were associated with the East, an enigmatic, irrational space from which the "rational," "proper," Enlightened Western Europe distanced itself, Grisebach's film challenges the simplistic East-West opposition, making it impossible to identify law and morality with one side only. For instance, in the American western the East is associated with the forces of civilization and the West is posited as uncivilized, untamed. Given that Grisebach flips the geography of the western, the symbolic place of the West is occupied by the East; thus, one would expect the East to be "the desert" or the wilderness to be tamed. However, the East (the Bulgarian village) is here already settled, and the West is represented by German contract laborers who are constantly on the move and thus positioned, through their mobility, as the opposite of the settled Bulgarians. On the other hand, while East-Europeans (in this case Bulgarians) continue to embody the idea of "the Eastern threat," both culturally (as "savage, uncivilized") and politically (as "ex-communist")—playing the role of "savage" Native Americans—it is the supposedly rational Western Europeans (the Germans) who are represented as aggressive, manipulative, and nationalistic while the Bulgarians appear (in most of the scenes) as genuinely hospitable. The simplistic dichotomy of the American western is further complicated by the allusion to a third type of characters (although they are only mentioned in passing) that belong neither to the native land of the hosts (the Bulgarians) nor to the group of guests (the Germans): refugees. Refugees are mentioned only once on the night when Adrian and the locals first encounter Meinhard during his night walk through the countryside. They pick him up in their jeep and give him a ride back to the work camp, instructing him that he ought to be more careful on account of the village's proximity to the Greek border which many refugees try to cross illegally (only to be shot by the police). Not only does the classical western not feature any refugees but the western hero, who dramatizes the conflict between freedom and law (i.e., the construction of national identity), could, in fact, be seen as a kind of voluntary refugee/exile who does not belong to the community and is willing to be deprived of official status, which however is a sign of his freedom rather than of his powerlessness or exclusion.

Grisebach's film seems to combine elements of all four phases in the western genre's evolution theorized by Wright. In the classical plot a lone gunfighter saves the town from villains. In Grisebach's film Meinhard, a lone construction worker, acts as a buffer zone or a mediator between hosts (Bulgarians) and guests (Germans). In the vengeance variation of the classical western the hero, failing to adjust to society, seeks vengeance. In Grisebach's film, the anti-hero, Vincent, failing to assert his power over the locals, and failing to attract the romantic attention of his object of desire (Vyara), seeks vengeance. In the transitional phase of the classical western the hero defends justice but is ultimately rejected by society. In Grisebach's film Meinhard defends the locals from the aggression of his fellow workers and compatriots but eventually becomes the object of aggression himself as some of the locals, whose shady business ventures he threatens, turn against him. In the professional plot of the classical western the hero is replaced by a group of professional gunfighters who "defend" society in exchange for money rather than out of commitment to ideals of law and justice. In Grisebach's film, the professional gunfighters are replaced by contract workers dispatched by Brussels to one of the eastern outposts of the EU to bolster its aging infrastructure in exchange for money rather than out of any genuine concern for the country's well-being. While the evolution of the American western reflects America's transition from a competitive market society to a planned corporate economy, Grisebach's Euro-western "catches up" with Europe in the next phase of economic development, neoliberalism: *Western* is no longer about bringing law and order to the uncivilized West but rather about bringing neoliberalism to a former communist outpost on the EU's eastern periphery. Thus the relationship between Germans and Bulgarians can also be thought of as that between "donors" and "receivers," between the EU and its poor member states whose European credentials are still perceived as somewhat suspect. From this point of view, Vincent's aggressive posture masks the donors' (the EU's) frustrated feelings of entitlement for keeping the EU boat afloat even as various poor member states threaten to capsize it at any moment.

Finally, the issue of masculinity, of "what makes a man," is as relevant to Grisebach's Euro-western, or "Eastern," as it is to the classical western. In the United States the revival of scholarly interest in the Western coincided with

America's second feminist movement. The preoccupation with masculinity-in-crisis is evident, for instance, in the uncharacteristic importance ascribed to the romantic subplot in westerns such as Ford's *The Man Who Shot Liberty Valance* (1962), which subordinates all issues—from the vanishing of the old West and the territorial debates, to the debates about law and order versus violence and vigilante justice—to the romantic subplot. In Grisebach's film, too, questions of the EU's expansion and of the ethical limits of neoliberalism are integrally linked to the exploration of masculinity in its relation to nationalism, with Vincent embodying a patriarchal, aggressive, and nationalistic concept of masculinity and Meinhard representing an alternative, nonhegemonic masculinity.

Grisebach's film thus explores some of the classical western's main conflicts but updates them for the neoliberal age and the European context. First, it reframes the classical western's conflict between law and morality as a conflict between the official relationships between European nations (especially Western and Eastern European nations) defined by their membership in the EU (exemplified by the EU-funded construction project in a poor EU member state) and, on the other hand, the unofficial, personal relationships between fellow Europeans defined in terms of "unconditional hospitality." Second, in contrast to the classical western's "legitimation of violence in a context of Puritan control over feelings," Grisebach's film questions the structural violence of neoliberalism exemplified by Vincent's perverse "legitimization" of stealing the water of the village in order to complete the EU-funded project meant to benefit the very same village. Third, rather than presenting and resolving "the conflict between key American values like progress and success and the lost virtues of individual honor, heroism, and natural freedom," the film presents and leaves unresolved the conflict between neoliberal values and a technocratic notion of European identity and, on the other hand, humanist values and the idea of a European identity free from territorial constraints and defined in terms of "belonging without belonging," embodied by Meinhard's nomadic figure. Fourth, rather than opposing Wilderness to Civilization in the contrasting images of the Garden and the Desert, the film depicts the product of the uneven nature of globalization by presenting the frontier, which in the classical western connotes excitement, dynamism, progress, danger, the unknown, and open possibilities, as an abandoned village on the edge of Europe populated by a handful of aging villagers whose children (like Adrian's) have either moved to the city or immigrated abroad. By structuring the film around the idea of the abandoned, stagnating frontier, the film undercuts the utopian claims of the classical western, calling into question the potential of the border to serve as a founding myth of European identity in sharp contrast to the potency of that myth in the construction of American identity.

As we shall see in the next chapters, if earlier migrant films fulfilled a "pedagogical" function—making visible the way in which the logic of exclusion/the logic of "Othering" functions—films made in the last decade or so build up on that "lesson": their aim is no longer simply to make visible what was previously invisible (the logic of exclusion) but rather to make an *ethical* claim about Europeans' relationship to non-European migrant Others. Many of these recent films rely on the trope of impersonation/disguise/performance to suggest that the *external, non-European* migrant Other is simply the *internal* Other (a particular racial/ethnic/migrant minority constitutive of the nation) *in disguise*, thus framing *the ethical claim* of hospitality in terms of a *categorical error*, an error resulting from "*misrecognition*" (that is, the non-European Other is not an absolute Other, just a misrecognized internal Other "in disguise").

Notes

1. Glenda Garelli and Martina Tazzioli, "Choucha beyond the Camp: Challenging the Border of Migration Studies," *The Borders of "Europe,"* 171. Although human rights organizations have proposed alternative methods of "detaining" refugees, these "alternatives" are driven by the same logic of economic efficiency. See "Dossier Migrants en Europe: Quelle Politique d'Accueil?" *Carto: Le Monde en Cartes*, no. 50 (November–December 2018): 14–23.
2. Fiorenza Picozza, "Dubliners: Unthinking Displacement, Illegality, and Refugeeness within Europe's Geographies of Asylum," *The Borders of "Europe,"* 239.
3. Ibid., 245.
4. Celik, *In Permanent Crisis*, 3.
5. Ibid., 7.
6. Ibid., 5.
7. Kohn, *Mediating Mobility*, 85.
8. Ibid., 24.
9. On the ethical importance of "foreignness," see Katarzyna Marciniak and Bruce Bennett, "Aporias of Foreignness: Transnational Encounters in Cinema," *Transnational Cinemas* 9, no. 1 (2018): 1–12.
10. Kohn, *Mediating Mobility*, 24. For a phenomenological reading of "home," see Margaret Morse, "Home: Smell, Taste, Posture, Gleam," *Home, Exile, Homeland: Film, Media, and the Politics of Place*, ed. Hamid Naficy (New York: Routledge, 1999), 63–74.
11. Kohn, *Mediating Mobility*, 89.
12. Ibid., 89.
13. Souad Osseiran, "'Europe' from 'Here': Syrian Migrants/Refugees in Istanbul and Imagined Migrations into and within 'Europe,'" *The Borders of "Europe,"* 186.

14 Ibid., 194.
15 Scheel, "The Secret Is to Look Good on Paper: Appropriating Mobility within and against a Machine of Illegalization," *The Borders of "Europe,"* 38.
16 Ibid., 60.
17 de Genova, "The Borders of 'Europe,'" 9.
18 Ibid., 24.
19 de Wenden, *La question migratoire*, 118.
20 On the important role migrants have played in expanding the politics of membership and the realm of the civic, see Saskia Sassen, "Membership and Its Politics," *Ethnic Europe: Mobility, Identity, and Conflict in a Globalized World*, ed. Roland Hus (Stanford CA: Stanford UP, 2010), 21–43.
21 See Giorgia Ceriani-Sebregondi, "Migrations internationales: vers un nouvel habiter?" *Travaux de l'Institut de Géographie de Reims*, no. 115–18 (2003): 59–74.
22 qtd in de Wenden, *La question migratoire*, 37.
23 See Paul Patton, "Marxism and Beyond: Strategies of Reterritorialization," *Cultural Critique* 8 (Winter 1987–1988): 197–216, and Kim Benterrak, Stephen Muecke, and Paddy Roe, *Reading the Country: Introduction to Nomadology* (Melboune: Re.press, 2014).
24 Thomas Nail, *The Figure of the Migrant* (Stanford, CA: Stanford UP, 2015), 12.
25 Maurice Stierl, "Excessive Migration, Excessive Governance: Border Entanglements in Greek EU-rope," *The Borders of "Europe,"* 210.
26 Rushdie qtd in Krishan Kumar, "The Nation-State, the European Union, and Transnational Identities," *Muslim Europe or Euro-Islam: Politics, Culture, and Citizenship in the Age of Globalization*, ed. Nezar AlSayyad and Manuel Castells (Lanham, MD: Lexington Books, 2002), 60. See also https://www.liberation.fr/debats/2018/09/20/migrer-une-condition-d-existence-du-vivant_1680151.
27 Francesco Cattani, "New Maps of Europe by Some Contemporary 'Migrant' Artists and Writers," *Europe in Black and White*, 55–66.
28 qtd in Aurora E. Rodono, "Nomadic Narratives: Migration Cinema in Germany and Italy," *The Cinemas of Italian Migration: European and Transatlantic Narratives*, ed. Sabine Schrader and Daniel Winkler (Newcastle upon Tyne: Cambridge Scholars Publishing, 2013), 188.
29 Kumar, "The Nation-State," 60.
30 Nail, *The Figure of the Migrant*, 3, my emphasis.
31 Hamid Naficy, "Framing Exile: From Homeland to Homepage," *Home, Exile, Homeland: Film, Media, and the Politics of Place*, ed. Hamid Naficy (New York: Routledge, 1999), 9.
32 Peters, "Exile," 32.
33 qtd in Peters, "Exile," 33, my emphasis.

34 Alexis Nouss, *La condition de l'exilé: Penser les migrations contemporaines* (Paris: Editions de la Maison des sciences de l'homme, 2015), 135.

35 Wendy Everett and Peter Wagstaff, *Cultures of Exile: Images of Displacement* (London: Berghahn Books, 2004), x.

36 Wendy Everett, "Leaving Home: Exile and Displacement in Contemporary European Cinema," *Cultures of Exile: Images of Displacement*, ed. Wendy Everett and Peter Wagstaff (London: Berghahn Books, 2004), 20.

37 Barbara Cassin, *Nostalgia: When Are We Ever at Home?* trans. Pascale-Anne Brault (New York: Fordham UP, 2016), 8.

38 Ibid., 63.

39 Ella Shohat, "By the Bitstream of Babylon: Cyberfrontiers and Diasporic Vistas," *Home, Exile, Homeland: Film, Media, and the Politics of Place*, ed. Hamid Naficy (New York: Routledge, 1999), 225.

40 Said, *Culture and Imperialism*, 332, my emphasis.

41 Gareth Millington, *Urbanization and the Migrant in British Cinema: Spectres of the City* (London: Palgrave Macmillan, 2016), 133.

42 Rancière, *The Politics of Aesthetics*, 90.

43 Ibid., 90.

44 Ibid., 92.

45 Badiou, *What Is to Be Done?* 134.

46 Ibid., 138–39.

47 Ibid., 136.

48 Rancière, *The Politics of Aesthetics*, 51.

49 Olaf Briese, "The Camp in the City, the City as Camp," *Walls, Borders, Boundaries: Spatial and Cultural Practices in Europe*, ed. Marc Silberman, Kren Till, and Janet Ward (London: Berghahn Books, 2012), 43–59.

50 Diken and Lausten, *The Culture of Exception*, 4.

51 For Agamben the subject who most immediately exemplifies the plight of "bare life" (the denial of political and legal representation) is the stateless refugee. See Anthony Downey, "Zones of Indistinction: Giorgio Agamben's 'Bare Life' and the Politics of Aesthetics," *Third Text* 23, no. 2 (2009): 109–25.

52 Agamben qtd in Diken and Lausten, *The Culture of Exception*, 5.

53 Halle, *The Europeanization of Cinema*, 6.

54 Liz, *Euro-Visions*, 107.

55 Ibid., 119.

56 Ibid., 127.

57 Malini Guha, *From Empire to the World: Migrant London and Paris in the Cinema* (Edinburgh: Edinburgh UP, 2015), 9.

58 Ibid., 132.

59 In an article published in *The New Republic* Josephine Livingstone and Lovia Gyarkye suggest that one possible reason scholars, writers, and curators have

been recently drawn to the flâneur might have to do with the waning of the Enlightenment idea of a universal subject and the backlash against identity politics. For critics of identity politics, "who would rather that knowledge were an uncolored thing," the flâneur represents "a fantasy of a time when a universal subject was a realistic proposition. [. . .] Anybody can be a flâneur. . . . But the reason anybody can do it is that the flâneur is nobody. [. . .] He is a default subject with no markers of identity. He is male and unattached, or simply a converted feminine mirror. . . . He is pure receptacle, a pair of eyes with no human relationships and a politics only of witnessing." A much more appropriate model for the mobile subject of globalization, they believe, is the cosmopolitan. Both the flâneur and the cosmopolitan are defined by mobility, but cosmopolitans exceed Baudelaire's narrow idea of flânerie in that "they are not just receptive to other cultures, but seek to develop and exercise a sense of intercultural mastery." As I have already shown, however, cosmopolitanism is not without its problems either (see the Introduction). https://newrepublic.com/article/141623/death-flaneur, accessed August 5, 2019. For a discussion of the *flâneur* as a moral rather than merely cultural ideal of world citizenship, see Bart van Leeuwen, "If We Are *flâneurs*, Can We Be Cosmopolitans?" *Urban Studies* 56, no. 2 (2017): 301–16.

60 Daniela Berghahn and Claudia Sternberg, "Introduction," *European Cinema in Motion: Migrant and Diasporic Film in Contemporary Europe*, ed. Daniela Berghahn and Claudia Sternberg (London: Palgrave Macmillan, 2010), 2.

61 For an analysis of the relation of European integration to colonialism, see Peo Hansen, *Eurafrica: The Untold History of European Integration and Colonialism* (London: Bloomsbury, 2015). For a postcolonial critique of the idea of "Europe" as a coherent, bounded entity, a "product" of the Renaissance, the French Revolution, and the Industrial Revolution, see Gurminder Bhambra's *Rethinking Modernity: Postcolonialism and the Sociological Imagination* (London: Palgrave Macmillan, 2009). Roberto M. Dainotto's *Europe (In Theory)* (Durham, NC: Duke UP, 2007) provides a parallel genealogy of Eurocentrism and imperialism but from within Europe itself, showing how modern theories of Europe have marginalized its southern region. For an alternative critique of Eurocentrism in terms of "self-colonization," see Alexander Kiossev's "Notes on Self-Colonizing Cultures," *After the Wall: Art and Culture in Post-Communist Europe* (Stockholm: Modern Museum, 1999).

62 Sandra Ponzanesi and Marguerite Waller, *Postcolonial Cinema Studies* (London: Routledge, 2012), 7. Like Ponzanesi, the editors of a recent volume on "border cinema" position border cinema within the tradition of Third Cinema's formally political aesthetics, although the Marxist concerns of Third Cinema have been replaced by concerns about "how digital aesthetics and expanded cinema impact and reflect identity . . . at a later stage of global capitalism" (6). See Monica Hanna and Rebecca Sheehan, "Introduction – Moving Images: Contested Global Borders in the Digital Age," *Border Cinema: Reimagining Identity through Aesthetics*, ed. Monica Hanna and Rebecca A. Sheehan (New Brunswick, NJ: Rutgers UP, 2019), 1–19. On "border cinema," see also *Transnational Cinema at the Borders: Borderscapes*

and the Cinematic Imaginary, ed. Ana Mendes and John Sundholm (New York: Routledge, 2018).

63 See *Postcolonial Cinema Studies*, ed. Sandra Ponzanesi and Marguerite Waller (London: Routledge, 2012).

64 Sabine Schrader and Daniel Winkler, "The Cinemas of Italian Migration: From *Il Cammino della Speranza* (1950) to *Into Paradiso* (2010)," *The Cinemas of Italian Migration: European and Transatlantic Narratives*, ed. Sabine Schrader and Daniel Winkler (Newcastle upon Tyne: Cambridge Scholars Publishing, 2013), 1–18.

65 Lars Kristensen, "Introduction," *Postcommunist Film—Russia, Eastern Europe and World Culture: Moving Images of Postcommunism*, ed. Lars Kristensen (London: Routledge, 2012), 3.

66 Encarnacion Gutierrez Rodriguez, "Transculturation in German and Spanish Migrant and Diasporic Cinema: on Constrained Spaces and Minor Intimacies in *Princesses* and *A Little Bit of Freedom*," *European Cinema in Motion: Migrant and Diasporic Film in Contemporary Europe*, ed. Daniela Berghahn and Claudia Sternberg (London: Palgrave Macmillan, 2010), 116.

67 Berghahn and Sternberg, "Introduction," 17, my emphasis.

68 Ibid., 22.

69 Ibid., 21.

70 Sandra Ponzanesi and Verena Berger, "Introduction: Genres and Tropes in Postcolonial Cinemas(s)," *Transnational Cinemas* 7, no. 2 (2016): 113.

71 Sandra Ponzanesi, "Europe in Motion: Migrant Cinema and the Politics of Encounter," *Social Identities* 17, no. 1 (2011): 73–92.

72 Ponzanesi and Berger, "Introduction," 112.

73 Tim Bergfelder, "Popular European Cinema in the 2000s: Cinephilia, Genre and Heritage," *The Europeanness of European Cinema: Identity, Meaning and Globalization*, ed. Mary Harrod, Mariana Liz, and Alissa Timoshkina (London: I.B. Tauris, 2015), 34.

74 Ibid., 44.

75 Ibid., 45. The vast majority of films supported through MEDEA belong to the "middlebrow" area of the "art cinema versus popular cinema" spectrum.

76 Jäckel, "Changing the Image of Europe?" 59–71.

77 Since 2010 *Eurimages* no longer considers the "European origin" of a project a criterion of eligibility, though it still assesses the European character of the project according to the point system stipulated in the regulations.

78 Jäckel points out the irony that a pan-European fund like *Eurimages*, whose mandate is to "promote European identity" with reference to a "single culture," often gives its support to films that foreground rather than obliterate cultural differences, with a particular preference for certain topics such as im/emigration, social inequalities, ethnic conflicts etc.

79 Mariana Liz, "From European Co-Productions to the Euro-Pudding," *The Europeanness of European Cinema: Identity, Meaning and Globalization*,

ed. Mary Harrod, Mariana Liz, and Alissa Timoshkina (London: I.B. Tauris, 2015), 78.
80 Ibid., 82.
81 Ibid., 81.
82 Rather than reclaiming Euro-puddings under the more acceptable name of "natural co-productions" supposedly representing a shared European identity, Baltruschart views European co-productions as just one instance of neoliberalism's equation of "culture" with "industry." See Doris Baltruschart, "Co-productions, Global Markets and New Media Ecologies," *Transnational Cinema in Europe*, ed. Manuel Palacio and Jorg Turschmann (Munster: LIT Verlag, 2013), 11–23.
83 Dina Iordanova, "Migration and Cinematic Process in Post-Cold War Europe," *European Cinema in Motion: Migrant and Diasporic Film in Contemporary Europe*, ed. Daniela Berghahn and Claudia Sternberg (London: Palgrave Macmillan, 2010), 51.
84 qtd in Daniela Berghahn and Claudia Sternberg, "Locating Migrant and Diasporic Cinema in Contemporary Europe," *European Cinema in Motion: Migrant and Diasporic Film in Contemporary Europe*, ed. Daniela Berghahn and Claudia Sternberg (London: Palgrave Macmillan, 2010), 36.
85 Petra Hanakova, "Staying Home and Safe: Czech Cinema and the Refusal to be Transnational," *European Cinema after the Wall: Screening East-West Mobility*, ed. Leen Engelen and Kris van Heuckelom (Lanham, MD: Rowman & Littlefield, 2014), 115.
86 Catherine Portuges, "Memory and Reinvention in Post-Socialist Hungarian Cinema," *Cinemas in Transition in Central and Eastern Europe after 1989*, ed. Catherine Portuges and Peter Hames (Philadelphia: Temple UP, 2013), 119–20.
87 Aga Skrodzka, *Magic Realist Cinema in East Central Europe* (Edinburgh: Edinburgh UP, 2012), 24.
88 Ibid., 28.
89 Ibid., 33.
90 Ibid., 34.
91 Massimo Locatelli and Francesco Pitassion, "Vesna Run Faster! East European Actresses and Contemporary Italian Cinema" *European Cinema after the Wall: Screening East- West Mobility*, ed. Leen Engelen and Kris van Heuckelom (Lanham, MD: Rowman & Littlefield, 2014), 37–54.
92 See Flannery Wilson and Jane Ramey Correia, ed. *Intermingled Fascinations: Migration, Displacement and Translation in World Cinema* (Newcastle upon Tyne: Cambridge Scholars Publishing, 2011).
93 Alberto Zambenedetti, "Multiculturalism in New Italian Cinema: The Impact of Migration, Diaspora, and the Post-Colonial on Italy's Self-Representation," *Beyond Monopoly: Globalization and Contemporary Italian Media*, ed. Michela Ardizzoni and Chiara Ferrari (Washington DC: Lexington Books, 2009), 245–68.

94 Giuliana Muscio, "Sicilian Film Productions: Between Europe and the Mediterranean Islands," *We Europeans? Media, Representations, Identities*, ed. William Uricchio (Bristol: Intellect Books, 2008), 177–94.

95 Mazierska, Kristensen, and Naripea, "Introduction," 2. Taking the German-Polish case, Kristin Kopp has demonstrated that if in German cinema of the 1990s, Poland embodied the Other against which a German national identity could affirm itself, when it came to negotiating the problematic identity of the former East Germans as equal citizens or colonized victims in reunified Germany, German cinema of the 1990s revived Germany's construction of Poland as a colonial space dating back to the second half of the nineteenth century. Conversely, comparing the dominant discourse of German aggression and Polish victimization in postwar Polish cinema to post-1989 Polish cinema, Ewa Mazierska has shown that not only are Germans represented in less negative terms but there is even an attempt to see them as victims and to recognize Poland's own war and postwar crimes.

See Kristin Kopp, "If Your Car Is Stolen, It Will Soon Be in Poland: Criminal Representations of Poland and the Poles in German Fictional Film of the 1990s," *Postcolonial Approaches to Eastern European Cinema: Portraying Neighbors on Screen*, ed. Ewa Maziersak, Lars Kristensen, and Eva Näripea (London: I.B. Tauris, 2014), 41–66, and Ewa Mazierska, "Neighbors (Almost) Like Us: Representation of Germans, Germanness and Germany in Polish Communist and Postcommunist Cinema," *Postcolonial Approaches to Eastern European Cinema*, 67–89, both in *Postcolonial Approaches to Eastern European Cinema*. However, this updating of "the Other" as "neighbor" characterizes *only* postcolonial approaches to East European cinema. Unlike other regions, notably Africa, Eastern Europe was colonized by its neighbors rather than by faraway empires, leading to a higher degree of cultural and ethnic hybridization during Soviet colonial rule, which was *not* predicated on racial difference.

96 On the politics of recognition, see Charles Taylor, "The Politics of Recognition," *Multiculturalism*, ed. Amy Gutmann (Princeton: Princeton UP, 1994), 25–75.

97 The following discussion is derived, in part, from an article published in Studies in European Cinema in 2011, available online DOI: 10.1386/seci.8.1.7_1.

98 On the intersectional approach to belonging, see Nira Yuval-Davis, *The Politics of Belonging: Intersectional Contestations* (Thousand Oaks, CA: Sage Publishing, 2011).

99 These three films can be fruitfully examined through the perspective of intersectional feminism.

100 The Orientalizing gesture through which the Roma are usually represented on screen undermines even critically acclaimed films like *Les Misérables* (Ladj Ly, 2019), a banlieue film praised for its unflinching portrait of the racial dynamic in a Parisian suburb. None of the reviewers who endorsed Ly's portrayal of second- and third-generation African and Maghrebi immigrants' disenfranchisement commented on the film's caricature of the suburb's Roma population as a belligerent, absurdly macho circus family.

101 See Angelica Fenner's illuminating reading of the film's decision to portray generic Turkish peasants rather than Kurdish refugees to appease Germans' and Swiss' ambivalence about immigration to Europe. Angelika Fenner, "Traversing the Screen Politics of Migration: Xavier Koller's *Journey of Hope*," *Moving Pictures, Migrating Identities*, ed. Eva Rueschmann (Jackson, MI: University Press of Mississippi, 2003), 18–38.

102 According to the myth, a coin (Charon's obol) placed in the mouth of a dead person would pay the toll for the ferry across the river to the entrance of Hades. Those unable to pay the fee would not be taken across.

103 Will Wright, *Sixguns and Society: A Structural Study of the Western* (Berkeley, CA: U of California Press, 1977), 3.

104 Ibid., 3.

105 Ibid.

106 Ibid.

107 Ibid., 4.

108 Ibid., 10.

109 Ibid., 12.

110 Ibid., 13.

2

Rethinking European Identity and European Cinema in the Age of Mass Migration: Between Abjection and Impersonation

As we have seen in Chapter 1, the subject of migration in European cinema is not new: most of the scholarship on the subject has been shaped by postcolonial theory, border studies, theories of Third cinema, ethnic and cultural studies, among others. I would argue, however, that what is particularly noticeable about recent studies of migration, European identity, and European cinema is their attempt to rethink Europe and European cinema from *a strategic position of weakness*, and to refigure *positively* the waning of national cinema—which for a long time was one of the three main categories through which European cinema was theorized, the other two being "art cinema" and "auteur cinema"—as an *opportunity* rather than a sign of European cinema's "new marginality" (Thomas Elsaesser).

I would like to propose that such attempts to rethink Europe and European cinema from a position of *tactical weakness* can be traced back to Italian philosopher Gianni Vattimo's influential notion of *pensiero debole* ("weak" or "post-foundationalist" thought), which refers to the exhaustion—but *not* the vanishing—of the project of modernity (the belief in reason, progress, history, the nation state, and so on). In *The End of Modernity: Nihilism and Hermeneutics in Postmodern Culture* (1991), Vattimo proposes that the postmodern is "not only [...] something new in relation to the modern, but also [...] a dissolution of the category of the new—in other words [...] an experience of 'the end of history' rather than . . . the appearance of a different stage of history."[1]

Instead of viewing the postmodern de-historicization of experience nostalgically or pessimistically, Vattimo believes that the ideas of Nietzsche and Heidegger

> offer us the chance to pass from a purely critical and negative description of the postmodern condition, typical of early twentieth-century *Kulturkritik* and its more recent offshoots, to an approach that treats it as a *positive possibility and opportunity*. Nietzsche mentions all of this [. . .] in his theory of a possibly active or *positive (accomplished) nihilism*. Heidegger alludes to the same thing with his idea of a *Verwindung* of metaphysics, which is not a critical overcoming in the _"modern" sense of the term[2] [. . .] [but rather] a going-beyond that is both an acceptance and a deepening.[3]

Analyzing the etymology of *Verwindung*, Vattimo underscores the connotation of "convalescence" (to be healed, cured of an illness), also linked to resignation, and the connotation of distortion ("to turn," "to twist"). One is cured of an illness and, at the same time, resigned to a pain or loss: "Metaphysics is not something we can put aside like an opinion. Nor can it be left behind us like a doctrine in which we no longer believe; rather, it is something which stays in us as do the traces of an illness or a kind of pain to which we are resigned. It is neither a critical overcoming nor an acceptance that recovers and prolongs it."[4] "Post-histoire," or "weak" history, as Vattimo understands it, is not yet another discourse that tries to legitimate itself on the grounds that it is more up to date and thus more valid or more authentic than the bankrupt discourse of modernity.

In her 2007 study *European Cinema after 1989*, film scholar Luisa Rivi appropriated Vattimo's idea of "weak thought" to theorize the exhaustion—but *not* the vanishing—of the nation and national cinema. For Rivi, the decline of Europe's master narratives does not mark their end; instead, these narratives are realized in declined ways "through the introduction and acceptance of concepts of plurality, alterity, difference, opaqueness, and heterogeneity,"[5] a process that involves Europe acknowledging its past myths and, instead of trying to overcome the past or recover it nostalgically, rethinking its master narratives to make them reflect the new social, political, and economic realities. Rather than discarding the concept of national cinema in favor of "postnational cinema," however, Rivi invites us to see post-1989 European cinema as "weak" or "declined" national cinema, one that acknowledges the different ways in which transnational forces and supranational bodies are altering the notion of national identity and national cinema. Along similar lines, in her book *Mythopoetic Cinema: On the Ruins of European Identity* (2017), Kriss Ravetto-Biagioli posits "European identity" and "European cinema" as existing "in ruins"—her version of Vattimo's and Rivi's "weak" or "declined" ontological status—but, like Rivi, rather than bemoaning the "ruination" of European identity and European cinema, Biagioli challenges the commitment to a discourse of identity, however inclusive, tolerant, and diverse, as politically dangerous—inasmuch as it gives rise to an endless reproduction of identifications that inevitably bring ever more radical forms of exclusion—championing instead what she calls "mythopoetics," a filmic critical practice that questions the constant need to provide new identities, including a "new Europe." Finally, echoing both Vattimo's reading of Nietzsche's "positive nihilism" and Rivi's reading of "weak national cinema" through Vattimo's *pensiero debole*, in his most recent book—*European Cinema and Continental Philosophy: Film as Thought Experiment* (2018)—Thomas Elsaesser, like Rivi and Ravetto-Biagioli, asserts that what he calls European "cinema of abjection"—populated by "abject" characters, who might or might not be migrants/refugees—promises to "reboot" Europe's political and ethical roots in Enlightenment humanist and universalist values (citizenship, justice, ethics, liberty, tolerance, and hospitality) from a position of *"tactical weakness,"* which references the weakness of the nation state as a political entity, the inherent vulnerability of democracy, and the "abjection" of the Other.

Not only are such attempts to rethink Europe and European cinema from a position of tactical weakness somewhat disingenuous, especially when considered in light of the "ethical turn" in the humanities and cinema studies, but they also risk sidestepping any serious consideration of the importance of gender and race in the construction of both national and European identity, and of the ways in which hospitality and humanitarianism remain embedded in Europe's racialized and gendered politics. Accordingly, the second part of this chapter seeks to make explicit the gender and racial dynamics of contemporary European migrant cinema by drawing attention to their increasing *genre hybridity* and to the trope of disguise or *impersonation*, which foregrounds the performativity of identity,[6] particularly in films imaginatively rethinking national and European identity through the lens of *gender* (section 2) and to the role *race* continues to play as an implicit frontier of "Europeanness" (section 3).

1 Rethinking European Identity and Cinema from a Position of "Tactical Weakness"

Seeking to rethink Europe and European cinema without falling back on identity politics, both Ravetto-Biagioli's *Mythopoetic Cinema* and Elsaesser's *European Cinema and Continental Philosophy* posit *self-critique* and *skepticism*—what Ravetto-Biagioli calls "mythopoetics," and Elsaesser, "film as thought experiment"—as essential to European cinema. Ravetto-Biagioli defines "mythopoetics," exemplified by the cinema of Sokurov, Angelopoulos, Abramović, and Godard, as a critical practice that questions the constant need to provide new identities, a "new Europe," and with it a "new European cinema." Distinguishing "mythopoetics" from the conventional understanding of the term as referring to a process of "mythmaking," "a creative practice that transforms ideas into themes, themes into narratives, and narratives into social meaning,"[7] she adopts a formalist approach to poetics, which focuses either on structural and stylistic features (following the example set by Aristotle's *Poetics*) or on narrative features (*a la* Todorov and Genette). If "mythmaking" is linked to identity construction and identity politics, taking as its object a certain filmic corpus, "mythopoetics" is a *filmic critical practice* with *no specific object other than the very act of critique*: *imploding* archetypal myths of national, ethnic, religious, and political identities, *questioning* what constitutes Europe in the age of neoliberalism, and *undermining* the notion of a "new European cinema." Insofar as "mythopoetic cinema" is about *crossing* historical, ethnic, national, religious borders, *contaminating* identities, cultures, and ideologies, *blurring* the line between the real, the historical, and the imaginary, *mixing* filmic styles and genres—thus refusing to provide us with yet another definition of a particular type of cinema reflecting a particularly "European" identity—it is indicative of a general predilection in recent scholarship on Europe for *fuzzy concepts* (see the Introduction). Distancing herself from studies attributing Europe's problems to "bad" identity politics that needs to be replaced by "a new, more ethical or realistic understanding of identity,"[8] Ravetto-Biagioli, nevertheless, insists that her notion of "mythopoetics" is deeply political—this, however, is a politics of *unthinking identity politics as such*. "European identity," in her view, should be seen as a dynamic process of constant self-erasure or self-questioning rather than an objective quality with a traceable history.

One distinctive feature of this "metaconcept" of European identity as an act of self-questioning or self-erasure is that it is, as Ravetto-Biagioli herself acknowledges, not specifically European—mythopoetic cinema as a critical practice "can emerge virtually anywhere, being connected not to political identities but to a kind of critique that, while connected to specific European philosophical traditions, is certainly not aimed at stabilizing 'Europeanness' of any kind."[9] Since "mythopoetic cinema" is a product of skepticism—skepticism regarding the existence of any kind of imaginary, whether personal, political, national, or supranational—the only thing that can be said of it is that it performs the work of deconstruction: it practices "unthinking," questioning the grounds from which our various imaginaries are drawn. Ravetto-Biagioli's only response to those criticizing the "groundlessness of critique" as "a form of cynicism, irony, hopelessness or passive nihilism, as an endless circuitous discourse"[10] is that critique or mythopoetics—the two being ultimately synonymous for her—does not offer easy answers or instruct us how to proceed ethically, but that is no reason for discounting it.

There are important continuities between Ravetto-Biagioli's "mythopoetics" and Aga Skrodzka's notion of "Second Worldness." According to Skrodzka, despite certain continuities between the colonization of Eastern Europe and that of the Third World, communist Europe is also a site of a unique colonialism that tends to be dismissed in postcolonial approaches to Europe. Under communism, East European and East Central European countries remained very conscious of their national identities and, unlike the Third World, were able to imagine their fate as common, thanks to their shared liminality, their shared convictions about their own (peripheral) Europeanness, and their shared role as a buffering agent.[11] On these grounds Skrodzka insists on preserving the particularity of the post-Soviet heritage, arguing that the interstitial space of "Second Worldness" occupied by ex-communist countries reflects a difference "stronger and older than the Cold War terminology, [a] difference that stubbornly persists in the era of European integration."[12] Invoking Jameson's observation that magic realism always emerges "from moments of socio-economic transitions and the accompanying coexistence of multiple representational codes,"[13] she views the discourse of "Second Worldness"—reflected in magic realist cinema—not as specific to East Central European cinema but as *intrinsic to certain sociocultural conditions and moments in history that arise in different parts of the world* (e.g., Latin America).

In short, both "mythopoetics," defined "as a critical practice that can emerge virtually anywhere, being connected not to political identities but to a kind of critique,"[14] and "Second Worldness," which Aga Skrodzka considers intrinsic to certain sociocultural conditions and moments in history that arise in different parts of the world, name *a certain skeptical tendency within European cinema* that obstructs any attempts at a positive definition of "Europe": mythopoetics is a "filmic critical practice" describable only as a resistance to committing to a particular ideology or imaginary, while "Second Worldness" represents a "counter-epistemological discourse," "a way to escape the positivist reality principle."[15] Insofar as both "Second Worldness" and "mythopoetics" posit a distinctly "European skepticism"—which interrupts, from within, *any* form of ideological and/or institutional discourse—as inherent to European cinema, both terms inscribe themselves in a long philosophical tradition (see the Introduction) of considering skepticism, doubt, and self-critique—viewed positively rather than negatively, as full of potential rather than as signs of weakness or vulnerability—as quintessentially European. Like Ravetto-Bagioli and Skrodzka, in *European Cinema and Continental Philosophy*, Elsaesser seeks to recuperate Euro-skepticism from a sign of Europe's decline and marginalization into an opportunity for rethinking European cinema as essentially free—free from the duty to function as a "window-on-the-world" or a "mirror-to-the-self," two metaphors predicated on *constructing identity through difference,* which Elsaesser proposes to replace with the metaphor of "double occupancy," for "window" and "mirror" still belong to a *discourse of representation* whereas "double occupancy" refers to the *constitution of identity* and is thus part of an *ontological discourse*. However, by replacing "window" and "mirror" with "double occupancy," Elsaesser is not really abandoning the legacy of ideological critique, for he is still very much concerned with the constitution and transformation of values and of the ideologies within which they have been inscribed—indeed, one of his main claims in the book is precisely that European cinema "is reworking its own legacy, the values and political ideals of the Enlightenment."[16] He thus still views European cinema as engaged in ideological critique, the difference now being that Hollywood is no longer the only object of that critique—instead, European cinema is beginning to reexamine its own ideological legacy. Neither does Elsaesser abandon the politics of representation embodied by the metaphor of the "mirror-of-the-self" as evidenced, for instance, by his proposal to supplement the three external narratives of Europe's declining geopolitical status with three *internal narratives of trauma* (demographics and biopolitics, the Holocaust, and Islam).

In his contribution to the volume *The Europeanness of European Cinema* (2014),[17] parts of which are reproduced in his 2018 book, Elsaesser proposes that "the new marginality" of European cinema, following its "demotion" to just another part of "world cinema," should not be seen as a loss but as a newly found freedom, which he theorizes, rather counterintuitively, as the freedom to impose on oneself certain constraints or limits. He sets out to challenge the established paradigms of European cinema scholarship in three main ways: (1) he claims to question the traditional binaries of art-commerce, Europe-Hollywood, auteur-star, realism-dream factory, movement image-time image; (2) he claims to go beyond paradigmatic approaches to European cinema in terms of classical film theory (ideological critique), cultural studies (the politics of representation and identity), and film-philosophy (Deleuze's movement image and time image); and (3) he claims to place Europe's new marginality within a broader context that includes not only the three main narratives of Europe's declining geopolitical status viewed from the outside but also "the three traumas of Europe" (partly overlapping with the three narratives), which reflect the three main anxieties tearing Europe apart. Ultimately, Elsaesser proposes a new model and method through which European cinema should be studied, one no longer based on the "Europe-Hollywood" binary, *and not even focusing on cinema,* but rather, on *what we mean by "Europe" today*.

Ironically, by associating European cinema with freedom—the freedom from commercial constraints and the freedom from having to represent the nation, which the rest of "world cinema" is, according to Elsaesser, still expected to do—Elsaesser's book actually bolsters, rather than challenging, the paradigm of constructing identity through difference. To begin with, when speaking of European cinema's "new marginality," Elsaesser uses the term "marginality" in a very specific, narrow sense. The very real marginality of certain types of cinema, for example, small national cinemas, is not comparable to what he calls "the new marginality" of European cinema—one would hardly refer to the marginality of Bulgarian cinema, for example, as "a highly prized freedom." Elsaesser uses the term "marginality" in the sense of a *privilege* rather than to denote something a certain type of cinema is automatically entitled to or capable of. Furthermore, even as he purports to challenge the traditional binaries of art-commerce or auteur-popular cinema, he describes European cinema's "new marginality" in exactly the same terms: European cinema is marginal in the sense of being free from commercial constraints (i.e., it *is* an art cinema, not popular cinema) and free from the requirement to represent the nation (i.e., it IS an auteur cinema, not a vehicle of nation-building). Surprisingly, arguing that European films now "share the generic label 'world cinema' where they compete with those from Turkey and Thailand, Iran and Mexico"[18]—a statement that sounds somewhat patronizing—Elsaesser chooses Haneke—a director whose work has been consistently discussed as embodying precisely the legacy of European auteur cinema—and specifically *The White Ribbon* (2009) as a case study of European cinema's new marginality understood as "freedom from either box office or social accountability."[19] Elsaesser's argument is that first, since the majority of European directors get most of their funding from noncommercial sources they are free from the constraints of the box office, and that, second, since national representativeness (and the constraints that come with it) is more the result of the festival circuit than an organic expression of the nation, and is mainly reserved for filmmakers from the emerging nations of Asia and the Far East of Africa, European filmmakers don't need to worry about "representing the nation." Ironically, although Elsaesser aims to demonstrate that Haneke is engaged in "performing the nation rather than representing it"[20] his own analysis of *The White Ribbon* concludes that the film is not so much about the origins of fascism as about "the origins of the nation state and national identity through the conflictual interplay of schoolteacher, State Church, feudal master and medical doctor, each standing for aspects of both the costs and benefits of progress and modernity winning over tradition and authority."[21] In short, although European filmmakers—of whom Haneke is supposed to be representative—no longer need to worry about representing the nation, they are still engaged in a self-reflexive analysis of national identity and the nation state!

In *European Cinema and Continental Philosophy*, Elsaesser revisits his earlier argument about European cinema's new marginality to propose, counterintuitively, that the future of Europe depends on reaffirming Europe's core Enlightenment values from a weak/marginal position he theorizes as "abjection." Throughout the book he develops a two-track argument about (1) film as "thought experiment" and (2) Europe as "thought experiment," ultimately claiming that cinema as thought experiment represents the most adequate response to Europe's political crisis. How can we rethink European cinema, Elsaesser asks, as "a political ethics" rather than a "window-on-the-world" or a "mirror-to-the-self"? Drawing on Deleuze, Badiou, Rancière, Agamben, Nancy, Žižek, and Levinas (only to distance himself from the latter), Elsaesser defines the most pressing political dilemmas facing Europe in terms of a threefold deficit: the deficit of democracy, the multicultural diversity deficit, and the social justice deficit. Making another (this time self-acknowledged) counterintuitive move, he wants to argue that these deficits can actually be seen as "assets" or "opportunities" for Europe to reboot its democratic principles, offering a more positive scenario "for the practice and future of democracy worldwide,"[22] an argument that could be said to attribute to Europe a quasi-messianic mission as the world's "savior." In the face of the current politico-ethical crisis, Elsaesser holds out European cinema as the last bastion of ethics and humanism, capable of nothing less than "rebooting" the values of the Enlightenment that real world actors and institutions (such as the EU) have proven themselves incapable of reviving. Two sections in Chapter 2—"What is cinema good for?" and "Cinema—humanism's last hope or the true face of technological determinism?"—sum up Elsaesser's high hopes for European cinema. Contradicting his own premise—that European cinema has become marginal and thus free from having to represent anything, or having to promote any ideology—Elsaesser positions European "cinema of abjection" as Europe's last hope—indeed, cinema's last hope—to reassert its status as the world's arbiter of "freedom, equality, and fraternity."

Perhaps not accidentally the philosophers Elsaesser draws upon—Rancière, Badiou, and Agamben—serve as "pillars" in another recent take on the relationship between politics and aesthetics, theory, and praxis, Nico Baumbach's *Cinema/Politics/Philosophy*, which traces these philosophers' engagement with the legacy of 1970s Althusserian film theory as "a discourse of political modernism" tying ideology critique "to an idea of a counter-cinema that perform[s] within film practice the very function of theory."[23] Like Baumbach's passionate defense of the legacy of "Grand Theory" Elsaesser's exploration of European cinema through the prism of continental philosophy can be seen precisely as continuing the legacy of film theory as a discourse of political modernism. On one hand, his project extends Rancière's critique of the Althusserian notion of art/ideology, which "corresponds to the surface of appearance but does not give us a means for knowledge."[24] Arguably, both Rancière and Elsaesser propose a different conception of the politics of aesthetics, one according to which politics is not something "applied" to art but something inherent to art, thus overturning the "binary opposition that dominated 1970s film theory between theory as knowledge and cinema as ideology."[25] On the other hand, inasmuch as Elsaesser ties philosophy—rather than ideology critique—to an idea of a counter-cinema (what he calls "a cinema of abjection") that performs within film practice the very function of philosophy, we could say that in his book continental philosophy performs a function similar to that of "theory" in the "political modernist" discourse of 1970s film theory.

If Rancière is concerned with "the politics of cinema as cinema," Elsaesser's notion of "film as thought experiment" is closer to the more familiar idea of cinema as "a political art": rather than exploring the relationship between politics and the cinematic medium, Elsaesser is mostly concerned with thematic and structural analysis of political themes in recent European films. Accordingly, to address the decline of Europe's Enlightenment values, Elsaesser situates recent European cinema within "a philosophical framework of cinema as a political ethics"[26] and approaches it as a "thought experiment"[27] by identifying "films that can be referenced to the core philosophical principles and political values of European democracy."[28] While Elsaesser presents his approach to European cinema as "thought experiment" as new, one could argue that all films can be seen as thought experiments inasmuch as all films construct a fictional/hypothetical world with its own system of values, which can then be discussed in terms of our practical system of ethical and political values and norms. In short, when Elsaesser writes that "it may be time to declare the very idea of a united Europe a political experiment badly in need of renewing itself as a philosophical thought experiment,"[29] he is describing what cinema does on a regular basis: imagining a world different from the one we live in. Furthermore, "cinema as thought experiment," which privileges films that invite ethical–political–philosophical readings and films functioning as "didactic parables or imaginary scenarios addressing hypothetical 'what if' situations,"[30] actually resurrects the idea of *expectations* and *obligations* Elsaesser claimed to have done away with by insisting on the "marginality" of European cinema as a source of its newly found freedom.

Reflections on "film as thought experiment" are not new: for instance, there are undeniable parallels between Elsaesser's idea of cinema as thought experiment and Badiou's concept of "le cinéma comme expérimentation philosophique."[31] According to Badiou, whenever cinema confronts us with a situation in which a choice has to be made, the situation can be described as philosophical. A situation is philosophical if it makes us think the event, the exception, if it shows us that, "entre l'amour et les lois ordinaires de la vie, les lois de la cité, la loi du mariage, il n'y a pas de commune mesure ... [La philosophie] va nous dire: 'Il faut penser l'évènement, il faut le penser ... il faut penser le changement de la vie.'"[32] Put differently, cinema-as-philosophical-experiment, or thought experiment, shows us that a different order of things is possible. Although Elsaesser makes no reference to Badiou's text, he does acknowledge that the idea of cinema as thought experiment is not specific to Europe's "new marginality"; rather, contemporary cinema as thought experiment is a sort of a sequel to the more personal/existential cinema as thought experiment that emerged in the aftermath of the Second World War and was characterized by "its reflexivity, its inward turn, as well as its unique form or ruminating, speculative self-scrutiny."[33] Indeed, Elsaesser goes as far as to suggest that inasmuch as European cinema is distinguished by "intense self-interrogation, political critique, and a probing of limits (of what it means to be European),"[34] it has always been "philosophical," that is, a "thought experiment." The only difference between contemporary European cinema as thought experiment, and the cinema as thought experiment that preceded it is the more overtly political engagement with the idea of community—in terms of "the Other as neighbor, stranger, antagonist and object of desire"[35]—compared to the earlier, more personal treatment of that subject.

One of Elsaesser's central assumptions is that while European films have become inconsequential both economically and ideologically, their increasing marginality "frees them from the burden of being 'representative,'" granting them "a new kind of autonomy,"[36] to which he attributes *political* significance. However, the claim that European films are "free" rests on a basic misunderstanding of ideology. To assert that European films no longer have to "reflect or promote a specific ideology"[37] presupposes an understanding of ideology as something with which a filmmaker *consciously* infuses their film—but this is not how ideology works. Moreover, it is doubtful that European films are no longer subject to symptomatic or allegorical readings (those based on the two abiding aesthetics of "the window" and "the mirror") to which, Elsaesser claims, Hollywood (and other) films still are—to insist that this is so is to promote an exceptionalist vision of European cinema as superior to other cinemas, which are unfortunately still "not free" of "having to be representative" or "having to reflect a particular ideology." We should also clarify that this "exceptional" status of being free from ideology and thus free to rethink classical philosophical values and ideas is reserved for Western European cinema only. Not only does Elsaesser not discuss any Eastern European or Central European films but his primary examples of the kind of cinema he believes capable of "rebooting" Enlightenment values are also drawn exclusively from the work of well-known Western European auteurs—Michael Haneke, Christian Petzold, Claire Denis, all festival darlings—who, oddly enough, are said to occupy a "marginal" place in the world of cinema.

Given the political significance Elsaesser attributes to the notion of "the abject" and to "the cinema of abjection," it is worth examining closely the meaning of this term in the context of Elsaesser's larger project. Elsaesser's use of the term "abjection," which transforms the negative connotations of "abject" into a perverse kind of freedom (as we saw earlier, he interprets the marginality of European cinema, similarly, as a kind of perverse freedom), asserted from "a position of extreme marginality and exclusion imposed by the Other,"[38] betrays the implicitly *therapeutic* drift of his overall argument. The notion of "abjection" could be seen as an optimistic reformulation of

Laurent Berlant's "cruel optimism" as an adjustment strategy (see Chapter 4), though Berlant underscores the perverse and ultimately damaging nature of "cruel optimism" whereas Elsaesser foregrounds the emancipatory potential of abjection as freedom, not freedom *from* something, but the freedom of having nothing more to lose, of having hit rock bottom. His rethinking of abjection as "freedom"—a sort of masochistic embracement of one's own self-abasement—and of trauma as "an opportunity" to reinvest the subject with a sense of agency serves the therapeutic purpose of creating the illusion of a supposedly powerless and traumatized European subject that continues to function in surprisingly effective ways. As he puts it in the chapter on Kaurismäki's *The Man without a Past* (2002) (featuring an amnesiac protagonist), amnesia (or, in psychoanalytic terms, repression), understood "as the psychological name for abjection,"[39] is a strategy of adaptation to a crisis that "reboots the system," that is, it is "a *productive pathology.*"[40] Here the concept of "abjection" as "the degree zero of what it means to be human today,"[41] implicitly indebted to Agamben's "bare life," is given a positive twist as a newly found freedom—the abject "has nothing more to lose, but also . . . no claims to make, thus commanding a particular kind of freedom that probes the limits of both freedom and the law."[42] Inscribing itself within the emancipatory appeal of "autonomy of migration approaches," Elsaesser's concept of "cinema of abjection" attempts to overturn the familiar negative view of experiences of marginalization, oppression, and exclusion by rethinking them as instances of (Kantian) "negative freedom," the freedom of having nothing more to lose, which Elsaesser compares to Herman Melville's Bartleby the Scrivener's "freedom to choose not to." While the intention behind this move—to undercut the victimization of abject Others (migrants and refugees, but also socially and economically disenfranchised "native" Europeans)—is understandable, it is doubtful that such "abject subjects" would consider themselves "free."

Elsaesser defines the "cinema of abjection" as an exploration of "what remains of us as human beings when none of the traditional bonds (marriage, family, clan, civil society, profession, nation, law, religion, language) can be relied upon to support a sense of self or identity other than the power of negativity itself,"[43] a definition that fails to identify what makes such films different from other films exploring the failure of any of the types of bonds listed above to provide a character with a sense of identity. His main examples are *I, Daniel Blake* (Ken Loach, 2016) and *Toni Erdmann* (Maren Ade, 2016), which feature protagonists "trapped in a seemingly relentless downward spiral until they 'hit bottom' or realize there is no bottom at all,"[44] that is, "abject characters," whom Elsaesser defines as "not necessarily migrants or homeless, not outcasts or marginal—but ordinary, sometimes well-to-do and seemingly established members of the community—who . . . find themselves falling out of their habitual lives for no special reason other than chance and bad luck, or who lose their footing."[45] Indeed, throughout the book Elsaesser uses the term "abjection" rather loosely, applying it to cinema (as in "European cinema of abjection"), to characters within a film (abject characters, reduced to a degree zero of what it means to be human), to an auteur (referring to self-imposed limits and constraints, for example, Haneke), to ethics (the ethics of abjection), to politics (the politics of abjection), to style (referring to a kind of minimalist approach to setting, acting, and plotting, for example, Dogme 95 films, Petzold's films), or to film spectatorship (designating films that purposefully withdraw their appeal to the viewer's empathy). The concept of "abjection" thus remains too broad to be meaningful.

Although Elsaesser acknowledges that he borrows the concept from Kristeva[46] he strips it from its original feminist and psychoanalytic significance, foregrounding instead the power the abject derives from being excluded or expelled, which "takes the form of provocative self-abasement ... [and thus] a gesture and an act that challenges the other to respond to the abject's particular kind of 'embodied truth.'"[47] It is precisely in this gesture of defiance that Elsaesser locates the abject's power. By borrowing only the structural rather than the substantive version of the concept of "the abject," the latter commonly associated with horror and melodrama—that is, with American cinema—Elsaesser implies that abjection in the structural sense is primarily or exclusively a European phenomenon. He also insists on a crucial difference between his concept of "the abject" and Agamben's "bare life," with which it shares obvious similarities although, like Kristeva's "abject," Agamben's "bare life" lacks one aspect central to Elsaesser's "abjection," namely "the power of those who do not claim power, the power that an existence which merely insists on being can exert over those that exclude it,"[48] the "uncanny" power of the victim-turned-abject, which "probes both the limits of freedom and the law."[49] Elsaesser also distinguishes his use of the term from another term often used synonymously with "bare life" and "abjection"—"precariousness"—specifying that he is using abjection in the structural sense of the term only, rather than as a sociological category descriptive of a particular person or group, which is the original meaning of the term "precarious." Unlike the precarious subject, who, as an object of pity and sympathy, still establishes a positive relation to the Other, such a positive relation to the other is suspended in abjection: the abject subject is in a "relation without relation" to the rest of the community and it is precisely in this "relation without relation" that its power and freedom lie. One wonders, however, what distinguishes Elsaesser's abjection, which he presents as "the ultimate ethical stance par excellence,"[50] from Levinas's understanding of ethics as "demands that present themselves as necessarily to be fulfilled, but which are neither forced upon me (by morality) nor are they enforceable (by law)."[51] Indeed, Elsaesser describes "the abject subject" in very similar terms, as one who makes no claims, who does not appeal to my empathy (hence the stress on "withdrawal of empathy" or "blockage of empathy"), and who has suspended any positive relation with me yet holds a certain power (understood as negative freedom) over me so that I cannot fail but recognize our shared humanity/abjection.

In the final analysis, the idea of "the abject" becomes just another way for Elsaesser to argue that the dismantling of all "grand narratives" (political and ethical) about Europe has reduced Europe to a tabula rasa, which, far from being a tragedy, should be seen as a chance for Europe to "reinvent" itself or, in Elsaesser's terms, (borrowing from the vocabulary of film remakes and franchise reboots) "reboot" itself. To put it bluntly, the advantage of hitting rock bottom is that it cannot get any worse—in fact, things are "logically" bound to get better. This "leap of faith," which reaffirms the Europeanness of Europe and of European cinema "as part of what it is not (yet), rather than against what it can no longer be"[52] depends on—indeed, demands—the transvaluation of the Enlightenment trinity of values from a position of "tactical weakness": "equality as abjection, fraternity as antagonistic mutuality, and freedom as the freedom to choose one's own limits."[53]

Not only does the other concept Elsaesser develops in parallel with "cinema of abjection"—"film as thought experiment"—suffer from the same definitional problems, but the connection he posits between abjection in the structural sense of the term (in the sense of rupture and transgression) and "film as thought experiment" is also mostly left unexamined. Although Elsaesser attempts to narrow down the concept of "film as thought experiment" by dating its emergence to the mid-1990s, the term remains frustratingly vague. The problem is that every film—not only the ones Elsaesser examines—constitutes a thought experiment inasmuch as every film is premised on a "what if?" Regardless of what different screenwriting manuals call it—the controlling idea, the action-idea, or the theme—the premise is "what a film is really about." Inasmuch as all films have a premise they are all "like" informal arguments that present evidence toward some conclusion. To argue that a certain class of films function as thought experiments in response to a specific problem—for example, Europe's political and ethical crisis—is to insist that only this specific class of films have premises. Furthermore, to claim that European cinema as thought experiment proposes a philosophical answer to a yet unresolved practical problem is redundant since all fiction films, insofar as they imagine a world, are informed by a particular worldview, are meant as reflections upon, rather than solutions to, real world problems, and can be said to borrow the rhetorical strategies of a thought experiment.

Although he claims that cinema as thought experiment does away with the two abiding aesthetics of "window" and "mirror," and that European cinema no longer derives its identity from its opposition to Hollywood, Elsaesser's very idea of Europe's new "abject position" is derived precisely from European cinema's loss of geopolitical and economic relevance vis-à-vis Hollywood (and Asian cinemas) with which it can no longer compete. In fact, Elsaesser himself invites us to see "Hollywood mind-game films" and

European cinema as thought-experiment as two versions of a conception of cinema emerging in response to "the crisis of cinema," both technological (the digital turn) and ethico-political (the auto-critique of Enlightenment values). Thus, Elsaesser still thinks the identity of European cinema is "face to face with Hollywood," and although their relationship is not necessarily one of power (both are posited as two responses to the same crisis of cinema), in keeping with his own notion of European cinema as "art" versus Hollywood as "industry/entertainment" (the book is full of anti-Hollywood asides), he argues that Hollywood mind-game cinema responds to the "merely" technological crisis of cinema while for European cinema is reserved the more important philosophical and ethical task of reinventing Europe and restoring our faith in humanism and universalism. Mind-game films are concerned with the individual and with epistemological questions about the nature of perception (hence they deal with parallel or alternate worlds), whereas European cinema as thought experiment is "above all concerned with ethical choices, the body politic, the collective and the community."[54] In short, Elsaesser reaffirms the familiar dichotomy of genre-oriented, individualistic American cinema versus socially oriented European art cinema, which he initially set out to deconstruct.

The self-contradiction plaguing the concepts of "abjection" and "cinema as thought experiment" is compounded by a lack of clarity in the nature of the connection Elsaesser wants to posit between the two—for example, it remains unclear how the emergence of an ethics and politics of abjection—where abjection is identified with "the voiding of interiority and subjectivity"[55]—in recent European films is related to the supposedly new *form* (the thought experiment) such ethics and politics assume. Do abject characters naturally lend themselves to the parable-like structure of the thought experiment, or, on the contrary, the minimalist, didactic structure of the thought experiment necessarily produces characters devoid of interiority and subjectivity? And what, concretely, is meant by this voiding of interiority and subjectivity? Sometimes, it seems to refer to the style of a film—the film deliberately denies us access to a character's internal life, *a la* Breson (in his discussion of Petzold's *Barbara* (2012) Elsaesser identifies schematic plots, minimalist mise en scène, and minimalist acting style as *stylistic features* typical of cinema as thought experiment)—but at other times it refers to abject characters who have been voided of everything that makes them human, having nothing more to lose and no claims to make (e.g., characters excluded from the community such as refugees, migrants, ethnic and racial Others).

Part of the problem is that Elsaesser treats as synonymous discourses as distinct as the ontology of film on one hand, and the European philosophical tradition since Descartes on the other, or, alternatively, epistemological skepticism on one hand, and minimalist film style on the other. For instance, he claims that the films of the Dardenne brothers place the viewer in an "ungroundedness that aims at insinuating a more general epistemological doubt (about other minds) than merely about the motives of (fictional) characters,"[56] thanks to the filmmakers' unique way of positioning the viewer as "at once close and distant, 'with' the characters and separated from them by what Luc Dardenne calls 'the secret.'"[57] Here there is a slippage from epistemological skepticism (regarding the existence of other minds) to film style (one that denies us access to the interior life of fictional characters) and social relations (the anxiety and fear that constitutes our relationship to the Other), from philosophy to film aesthetics to ethics and politics. To stay with the Dardenne brothers, as persuasive as Elsaesser's reading of their work might be, it fails to provide reasons for treating their films as representative of an entire class of films Elsaesser groups under the umbrella term "cinema of abjection": it's hard to see, for instance, how their camera's "hovering—between hesitancy and holding back"—which allows us to be "with the character" without soliciting, however, our empathy—and the importance of thresholds in their mise en scène, is representative of the "hypothetical" status of *all* films Elsaesser considers thought experiments. Here Elsaesser isolates a specific feature of the film style of *one* filmmaker and treats it as representative of a whole class of films ("cinema as thought experiment"), instead of examining the particular stylistic features that give the very different films grouped under this term (e.g., consider how different Haneke is from the Dardenne brothers) their hypothetical or experiment-like character.

On the other hand, Elsaesser regularly conflates the ontology of film with the history of post-Cartesian continental philosophy. For instance, in the section on the philosophical turn in film studies, he references Jean Epstein's notion of "photogénie"—cinema's leveling of the differences between the animate and the inanimate, treating both as "alive"—before turning, in the next paragraph, to the "auto-critique of the Enlightenment project"[58] by European intellectuals, an auto-critique responsible for "the loss of a binding value system and the apparent interchangeability of everything with everything else."[59] With the phrase "speaking of equality" serving as the only transition between the two paragraphs, the argument leaps from a discussion of cinema's leveling of differences (a "democratizing" tendency inherent in cinema as a medium) to a discussion of the erasure of democratic values like equality by postmodernism's leveling of differences, or, put differently, from a "good" type of indifference or equality (cinematic photogénie) to a "bad" type of indifference or equality (philosophical skepticism/deconstruction/relativism). Not only does Elsaesser fail to provide a reason for drawing an analogy between a feature of the cinematic medium (according to a particular film theory, in this case Epstein's theory of photogénie) and a historical feature of the European intellectual tradition (the collapse of grand narratives), but he also leaps from a discussion of film ontology to a discussion of a particular stage (the auto-critique of the Enlightenment project) in the history of a particular geographical place (Europe), thus committing the same error—that of conflating film ontology with film history—for which he later criticizes Deleuze.

Another instance of this conflation of film ontology with intellectual history is the discussion of the idea of film's *automatism* (in Deleuze and Cavell)—another feature pertaining, like photogénie, to the ontology of film—as synonymous with the loss of a binding system of values, a loss of "trust and belief in the world."[60] Here Elsaesser commits the same error for which he criticizes Deleuze's cinema books: he suggests that a specific, historically determined phenomenon (the waning of Enlightenment values) might, in fact, be inherent to (and thus explainable through) the ontology of film (its automatism, which might be seen as "breeding" cynicism and passivity). While it is true that, as Rancière has argued, the history of cinema has been driven by the question how "to tame the contingent (raw sensory data) that automatism brings to life, into 'fables,' that is, stories and narrative,"[61] it is not clear how this question can be extended to the political and ethical content of these stories and narratives, which is how Elsaesser wants to rephrase Rancière's argument, that is, to link automatism to humanism (the political and ethical values and ideals embodied in stories and narratives), raw sensory data to moral emotions (specifically empathy). Having earlier raised the question of the ethical import of cinema's photogénie, Elsaesser reframes the question in terms of "the ethical challenge of cinema's automatism,"[62] this time with reference to Cavell and Jean-Luc Nancy. All of the above proves ultimately detrimental to the fundamental premise on which Elsaesser's general argument rests: that the ethico-moral demands facing Europe and European cinema today are, in fact, inscribed in the medium of cinema as such, and that European cinema of abjection is the most appropriate answer to emerge in response to these demands or, put differently, that the ontology of cinema as a technological medium and, on the other hand, the history of ideas—specifically European intellectual history, and, even more narrowly, Europe's politico-ethical crisis in the wake of the loss of Enlightenment values and the undermining of universalism and humanism—are somehow interconnected.

Although the connection between the two tracks of Elsaesser's argument—cinema's ontology and Europe's history—gets lost in the second part of the book, it is worth considering the path Elsaesser proposes to follow (although he himself does not follow it consistently) if only to demonstrate that, ironically, the "solution" to the double-faced crisis—cinematic and European—Elsaesser eventually proposes is not substantially different from Deleuze's conclusion in his two cinema books. As I have argued in *The Image in French Philosophy* (2007), Deleuze's cinema books are representative of a certain strand within continental philosophy, whose attempt to critique metaphysics resulted in a strange "rebooting" (to use Elsaesser's favorite term) of metaphysics as a thinking pertaining to *impersonal* forces and *depersonalizing* experiences or, more generally, to what remains beyond subjectivity and representation. Recalling Epstein's notion of cinematic photogénie, that is, cinema's indifference to traditional distinctions between the animate and the inanimate, humans and things (an indifference to life that has, ironically, been read as evidence of cinema's affinity with life), Deleuze argues that the *evacuation of subjectivity* (what he refers to as "getting rid of ourselves")—exemplified by what he calls, in *Cinema II: The Time-Image*, "pure optical situations"—is the very purpose and meaning of philosophy: "To open us up to the inhuman and the superhuman (durations which are inferior or superior to our own), to go beyond the human condition: This is the meaning of philosophy, in so far as our condition condemns us to live among badly analyzed composites, and to be badly analyzed composites ourselves."[63] As we shall see, Elsaesser's discussion of "the ethical challenge of cinema's automatism"—which, as mentioned earlier, is from the start undermined by the unsubstantiated claim that specific politico-ethical values and ideas (such as the value of equality) are inherent in cinema as a medium in a meaningful rather than merely structurally analogous way—leads him to conclusions very similar to Deleuze's.

Elsaesser begins by invoking Nancy's contention, in his book on Kiarostami *L'evidence du film* (2001), that both classical and modern cinema are "reactionary"—the former because it presumes that the world makes sense, the latter because of its obsession with endlessly expressing the meaninglessness of the world. On the contrary, for Nancy, and for Elsaesser, the value of cinema is precisely that "it teaches us to live not just with impersonality, but also with meaninglessness [but] this we should see as a gift ... in being able to envisage how cinema can restore our trust and belief in a world, once we accept that it can cleanse 'the world viewed' of meaning and purpose."[64] The assumption is that revealing the values and ideals that used to give life meaning to be meaningless—or, in the specific historical context with which Elsaesser is concerned, revealing the values of the Enlightenment to be no longer binding—will somehow automatically lead to the rebooting of these values, thereby restoring our trust in the world. Not only is this not as self-evident as Elsaesser supposes it is, but the broader conclusion to which it leads him is even more problematic. Elsaesser claims that what all the philosophers he has referenced in preparation for his own argument about European cinema as thought experiment—Nancy, Cavell, Rancière, and Deleuze—have in common is the belief that "cinema is a powerful agent not for instantiating subjectivity or artistic expressivity but for getting rid of them, helping an ongoing and seemingly irreversible process of depersonalization of the sovereign subject and an exteriorization of all forms of interiority (soul, subjectivity, affect, desire)."[65] While the impersonal is, for Deleuze, the meaning of philosophy—inasmuch as philosophy aims to liberate us from the chains of subjectivity so that we can go "beyond the human condition"—Elsaesser reformulates Deleuze's "impersonal" into the

"the abject" without making explicit the liberties he takes in appropriating *a philosophical concept pertaining to the human* (opening up the human condition to the inhuman or the impersonal, to durations above or below human duration) to describe *a historically specific socio-ethico-political context* (opening up Europe to the Other or to the "abject," the exclusion of which is constitutive of Europe itself).

To sum up, if Deleuze's fantasy was "getting rid of ourselves" Elsaesser's project consists in getting rid of Europe's heroic narrative of self-identity, grounding this project in the medium-specific properties of cinema (notably automatism and photogénie) privileged by certain continental philosophers. In both cases, however, this "getting rid of" is imagined in terms of "self-purging"—purging ourselves of the anthropocentric point of view (Deleuze), purging ourselves of Eurocentrism (recognizing that Europe's identity is constructed through purging itself of "the abject"), and the abject subject purging herself of any claims to power (having nothing more to lose, no claims to make). This "purging" describes Elsaesser's methodology as well, that is, his tendency to borrow already existing concepts and, adapting them for his own purposes, "purging" them of their substantive content so as to retain only their "structural sense," for example, borrowing the structural aspect of Kristeva's concept (the sense of exclusion or expulsion of something considered as a threat to identity) and evacuating any substantive (psychoanalytic) meaning the term might have had. Similarly, Elsaesser approaches the *political principle of the right of mutual interference in the internal affairs of the other*, which describes the relationship between Brussels and EU member states—through *the (purely) formal (rather than substantive) structure of Levinasian ethics* (making no reference to any particular ethical imperative), which describes our relationship to the (ethnic, racial, national) Other. According to Elsaesser, both models based on "antagonistic mutuality" share an asymmetrical relationship with the Other. Anticipating the objection that the purely formal structure of Levinasian ethics may not serve as a solid basis for a democratic politics, Elsaesser proposes that the kind of politics made possible by adopting the formal structure of Levinasian ethics is one that, instead of promoting "the right to have rights," promises "the right to be" to those who are outside the nation and without citizenship,[66] the negative freedom of Bartleby the Scrivener's "I prefer not to." Not only is it unclear how abjection can be positively recast as something "forcefully willed" but the idea of abjection as negative freedom is, confusingly, also sometimes attributed only to those who are excluded from the community of citizens, while at other times Elsaesser invokes a "mutual abjection" without, however, illustrating it with examples.

Elsaesser develops further the idea of "purging"[67] by making a case for the purging of empathy (or affect in general) in European cinema as a way of countering the victimization of abject subjects and reinvesting them with agency. However, as I already pointed out, the link between these different discourses—(1) cinema as a medium, (2) the meaning and purpose of philosophy, and (3) the current state of Europe and European cinema—in short, the link between (1) photogénie and automatism as medium-specific properties, (2) the opening up of the human to the inhuman or the posthuman as the essence of philosophy, and (3) equality as an ethico-political value and ideal—is never explained but rather, treated as a given. In fact, the three propositions themselves rest on unexamined assumptions. For instance, Elsaesser assumes that European cinema's decline because of its economic marginalization and because of Europe's loss of its geopolitical status automatically renders it impervious to "ideological instrumentalization," a dubious proposition and one that Elsaesser's book, in fact, contradicts—after all, the main objective of his study is to demonstrate that European cinema has an important role to play in the revival of humanist and universalist values. Elsaesser's own definition of cinema as thought experiment points explicitly to the "ideological instrumentalization" subtending this view of cinema:

> Thought experiments deal in hypothetical situations, and thus are fictions, often presented in the form of a *didactic parable or an imaginary scenario*. However, thought experiments are also 'What if?' conditionals, and as such they are suppositions. *Conditionals and suppositions are ways of making inferences based on real world evidence, posited in such a way as to allow for deductions that can predict future outcomes.*[68]

Here one might ask: What is the purpose of a didactic parable other than to comment on a real world situation and recommend a certain course of action?

Discussing several examples of European "cinema of abjection" at a recent conference on European cinema,[69] including *Biutiful* (Iñárritu, 2010) and *The Other Side of Hope* (Kaurismäki, 2017), Elsaesser praised the former for presenting its protagonist as both a victim and a perpetrator of suffering and the latter for showing solidarity with the refugee without however obscuring existing asymmetries of power. If there was a certain sense of *déjà entendu* about Elsaesser's conference talk it was perhaps because the notion of "abjection," now used with reference to twenty-first-century European cinema in the context of the resurgence of ethno-nationalism and anti-immigrant neo-racism, can actually be seen as a reformulation of Elsaesser's own analysis, twenty years ago, of the attempts of postwar German cinema to negotiate the fascist past in terms of what Elsaesser called, in *Fassbinder's Germany: History, Identity, Subject* (1996), "vicious circles and double binds," referring to characters who are represented neither as oppressors nor as victims but as *both* at one and the same time.

Elsaesser ends his book by invoking Jean-Luc Nancy's notion of community (in *The Inoperative Community* [1991] and *Being Singular Plural* [1996]) and his understanding of "being-with" as a mutual abandonment and exposure to each other, a "mid-sein" (versus Heidegger's da-sein) in order to conclude, rather enigmatically, that *Europeans have nothing in common except the distances that separate us*. While Elsaesser's, Ravetto-Biagioli's, and Rivi's attempts to rethink European cinema as "weak," "mythopoetic," or "philosophical" constitute valuable contributions to theoretical debates about the idea of European identity and the identity of European cinema, they remain reluctant to give up completely the outdated association of "European cinema" with "art cinema" and "auteur cinema." Given that the themes of precarity and migration—which are not strictly European but global, inasmuch as neoliberalism's reach is global—are central to contemporary European films, European cinema can hardly be said to have "embraced its marginality" (Elsaesser); on the contrary, it is becoming increasingly global. Indeed, as Skrodzka's "Second Worldness," Ravetto-Biagioli's "mythopoetics," and Elsaesser's "cinema as thought experiment" suggest, this type of cinema is not specifically European but is "intrinsic to certain socio-cultural conditions and moments in history that arise in different parts of the world" (Skrodzka), being "a critical practice that can emerge virtually anywhere ... connected not to political identities but to a kind of critique" (Ravetto-Biagioli).

2 Genre Hybridity and the Performativity of (European) Identity: The Trope of Impersonation

As I suggested in the beginning of this chapter, one of the drawbacks of approaches to European cinema from a strategic position of tactical weakness is the lack of attention to the genre, gender, and racial dynamics of European migrant cinema. Attributing the box office failure of films like *Dirty Pretty Things* (Stephen Frears, 2002) and *In This World* (Michael Winterbottom, 2002) to their genre hybridity, Rebecca Prime suggests that we consider such films not as failed experiments at genre-crossing but as constituting an emerging new genre, "the refugee film."[70] Conversely, many critics consider films about migrant journeys to Europe mere variations on the road movie or the extreme road movie. According to Maria Ravisco, "the European film of voyage"—"any fiction film in which the journey, thematically and as a narrative structural device, shapes a tale of self-discovery and social knowledge in contact with otherness set across European contexts"[71]—provides a useful way to study the symbolic boundaries essential to the construction of a "European identity" insofar as the genre tackles "new modes of representing the nation by articulating the contrasts between different spatialities—local, national, transnational—as well as the experience of otherness."[72] Similarly, Michael Gott singles out the road movie as an appropriate entry point into debates on migration insofar as road movies cannot be studied adequately within a purely national context.[73] By identifying the differences between the American and European road movie, Gott hints at the similarities between the road movie and the migrant film: for example, whereas the American road movie, usually centered around a rebel protagonist, is concerned with challenging cultural norms, the European road movie travels "into the national culture, tracing the meaning of citizenship as a journey."[74] At the same time, the European road movie, specifically the migrant film, shares with American film noir a preoccupation with the underbelly of the (European and American) city, "its dark streets and urban passageways."[75]

For many critics who view the migrant film as a subgenre of the road movie, formal experimentation has become one of the criteria in critically appraising such films, as evidenced by the reviews of Boris Lojkine's *Hope* (2014), which praised the authenticity of the performances (by real migrants) and the in-depth research that must have gone into writing the script, but faulted the film for its "well-worn out tragic narrative trajectory"[76] and its lack of "expressionistic flourishes."[77] In the case of *Hope* this criticism is not entirely justified inasmuch as in this case the migrant story—the journey of a young Nigerian woman and a Cameroonian man across North Africa on their way to Spain[78]—is structured, quite originally, as a variation on a well-known Hollywood formula, the fake/pretend relationship movie, in which a romantic relationship of convenience eventually transforms into a real one. Furthermore, unlike most films about African migrants' journey to Europe, *Hope* focuses on the relationships between fellow migrants and the bonds of solidarity that bind them together or—more often than not—tear them apart, expanding the exploration of "hospitality" and "national identity" beyond the framework within which these are usually discussed (Europeans' hospitality toward non-European "Others"). By focusing on the Nigerian woman Hope, who is from the beginning positioned as an outsider requesting the hospitality of a group of Cameroonian migrants, who themselves are at war with other African migrant ghettos, all divided along national lines, the film shows that the lack of hospitality that eventually awaits most migrants is part of their experience long *before* they reach Europe.

While Gott and Ravisco regard migrant films as variations on the road movie, Jorg Metermann identifies melodrama as closer to the migrant film, inasmuch as "melodrama and migration possess a seemingly natural connectivity as central aspects of melodrama as a mode of experience overlap with dimensions of the experience of migration."[79] Melodrama intersects with the experience of migration through their shared concern with recognition: just as the melodramatic mode "processes deficits in justice emotionally, which can be read as deficits in recognition . . . [of] the dignity of a person," the "core of migration is recognition, at every level."[80]

Metermann convincingly demonstrates the proximity between melodrama and migration; however, he fails to consider the ethical and political implications of this comparison given the deeply conservative nature of melodrama, whose aim is generally, as he himself points out, "not change but enduring the endurable."[81]

In her analysis of the representation of ethnic and racial Others—who are often migrants and/or refugees—in European cinema and media, Ipek Celik also draws on genre theory, observing that "the kind of events that become central to the visibility and knowability of Europe's Others are thoroughly generic: ethnic and racial minorities are publicly visible in family melodramas in honor crimes, thrilling menaces to safety, and humanitarian 'disasters' or 'tragedies.'"[82] Rather than adopt a formalist approach to genre, however, she sets out to recuperate the affective intensities of genre usually dismissed in critical discourse, which tends to prioritize cognitive estrangement over emotional attachment in cinema. Borrowing Laurent Berlant's definition of genre "as an aesthetic structure of affective expectation . . . promising that the persons transacting with it will experience the pleasure of encountering what they expected, with details varying the theme,"[83] Celik analyzes the repetition of certain affects in events with a racial or ethnic dimension. Inasmuch as the affective expectations associated with particular genres form a certain "grammar of affects," "the dynamics of genres, in their repetition and failure of conventions, determine how ethnic and racial Otherness is reproduced as an affect, to be feared and to be pitied in Europe."[84] The importance of this increasing attention to affect in genre studies lies in the movement away from a representative framework to a symptomatic one, which "explores genres as forms that unfold affective pathologies and crises in Europe's relationship with its growing multiethnicity and multiraciality."[85]

Writing in 2010, Yosefa Loshitzky identified three evolving genres of films about migration: "journeys of hope" (depicting the hardships endured by migrants on their way to the Promised Land or the host country in Europe); "in the Promised Land" (examining "the encounter with the host society"), and films dealing with the second generation and beyond, exploring "the processes and dynamic of integration and assimilation and their counterparts, alienation and disintegration,"[86] for example, beur and banlieue films.[87] For Nilgun Bayraktar, however, one of the preeminent features of recent films featuring migrants and/or refugees is that "they are not immediately associated with stories of migrancy."[88] Reading the blurring of genres in recent migration cinema, and the blurring of aesthetic borders between cinema and contemporary art in the work of artists-filmmakers like Kiarostami, Farocki, Steve McQueen, Peter Greenaway, Chantal Akerman, and others as a reflection of Europe's concurrent geopolitical transformations, she suggests that "as European borders have become more flexible and deterritorialzied, expanding to embrace non-European territories and the routes back to European metropolises, the aesthetic borders between cinema and art have also become blurred, producing a new form of moving-image art that defies easy categorization."[89]

Although in *Immigration Cinema in the New Europe*,[90] Isolina Ballesteros locates "immigration cinema" within broader preexisting categories such as "social cinema," "world cinema," and "third cinema," and in relation to notions such as "gender, hybridity, transculturation, border crossing, transnationalism, and translation,"[91] like Bayraktar she underscores "the unmappable and hybrid condition of immigration cinema"[92] attributing it to its deliberate blurring of filmic conventions belonging to two or more genres. Even as she identifies the genres (comedy, melodrama, film noir, and the road movie) and film techniques (ethnographic documentary techniques) the majority of immigration films share, Ballesteros remains reluctant to view "immigration cinema" as a specific new genre, though she is also careful to distinguish "immigration cinema" from Naficy's "accented cinema," Ella Shohat's "diasporic and post Third Worldist films," Laura Marks's "intercultural cinema," and Verena Berger and Miya Komori's "polyglot films." While these labels distinguish migrant (made by first generation filmmakers) from diasporic cinema (made by second- or third-generation immigration filmmakers), and migrant/diasporic cinema made by immigrant/diasporic subjects from hegemonic cinema made by the symbolic representatives of the host/receiving societies, Ballesteros uses the term "immigration cinema" more inclusively, emphasizing its proximity to "world cinema" and "third cinema," with the second of which immigration cinema shares a similar aesthetics, mode of production, and ideological orientation. Ironically, having devoted her entire book to explicating the distinguishing features of "immigration cinema" Ballesteros eventually renounces the very term she has chosen, confessing that she is not comfortable with a term that might become "one of those universal categories used and imposed exclusively by First World film scholars and critics . . . who define these films' practices and authors' intentions mostly in opposition to Western cinemas."[93]

What the abovementioned studies fail to acknowledge is that in recent European cinema migration—including the European refugee crisis—is increasingly used as a background for other stories rather than supplying the main narrative, pointing to the gradual normalization of the crisis and perhaps to its banalization into an aspect of everyday life rather than an "event." Perhaps as a result of this, and contrary to those who view migrant films as just a variation of the road movie, migration now functions as the generalized mise en scène of a diverse range of genres that until recently were not associated with migration—for example, satires (*Diamantino* [Abrantes and Schmidt, 2018], *Happy End* [Michael Haneke, 2017], *Welcome to Germany* [Simon Verhoeven, 2016], *The Square* [Ruben Östlund, 2017], *Greed* [Michael Winterbottom, 2019]), westerns (*Western* [Manuel Poirier, 1997] and *Western* [Valeska Grisebach, 2017]), psychological thrillers (*The*

Workshop [Laurent Cantet, 2017], *The Double Hour* [Giuseppe Capotondi, 2009], *The Unknown Woman* [Giuseppe Tornatore, 2006]), melodramas in classical Hollywood key (*I Am Love* [Luca Guadagnino, 2009]), road movies and comedies (*Djam* [Tony Gatlif, 2017], *Eden Is West* [Costa-Gavras, 2009])[94]—rather than being confined within the migrant and diasporic cinema "ghetto." In short, an increasing number of genre-hybrid European films approach stories of migration through popular genres ranging from comedies and psychological thrillers to romantic dramas and science fiction rather than through the familiar lens of the "social problem" film.

This is especially evident in films featuring empowered female migrants—for example, *The Unknown Woman, The Double Hour, I Am Love, Bibliotheque Pascal* (Szabolcs Hajdu, 2010), *Marussia* (Eva Pervolovici, 2013)—which blend elements of different genres and often employ an unreliable female narrator—rare in cinema—positioning the female characters as "authors" of their stories rather than disempowered victims of sexual and national oppression, the dominant way in which they were represented in migrant films of the 1980s and 1990s. In *Marussia* the Russian Lucia and her six-year-old daughter Marussia wander the streets of Paris, suitcases in hand, looking for a place to sleep. A Russian Orthodox priest offers them shelter for one night, the second night they spend in a homeless hostel, the third night they party with a random acquaintance, the fourth night they spend secretly in a cinema, and the last night they spend in a hotel where they are invited by a Russian artist they meet accidentally. Rather than focusing on the gloomy aspects of the story, however, the film balances the depiction of the everyday challenges of illegal immigrants' nomadic life with the exciting unpredictability and joy that comes from living in the moment. Lucia's identity remains unknown as she keeps reinventing herself—changing her backstory—with every new person she meets. It's impossible to know if the stories Lucia tells about her past are true or not, or how long mother and daughter will continue living in the street—what matters is that they see themselves as the authors of their story/life.

The Unknown Woman tells the story of Irina—a Ukrainian illegal immigrant in Italy haunted by a horrible past, who insinuates herself in the life of a rich Italian family—not as a conventional story about the difficulties of integration into the host culture but as a mysterious narrative merging elements of film noir, psychological thriller, detective story, and melodrama. The narrative pace is deliberately disorienting, both spatially and temporally, and the mise en scène is heavily stylized. Although we see everything from Irina's point of view, her intentions and motives remain unknown to us. By echoing, yet subverting, Max Ophuls's 1948 melodrama *Letter from an Unknown Woman*, constantly shifting our allegiance to the migrant femme fatale protagonist, complicating the self/immigrant "other" with other pairs of dichotomies such as sexual victim/voyeur, mother/assassin, and judge/criminal, and setting the story in Trieste, "the most foreign of Italian cities and the most Italian of foreign cities,"[95] *The Unknown Woman* avoids the sentimentality and didacticism typical of most migrant films, presenting us with a portrait of a female migrant as a morally ambivalent, complex character.

In *The Double Hour*, which blends suspense, thriller, romance, film noir, and psychoanalysis, Sonia, who has recently moved from Slovenia to Turin, where she works as a chambermaid in an upscale hotel, meets Guido, a widower and former policeman turned security guard, at a speed-dating event. Their romantic relationship has barely started when during a stroll through the lavish forested estate where Guido works as a security guard, the two lovers are assaulted by masked robbers who tie them up inside the house while they ransack the place of its art treasures. When one of the robbers threatens to rape Sonia, Guido tries to stop him and is (seemingly) killed, while Sonia is wounded in the head. At that point, the semi-recovered and traumatized Sonia returns to work after three days of unconsciousness (although she keeps seeing the ghost of her lover). In retrospect all of this may or may not be the fantasy life of a woman in coma, who regains consciousness in the film's third act only to come upon photographs of herself she does not remember taking. Gradually, we discover that Sonia and her boyfriend conjured up a plan to pull a heist in the big private estate where Guido works and that she intentionally sought to meet Guido at the speed-dating event and win his trust by entering into a romantic relationship with him.

Like Lucia and Irina, Sonia is an unreliable narrator whose backstory is intentionally left ambiguous. She tells Guido that her father is Italian and that he left her after her mother died. Later, however, we find out that her father disowned her twelve years ago after she and her boyfriend robbed him. The point is that Sonia's immigrant background is not essential to the story. Her Eastern European identity is used simply as a plot device, thanks to East Europeans' already established stereotypical association with crime, corruption, and general "shadiness"/unreliability in Italian and (West) European cinema more generally. That "Eastern European" has become shorthand for "unreliable narrator" becomes evident in an early scene, in which the police stop Sonia and Guido during a romantic stroll and ask for their IDs. The scene is supposed to create suspense—will the police arrest Sonia, who we assume is an illegal immigrant?—although Slovenia joined the EU in 2004, which means Sonia has EU citizenship and perhaps even Italian citizenship (her father is Italian). In this scene, however, Sonia's "East European" identity automatically "translates" as "illegal" regardless of her actual citizenship status.

The sumptuous, eccentric visuals of *Bibliotheque Pascal* mix reality and fairy-tale elements with elements of burlesque and avant-garde cinema to tell an otherwise conventional story of sex trafficking in East European women. The film, told in both Romanian and English, opens with half-Romanian, half-Hungarian Mona being interviewed in a Romanian Child Protection Agency office after a long absence abroad. Mona's daughter has been taken away from her guardian, Mona's sister, and the authorities demand an explanation for Mona's long absence and for her sister's increasingly bizarre behavior, an explanation the film then offers us in an extended flashback before ending in the same office with Mona hoping that her story would persuade the authorities to return her daughter to her custody and arrest her aunt on child-exploitation charges. As we learn from Mona's story, she was sold to a sex trafficker and shipped off to an S&M brothel in Liverpool—"Bibliotheque Pascal"—which targets the S&M–related fantasies of its rich intellectual clientele in theme rooms offering role-playing games inspired by famous novels. Like *Marussia*, the film foregrounds the female migrant's status as a storyteller/unreliable narrator who seeks to recover some of the agency she has been deprived of by fabricating and embellishing her mundane story of hardship and prostitution into a fantastical adventure. If *Bibliotheque Pascal* develops the theme of sex trafficking within a magic realist scheme, *Trance* (Teresa Villaverde, 2006) abstracts the familiar "Natasha story" into a stylized, moody piece driven by hypnotic, Manoel de Oliveira-like cinematography, and Pedro-Costa-like mise en scène and narrative (the story moves through multiple places and encounters that could be real or imagined, memories or dreams, internal monologues or hallucinations).

I Am Love frames what is essentially a story of migration as a classical melodrama, conflating the sense of alienation experienced by the migrant with romantic dissatisfaction. The film opens in a snow-covered Milan as the upper-class Recchi family prepares for the birthday lunch of the aging paterfamilias and industrialist Edoardo Sr. At the lunch, Edoardo Sr. announces his retirement from the family business, which he leaves not only to his son Tancredi (named after Alain Delon's character in Visconti's *The Leopard*) but also to one of Tancredi's sons, Edoardo Jr., a perfect embodiment of the Recchi's aristocratic breed. Also at this lunch Edoardo Jr. introduces his mother Emma, Tancredi's Russian wife—whom, we later learn, he met in Russia many years ago during one of his art treasure hunting trips and brought back to Italy, as if she were just another "artwork" he acquired abroad—to his friend Antonio, a chef with whom Edoardo is thinking of going into the restaurant business. Apart from Edoardo Jr., the Recchis have another son, Gianluca, and an artistically inclined daughter, Elisabeta. Following the death of Edoardo Sr., Emma discovers that her daughter is lesbian, a discovery she will gradually come to view as a model for her own sexual transgression and liberation. While Emma and Elisabeta are engaged with exploring new personal and sexual horizons, the men of the family—Mancredi and his two sons—are attending important business meetings in London, where an Indian-American investor advises them to sell the family textile business, keeping the family name but making the business global (one of the specific selling points of the business proposal is the opportunity to go into business with Russia). Edoardo Jr., who is much closer in terms of sensibility to his mother (with whom he speaks Russian) than to his father, has difficulty accepting the mercantile, vulgar aspects of globalization, which his father and brother are eager to embrace, realizing that theirs is a slowly dying breed.

Although Emma has adopted and perfected all the mannerisms of the upper middle class into which she has been assimilated through marriage, she is not of their world. She attends to every single detail of the family meals with the utmost precision, knowing exactly what is expected of her, but during the parties following the dinners she retires to her room to rest or leaf through magazines absentmindedly. It is during one such moment, as she is looking through a magazine under the dim lamplight over the sofa, while the rest of the family are amusing themselves in the villa garden, that we catch a glimpse of her past in the form of fragmented dream images from her childhood in Russia, before she is abruptly awakened back to her well-mannered Italian life. The next time we are reminded of the absence of something essential to her sense of self is when, walking alone in the streets of San Remo, where Antonio plans to open a restaurant with her son, Emma stumbles upon a Russian Orthodox Church, but before she is able to go in and indulge in the nostalgia we have seen her briefly give in to, she glimpses Antonio passing by the church and follows him instinctively in a bravura sequence that pays homage to Hitchcock's *Vertigo* (1958). The two start a passionate affair, which ends up tragically with the sensitive Edoardo Jr.'s accidental death moments after he discovers his mother's secret affair.

Although Emma's nostalgia for her homeland is made narratively clear, it is important to note that her nostalgia finds expression in several different registers or on several different levels that are difficult to disentangle. On a most basic level, Emma's nostalgia manifests as a loss of self. Later in the film we learn "Emma" is not the character's real name but the name her Italian husband gave her when he brought her back to Italy. Shockingly, no one else in the family is aware that she has another name: the only person she entrusts with this secret is her lover, Antonio, telling him that she does not remember how own name, only the name they used to call her by when she was a child, "kitesh" (kitty). Toward the end of the film, after her son's funeral, Emma tells her husband that he no longer knows who she is. Here nostalgia is very directly linked to a radical loss of personal identity, of a sense of intimacy with oneself symbolized by the name one is given at birth. The rediscovery of this lost sense of self, the "homecoming" that is the object of nostalgia in the narrow sense of the term, is made possible through Emma's sexual awakening: in this way, the intimacy with one's self, the sense of coming from and belonging to a particular place (homeland) becomes conflated with the intimacy with another, the dissolution of one's sense of self that is typically associated with sexual surrender. Paradoxically, Emma recovers her

Russian identity—understood in the primary, corporeal, intimate sense—by experiencing the corporeal surrender or self-abandonment associated with sex. This conflation of Emma's "Russianness" with her sensual and sexual awakening suggests an organic view of national identity not as something alien and secondary, superimposed on one's sense of personal identity, but, in fact, constituting the very core of our sense of selfhood, something as unself-conscious and natural as the flowers we see impregnated by insects in the passionate sexual encounter between Antonio and Emma. To put it bluntly, and intentionally using a cliché, the yearning "to become one" or "to become whole" that is usually given the name of "sexual love" is inseparable, even dependent upon, the sense of being at one with oneself, being whole. Homecoming is possible, the film seems to suggest but only, as the ending makes clear, at a high price. Emma's "homecoming" begins in the paradisiacal countryside where she and Antonio make love, she tells him about her past, and prepares the traditional soup her grandmother taught her to cook (the film makes a big deal out of Emma taking off her fashionable, sophisticated Italian clothes and either being naked or wearing a casual, unflattering outfit that seems vaguely "Russian"). The tragic irony is that it is the very thing that symbolizes Emma's recovery of her "Russianness"—the Russian soup she prepares for Antonio, who then prepares it for Emma's son—that eventually causes, indirectly, Eduardo's accidental death during an argument with his mother. Thus, nostalgia is linked to the ability to feel at all: it is only when Emma begins an affair with Antonio that her nostalgia—the desire to recover her lost sense of self, her Russianness—becomes an active motor of sexual and personal liberation. In short, nostalgia is nothing other than love (hence the film's title).

Guadagnino makes Emma's "homecoming"/transgression not only a sexual one but also—in keeping with Sirkean melodramas like *All That Heaven Allows* (1995)—a class one. As in Sirk's film, Emma's lover is not only considerably younger than her but also from a working-class background. This is the point at which Emma's Russianness—and her nostalgia for her home—begins to seem less like an essential part of the narrative or the character and more of a flourish around the series of obstacles Guadagnino summons up to point up the drama in "melodrama." When, in the last third of the film, Guadagnino "zooms out" from Emma's story and returns to the Recchi family business and its fate in the age of global capital, the story of a Russian woman in Italy becomes secondary to the larger picture of the Italian upper middle class's anachronistic existence in the era of globalization, transforming the film into a sort of a sequel to Visconti's portrait, in *The Leopard* (1963), of the waning of the noble home of Fabrizio Corbero, prince of Salina, amid the social upheavals of 1860s Sicily. Emma's nostalgia for the homeland becomes "globalized" and given a material shape and value as the ineffable spiritual and affective connection to the "homeland" (Russia) is replaced by a profit-based proposal for selling the family business to foreign investors, including Russia. The status of "Russia" thus shifts from that of "home," the object of the migrant's nostalgia, to that of a potential lucrative business partner, an object of capitalist desire. Here the film draws, on one hand, an analogy between Emma, a Russian transplanted into the world of Italian nobility but who is not of this world and, on the other hand, the Italian nobility who continue to follow blindly age-old traditions and rituals, failing to realize that they are unable "to return home" (to return to bygone ways of life), that they are a vanishing species maladapted to the new laws of advanced capitalism and globalization. The film ends with an unresolved tension between these several conflicting levels of nostalgic discourse: Emma appears to have returned home—her transgressive desire is fulfilled—even as the Recchi family discover that one cannot go home in an age when "home" (e.g., the family business) is nothing more than a brand name. Thus, while *I Am Love* is the intensely personal story of a female migrant, it is also a commentary on the larger implications of the globalization of migration.

Despite their experimentation with a new genre and stylistic approaches to migration, in many ways the abovementioned films continue to tread on familiar ground. While the whimsical *Bibliotheque Pascal* grants its narrator a great deal of freedom in the construction of her story, it still relies on the established trope of the East European woman as an object of sex traffic. Similarly, the two Italian films intentionally center around white, Eastern European female migrants, rather than choosing a non-European female protagonist, to ensure the desirability of the female "Other" for the Italian (white) male viewer, who has yet to fully acknowledge the increasingly multiracial, multicultural nature of contemporary Italian society. Examining the gendered metaphor of the young Eastern European beauty in recent Italian cinema as an embodiment of Italian public opinion toward Eastern European migrants, Massimo Locatelli and Francesco Pitassio have demonstrated the continued relevance of the West/East axis in the construction of "the migrant" in Italian cinema as well as the persisting difficulty of defining Eastern Europeans migrants as truly "Other."[96] Most Italian films center on Eastern European female migrant protagonists either to attain easier audience identification with a white protagonist who comes from a similar cultural and religious background, or to make it possible for the Italian male protagonist to desire the "foreign" Eastern European "Other' without the risk of miscegenation.[97] Finally, in *I Am Love*, the exploration of the themes of migration, homelessness, and homesickness is subordinated to the strong *cinephilic* drive of the film, a nostalgia for a certain type of cinema now associated with a bygone era, namely sweeping Hollywood melodramas and European art cinema of the kind associated with the names of Visconti and Antonioni.

Unlike the films discussed above, *Steam: The Turkish Bath* (Ferzan Özpetek, 1998), *Unveiled* (Angelina Maccarone, 2005), *Dheepan* (Jacques

Audiard, 2015), *Eden Is West*, and, especially, *Diamantino* approach gender in more nuanced ways, emphasizing the *performativity* of both European and migrant identity by integrating an element of impersonation/performance/disguise/drag/gender fluidity in the plot. *Steam* traces the underexamined reverse (West-East) migration by following a successful Italian interior designer, Francesco, who, upon learning that he has inherited property in Turkey from his forgotten aunt Anita, travels to Istanbul to oversee the sale, leaving behind an unhappy marriage to Marta, his business partner. In Istanbul he finds out that the property is actually one of the last surviving hamams in the city. While he is hosted by the family employed to run the hamam, Francesco gradually loses his Western, rational veneer, falls in love with his host family's son, Mehmet, and decides to stay in Turkey. The radical transformation Francesco undergoes, in terms of gender identity, fits into a long line of similar cinematic representations of Westerners traveling East, going as far back as the Dracula story, which invests the East with all the erotic allure Istanbul has for Francesco, whose own married life in Rome is presented as stale. This storyline is not new, recalling classical melodramas like Sirk's *All That Heaven Allows* (1955), in which the transgression of social, class, and age boundaries is presented as emotionally and spiritually enriching. It is not only Francesco's dormant desires that Istanbul's enigmatic beauty reawakens, Marta also falls under the spell of the Orient. Resolving to confess her long-term affair with her business partner and end the marriage, Marta pays a surprise visit to Francesco, where she initially reacts bitterly to the discovery of her husband's affair with Mehmet, only to find out, to her surprise, that their affair reawakens her own feelings for her husband. Following a pattern typical of classical melodrama, Francesco is killed at the end of the film, as if to punish him for his sexual transgression, by a hitman hired by a powerful Turkish business woman, who wants to buy the hammam and the surrounding property in order to build a big shopping center, a business offer Francesco refuses in another reversal of the clichéd representation of Westerners as profit-driven businessmen and of Easterners as innocent victims. Regardless of how one views Özpetek's construction of Turkishness—as another instance of Orientalism or, conversely, as an example of "transnational Orientalism" that transcends Orientalism[98]— by depicting the West-East journey as deconstructing Italian/European identity through deconstructing gender identity, *Steam* foregrounds the performativity of gender, national, and European identity.

In *Unveiled* the performativity of (European) identity is similarly dramatized through the lens of gender, this time in a literal way: the protagonist, Fariba, a lesbian Iranian translator of German, escapes Iran (where being gay or lesbian is a crime punishable by law) by disguising herself as a man in order to enter Europe. After changing in the airplane's bathroom, she leaves behind her veil in a symbolic gesture representing the performativity of both personal (gender) and national/European identity

(Iranian, a supposedly religious identity versus German, a supposedly secular identity). In Germany Fariba's application for political asylum is rejected but luckily, she meets Siamak, a male refugee who commits suicide after hearing of his brother's execution back home. After taking on Siamak's identity Fariba is transferred to a temporary refugee hotel and finds illegal work at a sauerkraut factory near Stuttgart, where she meets and falls in love with a German heterosexual female coworker, Anne. Fariba ends up being deported to Iran but before the plane lands she changes back to her men's clothes in the bathroom, resolving to use her fake German passport (that Anne helped her get) to eventually return to Germany. The film makes it clear, however, that prejudices against refugees and foreigners in Germany, as well as Fariba's illegal status, will continue to jeopardize her stay there. By making "drag"—gender performance—an integral part of the story, and that which allows Fariba to enter Europe, Maccarone draws attention to the constructed nature of both gender and national identity, challenging the perception of *non-heteronormative relationships*—here treated as *synonymous with non-European identities*—as "illegal."

Dheepan is not principally concerned with exploring the challenges of integration faced by foreigners, in this case Sivadhasan, a former Tamil Tiger now living in the large, multiracial, multicultural housing project Le Pre-Saint-Gervais in Paris's northeastern suburbs. Instead, the film uses the conventional trope of the soldier suffering from post-traumatic stress disorder not to tell another story about the traumatic effects of war but, by combining it with the trope of identity as performance/drag, to point up, as in the other films above, the reversibility of roles/identities, that is, the "doubly occupied" nature of personal and European identity. Like Fariba (*Unveiled*), Aisha (*Diamantino*), Elias (*Eden Is West*), Samba and Wilson (*Samba*), and Marek (*Eastern Boys*) (see Chapter 3), Sivadhasan takes on a fake identity—that of a dead man—and a puts together a fake family (a woman and a girl, Yalini and Illayaal, both of whose families have been killed in the Civil War)—in order to buy a passport from the traffickers in the refugee camp and apply for political asylum in France. In the cover story he fabricates, he casts himself as one of the oppressed rather than an oppressor (he lies he was a journalist and peace activist for an NGO in Sri Lanka). Playing on the American genre of pretend relationship movies—either rom-coms, in which a man and a woman pretend to be a couple only to fall in love for real, for example, *While You Were Sleeping* (1995), *The Wedding Date* (2005), and *The Proposal* (2009) or "fake family" movies, for example, *We're the Millers* (2013)—*Dheepan* uses the trope of the pretend family to suggest that one's national or supranational identity is ultimately of less consequence than the structural place the Other occupies in the construction of one's identity. Despite the thousands of miles separating Sivadhasan from the civil war in his homeland, what he finds in his new home on the outskirts of Paris is just an extension of the structural dynamic that defined his identity/his role in Sri Lanka: there he was a Tamil Tiger soldier in a civil war, in Paris he is a caretaker who ultimately becomes entangled in a similar kind of "civil war" with the local drug dealers ruling the banlieue. What matters about the members of the local drug ring is *not* that they are French, or European for that matter, but rather, the structural role—that of "the enemy"—they perform in the construction of Sivadhasan's identity as a soldier. Thus, Sivadhasan finds himself perfectly "at home"—that is, constantly on the alert—in the supposedly foreign French territory, which turns out to be not that foreign after all. Drug alliances and political groups (like the Liberation Tigers) are both run as businesses, which accounts for their structurally reversible roles in the construction of Sivadhasan's identity[99] (Audiard makes explicit the literal (monetary) trace connecting the drug war in the Parisian suburbs to the civil war in Sri Lanka when he shows the local drug dealers, under the leadership of the Arab Brahim, the son of Monsieur Habib for whom Yalini works as a caregiver, strike up a deal with a colonel who entrusts Sivadhasan with procuring more weapons for the war back home).

The emerging genre of the "migrant/refugee comedy"—for example, *Eden Is West*, *Welcome to Germany*, *Diamantino*, *Plato's Academy* (Filippos Tsitos, 2009), *Né quelque part* (Mohamed Hamidi, 2013), *Cose dell'altro mondo/Things From Another World* (Francesco Patierno, 2011), *Welcome to Norway* (Rune Denstad Langlo, 2016), and others—dramatizes particularly well the "performativity" of European identity.[100] From its opening scenes the comedy/road movie *Eden Is West* relies on the trope of mistaken identity for comedic effect. The handsome Elias, an illegal immigrant from an unnamed country, braves the dangerous sea journey to Europe, but when the Greek Coast Guard "rescues" the boat he is on, he jumps into the dark waters of the Aegean and swims ashore, later waking up on the beach of a nudist colony, part of the luxurious Mediterranean Hotel Eden (Nicolas Provost's *The Invader* (2011) opens with a similar scene of a naked refugee washed ashore on a nudist beach).[101] Mistaken for a hotel employee, Elias scurries around the resort until a lonely middle-aged German tourist takes him into her bed. Eventually Elias escapes the resort's artificial paradise and heads out to Paris, a "mythical city" where he hopes to find a magician he met briefly at the resort who has promised Elias to find him a job, a reference to the unlikelihood (even for Europeans) of finding employment in the wake of the financial crisis. On Elias's trip to Paris, which takes him through "gypsy camps" and a factory exploiting the *sans-papiers*, the poor and disenfranchised generally help him while despicable middle-class Europeans abuse him in every way (including sexually). Although the film fails as a satire, it is representative of the trope of mistaken identity used by a growing number of films to challenge preconceived notions of "European identity."

Plato's Academy centers on four middle-aged loafers, three of whom own convenience stores at the same nondescript Athens intersection, where they spend their days drinking and commenting on the migrants (Albanians and Chinese) who have "invaded" their neighborhood/country: the Albanians have the nerve to be building a monument to cross-cultural understanding in the middle of the intersection, while the Chinese are finishing up a new Italian fashion store across the street. The divorced, depressed, middle-aged Stavros, the owner of one of the stores, is living with his demented mother who needs constant care, having suffered a stroke. One day an Albanian laborer passing by seems to recognize Stavros's mother, speaks to her in Albanian and, to Stavros's surprise, she responds in Albanian. Soon after she declares that the Albanian laborer is the son she had left behind in Albania as a young woman before she moved to Greece with Stavros, her other son. Stavros must now deal with the unpleasant idea that he might be Albanian—a literal rendering of Elsaesser's notion of "double occupation"—"the worst fate" that could possibly befall a Greek.[102] Stavros is gradually forced to live with this idea for the sake of his mother, who seems to regain her lucidity whenever her Albanian son is around. After his mother dies peacefully in her sleep, Stavros, now almost reconciled with the idea of not being fully Greek, invites his Albanian half-brother to her funeral only to have the Albanian confess that he is not sure Stavros's mother is really his mother (his claim that she is his mother rests on an old photograph in which the woman's physical resemblance to Stavros's mother is a matter of interpretation). Stavros goes berserk at the idea that the Albanian might have been trying to "pass" for a Greek and that not only his own Greek identity but now his hyphenated Greek-Albanian identity might also actually be fake: the idea of not knowing who he is, Greek or Albanian, is to Stavros even more intolerable than the idea of being Albanian, a perfect illustration of Freud's concept of "the narcissism of minor differences"—the pathological search for reliable and precise criteria for distinguishing "them" from "us" in complete denial of European identity as always already "doubly occupied."[103]

The title of Hamidi's *Né quelque part* (2013)—literally "born somewhere" but translated, ironically, as *Homeland*—dramatizes what is at stake in this comedy, which starts out as a sort of remake of *Le grand voyage* (2004) (an aging Maghrebi man—French-Moroccan in Ferroukhi's film, French-Algerian in Hamidi's—insists that his eldest son, born and raised in France, travel back to the home country, against the son's wishes) but then transforms into an absurd story of switched identities as the son (Farid, who has never been to Algeria and barely speaks Arabic) has his passport stolen by his cousin (also named Farid) in Algeria, and is thus forced to smuggle himself back into France as part of a group of illegal immigrants. The identity swap story is exploited not only for comedic effects but also to denaturalize the notion of national identity and citizenship by underscoring their aleatory aspect: it is eventually revealed that Parisian Farid's "Frenchness" was the result of pure chance as it was his cousin's father (his uncle) that was originally supposed to immigrate to France but at the last moment his brother left in his place (the trope of the "two Farids" exemplifies Elsaesser's notion of European identity as "doubly occupied," while also calling to mind Kieslowski's *The Double Life of Veronique* (1991), which deals with similar issues but in a more metaphysical/spiritual vein). When his Algerian neighbors learn that Farid has had his passport stolen, they compare his status to that of an illegal immigrant, a reverse *sans-papiers* in Algeria, which is more or less how the French consulate in Algeria treats him: in short, contrary to the misleading English translation of the film's title, *Né quelque part* deterritorializes national identity, insisting on the human bonds that bind us together, regardless of our birthplace, rather than on the constructed idea of the territorially bound nation. However, the film's postnational pretensions are undermined from within: by framing the story in terms of Farid's struggle to "prove" his "Frenchness"—here problematically conflated with "innocence" and contrasted with Algerian Farid's criminality—and to save the family property in Algeria (the ancestral home) from being bought by the government and used for public works, the film ironically reaffirms the organic notion of national identity and citizenship it purports to challenge.

Although *Diamantino* examines Portugal's colonial legacy, it does so in a radically different way from what are perhaps the most well-known cinematic explorations of this issue, Pedro Costa's films *Bones* (1997), *In Vanda's Room* (2000), *Colossal Youth* (2006), and *Horse Money* (2014), all set in Lisbon's slum Fontainhas, which houses many Cabo Verde immigrants. Costa's meditative approach could not be more foreign to the absurdist *Diamantino*, in which Aisha, a black lesbian secret agent of Cabo Verdean origins is sent on a mission to investigate the taxes of Portugal's legendary soccer player Diamantino (bearing a strong physical resemblance to Ronaldo). As in the films discussed earlier, she infiltrates his house by taking on a fake identity, that of "Rahim," a young male African refugee, whom Diamantino adopts as a way of dealing with the identity crisis he is battling in the wake of his failure to lead Portugal to victory at the World Soccer Cup. *Diamantino* relies on the trope of performance/disguise and gender fluidity to expose the constructed nature of "the Other" by superimposing and intentionally conflating various layers of "Otherness"—lesbian, non-European, and refugee. The film exposes the cracks in the notion of national identity by taking the organic concept of national identity literally: one of the subplots has the extreme right-wing government making use of the good-natured but vapid Diamantino in a nationalist ad campaign, whose sole purpose is "to make Portugal great again" by retracing its colonial greatness back to the Portuguese conquistadors' victory over the Moors, and thus over Portugal's own African heritage. In another subplot, Diamantino becomes part of a secret genetic project, financed by the government, to clone him and make an all-winning, golden national team to restore Portugal's former glory as a colonial power so that it can exit the EU. *Diamantino* challenges the patriarchal basis of the hegemonic concept of the (colonial) Portuguese nation by having its protagonist, the ultimate symbol of heterosexual male power, experience gender fluctuations as a result of the cloning project going wrong (he grows breasts). It is precisely this gender fluctuation that makes it possible for him and the lesbian Aisha to enter into an adoptive relationship, which is eventually transformed into a romantic one. The film suggests, quite literally, that genuine hospitality to "the refugee Other" demands a "gender transformation," a deconstruction of the chauvinistic, hegemonic, patriarchal concept of nationalism.

Importantly, rather than advocating an openness to Portugal's (and Europe's) "external Other" (the refugee) directly, *Diamantino* uses the figure of a mixed-race minority—the Cabo Verdean, here represented by Aisha—to demonstrate that what is considered "external" to the national and European "body" has always been part of that body, and through whose expulsion the Portuguese nation has constituted itself. Cape Verde, Portugal's former colony, whose inhabitants are of mixed European, Moorish, Arab, and African origin, serves as a constant reminder of Portugal's colonial history and of the "impurity" of the Portuguese nation. When Aisha poses as Rahim, an African refugee, and enters into a supposedly "fake" filial relationship with her adoptive father, she makes visible again a disavowed part of Portugal's colonial history. By having the internal Other (the Cape Verdean) take on the identity of a supposedly new, external Other (an African refugee), the film demonstrates that the external Other is just the internal Other in disguise: the only way the nation, and Europe, can enter into a hospitable relationship with the "external Other" is through acknowledging the internal Other constitutive of its identity.

Marian Crisan's intimate, unobtrusive dramatic comedy *Morgen* (2010) shares *Diamantino*'s absurdist tone and the staging of the migrant crisis as a story of impersonation, though Crisan's minimalist style could not be more different from *Diamantino*'s visual extravagance. The absurdity of borders, one of the film's central themes, is established in the opening scene, in which the protagonist Nelu, a middle-aged farmer living in a small border town in the northwestern corner of Romania, tries to cross the border on his way back home from a fishing trip in Hungary. Despite Nelu's protestations that both Hungary and Romania are in the EU, the officer demands a veterinary certificate for the fish, explaining that the fish is not in the EU and does not have the same rights (freedom of movement) as EU citizens, a status that, the scene implies, fish share with refugees. On his next fishing trip Nelu encounters a Kurdish refugee (Behran) trying to cross the Romanian-Hungarian border illegally on his way to Germany, where his son already resides. The rest of the film follows Nelu's unsuccessful attempts to smuggle the Kurd across the border—a friendly soccer game across the Hungarian border offers an ideal occasion but in the end, Nelu's plan falls apart—or find him work in town while waiting for the next opportunity. Although the two men do not speak each other's languages, they develop a bond; however, as in Kornél Mundruzcó's 2017 *Jupiter's Moon* (see Chapter 3), the viewer is denied access to Behran's inner feelings and thoughts—his lines are deliberately not subtitled—and invited to identify solely with Nelu.

Initially Nelu hides Behran in the cellar and lies to his wife that Behran is a Gypsy he hired to help fix up the roof. Thus, *Morgen* conceives the figure of the refugee (the external Other) through that of the Gypsy (the internal Other), although in this case a third term (Kurdish/Muslim) complicates the parallel drawn between these two terms. On one hand, the Kurd is imagined as a Gypsy in disguise—Nelu tries to appease his wife by lying to her that Behran is "just" a Gypsy—and the Gypsy as an illegal immigrant in disguise. On the other hand, often one of these three terms—"refugee"—is "skipped" and a direct connection is established between "Kurd" and "Gypsy"—for example, both Nelu's neighbors and the police refer to the Kurd derogatively as "a Gypsy," using the two terms interchangeably. In this context "Gypsy" refers not to a particular ethnic group but rather, to an umbrella term denoting the status of a "second-class" human being in Romania/the EU, a status shared by Gypsies, Kurds (non-Christians), and illegal migrants/refugees. Rather than different national identities or ethnic groups being conflated, specific ethnic, national, cultural, or religious identities are all reduced to the same common denominator, the common term for "the Other" in Romania (and in Europe), "the Gypsy." As we saw earlier, a similar process takes place in *Diamantino* (where the external, non-European Other—the Syrian refugee—is posited as an internal Other in disguise—the Cabo Verdean lesbian impersonating a Syrian refugee), and we find the same pattern in *Jupiter's Moon* (where the Syrian refugee is suspected of being a Gypsy in disguise) and *Welcome to Germany* (where a similar relationship of impersonation/disguise is established between the external other, an African refugee, and the internal Other, the second-generation German of Arab descent).[104]

Both *Morgen* and *Diamantino* can be fruitfully approached through Michael Billig's notion of "banal nationalism" (1995) insofar as they explore a grave sociopolitical issue (the refugee crisis) through popular culture, in this case sports, and more particularly soccer. In *Diamantino* the protagonist becomes part of a secret genetic project to create, though cloning, a golden national soccer team that will restore Portugal's former glory as a colonial power. Although *Morgen* does not focus on soccer, it presents the occasion of a cross-border soccer game as an opportunity to smuggle Behran across the border and, in a scene following the soccer game, shows Nelu, having a drink at the local bar, overhearing a few Romanian soccer fans expressing their anger at the increasingly multinational, multiethnic, and multiracial identity of Romanian soccer clubs, in which the majority of players are not Romanian but "Other" (South Americans, Portuguese, and Gypsies). A recent Australian comedy, *The Merger* (Mark Grentell, 2018), picks up on the same sports theme to tell a story that, while not set in Europe, deals with the repercussions of the European refugee crisis, envisioning sports (in this case football) as a possible solution to the resurgence of nationalism. The film focuses on a local football team, which, faced with the prospect of folding, renews its list of players with refugees from the local refugee support center (naturally the new team goes on to win the championship but not before facing the locals' anti-immigrant, racist attitudes). By posing the question of hospitality and of one's ethical relationship to the Other through the lens of the most popular sport, films like *Diamantino, The Merger,* and *Morgen* underscore the (literally) *performative* aspect of identity inasmuch as sports is itself a kind of performance, the "team" being a micro-community based on bonds of solidarity among members/players who otherwise have nothing in common.

The title of Verhoeven's *Welcome to Germany* (2016) echoes that of an earlier comedy about Turkish guest workers, Yasemin Samdereli's *Almanya: Welcome to Germany* (2011), which tells the story of three generations of the Yilmazes family whose grandfather left his village in Anatolia in the 1960s for work in the Ruhr. *Almanya* mines familiar national stereotypes for laughs before eventually degenerating into a sentimental melodrama upholding the importance of returning to one's roots. Verhoeven's film positions Diallo, the African refugee who is supposed to be the film's protagonist, as the newest incarnation of Germany's "Other" (replacing the Turk), but there are important differences between the two films. Samdereli's film fits squarely within an established tradition of films exploring the integration of Turkish immigrants in Germany and celebrating the values of multiculturalism. On the surface, the Germany of Verhoeven's film is already a multicultural society, in which second-generation immigrants of Arab descent like Tarek, the young man courting Mr. Hartmann's daughter, seemingly enjoy the same status and the same rights as Germans. However, as becomes evident in the course of the film—mainly through the character of Mr. Hartmann, the family patriarch and respected doctor under whom Tarek is doing his medical residency—ethnic and racial prejudices are not entirely a thing of the past. Mr. Hartmann is going through an age-related crisis, refusing to admit to himself that he is old and hating the whole world for it. Still, it is not always clear that his violent outbursts, of which Tarek is most often the implicit target, are motivated only by a denial of old age (in one scene Tarek confronts Mr. Hartmann and asks him point-blank if he finds Tarek "too dark-skinned"). Significantly, Mr. Hartmann's gradual warming up to Diallo, and his eventual decision to "welcome" him into his home, happens in parallel with (is dependent upon) his gradual acceptance of Tarek as a potential suitor for his daughter. As we already saw, in *Diamantino* hospitality toward the "external Other" (the non-European refugee) was figured through hospitality to an internal (to the nation) Other, the Cabo Verdean Aisha. In Verhoeven's film, too, the hospitality Mr. Hartmann extends to Diallo becomes possible only through Hartmann's acceptance of the internal Other, the second-generation German of Arab descent (Tarek), who still has to "pass for a German/European" even though he was born and raised in Germany.

Despite Verhoeven's good intentions, Diallo's character serves only as a plot device for triggering, and eventually resolving, the personal problems of each member of the Hartmann family. Diallo satisfies the recently retired Mrs. Hartmann's newfound hobby—charity—as she "upgrades" her charitable activities from donating clothes to the local refugee center to adopting "her own refugee" (Diallo) (playing on the adoption motif, which I discuss in Chapter 3). Diallo's relationship to Sophie, the Hartmanns's troubled daughter, is also defined in terms of how useful he might be to her (Diallo plays the role of her "matchmaker," bringing her and Tarek together). Diallo also proves his "usefulness" by playing the role of a "therapist" and reviving the relationship between Philip, Sophie's brother, and his estranged son (Basti) who is on the verge of failing fifth grade. Luckily for them, Diallo offers his tragic personal history (his whole family back in Nigeria was killed by the terrorist Islamist group Boko Haram) as a subject for Basti's class presentation, which brings the schoolteacher and the kids in the class to tears in an embarrassing scene that is all about how badly they all feel about Diallo's tragedy, rather than about Diallo's own feelings; later he offers his racial identity to Basti, who recomposes and re-records it in a clichéd, misogynistic hip-hop video, in which "black" means nothing more than "cool." Even Diallo's asylum application, on whose approval or rejection hangs his entire life, is used as just another occasion to repair the Philip-Basti relationship by "teaching" Philip a lesson about fatherhood.

Like *Diamantino*, Maren Ade's comedy-drama *Toni Erdmann* (2016), which explores the less popular, West-East trajectory of mobility, emphasizes the performative or ludic aspect of personal, national, and European identity weaving an absurd story about Winfried Conradi, a sixty-something man and practical joker, who leaves Germany to visit his estranged daughter Ines in Bucharest, where she has moved for work. To reconnect with his overworked daughter Winfried creates an alter ego, posing as "Toni Erdmann" (complete with false teeth and a shaggy wig), Ines's CEO's "life coach." Father and daughter spend a long day together, visiting the oil fields, from which Ines's multinational firm is planning to outsource labor thereby eliminating hundreds of jobs, crashing an Easter party at the house of a Romanian diplomat and her family, and bumping into each other again at a naked party at Ines's apartment. Central to the story is the notion of performance and the performativity of identity, which Ade explores both metaphorically and literally through Winfried's absurd alter ego. As the director has stated in interviews, this is a story about two people trying to break out of the roles they have been performing all their lives: for Winfried this means breaking out of the role of "the father" while Ines's "role-playing" concerns her inability to separate her work persona from her personal life (she schedules her personal life the same way she schedules her business meetings).

The theatricality of this kind of "performance," which perverts personal relationships into something monstrous and inauthentic, is brought home by Winfried's conversation with Anca, Ines's younger Romanian assistant in Bucharest. When Winfried asks Anca if Ines is a good boss, Anca gratefully acknowledges Ines's ability to provide her with good feedback on her "performance," and when Winfried fails to understand the meaning of "performance" Anca explains that "the art [of performing well at work] is to be able to explain to the client what they want," that is, to make them believe the company's plan for the client is actually the client's own idea. Here "performance" is understood as the art of manipulation and deception, a meaning that becomes clearer as we learn more about the nature of Germany's business presence in postcommunist Romania under the pretext of "modernizing" the country (as a foreman tries to convince a Romanian family living in squalor near the oil fields) but in reality exploiting its resources for Germany's and other foreign investors' own profit at the cost of eliminating thousands of Romanian jobs. Insofar as Romania's integration into the EU and its "Europeanization"[105] depends on its "good performance"—defined by EU business treaties, whose main purpose is obviously profit—European identity is here defined, literally, in terms of economic "performance" rather than in terms of a shared cultural identity or a common political project. Romania, as well as the rest of the ex-communist Eastern bloc, can prove itself "worthy" of being considered "European"—can "pass for European"—only as long as it "performs" well, which demands that "old-style," humanist values—like those represented by personal relationships—be sacrificed to neoliberal values (profit).[106] Winfried's adoption of yet another fake identity, that of Germany's ambassador, gives the lie to Germany's self-proclaimed reason for choosing to invest in Romania to help modernize the country's aging infrastructure (a motif also taken up in Grisebach's *Western*), although in reality it seeks to corporatize/EU-nize it. At the same time, however, the film does not disguise Winfried's own obliviousness to the social, economic, and political changes in the "new Europe" he lives in. The few days he spends with Ines in Bucharest serve as his introduction to the cynical neoliberal world his daughter has to navigate but from which he has been protected all his life. The Winfried-Ines relationship echoes the father-daughter relationship in Ken Loach's *It's a Free World* (2007), in which the younger generation must also give the older one a lesson in political economy under neoliberalism (see Chapter 4).

Ade's film juxtaposes the idea of "performance" demanded by neoliberal (business) ethics with Winfried's literal performance as the alter ego "Toni Erdmann," a fake persona whose fakeness, however, is so obvious that there is never any doubt as to who the "real" Winfried is: Ines always recognizes her father despite his disguises. By drawing attention to itself Winfried's "performance" remains sincere, a transparent disguise he wears with the intention of reviving, in a playful way, his personal relationship with his daughter rather than with the intention of deceiving her. Ironically, Ines's and Winfried's emancipation from the roles in which they are trapped, and the reestablishment of a genuine relationship between them becomes possible only through a conscious act of role-playing which, in Winfried's case, involves donning a literal disguise and, in Ines's case, getting naked (at the party she organizes at her place to boost up her work team's spirit) in order to free herself from the expectation of "successful performance" she has internalized to such a perverse degree that she has actually hired a personal coach (with whom we see her skyping in one scene) to teach her to control her body language better.

Although Ines initially resists her father's playful interventions, which she dreads as embarrassing and generally bad for business—Winfried constantly jeopardizes her business hopes and deals—she gradually loosens up and eventually responds to her father's invitation to "play": for example, she humiliates one of her colleagues (who has been sexually harassing her) by making him ejaculate on a petit four, which she then eats demonstratively and without the least bit of passion, and she impulsively decides to "turn" (as in "detournement") the business lunch she organizes at her place to boost up her team's spirit into "a naked lunch" (which Anca hilariously interprets in the empty business lingo they have all been using as "a challenge." a challenge in which she is all too willing to participate, lest her "performance review" suffer). Here the film plays with another meaning of "performance" as an act of emancipation from (self-)inhibitions, a familiar trope perhaps most memorably treated in Lars von Trier's Dogme 95 film, *The Idiots* (1998), in which a group of adults challenge bourgeois norms by seeking their "inner idiot" and "spazzing out" (behaving as if they were developmentally disabled) in public *pour epater la bourgeoisie* or, in *Toni Erdmann*, *epater* Europe's "nouveau riche" embodied perfectly by Ines's CEO's Russian wife, who at one point declares she likes living in Frankfurt and France because she finds countries with a middle class relaxing.

Like the films discussed so far, *The Workshop* (Laurent Cantet, 2017) and *Stranger in Paradise* (Guido Hendrikx, 2016) *stage* contemporary debates around immigration, class and race, neoliberalism, and the resurgence of nationalism within an explicitly *performative* context. Although *The Workshop* is not *about* migration, its premise—a group of students in a fiction workshop are co-writing a crime thriller and must decide who the perpetrator(s) and the victim(s) should be—underscores the importance of the imagination/fiction/performance in the construction of personal and national imaginaries. The creative writing technique of "brainstorming" demands that students and teacher *rehearse/perform* different points of view as they look for the most realistic fictional "perpetrator" and "victim" for their story. On the other hand, working with a professional actor but with real asylum seekers, *Stranger in Paradise* rehearses two possible answers to the refugee crisis in the form of what Elsaesser calls a "thought experiment." While formally intriguing, however, politically both films remain somewhat opaque, reflecting the difficulty of envisioning a concrete sound political solution to Europe's current predicament.

In Cantet's film the students represent the vision of a multiracial, multiethnic, postcolonial France as seen through the eyes of their teacher (Olivia). Responding to his peers' suggestion to make the murder victim in the novel they are co-writing black or an Arab, Antoine asks: Why not make the victim white and the killer Arab or black? Similarly, we might ask Cantet: Why not make the teacher black or an Arab rather than staging France's multiculturalism, yet again, from the supposedly "neutral" point of view of the white upper-middle-class Parisian Olivia? Antoine proves to be a "difficult student." Genuinely wanting to help Antoine but also to use him to develop one of her own fictional characters in a book she is writing—reminding us that there is a fine line between empathy and exploitation—Olivia criticizes Antoine for "mixing up everything." The same could be said of Cantet's film, in which the possible motivations for Antoine's potential future act of violence, which looms over the entire story only to be averted at the last moment, pile up quickly without ever adding up. The opening shot plunges us directly into a video game featuring a lonely Viking-type warrior climbing up snow-peaked mountains and shooting into the sun (perhaps a reference to *The Stranger*, in which the sun bearing down on Merseault on the beach, just moments before killing the Arab for no reason, also plays an important role). We seem to have entered Haneke territory, specifically the Haneke of *Benny's Video*—Cantet appears to be setting up another didactic story about the harmful effects of video games on impressionable young minds. Indeed, a few scenes later we see Antoine watching a commercial for the French Army, which, he tells Olivia later on, he plans to join. However, the opening shot is echoed at the end of the film, this time within the film's diegesis, as Antoine decides not to shoot Olivia or himself (both presented as possible courses of action) and instead shoots into the sun. With this, the first potential motivation for his future perfect act of violence—media violence—is discarded as the first in a series of red herrings.

The film then suggests another possible motivation for Antoine's actions: we see him watching a YouTube video of a speaker espousing extreme right-wing views. The problem, the speaker argues, are not foreigners and borders as such but globalization and EU bureaucrats who have opened the borders, thereby jeopardizing not only France's sovereignty but also its immunity, its national and cultural identity (and by extension European identity). Tellingly, the "threat" to French identity is articulated not through reference to the refugee crisis, as one might have expected, but through invoking the "internal threat" to "Frenchness" represented by culturally, religiously, and racially internal "Others" (such as Malika and Bouba, two of Antoine's classmates), evidence that "old" postcolonial wounds have not healed. But, as with media violence above, the xenophobia and nationalism that explode during class discussions, testifying to the failure of multiculturalism, are eventually also discarded as a possible explanation for Antoine's "future perfect" act of violence.

With this second red herring out of the way a third one is thrown into the already heady mix. This time it's a question of something more tangible—the impressive remains of the once busy La Ciotat dockyard that closed down twenty-five years ago but is still visible in the background of the idyllic outdoor classroom. An obvious reference here is to Fernando Leon de Aranoa's *Mondays in the Sun* (2002), which follows a group of unemployed workers at a dockyard in the Spanish port city of Vigo after the dockyard has shut down. Rather than follow the unemployed workers, passively resentful in their acceptance of their predicament, as de Aranoa does, Cantet focuses on a group of teenagers—whose families were all affected by the unemployment crisis—as they brainstorm ideas for a novel in which one of the disaffected Ciotat workers decides to take revenge and thus becomes a murderer. This part of the story includes a "field trip" to the abandoned dockyard during which one of the laid-off workers reminisces about the town's great industrial past, which some of the students are eager to reclaim. Part of that history is recalled visually through images from the town's film archive, one of which—a shot of workers leaving the dockyard at the end of the workday—can be read as a double "quote," referencing the Lumiere brothers' *Workers Leaving the Factory* (as well as *Arrival of a Train at La Ciotat*, another possible source of pride for locals) and the opening of Karel Reisz's British New Wave *Saturday Night and Sunday Morning* (1960). When Malika suggests tapping into their town's rich industrial history in order to reclaim the feeling of pride residents of La Ciotat used to feel for their hometown, Antoine scornfully dismisses her idea as sentimental. Later, however, he goes down to the harbor and admires, though with resentment, the expensive yachts that the once impressive industrial giant of a dockyard is now reduced to servicing, providing only minimal employment in comparison with the past when a large portion of the town's population worked at the dockyard. Clearly, class differences, not only between the people of La Ciotat and the rich yacht owners we never see, but also between "the two Frances," that of the metropolitan center (Paris) and that of the periphery (La Ciotat), shape the worldview of Antoine and his classmates: for example, following their first class the students exchange their first impressions of Olivia, whom they see as a white, well-educated, privileged Parisian, for whom the time spent in "the provinces" is a well-paid vacation rather than a real job. However, even class differences and precarity are just another narrative distraction eventually dismissed as a possible explanation for Antoine's act. A final red herring is provided by terrorism, with the Bataclan massacre inevitably coming up in class discussions as students, notably Antoine, try to dissect the psychology of terrorists and the traumatic effect such events have had on the French national psyche. In the end, this line of thought is also dropped as insufficient explanation for Antoine's "difference" from other students.

The "workshop" of the film's title refers to a particular kind of class format often used in creative writing university departments, whose purpose is to encourage students to freely exchange ideas on each other's work-in-progress, but it also describes, metaphorically, what Cantet's film itself does (or at least what Cantet sees his film as doing)—"work-shopping" the socioeconomic, political, and cultural challenges faced by France. "Workshop" also refers to the quasi-detective work in which the film engages the viewers as we try to evaluate all of the suggested possible motivations for Antoine's future perfect act of violence. Ultimately, however, Antoine's final act remains unpredictable—what happens at the end of the film takes us by surprise. However, the real reason for the surprise becomes clear only in the closing scene, when Antoine comes by the workshop to say goodbye and reads aloud a passage he has written, a passage that dismisses as incorrect all possible explanations we might have had, ultimately rendering his act politically opaque. It is only now that we understand what makes Antoine different from the other students and why they formed a united front against him as soon as they heard the first piece he wrote for the class. The reason they condemn that piece as crossing some implicitly accepted limit of what is permissible is precisely the reason Antoine identifies in his farewell letter to the class: the violence of his passage, and of all his provocations in class, makes everyone uncomfortable because they, including the teacher, remain unable to ground Antoine's behavior in any kind of identity politics. If Antoine's provocations targeted specific people or groups of people at least they could be understood as expressions of xenophobia, racism, nationalism etc. What the students—and Olivia—cannot stand/*under*stand is the non-identitarian position Antoine represents. In one seemingly trivial scene the other students are waiting for Olivia, passing the time exchanging "pleasantries," mocking one another's racial and cultural identities, something they can do precisely because their identities are inscribed in easily recognizable and thus comprehensible identity politics, something they all share despite their religious, ethnic, and cultural differences. Antoine, however, does not subscribe to any identity politics, and it is this that makes *him*—rather than them—the ultimate "Other."

While the various possible motivations suggested for Antoine's potential act of violence seem to make his character more complex, supposedly posing various moral and political questions, in reality the proliferation of possible motifs for his final act follows a simple generic logic, that of the crime film: instead of suggesting different possible suspects and eliminating them one by one until the real culprit is revealed, Cantet multiples the number of possible explanations for Antoine's act only to discard them, one by one, until all we are left with is the (boring) proposition that Antoine (would have) committed murder simply out of boredom. Although this genre logic seems to strip Antoine's future perfect act of any possible political significance—insofar as the crime film operates according to the principle of elimination (of suspects and possible motivations) whereas politics operates according to the exact opposite principle of total engagement and identification with a definite set of beliefs—the dominance of the logic of genre over psychological or political logic (for both politics and psychology are associated with the notion of a character as an autonomous agent whose actions embody his beliefs, whereas genre is associated with conventions, whose force outweighs any autonomous decisions a character might make) is *not apolitical*. Indeed, one might argue that by framing Antoine's arc as that from a young man with extreme right-wing political views, who would have killed because he enjoys killing those (ethnically, racially, culturally) different from him—incidentally, a desire to kill that is conflated, on several occasions, with Islamic radicalization, which is itself highly problematic—to a young Camuesque existentialist who would have killed out of sheer boredom, the film not only conflates two very different discourses—one political, the other existential/philosophical—but even seems to suggest that any kind of radicalization can be "explained" as simply an extreme form of existentialist angst. And *that* line of thought has *political* implications: although the overall arc of the story is clear enough—the teacher leading the workshop realizes that one of her students, Antoine, shares dangerous extreme right-wing views that might lead him to commit a violent act—the film ultimately undercuts this reading by reducing what initially appears to be a particular xenophobic worldview to a purely existential or philosophical problem reminiscent of Camus's *The Stranger* (in Antoine's final piece of writing for the class, with which he dismisses those who might have interpreted his potential act of murder as having a particular political significance, Antoine explains that to say he killed someone *because* he was an Arab or a Jew would make the murder comprehensible, even if morally wrong).

Straddling the border between fiction and documentary, *Stranger in Paradise* rehearses two possible answers to the refugee crisis before presenting us with the actual one. Divided into three parts, the film invites us to identify with a handsome blond European man, a "teacher" at an immigration center in Sicily, who is revealed in the film's coda to be a professional actor. In part I, the well-spoken, reasonable sounding "teacher" explains to a classroom full of refugees how much each one of them costs Europe and why the European welfare state is not set up to help everyone who needs help. Citing Europe's post–Second World War reconstruction as a model they should follow, he advises the refugees to return to their countries and try to rebuild them the way Europe rebuilt itself after the war. In part II, the same "teacher" praises the refugees for their courage in undertaking the dangerous journey to Europe and questions them about their dreams and aspirations for the future. Citing the economic advantages of opening up Europe's borders, he also "reminds" the refugees that their current predicament is the product of Europe's colonial legacy: given that Europeans became rich by exploiting Africa's natural and human resources they ought to share some of their accumulated wealth with the victims of European colonialism. Not only is this picture of Europe superficial and misleading, failing to acknowledge the different colonial histories within Europe and the neocolonial position now occupied by certain European countries, whose citizens are hardly representative of "the rich Europeans" the "teacher" refers to, but it also advocates merely a *conditional hospitality* by suggesting that Europe should welcome migrants *only because there are legitimate grounds for this (i.e., colonialism)*. Indeed, when the "teacher" passionately argues that Europe should welcome refugees, because it *needs* them to do the jobs *Europeans don't want to do*, he seems to be grounding hospitality in a new form of neocolonialism.

In part III, the "teacher," now playing the role of an immigration official, interviews the refugees one by one to establish the validity of their asylum claims and then reads their "verdicts" aloud, denying asylum to all but three of them. Relying on a set of unequivocal laws that do not leave any room for interpretation, the teacher's final judgment renders the difference between life (a permit to stay in the Netherlands) and death (deportation) a matter of absurd, seemingly random, rules and exceptions: for example, those coming from a "country of safe origin" are automatically denied asylum, except if they are gay, lesbian, or transsexual, as if the threat to one's gender identity is more important than the threat to one's ability to support oneself financially; those who had the misfortune of being fingerprinted in the first European country they entered, are automatically denied the right to seek entry into another European country, as per the Dublin Agreement. In the film's coda the actor playing "the teacher," waiting for his ride back to the Netherlands, chats with a group of passing refugees from the center about the film he has been working on, how much it costs, and what the film's festival prospects are.

The decision to use a professional actor but real refugees—who knew the "teacher" was an actor without necessarily knowing exactly how the conversations in the classroom would unfold—produces some interesting results. On one hand, the tripartite structure and the recurring role of the "teacher" create the impression that each part "rehearses" a different response to the migrant crisis. This is true in a double sense, both metaphorically (inasmuch as each part invites us to imagine a particular scenario) and literally (inasmuch as each part features an actor, who is really performing/rehearsing particular scenarios with the refugees, with the typical director-actor relationship reversed in this case since the "director"/"teacher" is an actor while the refugees are not actors). On the other hand, even though the same actor appears in all three parts, only the first and second part can be really said to "rehearse a scenario," a possible way of looking at the refugee crisis (there is a further "doubling" here inasmuch as each part rehearses a possible scenario and, at the same time, is a rehearsal itself because it involves an actor playing a role, namely the role of rehearsing a scenario), in contrast to the third part, which is meant to offer a realistic depiction of the procedure by which immigration authorities evaluate asylum claims (even though to do so it still employs a professional actor).

The fact that the part of the "teacher" and "immigration official" is played by the same actor suggests that what were supposed to be different ways of looking at the crisis—anti-refugee, pro-refugee, and the point of view of immigration law—are actually different aspects of the same European perspective. Looked at in this way, the European response to the crisis appears fraught with contradictions: the cost analysis of the crisis (part I) does not acknowledge Europe's colonial history; the utopian embrace of the economic, cultural, and genetic benefits of migration (part II) is not reflected in any way in the current immigration law (part III); immigration law (part III) does not take into account the cost of closing boundaries, erecting new borders, and detaining asylum seekers but only asylum seekers' potential cost if they are allowed to stay in Europe, and so on. Since the film's intended audience cannot be Europeans—we already know how we think of the refugee crisis and generally identify with one or the other of the two views presented in parts I and II—the "teacher" cannot be said to be addressing us (the viewers). He must then be addressing/"teaching" the refugees. But what exactly is he "teaching" them? What is the "lesson" they are supposed to learn? The lesson in part I is that Europe sees them not as individual human beings, with their particular histories and their individual plans for the future, but as numbers (the euros they cost Europe). The lesson in part II is delivered in a veiled patronizing manner as the "teacher" sets out to "emancipate" refugees by "enlightening" them about their own colonial history, their "rights," and their victim status. The refugees learn that it is only thanks to European colonial guilt that they have certain rights, including the right to migrate and be granted asylum in Europe. It is only in part III that both viewers and refugees are addressed as "students" as we are given a quick survey of immigration law, which does not appear to be based on either of the two perspectives presented in the first two parts.

Given that, as the director has stated in interviews, the refugees were made aware of the whole setup before shooting began, we must conclude that the blurring of fiction and documentary is intended to produce a certain effect on the viewers. By making us question whether the views we hear expressed in the three parts of the film are "real" or not, the film seeks to undermine these views' presumed validity: in short, the character of the teacher functions as a Brechtian alienation device, making it impossible to fully identify with/accept any of the views presented in the film. But the inclusion of the actor/"teacher" serves another function as well: by "contaminating" the reality of the situation, it also "contaminates" the refugees' responses so that we cannot be certain of their authenticity. The director himself has said that what he wanted to explore was the power relationship not only between Europe and the refugees but also between the film crew and the refugees. Although the refugees were instructed to react as truthfully as they could to the situation created in the classroom, it was hard to know whether what they said was what they really wanted to say or they said it because they thought that's what the director and crew wanted to hear.[107] Thus, while *Stranger in Paradise* shows refugees how Europe sees them, perhaps the most important "lesson" of the film is that we can never know *how they see us*.

3 Race: The Implicit Frontier of "Europeanness"?

In European cinema the preoccupation with screening "the Other" is not new—it can be traced back to German Expressionism and its endless repertoire of figures like the robot, the Golem, the somnambulist, the vampire, and the homunculus, disguised representations of "the threatening presence of the Jew, the Gypsy, and the Bolshevik as symbols of the menacing East."[108] *La Haine* (directed by a French Jew) is probably the most referenced milestone reflecting the substitution of the new Others—postcolonial Arabs, South Asian Muslims, and African blacks[109]—for the "Jew" as the classical other of "old" Europe. At the same time, there are clear continuities between cinematic representations of Europe's "Other(s)" and representations of African-Americans in American cinema, making a case for seeing Europe's "Others" as part of the "Black European experience."[110] Ironically, seeing Europe's "Others" (Jews, the Roma, migrants, refugees etc.) as *metaphorically* part of the "Black European experience" simply reaffirms the assumption that "Black" and "European" are mutually exclusive notions, rendering invisible once again the extent to which the question of "Europeanness" remains invested in a postcolonial politics of race.

One could argue that the "performativity" of European identity I have been trying to articulate through the trope of impersonation, disguise, or performance in recent films—especially in the particular case of the trope of "passing for European," understood both literally and metaphorically—has its precedent in the trope of "passing for white" in American cinema. In this context, Elsaesser's notion of European identity as "doubly occupied" could be seen as the extension of Du Bois's concept of African American "double consciousness" into a European context. In one of Douglas Sirk's most celebrated Hollywood melodramas, *Imitation of Life* (1959), Lora Meredith, a widowed mother and aspiring actress, takes into her home a black single mother (Annie and her daughter Sarah Jane) and her mixed-race daughter Sarah Jane; although the situation is supposed to be only temporary, Annie persuades Lora to let her stay and take care of the household so Lora can pursue her Broadway career. Sirk's film zeroes in on Sarah Jane's struggle with her mixed-race identity and her attempts to pass for white even at the cost of rejecting her own mother. The phenomenon of "passing for white" has been one of the central concerns in the critical reevaluation of the often maligned melodrama genre, with many scholars drawing on Du Bois's concept of "double consciousness," the sensation of always looking at one's self through the eyes of others and thus always seeing oneself as an "Other"—articulated first in the 1897 *Atlantic Monthly* article "Strivings of the Negro People" and later republished under the title "Of Our Spiritual Strivings" in the 1903 book *The Souls of Black Folk*—to theorize racial identity in Sirk's films.

Despite certain continuities between "passing for white" and "passing for European," however, the problem of race in European cinema is differently inflected than that in American cinema, the reasons for that having no doubt to do with Europe's colonial legacy, which continues to shape perceptions of race and the "Other" in Europe. Paul Gilroy attributes Europe's disavowal of race to what he calls two "disabling scripts," the first dismissing race as being "of no consequence whatsoever,"[111] the second reducing race to "an experiential and therapeutic question that identifies a zone of feeling . . . considered to be emphatically prior to all political considerations."[112] To counter these discourses, he suggests excavating the little known facts of Europe's imperial history, which remind us of the constitutive role of strangers, aliens, and blacks in the construction of European identity and European institutions. It is only by rethinking the figure of the migrant as "part of Europe's history rather than its contemporary geography that we can avoid framing the issue of race in terms of a 'migrancy problematic.' The postcolonial migrant needs to be recognized as an anachronistic figure bound to the lost imperial past. We need to conjure up a future in which black Europeans stop being seen as migrants."[113]

As we saw earlier, a wide range of films spanning different genres—from *Diamantino* and *Welcome to Germany* to *Jupiter's Moon* and *Morgen*—continue to rely on the trope of impersonation and the figure of *the intermediary* presumably to "soften" the shock of the European's encounter with the external/refugee Other, who is often presented as an internal Other (whether a mixed-raced Other, a religious Other, or a Gypsy) "in disguise." Contrary to popular proclamations that Europe is becoming "post-racial," the majority of recent European films continue to obfuscate biological racism, displacing the question of racial identity onto that of legal status (see Balibar and Wallerstein's discussion of differentialist racism in the Introduction). In this context it is instructive to compare an earlier film like *Otomo* (Frieder Schlaich, 1999) to recent films like *Illegal* (Olivier Masset-Depasse, 2010), *The Invader* (Nicolas Provost, 2011), and *Samba* (Olivier Nakache and Eric Toledano, 2014) in order to make explicit the degree to which race continues to function as an implicit or explicit frontier of Europeanness.[114]

Otomo is based on the real story of a Cameroon illegal migrant, Frederick Otomo, living in Stuttgart without citizenship papers. Otomo was killed on August 9, 1989, after killing two police officers who tried to apprehend him under the pretext that he refused to comply with the orders of a racist ticket controller on the subway. In the film's silent opening sequence, whose minimalist style and cool protagonist recall Melville's stylized noir *Le Samourai* (1967), Otomo is seen packing his personal belongings, about to leave the hotel where he has been living in secret. As we follow him through the last day of his life, we quickly begin to see him as the Germans did—a hunted man. Otomo's racial identity defines the terms of all his encounters with others: at the unemployment office he is refused work under the pretext that he doesn't have residence papers, though it's clear that he is rejected because of his race rather than because of his legal status; when the police learn that Otomo has applied for a job at Daimler-Benz, one officer jokingly declares he wouldn't want to be in a car assembled "by one of them" (i.e., blacks); there is a clichéd reference to black men's "exceptional virility" when the German police officers resentfully note that German women would rather pick up a black man than a German; the hotel manager decries the "watering down" of the German nation, observing with regret that "it used to be, at least the [taxi] driver was German" whereas now refugees (i.e., blacks) have infiltrated all businesses; finally, a scene of Otomo meeting a little girl by the river explicitly references the scene of Boris Karloff's monster befriending little Maria in James Whale's *Frankenstein* (1931).

It is eventually revealed—through a letter from Otomo to the German president, which the police find when they search his hotel room—that Otomo had to flee his native Cameroon because his father was a German sympathizer—he fought with the German army in Cameroon between 1910 and 1918 but after the Germans left it became too dangerous for him to stay there. This fact, however, is of little consequence for the Germans, whose only response is to comment sarcastically that "German sympathy can come in handy. So can German shepherds. We have some Polish men with German shepherds in our building. They have become German citizens!" When, in an earlier scene at the unemployment office, some unemployed Germans mock Otomo's shoes, another unemployed man reassures Otomo the Germans will get him new shoes once he is hired, but a third one advises Otomo not to trust such promises because the shoes the employers provide are made in Poland and banned in Germany for failing to meet safety standards. These scenes draw an implicit parallel between the status of black immigrants in Europe in the wake of decolonization and the status of the "internal (white) Others" through whose symbolic expulsion German—and European—identity has been historically constituted, whether it is the Polish Jews of the Second World War or, after 1989, Poles and other Eastern Europeans, who, like Otomo, can never attain the status of "properly European" even if they are granted legitimate citizenship status.

Recent films about "illegal" migrants and refugees have done nothing to challenge the conflation of race with legal status. Masset-Depasse's *Illegal* tells the story of two illegal Russian immigrants—Tania, a former teacher now working as a cleaner, and her thirteen-year-old son Ivan—living in Belgium. Tania is arrested in the street and sent to an immigration detention center for women and children, where she refuses to disclose her name, hoping to be released soon. She befriends Ayssa, an African woman who has spent eight months at the center and barely survived numerous attempts of forceful expulsion from Belgium, every time being severely beaten up by the shifts. Ayssa is the only illegal we see brutally beaten up, over and over again. The center refuses to hospitalize her until one day she hangs herself in the shower. Ayssa's story makes reference to the heated debate in Belgium around the forced expulsion of illegal immigrants sparked by the death (in 1998) of Semira Adamu, an African immigrant who didn't survive the violence used during her expulsion. Although her death was the reason of a thorough revision of the expulsion procedures in Belgium, in *Illegal* it is the attempt at the forceful expulsion of the white, Russian illegal—not the death of the African illegal—that draws the media's attention to the strong-arm approach of the police to deportations: tellingly, unlike Ayssa, who meets a tragic end, in the film's final scene Tania is seen reunited with her son. Fernand Melgar's documentary *Vol Special* (2011), set in a Geneva detention center—and ending, like *Illegal,* with the death of one African illegal during his forceful expulsion—also foregrounds the importance of race in the construction of Europe's unwanted "Others." There are numerous scenes in which African inmates gather together to sing about their predicament, yet their songs rarely make mention of their shared illegal status, recounting instead their shared stories of abuse by the white man.

Opening with a long take of a naked woman in a pose that recalls Courbet's famous painting *The Origin of the World* (1866), featuring an almost anatomical description of female sex organs, *The Invader* draws on various stylistic and narrative elements of film noir, including the femme fatale who causes the male protagonist's downfall. While the opening shot can be read as a reference to the noir interpretation of the idea of woman as the origin of the world—the idea of woman as the origin of all evil and the downfall of man—since *The Invader* is a film about an illegal immigrant this reading is complicated by the themes and preoccupations specific to migrant cinema, namely the relationship between Europe (the beautiful, sophisticated, bourgeois white woman, Agnes) and the disenfranchised, abject, black, illegal immigrant (Amadou, "the invader" of the title). The film's opening shot recasts film noir's deadly erotic relationship between Woman and Man as the conflicted relationship between the EU and the refugees trying to enter it and, at the same time, between Europe, in its self-definition as "raceless"/white, and those racially "Other" who continually challenge this self-definition (rooted in misrecognition). In the film's imaginary, the EU is "the origin of all evil," remaining unresponsive to the claims of non-European, nonwhite "Others."

In fact, the opening sequence can be read as both a critique *and* an endorsement of the racial divide that undergirds Europe's self-perception. Following the close up of Agnes' genitals, we see Amadou and another black man washed up ashore a nudist Mediterranean beach, shorthand for Europe-as-paradise (recalling the opening of *Eden Is West*). The naked white woman gets up and walks calmly toward the sea until we see, from her exoticizing point of view, Amadou's half-naked, well-built body emerge, Venus-like, from the sea. This shot positions Amadou as an ominous presence invading the prelapsarian/pre-migrant crisis, racially homogenous space of the white nudist colony/Europe. Although the encounter between Agnes and Amadou is represented as one between Woman and Man (Agnes representing Eve and Amadou standing in for Adam), sexual difference is figured through the prism of race. The rest of the film tries, unsuccessfully, to interweave the two parallel stories already suggested in the opening sequence: Amadou's *amour fou* story (he is smitten, predictably enough, with the reserved, white bourgeois Agnes) and the critique of the EU's treatment of the refugee crisis.

Following the opening sequence, Amadou is seen working illegally on a construction site, from which he is forced to run when the police arrive for inspection. Returning to the squat where he lives with other illegals, he finds his sick friend gone. Their shady employer takes Amadou to the Boss, who lies to him that his friend has run away without paying for the residency and work permit the Boss has procured for both of them. Amadou is now saddled with a debt of 4000 euros and with a barely hidden thirst for revenge (his friend, we assume, was killed by the Boss). His revenge will have to wait—he will come back for it at the end of the film, significantly right after being rejected by Agnes. Amadou overhears his Boss talking to an attractive white woman (Agnes), a real estate developer, who informs the Boss that she will no longer work with him because she disapproves of him hiring illegal immigrants. Amadou follows Agnes to her husband's lecture, where he tells her bluntly that he desires her. After they spend the night together he insists on seeing her again, but Agnes keeps her distance. Amadou wanders the streets, thinking about her and waiting for another chance to see her. Realizing that Amadou stole the keys from her loft, Agnes sends a colleague to collect the keys and give Amadou money as a way of discouraging him from pursuing her further. In accordance with the film noir trope of the icy cold, blonde femme fatale driving the noir hero to acts of violence, or at least unleashing the violent tendencies that have been lying dormant within him, Amadou takes the rejection hard, going on a gruesome killing spree (he murders both his former employer and the Boss). In the film's closing scene, having managed to sneak into Agnes's apartment, Amadou stands naked at the foot of her bed, in which she is sleeping peacefully next to her husband. After cutting to a medium shot of the two of them sleeping, the camera pulls back to reveal Amadou lying in Agnes's husband's place; however, this time Amadou is alone in bed.

The film desperately tries, and fails, to integrate the romantic subplot with the larger social critique of the treatment of illegal immigrants and refugees in Europe. At one point, Amadou randomly walks into a church, which has been turned into a squat for illegal immigrants and homeless people. A slogan hanging on the church façade reads "Hunger strike. Silence is a sign of complicity!" The appearance of this slogan in the middle of the film, after we have been made aware of Amadou's precarious status but before he goes on a killing spree, may be taken to suggest that Amadou's violent act is justified (if silence is a sign of complicity, his act can be justified as being "in the name" of the struggle of the destitute), a politically problematic stance that the film neither openly endorses nor, however, takes responsibility for. Indeed, it is precisely the conflation of a clichéd romantic story with a social commentary about the refugee crisis that makes *The Invader* a politically regressive film. Told from Amadou's point of view, the story invites us to sympathize with him so that when the rich white woman rejects him we are expected to see him as a victim and her as an aggressor who took advantage of him, despite the fact that a woman has every right not to want to extend a one-night stand into an affair. Conflating romantic disappointment with the feeling of exclusion and rejection experienced by those making a claim of belonging to Europe, *The Invader* positions Amadou as a victim whose only chance of becoming a subject, in Rancière's sense of subjectivization, is through a literal act of violence. In addition to the problematic conflation of romantic disappointment with political disenfranchisement, and of sexual difference with racial difference (in the opening sequence), the film regularly figures racial identity in terms of legal (immigration) status. For example, after Agnes rejects Amadou, he spends a relaxing night getting drunk with a group of much younger American girls, who are portrayed as welcoming and generous, treating him as an equal and taking no notice of his race, which presumably does not translate into "illegal" in their minds the way it does in the European Agnes's mind.

The mutual entanglement of racial identity and legal status can be seen in another film tracing the romance between a white bourgeois French woman and an illegal black immigrant, *Samba*, in which the question of who belongs to Europe, defined in terms of legal status and embodied in the Holy Grail of the residency permit, is initially posited in terms of race, inviting us to read the film as a critique of Europe's self-definition as racially white and of the mutual imbrication of racial identity with legal status. Ultimately, however, the film posits legal status as trumping racial identity in deciding who belongs to Europe. Samba, an illegal immigrant from Senegal who settled in Paris ten years ago, is working a low-paying job as a dishwasher in the back of a fancy restaurant. He has already applied for a residence permit; however, when he brings a job contract from his employer to Immigration Services they inform him that his permanent residence application has been denied and promptly send him to a detention center, where he meets Jonas, another illegal immigrant from Senegal. Jonas asks Samba to promise him that if he ever gets out, he will track down Jonas's lover. It is at the detention center that Samba meets Alice, a white senior executive suffering from a "burnout," on a "charity sabbatical" from her demanding job. Samba is released from the center but only on the condition that he leave the country. Samba returns to the apartment he shares with his uncle, a legal resident of France, who advises him to be inconspicuous by dressing like a European businessman and avoiding train and subway stations. Samba does just that. In a scene that illustrates the conflation of race with legal status, we see Samba riding the Paris metro, dressed like "a European businessman," newspaper in hand, anxiously looking around, paranoid that someone might see through his disguise (another instance of the trope of "passing for European"). Given that all the people he imagines staring at him with suspicion are white (he is the only black person in the subway car, something inconceivable to anyone who has ever taken the metro in Paris), the scene makes it unclear—perhaps intentionally—whether the real source of Samba's anxiety and paranoia is his racial identity or his illegal status.

As the romantic relationship between Samba and Alice evolves, Samba finds a job as a security guard in a mall. However, one night there is a break-in and Samba is forced to run before the police arrive on the scene. Using his uncle's residence permit to look for work, Samba runs into Wilson, another illegal immigrant who introduces himself as Brazilian but later confesses he is really of Maghrebi origin (he decided to pretend he is Brazilian after seeing how much easier it is for Brazilians, race-wise, in Paris). The issue of race is foregrounded, again, in a later scene when Wilson takes Samba to a guy running his own black market for fake IDs from the back of a grocery store. As the three men haggle over prices, Wilson is shocked to learn that fake IDs for blacks are considerably cheaper than those for whites, while fake IDs for Chinese are even cheaper than those for blacks. The scene demonstrates the commodification of race in the construction of legality and illegality with immigrants' desirability and acceptability being rated in accordance with the desirability and acceptability of their race. The fact that throughout the negotiations Wilson acts as Samba's translator, translating into French everything the fake ID seller says to Samba, despite the fact that Samba speaks perfect French, hints at yet another, even more hidden racial "ranking" of immigrants according to their provenance within France's former colonial territories, the Maghrebi Wilson being, unlike Samba, visibly indistinguishable from a white man.

Samba spends most of the film running away from the French authorities, that is, from "the white man"; and yet, in the end his life is put in danger not by a white man but by another black immigrant, Jonas, who, having been released from the detention center, comes looking for Samba after hearing about Samba's sexual relationship with Jonas's lover. At the end of the film Jonas and Samba find themselves on opposite sides of the law, with Jonas already a legal resident and Samba still *sans-papiers*, a divide that in the end proves more important than their shared racial/postcolonial identity. In the altercation between Samba and Jonas, the latter dies and, although the film doesn't make this explicit, we are led to understand that Samba has stolen Jonas's resident permit and is finally able to stay in Paris with Alice while his uncle returns to Senegal. The happy ending sees Alice return to work spiritually, emotionally, and sexually "renewed" by her romance with the illegal black immigrant while Samba attains his dream of becoming, improbably, the Chief Chef of Le Garde Republicaine![115]

Following an already established pattern of staging "the first encounter" with the (refugee) Other—a trope with a long colonial history—either as an abrupt interruption/rude awakening of a leisurely sailing trip (e.g., Wolfgang Fischer's 2018 *Styx*, discussed in Chapter 3) or as an interruption of daily work (e.g., Emanuele Crialese's 2011 *Terraferma*, discussed in Chapter 4), the coming-of-age drama *Once You Are Born You Can No Longer Hide* (Marco Giordana, 2005) has Sandro, the young son of a middle-class Italian family living in the northern city of Brescia where his father owns a factory, fall overboard in the Mediterranean during a yachting vacation with his father only to be rescued by a boat of refugees, with some of whom—particularly the Romanian youth Radu and his sister Alina—Sandro becomes close, so close in fact that when the boat is intercepted by the Italian coast guard Sandro insists on accompanying his Romanian friends to the refugee processing center rather than agreeing to be sent home. Leaving aside the question of the credibility of this part of the plot, a more cynical reading of which might see it as the European boy's wish "to play refugee," it is important to question the choice of two Romanian refugees, rather than, say, two African refugees, who in fact represent the majority of refugees on the boat, as Sandro's saviors/friends. This choice reveals the racial limits of the European liberal imagination, for as much as Giordana's film purports to advocate a more hospitable relationship to the migrant Other, like the other films discussed above it resorts to using an "intermediary," a figure that is Other to the Western European self yet not absolutely (i.e., racially) Other—here a white Eastern European youth who comes from a country with clear linguistic and cultural links to Italy—to make the advocated "hospitality" to the Other more "palatable," especially since the film later develops the notion of hospitality, once again, through the trope of adoption (see Chapter 3). Since the notion of Sandro's "liberal" white family adopting black "refugee children" is apparently unthinkable, the choice falls upon two white attractive Romanian teenagers who could easily "pass" for Italian.

At the same time, although at first the film positions Radu as Sandro's savior, which accounts for Sandro's fraternal devotion to him, eventually Radu himself breaks that trust by robbing Sandro's family and running away, abandoning his sister whom he had forced into prostitution; in short, the film reaffirms the Western European stereotype of the cunning Eastern European who cannot be trusted. The film's ambivalent politics is, in fact, embedded in its title, which is at odds with the film's liberal pretensions. On one hand, Sandro's accident, which transforms him, in a matter of seconds, from the child of a middle-class Italian family living in Italy's prosperous North into a nameless refugee (to protect Sandro from the Sicilian traffickers Radu tells them that Sandro is a Kurdish refugee like him) is meant to underscore what we owe one another as human beings rather than as citizens of particular nations. This idea is succinctly captured in the shot of Sandro, all alone, in the water, a shot that we also get in *Styx* (2018) when Kingsley (the African refugee boy) pushes Rike off the boat, leaving her alone in the water for several minutes. Such symbolic, quasi-baptismal shots of Europeans floating in the Mediterranean seem to offer a different reading of the term "refugee," considering it not as a legal status, but rather along the lines of Agamben's "bare life," which all humans share. However, such a reading is compromised by the very title of the film—*Once You Are Born You Can No Longer Hide*—which Sandro discovers, to his surprise, to be the name of one of the African refugees working in the detention center. Not only does the name suggest, problematically, that "refugee" is not something one "becomes" (i.e., it is not a matter of legal status) but also something one already "is," though it frames the status of "refugee" in terms of *racial difference/visibility*, leaving unchallenged the presumed equivalence between "refugee," "illegal," and "black."

Notes

1 Gianni Vattimo, *The End of Modernity: Nihilism and Hermeneutics in Postmodern Culture* (Cambridge, UK: Polity Press, 1991), 4.
2 Ibid., 11.
3 Ibid., 172.
4 Ibid., 175.
5 Rivi, *European Cinema*, 32.
6 On the performativity of gender see Judith Butler, *Gender Trouble: Feminism and the Subversion of Identity* (New York: Routledge, 2006).

7 Kriss Ravetto-Biagioli, *Mythopoetic Cinema: On the Ruins of European Identity* (New York: Columbia UP, 2017), 4.
8 Ibid., 5.
9 Ibid.
10 Ibid., 235.
11 Skrodzka, *Magic Realist Cinema*, 8–9.
12 Ibid., 14.
13 qtd in Skrodzka, *Magic Realist Cinema*, 16.
14 Ravetto-Biagioli, *Mythopoetic Cinema*, 5.
15 Skrodzka, *Magic Realist Cinema*, 15.
16 Thomas Elsaesser, *European Cinema and Continental Philosophy: Film as Thought Experiment* (New York: Bloomsbury, 2019), 31.
17 Thomas Elsaesser, "European Cinema into the Twenty-First Century: Enlarging the Context," *The Europeanness of European Cinema: Identity, Meaning and Globalization*, ed. Mary Harrod, Mariana Liz, and Alissa Timoshkina (London: I.B. Tauris, 2015), 17–32.
18 Ibid., 18.
19 Ibid., 25.
20 Ibid., 28.
21 Ibid., 30.
22 Elsaesser, *European Cinema*, 85.
23 Nico Baumbach, *Cinema/Politics/Philosophy* (New York: Columbia UP, 2019), 8.
24 Ibid., 25.
25 Ibid., 35.
26 Elsaesser, *European Cinema*, 5.
27 Elsaesser's metaphorical use of the term "thought experiment" does not correspond to the strict definition of "thought experiment" in philosophy or ethics.
28 Ibid., 3.
29 Ibid.
30 Ibid.
31 Alain Badiou, *Cinema: Textes rassembles et presentes par Antoine de Baccque* (Paris: NOVA Éditions, 2010), 327.
32 "Between the event of love and the ordinary rules of life (the laws of the city, the law of marriage) there is no common measure . . . [Philosophy] will tell us: 'We must think the event. . . . We must think the transformation of life'" (my translation). Ibid., 327.
33 Elsaesser, *European Cinema*, 4.
34 Ibid., 4.

35 Ibid.
36 Ibid., 8.
37 Ibid.
38 Ibid., 15.
39 Ibid., 204.
40 Ibid., 15.
41 Ibid.
42 Ibid.
43 Ibid., 131.
44 Ibid., 129.
45 Ibid., 132.
46 See Julia Kristeva, *Powers of Horror: An Essay on Abjection* (New York: Columbia UP, 1984).
47 Ibid., 138.
48 Ibid., 140.
49 Ibid.
50 Ibid., 211.
51 Ibid., 210.
52 Ibid., 17.
53 Ibid.
54 Ibid., 64.
55 Ibid., 69.
56 Ibid., 77.
57 Ibid.
58 Ibid., 30.
59 Ibid.
60 Ibid., 44.
61 Ibid., 51.
62 Ibid., 53.
63 Deleuze, *Bergsonism*, trans. Hugh Tomlinson and Barbara Habberjam (New York: Zone, 1991), 27–28.
64 Elsaesser, *European Cinema*, 53.
65 Ibid., 53.
66 Ibid., 119.
67 Elsaesser's notion of abjection is indebted to Lyotard's concept of "the second inhuman" referring to "our debt to our own humanity as something that "needs no finality" (Lyotard 7): "Given the degree to which the very ideas of 'humanity' and 'humanism' have become contested, abjection strategically upholds the human against the post-human" (Elsaesser, *European Cinema*,

160–61). See Jean-Francois Lyotard, *The Inhuman: Reflections on Time*, trans. Geoffrey Bennington and Rachel Bowlby (New York: Polity Press, 1988).

68 Elsaesser, *European Cinema*, 59.
69 Thomas Elsaesser's conference talk, http://www.lestudium-ias.com/event/ruins-and-margins-european-identity-cinema-european-identity-era-mass-migration.
70 See Rebecca Prime, "Stranger Than Fiction: Generic Hybridity in the Refugee Film," *Post Script* 15, no. 3 (2011): 57–67. See also Schurmans, "The Representation of the Illegal Migrant in Contemporary Cinema." Schurman distinguishes films with a classical narrative structure that often feature as an "intermediary" a Western man going through an existential crisis, which his encounter with the illegal migrant helps him overcome, from films working through allusion/metaphor without the use of an "intermediary."
71 Maria Ravisco, "Nation, Boundaries and Otherness in European 'Films of Voyage,'" *We Europeans? Media, Representations, Identities*, ed. William Uricchio (Bristol: Intellect Books, 2008), 142.
72 Ibid., 143.
73 Michael Gott, *French Language Road Cinema: Borders, Diasporas, Migration and "New Europe"* (Edinburgh: Edinburgh UP, 2016), 1–18.
74 Ibid., 10.
75 Ibid., 155.
76 https://www.hollywoodreporter.com/review/hope-cannes-review-705847, accessed August 6, 2019.
77 https://variety.com/2014/film/festivals/film-review-hope-1201206198/, accessed August 6, 2019.
78 *14 Kilómetros* (Gerardo Olivares, 2007) tells a similar story.
79 Jorg Metermann, "'E Giusto vivere cosi?' Contemporary Melodrama and Migration," *The Cinemas of Italian Migration: European and Transatlantic Narratives*, ed. Sabine Schrader and Daniel Winkler (Newcastle upon Tyne: Cambridge Scholars Publishing, 2013), 251.
80 Ibid., 252.
81 Ibid., 261.
82 Celik, *In Permanent Crisis*, 20.
83 qtd in Celik, *In Permanent Crisis*, 21.
84 Ibid., 20–21.
85 Ibid., 130.
86 Loshitzky, *Screening Strangers*, 15.
87 Santaolalla traces the evolution of the genre of migration cinema from an initial focus on social problem narratives and stories of victimization to later depictions of immigrants in a wider range of private and public spaces. See Isabel Santaolalla, "Body Matters: Immigrants in Recent Spanish, Italian and Greek Cinemas," *European Cinema in Motion: Migrant and Diasporic Film in Contemporary Europe*, ed. Daniela Berghahn and Claudia Sternberg (London: Palgrave Macmillan, 2010), 152–74.

88 Loshitzky, *Screening Strangers*, 54.
89 Nilgun Bayraktar, *Mobility and Migration in Film and Moving Image Art: Cinema Beyond Europe* (New York: Routledge, 2017), 6.
90 Ballesteros, *Immigration Cinema*.
91 Ibid., 3.
92 Ibid.
93 Ibid., 17.
94 For a discussion of European migrant cinema in terms of genre (specifically the road movie and the observational documentary) and postcoloniality, see Sandra Ponzanesi, "Of Shipwrecks and Weddings: Borders and Mobilities in Europe," *Transnational Cinemas* 7, no. 2 (2016): 151–67.
95 Tornatore qtd in Nathan, *Marvelous Bodies*, 87.
96 Locatelli and Pitassio, "Vesna Run Faster!" 38.
97 Ibid., 44.
98 Elisabetta Girelli, "Transnational Orientalism: Ferzan Özpetek's Turkish Dream in *Hamam* (1997)," *New Cinemas: Journal of Contemporary Film* 5, no. 1 (2007): 23–38.
99 For an alternative reading of the structural similarities Audiard sets up between Sri Lanka and the French suburbs, see "Why Dheepan's Take on Immigration Isn't Helpful," in which Caspar Salmon argues that *Dheepan*'s reliance on genre (the revenge drama, the western) associates refugees with "the stigma of lawlessness." https://www.theguardian.com/film/filmblog/2016/apr/20/dheepan-immigration-depiction-selective-jacques-audiard-multiracial-france, accessed August 6, 2019.
100 A number of recent TV comedies, for example, the British *Home* (2019) and *Don't Forget the Driver* (2019), also explore the refugee crisis and illegal immigration. On the more serious side is the French TV show *Eden* (2019).
101 The visual motif of Europe as a nudist paradise pops up in *Eden Is West*, *The Invader*, and *Jupiter's Moon*: on one hand the image deconstructs the naïve idea of Europe as a paradise of luxury and freedom (the luxury *of* freedom) while, on the other, it reaffirms the idea of Europe as Eden in danger of being "polluted" by non-Europeans.
102 *Xenia* (Panos Koutras, 2014), whose title can be translated as "hospitality," explores similar issues as it follows two half-Albanian brothers searching for their Greek father after their Albanian mother dies.
103 Other examples of performativity and disguise in European films include *The Italian* (Olivier Baroux, 2010), in which the son of Algerian immigrants in Marseille pretends to be Italian, and *The Island* (Kamen Kalev, 2011), in which a Bulgarian man living with his French girlfriend pretends to be German.
104 In *Greed* (Michael Winterbottom, 2019), too, the figure revolting against the structural violence of neoliberalism, embodied here by a high-street fashion tycoon, is a postcolonial racialized Other—a Sri Lankan woman, now a UK

citizen and one of the billionaire's high-level staffers—rather than the Syrian refugees recently landed on the beach.

105 The re-education/Europeanization of the former countries of the Eastern bloc, for example, in matters of racial tolerance, is explored from a comedic point of view in Christian Mingiu's *Occident* (2002), in which Romanians are taught that "gypsies are people too" and that a "Black European" is not the oxymoron they think it is.

106 In its depiction of the neoliberal restructuring of a former communist society as a case of unscrupulous devouring, which can be stopped only through some kind of pagan ritual, the film draws on one of the oldest cinematic tropes in vampire lore, that of the vampire repelled by a garlic bouquet or, in this case, by a Bulgarian pagan Kukeri mask.

107 https://variety.com/2016/film/festivals/guido-hendrikx-immigration-doc-stranger-in-paradise-idfa-1201921740/, accessed August 6, 2019.

108 Loshitzky, *Screening Strangers*, 8.

109 Bottici and Challand identify Walter Laqueur's *Last Days of Europe: Epitaph for an Old Continent* (2007), which introduced the problematic category of Islamo-fascism to explain why Europe is at risk, as an important reference in the substitution of the Muslim threat for the older myth of the Eastern threat.

110 Greg de Cuir Jr., "The Feather Collectors: Erased Identity and Invisible Representations of the Roma in Yugoslav Cinema," *The Europeanness of European Cinema: Identity, Meaning and Globalization*, ed. Mary Harrod, Mariana Liz, and Alissa Timoshkina (London: I.B. Tauris, 2015), 108.

111 Paul Gilroy, "Foreword: Migrancy, Culture, and a New Map of Europe," *Blackening Europe: The African American Presence*, ed. Heike Raphael-Hernandez (London: Routledge, 2004), xv.

112 Ibid., xvi.

113 Ibid., xxi.

114 *Amin* (Philippe Faucon, 2018) tells a story very similar to that in *Samba*.

115 Abdellatif Kechiche's *Poetical Refugee/La faute a Voltaire* (2000)—which follows Jallel, a young illegal North African immigrant in France as he struggles to find employment and hide from the authorities, all the while sharing solidarity with other social outcasts in Paris—can be seen as an earlier version of the basic story told in *A Season in France, The Invader,* and *Samba*.

3

The Figure of the Migrant and Cinematic Ethics

As we saw in the previous chapter, one of the central premises in Elsaesser's latest book is that European cinema has been "demoted" to just another part of "world cinema," a "demotion" Elsaesser invites us to read as a golden opportunity for Europe and European cinema rather than a sign of its impending fade into oblivion, allegedly because, having been relegated to the margins, European cinema is now free from the burden of having to reflect specific values or of having to represent either the "nation" or "Europe." As we shall see, however, European cinema is by no means "free of having to reflect certain values"; on the contrary, it is expected to *bear witness* to a continually unfolding migrant and refugee crisis. Like the Holocaust, the migrant crisis has become crucial to redefining European identity along ethical and humanitarian lines, prompting scholars to rethink the Eurocentric conflation of humanitarian with European values.

Needless to say, European films about "illegal" migrants and refugees predate the 2015 refugee crisis: consider, for instance, fiction films like *Moonlighting* (Jerzy Skolimowski, 1982) (a Polish businessman living in London brings a handful of workers from Warsaw to renovate his house but after Solidarity is crushed and Martial Law is declared in Poland the Poles overstay their tourist visas while trying to stay afloat through petty crimes), *300 Miles to Heaven* (Maciej Dejczer, 1989) (two boys escape communist Poland, hidden under a truck, and end up in Denmark, where they have to struggle to obtain political asylum), *Lettres d'Alou* (Montxo Armendariz, 1990) (a Senegalese man who enters Spain illegally and is deported decides to cross the border illegally again), *Winter Flowers* (Kadir Sozen, 1997) (a Turkish immigrant living in Germany with his family is deported after his residence permit expires and decides to cross the border illegally again), *Saïd* (Llorenc Soler, 1998) (the status of an illegal Moroccan immigrant in

Spain becomes jeopardized by a violent encounter with skinheads), *Bwana* (Umanol Uribe, 1996) (a Spanish family on a weekend trip to a remote beach on the Almeria coast encounter an illegal immigrant who has made the crossing from Africa by raft), *Last Resort* (Pawel Pawlikowski, 2000) (a young Russian woman and her son arrive in London expecting to meet her fiancé but when he does not show up they are confined to a small seaside town while their claim for asylum is being processed), *Marie-line* (Mehdi Charef, 2000) (a French woman overseeing the cleaning crew in an office building is forced to hire illegal immigrants and must then defend their rights), *Poniente* (Chus Gutierrez, 2002) (a Spanish woman returning to her hometown to take over her family's tomato farm must confront the locals' racism against the illegal immigrant workers she employs), *Agua con sal* (Pedro Perez Rosado, 2005) (a Cuban woman comes to Spain as a hopeful student only to become an illegal immigrant), *Crossing Borders* (Carlos Iglesias, 2006) (two Spanish men, having lost their jobs, are forced to immigrate illegally to Switzerland), and documentaries like *The Other Europe* (Poul-Eric Heilbuth, 2006), *The Fortress* (Fernand Melgar, 2008), *Vol Special* (Fernand Melgar, 2011), *L'Escale* (Kaveh Bakhtiari, 2013), *Land in Sight* (Antje Kruska and Judith Keil, 2013), *Willkommen auf Deutsch* (Hauke Wendler and Carsten Rau, 2014), *Neuland* (Anna Thommen, 2013), *The Land Between* (David Fedele, 2014), *Closed Sea* (Andrea Segre, 2012), and others.

Nevertheless, and perhaps unsurprisingly, since 2015 the number of films featuring "illegal" migrants and refugees has grown dramatically, from documentaries like *4.1 Miles* (Daphne Matziaraki, 2016), *The Good Postman* (Tonislav Hristov, 2016), *Bienvenue au Refugistan* (Anne Poiret, 2016), *Dog Years* (Rocky Rodriguez, Jr., 2017), *La Ville Monde* (Antares Bassis, 2018), *Libre* (Michel Toesca, 2018), and *Refugee* (Alexander Farrell, 2018) to fiction films like *Dheepan* (Jacques Audiard, 2015), *Shanghai Belleville* (Show-chun Lee, 2015), *Mediterranea* (Jonas Carpignano, 2015), *Fire at Sea* (Gianfranco Rosi, 2016), *Welcome to Germany* (Simon Verhoeven, 2016), *Corps etranger* (Raja Amari, 2016), *The Citizen* (Roland Vranik, 2016), *The Order of Things* (Andrea Segre, 2017), *Happy End* (Michael Haneke, 2017), *The Other Side of Hope* (Aki Kaurismaki, 2017), *Jupiter's Moon* (Kornél Mundruzcó, 2017), *The House by the Sea* (Robert Guediguian, 2017), *Amin* (Philippe Faucon, 2018), *Fortuna* (Germinal Roaux, 2018), *Diamantino* (Gabriel Abrantes and Daniel Schmidt, 2018), *Happy as Lazzaro* (Alice Rohrwacher, 2018), *Styx* (Wolfgang Fischer, 2018), *Transit* (Christian Petzold, 2018), *Meltem* (Basile Doganis, 2019), *Atlantique* (Mati Diop, 2019), and others. Virtual reality has been increasingly promoted as an "empathy machine," with VR works like Nonny de la Peña's *Hunger in Los Angeles*, Chris Milk's *Clouds over Sidra* and *The Last Goodbye*, Stanford University's Virtual Human Interaction Lab's *Becoming Homeless,* and Alejandro Iñárritu's *Carne y arena* (2017) purporting to deepen the user's empathic identification through visual and aural immersion and positing neuroscience (with its understanding of affect as "hardwired") as "the new universal" in the wake of waning Enlightenment universalism. VR's perfect simulation of the purely physical experience of a refugee does not, however, help us understand the person forced into that situation, since the experiences for which VR claims to produce empathy (e.g., being a refugee) "are not fundamentally about the immediate physical environment."[1] In the words of game developer Robert Yang, "If you won't believe someone's pain unless they wrap an expensive 360 video around you, then perhaps you don't actually care about their pain."[2]

1 The Blind Spots of "the Ethical Turn"

The "ethical turn" in the humanities and social sciences has produced a whole new subfield within cinema studies.[3] In one of the representative studies on the subject, *Film and Ethics: Foreclosed Encounters* (2010), Lisa Downing and Libby Saxton locate all of the following under the umbrella term "the ethical turn"—Levinas's philosophy, late Derrida's philosophy of ethics, the ethical dimension of Lacanian psychoanalysis, and the "ethics of looking" in feminist, queer, and postcolonial theory—while, at the same time, distinguishing the continental tradition's "ethical turn" from the analytic tradition's concept of ethics, "a positivistic and humanist model of 'virtue ethics' dealing with morally practical questions of obligation, a tradition at odds with continental thought which challenges the supremacy of the human subject and stresses the unassimilable otherness of the Other."[4] The emphasis on ethics as "a process of questioning rather than a positivistic exercise of morality"[5] is important to Downing and Saxton, who believe their definition of ethics serves as a sort of "insurance" against critiques of "the ethical turn" or "ethical ideology," such as that by Badiou and Rancière, for instance. And yet, what Badiou calls "ethical ideology" is not equivalent to the analytic philosophy's concept of ethics as "prescriptive moral codes and rules," which is the actual target of Downing and Saxton's critique.

Downing and Saxton's main avenue of defense of the continental against the analytic notion of "ethics" is to demonstrate the irreducibility of Levinas's philosophy to a "bland and empty injunction to respect otherness."[6] On the contrary, they argue, Levinas's project in *Totality and Infinity* (1961) is to answer the question: How can one get away from Western philosophy, which he describes as an ontology or "egology"—a "reduction of the other to the same"—and conceive of a relationship with an other that does not "immediately divest it of its alterity?"[7] or, as Levinas puts it, in *Otherwise Than Being or Beyond Essence* (1974), how can one describe without betraying Levinas's "ethical relation without relation," which preserves "the strangeness of the Other, his irreducibility to the I, to my thoughts and possessions, his transcendence, his absolute and irrecuperable alterity"?[8] Downing and Saxton are right to frame Levinas's project within a broader intellectual tradition of ethical thought characterized by a profound skepticism toward representation and signification (a tradition Martin Jay ties to the Hebraic taboo on images) inasmuch as for Levinas the Other comes "without mediation" and "signifies by himself."[9] In their comparative analyses of films dealing with "the ultimate trauma," the Holocaust, Downing and Saxon privilege Levinasian films—for example, Lanzmann's *Shoah* (1985)—which register the trauma only through its unrepresentability and unintelligibility, privileging speech over image. Supposedly, it is only through a refusal of representation that the meaningfulness of the Other—a meaningfulness prior to representation and irreducible to knowledge—can be preserved.

This, however, leaves unanswered the question of how a visual medium like film can allow us to enter into an ethical relation with the Other if the Other is forever to remain beyond the perceptual field, or what is to prevent this very refusal of representation from eventually becoming a genre element one expects from any film dealing with the ethics of the Other. Should films avoid visual representations of the Other *in order to* remain "ethical"? Doesn't the notion of aesthetics as "prescriptive aesthetic codes and rules" contradict Levinasian thought, which seeks to get away from any [moral] prescriptions and rules? How can the critique of representation as such, under the pretext of respecting Levinas's thought, be reconciled with Levinas's other, equally important idea, that there is no ethics without risk, that, as Downing and Saxton themselves put it, "ethics becomes unethical if it does not expose itself to the possibility of betrayal and contamination inherent in political and juridical discourse, in the attempt to establish laws and rights"?[10] The way Levinas has been incorporated into cinema studies has led many scholars to assume that the refusal of representation somehow *guarantees* an ethical relationship to the Other, an idea that, in fact, goes against the spirit of Levinasian thought. Downing and Saxton fail to address Badiou's principal objection to the "ethical ideology" he associates with Levinasian ethics and with the sentimental ideologies of liberalism, namely the objection that there is no ethics in general, no general principle of human rights, because what is (deemed) universally human is always rooted in particular truths. It is not clear how Levinasian ethics can escape this critique given that the notion of "the Other" refers precisely not to a particular individual but to an abstraction. In the final analysis, Downing and Saxton's defense of ethical criticism against allegations that it is not political, or not political enough, rests on shaky grounds—to demonstrate the political potential of ethical criticism they propose an "ethico-political" approach by "locating the ethical in branches of film theory (feminist, queer, postcolonial) that are more usually thought of as political"[11] and that are particularly concerned with the politics (and thus the ethics) of looking, with problematizing "the right to look." It seems, however, that they are simply substituting one term (ethics) for another (politics).

Having located the ethical in specific branches of film theory, Downing and Saxton propose that "the ethical is the context in which *all* filmmaking takes place, since the creation and reception of a work of art always already engage desire and responsibility (for both artist and audience),"[12] urging us to expand the application of ethics beyond documentary cinema to which it has usually been limited. Thus, they have trouble defining the boundaries of the ethico-political approach they argue for, constantly shifting between *too broad*—"every aesthetic decision has an ethical dimension,"[13] that is, the camera's apparent neutrality does not signify moral indifference but a refusal to inscribe a moral perspective or an appropriate moral response from the spectator—and *too narrow* (only specific theories, such as feminist, queer, and postcolonial, are concerned with ethics) definitions of what "cinematic ethics" might look like. This definitional ambivalence could perhaps be seen as a reflection of the long-standing, unresolved philosophical problem of the relation between aesthetics and ethics, which Downing and Saxton trace from Kant, through Schiller, to Hegel. Taking its cue from Schiller's critique of Kant's privileging of the formal drive (to complement which Schiller introduced the sensuous drive), and challenging Hegel's demand for a correspondence between the Idea and its sensuous representation, ethical criticism reminds us that formally pleasing scenes of suffering are ethically problematic, just as films with a clear "moral message" are not aesthetically satisfactory, but in this constant arbitration of the "correct dosage" of ethics and aesthetics, ethical criticism cannot but open itself to the risk of turning into an "ethical ideology" that endlessly reapportions a relationship between two terms—ethics and aesthetics—that cannot be so easily defined themselves.

The subtitle of Downing and Saxton's book suggests that something has so far foreclosed or prevented the encounter between film and ethics or that they were bound to encounter each other (presumably because of certain affinities they share) but were prevented from doing so. The authors' comparative analysis of films they consider exemplary of ethical cinema—films they locate at the intersection of ethics, politics, and post-coloniality and thus at the intersection of theoretical work such as Derrida's reflections on hospitality and reconciliation, Spivak's work on responsibility and on the singularity of the subaltern, and Anthony Appiah's work on identity and cosmopolitanism—renders ethical criticism indistinguishable from postcolonial criticism so that an "ethical" representation of the Other appears to be simply one that allows the Other to represent herself, "tell her story." In contrast to white conscience films, which purport to critique global capitalism—for example, *The Constant Gardener* (2005) and *Hotel Rwanda* (2004)—but, in fact, subordinate Africa to a Eurocentric moral discourse, films like *Bamako* (2006), Downing and Saxton believe, offer the same critique but from the point of view of African characters and using a narrative influenced by African oral traditions, dismantling from within the dominant Western linear narrative.[14] Yet, one wonders what it means to praise *Bamako* for being concerned not just with the "ethics of globalization" but with "the globalization of ethics."[15] Isn't this simply a way of describing the proliferation of points of view and fields of reference in an increasingly globalized world rather than proving the emergence of a new type of cinema supposedly "beyond representation" à la Levinas? The question of how films negotiate asymmetrical power relations between characters, as well as between viewers and characters—particularly characters' suffering on screen—is by no means new or limited to "ethical criticism," yet even here Downing and Saxton fail to articulate ethical criticism's *specific* contribution to debates around ethics and politics. Instead, they remind us that most mediated suffering reflects the legacies of Western colonialism and imperialism and simply reiterate the two sides of the debate: those who maintain, like Sontag, that the discourse of pity and sympathy serves only to absolve the viewers from responsibility for the suffering they see represented on the screen, and those who believe, like Boltanski, that there is nothing "inherently pernicious in mediated witnessing of suffering," emphasizing instead "the ethico-political agency and responsibility of the viewer."[16] Ultimately, Downing and Saxton's study leaves us wondering how, or if, the incorporation of Levinas's notion of the Other enriches already familiar postcolonial readings of Eurocentrism.

The debates around what constitutes the proper basis for a genuine ethics have been accompanied by discussions about what constitutes a genuinely ethical cinema, as distinguished from what some have disparagingly called "a cinema of duty" (Sarita Malik's term). Analyzing the problems inherent in the "cinema of duty," Isabella Ballesteros observes that although on the surface immigration films seem to articulate a new cinematic ethics by providing "a symbolic space of both conflict and solidarity, a space for activism and the articulation of ethics and social justice,"[17] immigration films articulating a postcolonial white guilt—stressing the values of nomadism, moral consciousness, conscious strangeness, cosmopolitan commitment—"reveal more about white intellectuals and filmmakers than about the subjects they are trying to imagine or describe."[18] Put differently, their ethical commitment "is less about the nonwhite Other than it is about crises in national identities and how they are articulated both privately and publicly."[19] To illustrate her point, Ballesteros analyzes the rhetoric of expiation in a number of white savior narratives constructed around a white protagonist who, in rescuing people of color, "purges himself of whiteness and frees himself from the guilt and responsibility while also becoming a hero"[20] with whom the audience identify, becoming similarly absolved of their white guilt.

Although in her book *In Permanent Crisis* (2015), Ipek Celik does not focus specifically on immigration cinema, analyzing instead the ways in which mass media depictions of migrants and refugees shape cinematic portrayals of ethnic and racial Otherness in Europe, she draws attention to the emergence of a global moral economy of humanitarianism, which positions refugees, migrants, and minorities in Europe either as victims, calling for humanitarian intervention, or criminals, justifying the securitization of Europe. For Celik, pity and fear are the dominant affective registers in which racial and ethnic Others in Europe are represented as evidenced by the overrepresentation of refugees, migrants, and ethnic minorities in stories of crime and deviation such as illegal migration and religious fundamentalism. While pity and fear are part of the visibility and knowability of migrant Others, they are not political affects because they deprive the Other of agency.[21] Notwithstanding the shift in recent debates on violence in political philosophy from physical violence to structural or systemic violence and precariousness—experienced by many—migrants, refugees, and ethnic minorities continue to figure discursively as the only (or the most likely) victims of violence. As Graham Huggan observes cynically, with reference to the perversion of ethics into a marketing strategy, "cultural and ethnic otherness has become part of a booming alterity industry, making marginality a valuable intellectual commodity."[22]

Analyzing the conceptual functions of "Europe" in recent European films featuring migrants, Maria Stehle and Beverly Weber, in their forthcoming book *Precarious Intimacies: The Politics of Touch in Contemporary European Cinema*, assert that more often than not "Europe" functions as "a form of symbolic violence enacted (ironically) through gifts of welcome" inasmuch as, far from challenging the relationship of power between giver and giftee, the majority of films embed the act of hospitality in the idea of Europe as "the giver" and Europeanness as "the gift." Rather than acknowledge the role Europe has played in producing the conditions leading to forced migration in the first place, most recent films seek to awaken compassion for European characters by focusing on their feelings of helplessness and/ or guilt for failing to help refugees and migrants. Drawing on Derrida's distinction between conditional and unconditional hospitality—in the case of conditional hospitality the "foreigner" must request hospitality in a language that is not their own but one imposed by the space into which they seek admittance,[23] whereas unconditional hospitality demands the suspension of the very distinction between "guest" and "host," thus making the relationship between the two illegible as "hospitality"[24]—Stehle and Weber foreground the ways in which hospitality "offered in the context of economic structures that produce precarity, intersects with affect and intimacy as/and power" and thus remains embedded in Europe's colonial history and rendering impossible a reciprocal relation of hospitality between colonizer and colonized. In a yet unpublished article, Seung-hoon Jeong offers a more optimistic reading of hospitality and gift-giving by breaking up Levinas's unit of "self" and "Other" to reveal a "faceless Third"—what

Jeong calls "an abject-stranger"—whose otherness is indeterminable as friend or enemy, and who is better theorized through an ethics of "the neighbor" (Kenneth Reinhard, Eric Santner, Slavoj Žižek)[25] rather than "the Other." In the films Jeong analyzes "the hierarchy of the sovereign, the subject, and the abject is dismantled into the equality of abject-neighbors, who connect immediately to the other's very abjectness beyond cultural mediation or identity labels," and who walk *side by side* rather than *facing* (Levinas) each other.[26]

2 The Ethical Stakes of European Migrant Cinema

As I already suggested in the previous chapters, regardless of their stylistic and genre differences, the majority of recent migrant films can be said to share a preoccupation with the *ethical* limits of Europeans' responsibility to the "illegal" Other rather than with the Other's *cultural* difference. What is at stake in these films' ethical stance is the aporia, articulated by Derrida and Rodolphe Gasché, between unconditional and conditional hospitality.[27]

2.1 Hospitality, or the Value of a Life

In contrast to Levinas-inspired reflections on ethics and the Other in cinema, the way in which many films, starting with the Dardenne brothers' *La promesse* (1996), engage with the question of hospitality could be described as literal or unequivocal: they test the ethical limits of belonging to Europe by presenting a white European citizen with the dilemma of evaluating the literal value of a legal or illegal immigrant's life against that of their own or, in some cases, reverse the roles so that it is the migrant, rather than the white European, who must make the difficult choice. In this respect *La promesse*, which centers on the conflict between Roger, an illegal immigrants trafficker, and his teenage son Igor, who decides to help the family of one of those immigrants after the immigrant's accidental death (which Roger covers up), anticipates later films like Daniele Luchetti's *Our Life* (2010), in which the Italian protagonist has to cover up the accidental death of an illegal Romanian immigrant in order not to lose his own job, or Catherine Corsini's *Three Worlds* (2012), in which the French protagonist accidentally kills an illegal Moldovan immigrant and has to cover up his death in order to get the promotion and the marriage he has been working toward all his life. The Dardennes' later film *Lorna's Silence* (2008) reverses the question: this time it is the Albanian immigrant, Lorna, who must decide how much is worth the life of the Belgian citizen, the junkie Claudy, with whom she is in a sham marriage for the purpose of getting her citizenship. Lorna's plan is to divorce Claudy and have another fake marriage, this time to a rich Russian, in order to raise enough money for her and her boyfriend Sokol to open a snack bar in Belgium and get married. Everything goes according to plan until Fabio, the Italian mobster who has orchestrated the whole plan, refuses to wait for Lorna and Claudy's divorce, for fear of losing his Russian client. Despite Lorna's attempts to save Claudy, Fabio orders Claudy killed so that they can proceed with the original plan. Fabio tries to "buy back" Lorna by offering her 1,000 euros (supposedly for staying with Claudy and helping him out with his addiction), which she initially refuses but later takes, presumably to pay for the snack bar. After finding out she is pregnant (her pregnancy is never confirmed, serving as a symbolic expression of her feelings of guilt over Claudy's death), Lorna abandons her plans with Sokol, indirectly cancelling the 1,000 euros money transaction. The dilemma of evaluating the cost/price of one's life, or one's love/trust, is a motif that runs through many other films, which translate abstract ethical dilemmas into the mundane, vulgar language of money/exchange. Insofar as *Lorna's Silence* reflects on broad moral questions (do the ends justify the means?) through the prism of a pragmatic question (to what lengths are immigrants willing to go to secure the ultimate "official" symbol of belonging, the coveted EU citizenship that increasingly functions as a precondition for social and economic mobility), it simultaneously poses the question of the limits of neoliberalism: Is everything in life calculable, measurable in euros (hence numerous scenes in the film feature people counting and exchanging money or talking about money), and is there a place for ethics in this kind of world? Thus, the ethical limits of European identity are revealed to be inextricable from the ethical limits of neoliberalism.

The motif of the white European citizen faced with the impossible ethical task of evaluating the cost of another person's (legal or illegal immigrant) life reappears again in Loach's *It's a Free World* (2007), in which a group of illegal Eastern European immigrants, whom the white, British protagonist Angie owes money, kidnap her son and threaten to kill him. One of them tells Angie a story about a fellow immigrant's son, who lost his arm in a work-related accident for which the employer denied any responsibility and refused any recompense. Does she think that her son's life is worth more than that of this man's son, the kidnapper asks Angie. The question of the comparative literal value of a European's life versus that of an illegal immigrant, comes up again in Catherine Corsini's *Three Worlds* (2012), in which, in response to a French hospital's request that she donate the organs of her dead husband, Vera, the widow of an illegal Moldovan immigrant, furiously condemns France for exploiting immigrant bodies and asking them to donate their organs, the very organs that many immigrants have to sell to gain entrance to France. When Vera demands to know how much she will get for her husband's body, she is told that the human body is not a commodity and organs are donated freely. Where Vera comes from, however, everything has a price (a kidney is worth 30,000 euros, an eye 8,000 euros)—an immigrant's body is her only capital. The incompatibility of these two parallel "stock exchange markets"—one, in which organs are used as currency to enter the EU, and the other in which the EU requests illegal immigrants to donate their organs after refusing to pay them minimum wage or grant them legal status—is also dramatized in Damian Kozole's *Spare Parts* (2003), whose very title references the expendability of immigrant lives from the perspective of fortress Europe.

Atlantis 2003 (Michal Blaško, 2017)—the title plays on the connotations of Atlantis, here standing for "Europe," as a fictional/lost paradise[28]—is a road movie that could be seen as a variation on the biopolitical migrant film, in which migrants and refugees are forced to sell their organs in exchange for fake passports, becoming literally "bodies without organs," although Blaško is more interested in exploring the skewing of ethical values (everything is for sale, including love and trust) and the limits of ethical responsibility between refugees, rather than between Europeans and refugees. Set four years before Slovakia became part of the Schengen Area, the film follows a young Ukrainian couple, Martin and Denisija, as they try to cross the border into Slovakia illegally.[29] We gradually learn that the hardened Martin has struck a deal with their traffickers in Slovakia to "sell" them his girlfriend (who will presumably become another "Natasha") in exchange for a fake ID to continue his journey to Germany. At the last moment Martin, a refugee acting at the same time as his girlfriend's smuggler, changes his mind and decides to escape with Denisija but it's too late: the traffickers come to "collect their payment" earlier than agreed. In the last scene Martin is seen traveling alone, with a fake passport, on the train to Germany.

The same principle operates in those films in which a European must choose between his own life and that of another European (rather than a non-European migrant) or is forced to monitor/control his fellow man (echoing the culture of spying and reporting in formerly communist countries), for example, *The Measure of a Man* (Stephane Brizé, 2015)—in which an unemployed man, having lost his job as a factory worker, goes through a series of humiliating retraining courses before landing a job as a security guard in a supermarket where he is forced to spy on his coworkers—and its Portuguese equivalent, *Saint Georges* (Marco Martins, 2016), in which an unemployed factory worker and boxer (Jorge) struggling to keep his Brazilian wife and their son from leaving the country is forced to become a debt collector whose job is to intimidate his fellow countrymen who have defaulted on their loans. Jorge is faced with the dilemma of choosing between his financial and personal well-being (under the threat of losing his family) and the financial and physical well-being of regular Portuguese people struggling, like him, to make ends meet. As elsewhere, the question of the "price" one has to pay to stay financially afloat is framed in ethical or moral terms, that is, monetary debt is "translated" as ethical/moral debt, highlighting the dependence of neoliberalism's ostensibly objective, empirical socioeconomic nature on normative/ethical presuppositions (Chapter 1).

The regularity with which the discourse of the body as commodity, of bodies literally without organs, comes up in various films featuring migrants and refugees calls to mind Shakespeare's *The Merchant of Venice*, in which the Jewish usurer Shylock lends money to his Christian rival, the merchant Antonio, but demands a literal pound of Antonio's flesh as security. The absurd nature of the bond, which figures the human body as capital, is echoed in Scene 3, in which, after Lorenzo, a Christian, has eloped with his daughter, Shylock responds to a pair of Christians taunting him for intending to take a pound of Antonio's flesh:

> I am a Jew. Hath not a Jew eyes? Hath not a Jew hands, organs, dimensions, senses, affections, passions [. . .]?
> If you prick us, do we not bleed? If you tickle us, do we not laugh?
> If you poison us, do we not die? And if you wrong us, do we not revenge? If we are like you in the rest, we will resemble you in that.[30]

It is enough to replace "Jew" with "illegal immigrant" or "refugee" in Shylock's speech to hear its reverberations in the biopolitical films[31] analyzed in this chapter, particularly in those moments when a white European citizen is forced to "calculate" how much a human life is worth by choosing between his or her own life and that of an (illegal) Other. These similarities between *The Merchant of Venice* and recent films may not appear that surprising once we recall that, as Yosefa Loshitzky has argued, the illegal immigrant/refugee has now replaced the Jew as the "classical" Other of old Europe.

Although the French-Romanian comedy *Of Snails and Men* (Tudor Giurgiu, 2012) doesn't feature any immigrants or refugees, it shares common ground with the films mentioned earlier. Set in 1992, during Romania's "democratic transition period," the story centers around the closing down of a car factory, which employs most of the town's male population, following a deal with a French firm, which presumably intends to transform the factory into one canning snails while keeping 300 of its employees and laying off the rest. In reality, the French firm intends to sell the equipment and close the company for good. Unlike the workers in Perdo Pinho's *The Nothing Factory* (2017), who occupy the plant where they work after learning it is going to be dismantled, the workers in Giurgiu's film, led by the charismatic union representative Gica, have another plan: to buy the factory themselves by donating sperm to an American sperm bank, a "solution" which, as absurd as it sounds, is reminiscent of the organ donor theme in many migrant films, the difference this time being that those forced to sell their organs/sperm are citizens, not migrants, and what they seek to obtain is not a permission to enter Europe but a "permission" to lead a normal life in their own, European country. When the 300 men storm the sperm clinic, they are informed that their "product" is not worth much: the clinic's foreign clients demand handsome, well-educated, blond/ Aryan, preferably Danish, donors, not Romanian workers. The workers are faced with the complete devaluation of their only "capital," their bodies: their "worthlessness" is figured not only in terms of class—the proletariat's presumed lack of education makes it genetically undesirable for the purposes of reproduction—but also in terms of ethnicity (the Romanians' genetic value is considered inferior to that of the North Germanic ethnic group to which the Danes belong). In short, unlike refugees, Romanian workers turn out to be worthless even as "spare parts."

While the films discussed earlier pose the question of ethics as one of the literal value of European and migrant lives, a growing number of films frame the ethical dilemma within a coming-of-age story, which however becomes inflected differently depending on whether the protagonist is male or female. Films featuring male protagonists approach the question of an ethical relationship to the migrant Other through a teenager's/young man's struggle with paternal authority/aggressive masculinity (embodied by a father or a father-like figure). Inasmuch as both *Spare Parts* and *Daha* (Onur Saylak, 2017) explore the ethics of human trafficking within the context of a coming-of-age story, in which an initially innocent "apprentice"/bystander (Gaza in *Daha* and Rudi in *Spare Parts*) "comes of age" by becoming dehumanized, "toughening up" into a sadistic torturer and jailer of refugees,[32] they recall the Dardennes' earlier coming-of-age film *La promesse* (1996), in which moral awakening happens through a challenge to patriarchal authority (a teenaged son confronts his father, a slum landlord for illegal immigrants, over the moral implications of his exploitative business). In *Daha* teenaged Gaza works for his father Ahad, who owns a small truck for transporting fruit and vegetables along the Turkish coast, which he uses to smuggle Syrian refugees into Turkey and across the Turkish-Greek border, keeping them in a dark basement under his garage while he waits for good sailing weather. *Spare Parts* centers on former Slovenian speedway champ Ludvic, a middle-aged divorcee who spends most of his time drinking, smoking, and whining about globalization and the EU, and his young assistant Rudi as they run a lucrative business transporting Albanians, Turks, and Macedonians over the border into Italy. Rudi is at first appalled by his boss's unscrupulous exploitation of refugees and even breaks off his relationship with him but later resumes working for Ludvic. By the end of the film, Rudi, already hardened, takes over the business and hires a new assistant, another innocent, naïve youth like his former self. By the time Rudi and the other smugglers inadvertently cause the death of an African family (who suffocate in the trunk of the car used to smuggle them across the border), Rudi is able to get rid of their bodies without any pangs of conscience. *Young Tiger* (Cyprien Vial, 2014), set among the rarely screened Sikh community in Paris and tracking an illegal Punjabi teen's journey from clandestine outcast to human trafficker, is another coming-of-age story in which Many's moral choice is, once again, framed in terms of resisting patriarchal authority, here embodied by the trafficker's surrogate father figure. Rather than exploring cultural alienation, the film focuses on Many's conflicted loyalties to his family back home and to his smuggler who finds him illegal work, and the growing ethical and moral problems these loyalties present for him.

Unlike the aforementioned films, those with female protagonists frame the ethical dilemma through a feminist lens, focusing on questions typically explored by coming-of-age female stories, such as the right to one's body and female solidarity. *Fortuna* (Germinal Roaux, 2018) tells the story of a thirteen-year-old Ethiopian girl who, after crossing the Mediterranean, finds refuge in a Swiss Alpine Catholic monastery, where she falls in love with another refugee, Kabir, and becomes pregnant. When the police visit the monastery, Kabir is either arrested or disappears, leaving Fortuna even more alone than before. Most of the reviews of the film point to its spiritual and political dimension, or to the combination of elemental mysticism and the harsh reality of refugees' lives. The refugee crisis is not Roaux's main preoccupation, however—as he admits in an interview, his main interest lies in coming-of-age stories. The refugee story is used to point up the already unsettling, often solitary experience of entering adulthood. The final scene, in which Brother Jean discusses with a representative of social services what to do about Fortuna's pregnancy, folds the practical question of what to do with a pregnant adolescent refugee, whose chances of being adopted by a local family are almost nonexistent, into the larger, ethical question of how much can we really know the Other. The conflation of the ethico-political with the spiritual dimension is further underscored by the director's conscious choice to shoot in black and white, a decision predicated on the clichéd equation of black and white cinematography with a minimalist style, replete with the requisite Christian allegories (many scenes are framed as quasi-nativity scenes, and Fortuna's close relationship with a donkey is a clear reference to Bresson's 1966 *Au Hasard Balthazar*). Ultimately, Fortuna's refugee status is not that important to the film, which is more interested in her physical experience of abandonment and displacement than in her legal status, in her woman's rights over her body (the decision whether or not to keep the baby) than in her refugee rights.

Talkhon Hamzavi's *Parvaneh* (2012) is set, like *Fortuna*, in the Swiss mountains, and tells the story of another young (in this case Afghan) female refugee, Parvaneh, living alone in a transit center for asylum seekers outside Zurich. Upon hearing of her father's illness Parvaneh travels to Zurich to send her family money but the Western Union clerk refuses to let her send the money because she doesn't have a valid ID and is under eighteen. After trying unsuccessfully to solicit passersby to lend her their ID, Parvaneh finally convinces a Swiss teenaged girl to help her. The girl demands a portion of the money for her "services." The two girls form an unlikely friendship, bonding over their shared loneliness and alienation (here the film relies on a stereotypical contrast between the Swiss girl, who seems to have everything except her mother's love, and Parvaneh, who is physically separated from her family yet still very close to them). By the end of the story, their relationship has transformed from "donor" and "receiver" or "exploiter" and "exploited" to "sisters." Tellingly, as in the films discussed earlier, the transition to a genuine relationship of hospitality is figured symbolically through the Swiss girl returning the money she took from Parvaneh "as payment," a gesture redefining the nature of their relationship from one of convenience or profit to one of sisterhood. Not only does the film represent the inauguration of a genuinely ethical relationship to the Other through the cancellation of a monetary exchange—as in *Lorna's Silence*—but it also frames the ethical gesture of openness to the Other in terms of female solidarity: when a young man sexually harasses Parvaneh, the Swiss girl defends Paravaneh, who later returns the favor.

Desert Flower (Sherry Hormann, 2009), which tells the true story of Waris Dirie, a Somali refugee who became a top fashion model and social activist fighting to raise awareness about female genital mutilation, is not a film specifically *about* migration; rather, it uses the migration to tell a story about female empowerment (which the film conceives, ironically, in terms of her using her body as capital), an approach taken by many films featuring female migrants. Although Waris tells a BBC journalist that the day that changed her life was not the day she was "discovered" by a famous fashion photographer but the day her mother arranged for Waris's genital mutilation, this confession comes too late, after the film has already framed her emancipatory journey in terms of the nomad-to-fashion model story. Insofar as the film mixes elements of the migrant film with elements of the feminist film, while keeping the migrant's body center stage, it could be seen as a variation on the biopolitical migrant film, which foregrounds the ways in which the body of the migrant/refugee is reduced to human waste or "spare parts" for rich white Europeans, the difference here being that Waris's "value" is presented as "capital" rather than "waste." Her "value" is measured in terms of her body's profitability to the fashion industry. Indeed, her cynical agent estimates Waris's "value" to be so high as to justify violating the law in order to grant her legal status—the agent thus spends a considerable amount of money on a fake passport for Waris. The scene of Waris's photo shoot with the fashion photographer who "discovers" her dramatizes the "conversion" of Waris's human value into capital. Aiming for expressive shots the photographer asks Waris whether she is nostalgic for her home and her mother. As the camera clicks away it registers indifferently Waris's wordless responses to those questions, divesting them of their personal importance to her and reducing them to abstractly expressive shots of an exotic, racialized Other onto which the viewer is invited to project whatever they want.

2.2 The Trope of Adoption

If the question of the ethical relationship to the migrant Other is often posed in the literal (bodily) terms I have just discussed, the answer is equally often framed in terms of literal or metaphorical adoption. Here Alfonso Cuarón's *Children of Men* (2006) is particularly prescient, revolving as it does around a worldwide crisis of reproduction as a result of falling fertility rates and the miraculous pregnancy of an African refugee, who becomes humanity's sole hope for survival. Based on a 1992 novel by the crime author P. D. James, the film follows Theo, a former political activist recruited by his ex-lover, the leader of an anti-government resistance movement, to procure transit papers for the pregnant African refugee and escort her to safety, outside Britain, which locks up any asylum seekers blaming them for all its social, economic, and political problems.[33] The issue of reproduction as it relates to Europe's declining fertility rates is regularly taken up in European migrant cinema either literally—*Dirty Pretty Things* and *Spare Parts*, both referencing the harvesting of refugees' and migrants' bodies for "spare parts" to be sold to Western Europeans; and *Problemski Hotel*, in which Marina almost kills her baby to "buy" herself illegal entry into England—or metaphorically through the trope of adoption in films like *Diamantino, Le Havre* (Aki Kaurismaki, 2011), *The House by the Sea* (Robert Guediguian, 2017), *Welcome* (Philippe Lioret, 2009), *Eastern Boys* (Robin Campillo, 2013), *Jupiter's Moon* (Kornél Mundruzcó, 2017), *Good Morning, Aman* (Claudio Noce, 2009), *Con il sole negli occhi/ With the Sun in Their Eyes* (Pupi Avati, 2015), and others.[34]

Pawel Pawlikowski's *Last Resort* (2000), in which a Russian woman and her son accidentally become political refugees in a seaside town after the woman's English boyfriend abandons her, but are then welcomed by another Englishman, the local amusement park manager who becomes the Russian boy's surrogate father, anticipates the articulation of the notion of "hospitality" to the migrant Other in terms of the adoption motif. As we already saw, *Diamantino* figures hospitality to the refugee Other through the trope of adoption by having Diamantino adopt the lesbian Cape Verdean Aisha, who infiltrates his house by impersonating a young male African refugee. The gender fluctuation Diamantino experiences makes it possible for their adoptive relationship to eventually transform into a romantic one. In *Man at Sea* (Constantine Giannaris, 2011), a Greek tanker intercepts a refugee boat in the Mediterranean and the captain takes them on board against the orders of his shipping company and to the overwhelming disapproval of his own crew. His plan to deliver the refugees to various human rights organizations falls through, leaving the refugees stuck on the ship, which creates tensions among the crew and the captain and his wife, the latter still mourning for their drowned son, to whom one of the younger refugees bears a striking resemblance. Similarly, Andrea Segre's

First Snowfall (2013) traces the burgeoning friendship/surrogate father-son relationship—born out of shared grief—between an African refugee displaced in the northeastern part of Italy, where he lives in a refugee center with his baby daughter and mourns the death of his wife in childbirth, and an Italian boy who mourns the death of his father in an avalanche.

In *Le Havre*, which tells the story of an aging shoeshiner (Marcel) in the port city hiding an African illegal immigrant (the young Idrissa), the motif of adoption as a metaphor for a genuine relationship of hospitality between Europeans and refugees also plays a central role. The film depicts helping refugees as something self-evident, not a conscious decision that one has to mull over but an instinctive, natural human response—not a political issue but an unwritten ethical law. As the story unfolds the entire neighborhood transforms into Idrissa's adoptive family, hiding him from the authorities and taking care of him. Marcel's devotion to Idrissa is so sincere and complete that it even leads him to ignore his sick wife, who is ultimately cured of what appeared to be a terminal illness precisely through, as a metaphorical reward for, Marcel's act of unconditional hospitality to Idrissa. By contrast, in Lioret's *Welcome*, which tells a similar story, the hospitality the European character (Simon) extends to a refugee boy (Bilal) is not unconditional. Seventeen-year-old Iraqi-Kurdish Bilal has crossed Europe on foot, trying to reach London where his girlfriend has recently immigrated with her family. He is caught in Calais and sent to a refugee camp. Bilal decides that his only option to reach England is to swim across the English Channel, so he signs up for swimming lessons with Simon, a middle-aged swimming coach in Calais who is in the process of divorcing his wife. Initially unwilling to get involved, Simon eventually befriends Bilal, acting like his adoptive father although, as it becomes clear, mostly for personal reasons, namely to win back his estranged wife, with whom he doesn't have any children. Bilal's character is thus reduced to an inciting incident in Simon's personal story of redemption.

Something similar happens in *The House by the Sea*, which is set in a quiet town near Marseille, once a lively resort whose inhabitants have either died or sold out and left. The story revolves around the reunion of elderly restaurant owner Maurice's adult children—two brothers, one of whom has been running the cheap restaurant and the other a recently fired executive with literary ambitions, and their sister Angele, a theater actress—who find themselves, in the wake of their father's stroke that leaves him unresponsive, with the burdensome project of taking care of the family estate. This is Angele's first return to her father's home following an earlier tragedy (the accidental death of her daughter) for which she never forgave Maurice. What starts out as a family drama suddenly changes direction in the third part of the film as the three siblings, having been warned by soldiers patrolling the area of a boat of refugees capsizing somewhere along the coast, discover three North African refugee children (one girl and her younger twin brothers, an obvious mirror image of the three French siblings) hiding in the woods nearby. The late introduction of the refugee crisis subplot appears forced, however, especially when it becomes obvious that the generosity and hospitality with which the three siblings, especially Angele, welcome the children is ultimately made to serve Angele's personal, emotional needs: the three children are supposed to heal the pain Angele has felt all these years by filling the empty place of her dead daughter and allowing Angele to finally have her emotional catharsis. The adoption metaphor here implies a conditional hospitality, the condition being that the refugee children prove themselves "useful" or "necessary"—even if it is only emotionally—to the "long-suffering" white European mother.[35]

In contrast to *The House by the Sea*, *Eastern Boys* traces the gradual transformation of a mutually exploitative sexual relationship into an adoptive one based on filial love and unconditional hospitality. The film follows Marek, a young Ukrainian illegal immigrant in Paris, who begins an affair with Daniel, a French businessman. After taking part in an orchestrated invasion of Daniel's apartment, which ends up with Marek and his East European hustler friends stripping Daniel of all his possessions, Marek visits Daniel again, this time alone, offering his sexual services for cash. Soon Marek and Daniel begin a regular affair but over time their relationship evolves and as Daniel learns more about Marek's personal life (his real name is Rouslan and he is from Chechnya, both of his parents having died during the war), he becomes less interested in him as an object of sexual pleasure. Eventually Rouslan moves in with Daniel and learns to speak French while Daniel encourages him to break his ties with the gang of hustlers. The film ends with Daniel applying to legally adopt Rouslan. If the first part of the film, which tracks Daniel's and Rouslan's affair, presents both characters as exploiting each other, in the second part their sexual relationship transforms into a legitimate, filial one. Tony Gatlif's *Djam* (2017) also draws on the metaphor of adoption but in the reverse direction: instead of a Western European "adopting" either an Eastern European illegal migrant (as in *Eastern Boys*) or an African refugee (as in *Diamantino* and *Le Havre*), in *Djam* it is a Greek girl who metaphorically "adopts" a temporarily homeless French girl.

Heavily influenced (visually and narratively) by *Children of Men*, with echoes of *Blade Runner* (Ridley Scott, 1982), *Wings of Desire* (Wim Wenders, 1987), *The Exterminating Angel* (Luis Buñuel, 1962), and Tarkovsky's iconic levitation scenes, and drawing on several genres, including dystopian, retro-futuristic science fiction, superhero films, neo-noir, and supernatural thrillers, *Jupiter's Moon* begins with a title card informing us that Jupiter has sixty-seven moons, but "Europa" is the only one that might be capable of supporting life. Rather than finding "a cradle of life" in Europe, the film's protagonist, a young Syrian refugee named "Aryan" (yet another framing of the refugee crisis in terms of the Holocaust) is gunned down as soon as he enters it.³⁶ The film opens with the requisite sequence of a group of refugees embarking on a dangerous boat trip somewhere on the outskirts of Hungary. As immigration authorities begin firing into the water, Aryan is separated from his father and runs into the nearby forest where he is pursued by a worn-out cop, László, who eventually shoots him; however, instead of dying, Aryan floats above ground before dropping back down.³⁷ Later, Aryan finds himself in a refugee camp near Budapest where a corrupt surgeon (Stern) fired for malpractice (after operating drunk on a young man, thus causing the man's death) witnesses his levitation skills and decides to exploit Aryan by having him perform "miracles" for terminally sick patients. The film paints a macabre picture of a Europe, in which everyone is corrupt and living in bad faith: Stern is hoping to "pay an old debt," convinced that his ethical responsibility for the death of his patient can be measured in euros, Stern's lover (a nurse) is helping Stern raise money by accepting bribes from refugees, while the cynical László has no problem blackmailing Stern, threatening to expose Stern's illegal deal with refugees if Stern refuses to cover up László's unjustified shooting of Aryan.

Here, too, the European-refugee relationship is figured through the metaphor of adoption. When one of Stern's patients asks him whether Aryan is his son Stern responds affirmatively and while at that point he is lying, thinking of Aryan more as "his refugee" rather than as his son, the second part of the film, after Aryan's father's death and Stern's transformation from Aryan's exploiter to his most fervent "disciple," explicitly frames their relationship as that between a father and his adoptive son. Following the pattern already established in some of the other films analyzed earlier, the character of the refugee here serves as a mere trigger/mirror for white man's guilt and eventual redemption as well as a metaphor for a higher, spiritual/religious realm with which Europe has supposedly severed its former connection: thus, at one point Stern tells Aryan, "I wanted to keep you only for myself. . . . But you brought us a message. People forgot to look up. We live horizontally, in our networks." By denying the viewer access to Aryan's private feelings and instead treating the figure of the refugee as symbolically representing another, spiritual realm "outside history," the film perpetuates "the denial of coevalness" to non-Europeans of which traditional anthropology, history, and sociology—as we saw in the preceding chapters—have been found guilty. Indeed, *Jupiter's Moon* goes even further by explicitly making Aryan, a Muslim, into a Christ-like figure (when Stern asks him about his life back in Syria Aryan responds that his father was a carpenter). As a Christ-like figure with a gift for levitation Aryan alternates between the two faces of God, those of the New and Old Testament, sometimes acting as a benevolent angel who saves the suffering by killing them gently (he mercifully grants an old, sick woman her death, and there are a number of times throughout when civilians, noticing Aryan suspended in the air above them, fall to their knees in prayer), and at other times as an exterminating angel punishing mercilessly those who deserve to be punished (he drives a neo-Nazi to suicide). When Stern and Aryan show up at the neo-Nazi's apartment, he takes one look at Aryan before asking Stern whether he has started recruiting gypsies. Stern's response is to tell Aryan to "do his best" to impress (that is, punish) the patient. If *Diamantino* frames anti-refugee attitudes in terms of racial discrimination against Cape Verdeans, *Jupiter's Moon* reframes them in terms of Hungary's largest ethnic minority (the Roma), as does the Romanian comedy *Morgen* (the Roma are also Romania's largest ethnic minority). In short, in these films the refugee functions both as a figure of salvation/redemption[38] *and* a figure of punishment.

Insofar as it traces the transformation of a morally discredited European (Stern) from a jaded neo-racist exploiting his personal relationship with an "illegal alien" (a Syrian refugee) into the alien's ultimate protector, *Jupiter's Moon* recalls another dystopian sci-fi movie, Neill Blomkamp's political satire *District 9* (2009), in which a white South African transforms from a blind persecutor of illegal aliens into a politically emancipated defender of their rights. In *District 9*, a naïve bureaucrat (Wikus) is tasked with overseeing the mass eviction and relocation, backed by the privatized corporate security militia, of a million aliens, derogatorily called "prawns," stranded on earth for the past twenty years, from their current militarized ghetto home on the outskirts of Johannesburg to a rural "concentration camp." In the course of the eviction procedure, Wikus is exposed to an alien chemical and as his mutant DNA begins to transform him into an alien capable of operating powerful alien weaponry he becomes a coveted object both for the corporatized militia, who plan to harvest his tissue and body parts to create new biological weapons, and for the Nigerian gangsters who have been ruling over District 9 and buying off the aliens' illegal weapons. Suddenly finding himself betrayed by the company for which he has worked all his life, as well as by his own species, the half-human/half-alien Wikus teams up with a couple of "prawns" who can help him become human again if he helps them leave earth. Initially driven by purely selfish motives, Wikus gradually transforms into a freedom fighter defending the rights of dispossessed illegal aliens, a transformation that parallels his transition from human to alien. Although South Africa's specific history of racial relations complicates the comparison with *Jupiter's Moon*, it is notable that as an explicit allegory about a country still dealing with the after-effects of apartheid *District 9* frames the idea of a hospitable relationship to the Other (here the ultimate Other, aliens) in exactly the same way as films like *Diamantino* and *Welcome to Germany*, namely, through constructing the external Other as an impersonation of an internal Other: in the South African context, "illegal aliens" stand in both for black South Africans, the object of white South Africans' racism, *and* for Zimbabwean refugees, the object of neo-racist attacks by same-race (black) South Africans.

2.3 Ethics as Masochistic Self-Critique, or White Man's Guilt

In the Swiss multiple award-winning short film *Bon Voyage* (Marc Raymond Wilkins, 2016), a Swiss couple (Jonas and Silvia) enjoying a sailing holiday in the Mediterranean come upon an overloaded Syrian refugee boat about to sink. They call the Libyan coast guard but then lose the boat out of sight; the following morning they find themselves drifting, surrounded by dead bodies. Jonas and Silvia manage to pull a few survivors out of the water only to be confronted by their inevitable question: "Why did you sail away?" When Jonas refuses to steer the boat toward Europe at the refugees' request (he won't break the law, even for them), they tie him and Silvia up and take control of the boat; later, however, a rope gets twisted around the propeller and the refugees, in need of Jonas's help, are forced to untie them. This time Jonas lies he will steer the boat toward Crete, but instead calls the Libyan coast guard. Jonas and Silvia watch in disbelief as the Libyans violently transfer all the refugees—with the exception of a little girl whose mother hides her under a bench—to their boat. As the Libyans sail away, the girl climbs out of the boat and stands between Jonas and Silvia, a silent visual reminder of the horror for which they bear responsibility. Although it tries to individualize the refugees by giving them a voice and the agency to take control of their fate, however temporarily, *Bon Voyage* is *not* about the refugees but about the European couple's guilt, of which the Syrian girl remains merely a symbol.

As we saw in the Introduction, and as Pascal Bruckner argued forcefully in *The Tears of the White Man: Compassion as Contempt* (1983)—which mercilessly dissected the hidden superiority, under the guise of an "ethical stance," underlying Europe's "strategic" self-deprecation and "masochism" in the wake of anti-colonial movements—self-criticism and self-hatred have been, historically, the defining characteristic of Europeans. Ironically, even as Bruckner exposed Europe's self-hatred as just another manifestation of Eurocentrism he somehow managed to recuperate Europe's alleged superiority by framing this systematic self-criticism as an openness to other cultures (because to be critical of oneself one needs to be able to see oneself through the eyes of others), a quality that Europe can, he believes, "teach" other cultures:

> If there is one lesson Europe can teach others, it is self-criticism, something that we practice systematically. [. . .] Europe was scarcely born when it began to oppose itself, and because of having placed its own enemy within its heart, could open itself to other cultures without being swallowed up. It is the only culture that has been capable of seeing itself through others' eyes [. . .] the only civilization in history to have been able to reflect on its

own misdeeds. [...] The Old World's example has made it impossible for any nation today to escape from the obligation to criticize itself.[39]

Just as white man's postcolonial guilt often masquerades as compassion, too often the self-congratulatory, masochistic self-critique of migrant films disguises a deep-seated Eurocentrism.

This is to say that too often the "ethical turn" in the form of an "immeasurable debt to the Other" takes the form of self-loathing and self-flagellation; indeed, the most fascinating—and bewildering—aspect of recent scholarship on Europe and European cinema has been the transformation of the popular negative rhetoric of decline, decay, self-destruction, trauma, marginalization, Euro-skepticism, even Europhobia, into an implicit basis for a shared European identity and a source of political and ethical renewal for Europe: it's not a coincidence that the majority of winners of the prestigious LUX prize belong to what Anne Jäckel has called "an anti-European European cinema."[40] For Ravetto-Biagioli, precisely the strong anti-Europeanism of "mythopoetic cinema"—exemplified by the films of Jean-Luc Godard, Alexander Sokurov, Marina Abramovic, and Theo Angelopoulos—makes it "European." Along similar lines, in his discussion of Pierre Morel's film trilogy—*District 13* (2004), *Taken* (2008), and *From Paris with Love* (2010)—Neil Archer emphasizes the tension between self-hatred and self-love that characterizes European cinema's new "Europhobia-as-Europeanness" sense of identity. For Archer, it is precisely these films' shared Europhobic stance, revealing "a paranoid vision of the new Europe of porous borders, overcrowded metropolises and ethnic tensions,"[41] that constitutes their Europeanness, for "it is the very possibility of rejection, especially of dominant or fixed notions of identity that connotes a European idea (or even ideal)."[42] Archer points to film noir (on which Morel's trilogy draws) as a model for the contradictory coexistence of self-hatred and self-love. Recalling Edward Dimendberg's reading of film noir as both dystopian and utopian—inasmuch as "dystopian representation may also be utopian by virtue of its 'unsentimental illumination' of urban space,"[43] Archer asserts that, despite the apparent absence of traditional images of Paris as "the city of love," or rather, precisely thanks to this absence, the legacy of French poetic realism and of the wider tradition of the French polar, is still very much alive in Morel's trilogy. Although Morel's films paint a dystopian image of "contemporary Europe as a locus for global anxieties (uncontrolled immigration, declining economic power, terrorism, impotence of law and order),"[44] they also point up Europe's utopian imaginary, which finds expression in the films' attention to "counter-authoritarian practices and styles such as parkour or gangster chick"[45] so that the films "exploit our worst fears about Europe *only so we might love it all over again*—in the cinema, at least."[46] It appears that anti-Europeanism has become European cinema's big selling point.

Some have questioned the sincerity of this Europhobic stance. Speaking of the 2011 film *The Artist*, Mary Harrod, Mariana Liz, and Alissa Timoshkina admit to being tempted "to read [the 'masochistic strain given thematic expression by Valentin's period of increased self-loathing'] . . . in relation to a significant trend for self-definition through negative representations of Europe in its cinema."[47] European cinema, they argue, no longer defines itself in opposition to its traditional big "Other"—Hollywood; instead, "Europe itself may at times be the principal other in European cinema," so that "negative perceptions of Europe—even Europhobia—[are] central to the Europeanness of European cinema."[48] Having lost its external "Big Other" (Hollywood) as a source of identity, European cinema internalizes this opposition, now deriving its identity from its opposition to itself. However, as Harrod, Liz, and Timoshkina go on to remind us, too often Europe's "self-deprecation is . . . a strategy signaling knowingness and therefore a kind of perverse superiority."[49] It is precisely such "strategic" self-deprecation that drives Elsaesser's argument about European cinema's "new marginality," which he reads as freedom from the burden of having to reflect specific values.

Far from being "free from having to reflect certain values," European cinema is, in fact, expected to revive the ethical and humanitarian values of the Enlightenment and endowed with the ethical task of "bearing witness." Indeed, one of Elsaesser's primary examples of cinema as "thought experiment"—Michael Haneke's cinema—has become central to debates around the ethics of the image and the ethics of film spectatorship, demonstrating the increasing *expectation* that European cinema will engage with ethical and moral questions rather than simply enjoying its newly found freedom-as-marginality, something for which Elsaesser himself *praises* European films, specifically Haneke's, in his latest book.

Haneke belongs to a European tradition of modernist filmmakers that includes directors like Bresson, Antonioni, and Tarkovsky: for example, in interviews included on the DVD releases of *The Seventh Continent* (1989) and *Caché* (2005), Haneke readily acknowledges his interest in characters whose motives cannot be explained and in situations or conflicts that cannot be resolved. And yet questions of guilt, shame, responsibility, and Sartrean bad faith recur throughout Haneke's films, pointing, perhaps, to a (disguised) return of the religious in contemporary European cinema. Haneke's belief in the emancipating potential of an aesthetic of fragmentation, dissonance, and displeasure seems to place him within the tradition of the Frankfurt School's critique of mass culture. For Adorno, who identified the fragment as the last vestige of truthfulness in a mass society ruled by the culture industries, the goal of aesthetic experience was to overcome the attitude of "tasting" and "savoring," for in a false world all pleasure is false, including aesthetic pleasure. Rather than encouraging art to simply negate this false world, Adorno foregrounded the critical and demythologizing potential of mimesis—the modernity of art, he insisted, lies in its mimetic relation to a petrified and alienated reality, not in the direct negation of that reality, which would produce merely a "jargon of authenticity."

Still, despite the commonalities between Haneke's and Adorno's views on the status of the aesthetic under the conditions of mass culture, the sheer moral earnestness of Haneke's films remains at odds with Adorno's critique of pathos, seriousness, and responsibility in art. For Adorno, the more art tries to be dignified, the more ideological it becomes: the dignity of art demands that it give up the pretension of dignity. By contrast, Haneke's perversely pedagogical films are pervaded by an unmistakable sense of gravity—moral, ethical, political, and aesthetic—that no amount of wit or irony (let alone humor, of which there is little in Haneke) can dissipate, and by a punitive moralism that appears untimely and slightly embarrassing against the background of postmodernism's signature stance of affected affectlessness. If there is one filmmaker whose work conveys a sense of affectlessness and, *at the same time*, uncompromising moralism, it is David Lynch. When Jeff Johnson described Lynch as a "Po Mo Puritan," whose cool "postmodern" visuals and convoluted narratives conceal an untimely, Old Testament-like vision of the world divided between the "Forces of Evil" and the "Forces of Good," he could have been talking about Haneke.[50]

In Haneke's cinema of cruelty, we (Europeans) are all guilty by default. At one point in *Code Unknown* (2000), for instance, Haneke draws a parallel between two sets of photographs taken by Georges (a war photographer): the first set (seen in a montage sequence) consists of photographs Georges took in Kosovo, the second one (also a montage sequence) appears toward the end of the film and includes snapshots of people riding the Paris subway. The second montage sequence is accompanied by Georges' voice-over as he reminisces about his experience in Kosovo rather than commenting on the photographs we see. He recalls a time when he was mistakenly taken hostage. His original Taliban guard was eventually replaced by an American guard, who, in answer to all of Georges's questions, would ask him again and again, "What can I do for you?" This question, repeated several times over the blank faces of subway passengers, implicates them—and us, the viewers—visually and morally in the Kosovo atrocities, regardless of their actual knowledge of them. During the montage sequence Georges reflects: "It's easy to talk about 'the ecology of the image' and 'the value of the non-transmitted image.' But what really matters are the end results." The media are bound to present a skewed image of other people's suffering, and often use it to bolster up their own image as a vehicle of democracy. However, defending the "ecology" of the image, insisting on its undecipherability—on the absence or unknowability of a code—can be just as easily exploited as a justification for moral and political apathy. To question the ethics of media coverage of human suffering in Kosovo might be necessary, Haneke "teaches" us, but to claim that media coverage does not tell us—or cannot tell us—anything about what's going on in Kosovo, that the media only mediates a reality that continually recedes from us, is to wash our hands of this reality and justify forgetting it. Whether we believe there is no "code" (no possibility for an authentic relationship to the Other), or there is a code but it's unknown/unknowable (as in the film's title), we (Europeans, or rather Western Europeans) are always responsible, always guilty.

One of Haneke's most acclaimed films, and the one Elsaesser analyzes in detail in his latest book (see Chapter 2), *The White Ribbon* (2009)—a group-guilt drama set in a small German village just before the First World War and exploring "the roots of evil" through a series of mysterious acts of cruelty perpetrated apparently by no one—could be seen as the sadistic cinematic equivalent of Kracauer's *From Caligari to Hitler: A Psychological History of the German Film* (1947), in which Kracauer famously argued that certain prevailing social attitudes in Weimar Germany, reflected in the expressionist cinema of the period, "prefigured" the rise of fascism. *The White Ribbon* distills the numerous contradictions inherent in allegorical-pedagogical films[51] that purport to be political: the film was, at one and the same time, *praised* for its universal significance as a critique not only of fascism but of *any* totalitarian ideology (although the Baron employs a number of Polish workers, there is no quasi-Jewish Other that would serve as the target of the Germans' resentment, suggesting that the enemy might be within)[52] *and critiqued* for eschewing the question of moral responsibility by judging everyone—and thus no one—"guilty" by default.[53]

Like *The White Ribbon* Haneke's latest, *Happy End* (2017), is representative of the critically acclaimed masochistic self-critique characteristic of "anti-European European cinema." The film revolves around the Laurent clan, an aristocratic family in Calais headed by the misanthropic octogenarian Georges, who, having helped his wife suffering from dementia end her life years ago, is now suffering from incipient dementia himself and looking for someone to help him commit suicide. Georges's workaholic daughter, Anne, has taken over the lucrative family construction and transport business and is engaged to her British lawyer handling a new UK deal. Anne's brother, Thomas, is divorced and living in the family mansion with his new wife and their newborn son. Eve, Thomas's potentially sociopathic, computer-savvy daughter from his first wife, might or might not have caused her mother's drug overdose that sends her to the hospital thus forcing Eve to move into the palatial family home. There are also Anne's estranged son, deeply troubled by his family's complicity in the class system, who, through his negligence as construction site supervisor, puts the family firm in line for a huge civil suit and, finally, the family's Moroccan servants Rachid and Jamila, whose living quarters are in the basement and who are treated with benign racist condescension. Haneke's catalog of family dysfunctions of the European haute bourgeoisie, arguably intended as a catalog of the "sins of Europe," position it as a sort of sequel to his debut feature, *The*

Seventh Continent, which deals with the suicide of a bourgeois family. The differences between the two films have to do with the scale of the suicide—in the earlier film it's a collective (family) suicide, while in the recent one it's the attempted individual suicides of the family patriarch, Georges, and of the youngest family member, Georges's granddaughter Eve—and with the significance of their act (personal and literal in the earlier film, social and symbolic in the later film). If *The Seventh Continent* is a personal exposé of urban alienation exploring suicide as an existential choice in the face of modern life's vacuity, *Happy End*'s masochistic self-flagellation for Europe's colonial guilt entertains the idea of suicide as (in Haneke's eyes at least) a fitting punishment for Europe's sins encapsulated in the Laurent clan's self-absorption and obliviousness to the refugee crisis.

Although Haneke is unquestionably the master of "anti-European European cinema," he is not the only one. We witness the same perverse reversal of roles, typical of anti-European European cinema, through which the guilty white man comes to occupy the position of "victim"—*victim of his awareness of his guilt*—in films like *The Order of Things* (Andrea Segre, 2017), *Styx* (Wolfgang Fischer, 2018), and *The Unknown Girl* (Jena-Pierre Dardenne and Luc Dardenne, 2016). Segre has made several films about migrants, both documentaries and dramas,[54] but what is new about his latest, the morality tale *The Order of Things*, is that it flips perspectives, assuming the point of view not of a migrant but of a policeman (Rinaldi) working for the European task force in charge of immigration control. On one of his trips to Libya—where the Italian government has sent him to negotiate an agreement that would oblige Libya to prevent refugees from illegally crossing into Italy and host them in detention centers, in return for financial aid from the EU—Rinaldi is approached by one of the refugees in the detention center, Swada, a Somali woman who is trying to reunite with her husband in Finland and whose brother has just died (murdered by Libyan prison guards). Segre tries to present a more complex picture of the refugee crisis, deliberately refusing to depict refugees merely as victims and Europeans (or representatives of Europe's immigration authorities) as unethical perpetrators of human suffering. Indeed, the film seems to accomplish the impossible task of making the viewer empathize with Rinaldi, an otherwise efficient representative of the law, who is led to question his own ethical responsibility when he becomes accidentally acquainted with Swada. One might argue that his willingness to help Swada is hypocritical—after all, if *she* has the right to be helped then *all* refugees incarcerated in the detention center have the same right, yet Rinaldi never considers the possibility of helping all of them. However, by singling out Swada and focusing on Rinaldi's personal relationship with her the film suggests that ethics must always be grounded in individual cases or else it becomes a meaningless abstraction. The object of the unwritten ethical law cannot be a mass of refugees but only the single individual. Thus, the real standard by which Rinaldi's ethics is to be judged, at the end of the film, is not his generally principled, well-intentioned insistence on treating refugees humanely and punishing those responsible for human trafficking but rather his conscious decision *not* to help Swada after all, even though he has already arranged her escape to Finland.

The reason why Rinaldi changes his mind is not given, though we can assume his decision is motivated by his awareness that even if he helps Swada there are many others he cannot help, by a general fatigue (from which his French colleague also suffers, prompting him to resign from his current post) and by the inertia of accepting "the state of things" even at the cost of the inevitable pangs of conscience, of which Rinaldi is very much aware. At first, the film suggests that although Rinaldi is a good man— he does his job conscientiously while seeking to uphold certain ethical standards, including the rights of refugees to be treated humanely—he is not (yet) an ethical subject, because he is concerned (only) with upholding universal human rights in principle. It is only when he meets Swada, who makes a personal ethical demand on him, that Rinaldi is really faced with the ethical implications of his work. He responds to her ethical demand— he arranges for her escape—but his ethical response is then revealed to be unethical precisely because it is not generalizable into a universal ethical law (he cannot help all refugees escape). Although the film initially questions the notion of ethics as a universal, abstract principle and demands a passage through the singular, the individual, ultimately it rejects the response to a singular demand as unethical precisely because it is not generalizable to a universal principle.

It is in this irreconcilability between the singular and the universal that the film's tragedy lies, and it is also thanks to it that Segre succeeds in establishing empathy for Rinaldi despite the latter's ultimate indecision. Rinaldi is positioned as a tragic character, a perfect illustration of Aristotle's definition, according to which although a tragic character has a fatal flaw the audience should feel pity for him because he is a good person who falls from good fortune not because of some depravity or vice but "through no fault of his own." Ironically, although the film seems to (want to) judge Rinaldi for his weakness (for his backtracking from the decision to help Swada), it ends up providing him with an implicit alibi by suggesting that what happens to Swada and the other refugees is not his fault but the fault of the EU's "senseless and unethical immigration policies," thereby locating the ultimate ethical authority in some abstract, nebulous realm (the EU). Thus, while the film questions the politics of accepting "the order of things" it also reaffirms "the order of things": it absolves Rinaldi by revealing the full measure of the ethical dilemma he faces, and redirects the blame/responsibility to various EU institutions.

One could also argue, however, that the ethics of the film lie not in presenting its protagonist with an ethical choice—he actually makes the "correct" ethical choice when he decides to help Swada—but rather in presenting him with an ethical dilemma that is, by definition, unresolvable (because of the loop from the universal to the particular and back to the universal). Paradoxically, Rinaldi's *realization* of the dilemma is precisely what makes him an ethical character and solicits our identification with him. In fact, not only does the film depict Rinaldi as a man of integrity but it also succeeds in positioning him as a victim *as a result of* (because of) his awareness of the ethical dilemma. Inasmuch as Rinaldi's knowledge of his own complicity in the unethical treatment of refugees exonerates him, to an extent, from the guilt he obviously feels, the film confirms Richard Dyer's astute observation that "white liberal guilt at its most performative has the additional effect of diverting attention from the facts of white racism to how badly the Enlightened Liberal feels about it."[55] Something similar happens, as we already saw, in *Fire at Sea*, which displaces our empathy from the refugees to how badly the enlightened European (the doctor) feels about the refugee crisis.

The opening sequence of *Styx* (Wolfgang Fischer, 2018)[56] introduces us to an efficient German doctor (Rike) who is part of a medical team dispatched to the site of a car accident. The film then shifts gears as we watch Rike prepare for a long, solitary sailing journey to Ascension Island. The first third of the film is devoted to tracking Rike's daily routine of navigating the boat and enjoying the solitary pleasures of going for a swim in the ocean, basking in the sun, reading *The Creation of Paradise: Darwin on Ascension Island*, an illustrated book about Darwin's ecological experiment,[57] and watching the sunset. A heavy storm briefly interrupts her idyllic journey, a natural disaster for which Rike is, however, very well prepared and even forewarned by a fellow skipper. The film establishes Rike as a self-sufficient woman while also underscoring her privileged status as a white European (she is German) for whom sailing alone through the Atlantic Ocean is a well-planned and secure (there are numerous shots of the reliable equipment for navigating the boat and charting the journey at Rike's disposal) pleasure trip to a romantic destination, Darwin's artificial paradise, rather than a life-threatening journey she is forced (by circumstances beyond her control) to go on. It is not the storm that ultimately disturbs Rike's journey but the fishing trawler overcrowded with refugees she notices after the storm clears. She makes a distress call to the Coast Guard, who promise that help is on the way and order her not to intervene. Rike waits in vain as she watches refugees fall or jump to their death. One boy (Kingsley) swims over to her boat, on the brink of dying from dehydration and exhaustion. Rike takes care of him but when he pleads with her to save the others (his sister is on the boat) she explains to him they have to wait for help because her boat is too small.[58] Desperate, the boy continues to plead with her for help while Rike repeats her distress calls to the Coast Guard, who stop promising help and, instead, demand that Rike confirm she will obey the order not to intervene (preventing Rike from intervening appears more important than sending out help), and to the other skipper (the one who warned her earlier about the storm) who refuses to help, explaining that he cannot risk his job, to which Rike replies, "You are obliged to." Realizing that no help is forthcoming any time soon Rike makes a fake distress call: she reports that her own boat is sinking and proceeds to turn off her radio and sail back to the refugee boat to look for survivors. Predictably, the Coast Guard respond to her distress call quickly and send a rescue team to transport the few remaining survivors and the dead refugees' bodies to Malta. Placed under surveillance and informed that she is now part of an "inquiry," Rike is asked to fill out a number of forms, a request to which she does not respond, seemingly in shock from the moral apathy she has just witnessed. Although Rike responds to Kingsley's plea to do something by telling him she has "no answers," the film's position on the "right" response to the refugee crisis is clearly spelled out through the choice of a medical doctor as a protagonist and through Rike's own response to the fellow skipper, who declines to help her, that he is "obliged to help," a response that posits the Hippocratic oath as an ethical model for Europe's response to refugees: the ethical (ethico-medical) response to a single, white European citizen in distress (the car accident in the opening sequence) ought to be the same as the collective response to non-European refugees in distress, and it should supersede any national or supranational laws and regulations regarding immigration.

While the choice to tell the story from the point of view of a medical professional seems to invest the film with the ethics of hospitality advocated by enlightened liberal Europeans—positing Rike's individual ethico-medical response as a universal law—it could also be read in the opposite way, namely as suggesting that Rike's response to the situation was dictated by her professional training, thus making it impossible to be universalized into an ethical law. Furthermore, although the focus here is not on "white man's guilt," as it was in the films discussed earlier (given Rike's limited resources she could not have done anything more than she did), given that Rike is the protagonist, it is her horror, bordering on emotional numbness, at the Coast Guard's moral apathy—rather than the refugees' response to being rescued accidentally (thanks to Rike's fake distress call) or even their death (most of them die before the arrival of the Coast Guard)—that takes center stage at the end of the film. Although *Styx* deliberately tries to subvert the clichéd white savior narrative, it still invites the viewer to identify with the emotional response of the failed white savior, to *both* "feel bad" *with her* (morally shocked, rather than guilty) at the cynicism of the Coast Guard—the latter remaining conveniently invisible (we only hear their voices) so that responsibility for the loss of human life is, once again, displaced onto anonymous EU authorities—*and*, perversely, to feel bad that Rike, a woman of integrity, has had her idealized notion of moral and ethical duty, embodied by the Hippocratic oath, unceremoniously crushed and exposed as fake, as fake as Darwin's artificial paradise she was so excited to discover on her luxurious journey of "self-discovery." *Styx* juxtaposes the white European's dream of an "artificial paradise" (Darwin's "Edenic garden") with the refugees' dream of Europe as an (equally artificial) paradise, which becomes, for the majority of refugees, their burial site. It's impossible to miss the cruel irony that while both Europeans and refugees dream of an artificial paradise, the refugees' romantic idea of Europe as "Eden" is exposed as "artificial" in the sense of "false," whereas scientists believe Darwin's experiment in producing a self-sustaining, self-reproducing ecosystem could be used to create future colonies on Mars. Still, Rike's failure to reach the paradisical island that was her final destination reveals the European's paradise, too, like the refugees' idea of Europe-as-paradise, to be a "lost paradise": the film's opening shots of domesticated monkeys wandering in the parking lots of Malta, rather than swinging wildly from lush palm trees Rike dreams of, introduce early on this idea of "paradise" as *always already* lost.

In *The Unknown Girl*, the Dardennes' overly symbolic collective guilt drama, a young female doctor (Jenny) becomes obsessed with finding out the name of a dead woman after she fails to let her into her clinic late one night. Like the films discussed in Chapter 2, *The Unknown Girl* implicitly conflates racial identity with immigrant status: although Jenny knows nothing about the dead woman, having only seen the video footage from the surveillance camera, she automatically assumes the dead black woman is an illegal immigrant; in short, the film becomes a vehicle for the atonement of white guilt. The object of Jenny's self-directed criminal investigation provides her—the educated and financially stable white woman—with the desired emotional catharsis; worse, when at the end of the film the dead woman's sister confesses to Jenny her own feelings of guilt over her sister's death, her confession sounds terrifyingly close to an apology, as though she were apologizing to Jenny for having made her feel guilty "in vain" thereby absolving Jenny of her "imaginary" guilt. Although the film is titled *The Unknown Girl* and the whole story revolves around finding out the name of the girl as a symbolic gesture of restoring her identity to her (presumably a reference to the thousands of African illegal migrants who perished in the Mediterranean, remaining nameless), the story focuses on Jenny, cast in the familiar role of the white savior who must fight on behalf of the nameless and the voiceless, while the dead girl (whose name, we learn at the end, is Felicia), whose ghost haunts the entire film, is present merely as a symbol of white guilt. Like *Styx*, *The Unknown Girl* frames the ethical question of what we owe one another as human beings in terms of medical ethics, but while *Styx* suggests that medical ethics ought to serve as a universal model in arbitrating the ethical response to refugees, *Girl* reveals the limits of this model: after all, it is precisely *because* the earnest Jenny follows strictly the rules of the medical profession—not allowing oneself to be carried away by emotions, which would interfere with making a good diagnosis, and not letting patients in the clinic past clinic hours when doctors are tired and cannot make the proper diagnosis—that Felicia dies.

2.4 The Ethics of Affect: Between Affective Over-investment and the Withdrawal of Affect

How, then, do we distinguish a genuinely ethical cinema from the "cinema of duty"? Does the discourse of pity and sympathy serve only to absolve the viewer from responsibility for the suffering represented on screen and, if this is the case, should we assume that the deliberate draining of affect guarantees a more authentic, ethical relationship to the migrant Other? Shot in over twenty countries, Weiwei's *Human Flow* (2017) presents a sweeping view of the global refugee crisis. Although at one point Weiwei offers a "definition" of refugee—"someone who has reasonable fear of being persecuted in his country for religious, political, ethnic and other reasons"—the very fact that he feels it necessary to travel through twenty-three different countries to get a "representative" idea of the global scale of "human flow," rather than examining in detail one country, or even one group of people in one country and their reasons for migrating, suggests that what concerns him is the global reach of the phenomenon, *the spectacle* of migration, rather than its historical particularities, causes, and effects. Weiwei's aestheticization of migration is already evident in the film's opening peaceful shot of a boat on the sun-kissed Mediterranean sea: since the boat is not immediately recognizable as a refugee boat the image remains aesthetically pleasing in its vagueness. The film closes with a similar shot—an enormous pile of safety jackets on the coast, which becomes "readable" only when the camera reaches a certain distance from the pile, before it dissolves again into the unreadability of an abstract painting. Weiwei's primarily aesthetic concerns—his interest in what migration *looks like*, rather than in *what it means*—is also evident in the overall lack of balance between the aesthetic and documentary/reporting modes: the startling, often surreal beauty of many of the shots sits uncomfortably with the more conventional documentary parts, in which Weiwei burdens the screen with statistical information and interviews a wide range of experts only to provide us with informational bits easily accessible via any news channel. When we do get some respite from the information overload it is generally through heavy-handed metaphors, as when Weiwei spends some time on portraying the transportation of a tiger from Egypt to South Africa, where, presumably, a better life awaits him, showing the great bureaucratic lengths to which animal activists and the governments involved are willing to go, opening national borders for the sake of a single animal but keeping them closed to millions of human refugees.

One of the most illuminating moments in the film comes toward the end when Weiwei visits the refugee camp inside Berlin Tempelholf. The little girl he interviews there complains of being bored most of the time and not being allowed to leave the camp without her parents. Here, finally, Weiwei's self-serving humanitarian concerns cannot overshadow the purely existential aspect of the refugee experience. One of the humanitarian workers Weiwei interviews explains that what they are trying to do in he camp is make the refugees feel human rather than just a number. Unfortunately, despite his humanitarian intentions—or perhaps precisely because of them—Weiwei never accomplishes the same for the millions of refugees we glimpse briefly in *Human Flow*: they remain numbers rather than individual human beings. At the same time, and ironically, precisely by limiting his interest to the purely cinematic look of migration—focusing on the framing and composition of individual images and on the rhythm of editing similar images taken in very different parts of the world (the repetition of the same type of shots, or of shots taken from the same distance in different countries or continents)—Weiwei manages to convey the anonymity of refugee camps, spaces that evoke the "any-space-whatever" (Deleuze) of the post–Second World War period.

Weiwei's concern with the perceptual limits to grasping migration rather than with understanding the reasons behind it might account for the prevalence of high overhead drone shots that seek to capture the sheer scale of people's movements across the globe, often evoking the Kantian mathematical sublime. The film's visual and narrative abstractness is matched on the affective level: intending the film as a general appeal to our humanity, Weiwei inserts himself in almost all the shots, covering distraught refugees with a blanket, offering them hot tea or listening, with empathy and understanding, to their tragic stories. On many occasions the self-congratulatory feel of such shots, which emphasize the humanitarian role Weiwei believes himself performing, becomes too uncomfortable to bear, as when Weiwei playfully exchanges passports with one refugee and tells him that he "respects his passport," adding as an afterthought that "he also respects him." Weiwei's repeated quasi-political gestures in the film notwithstanding—in one scene he takes a selfie holding a handwritten sign "#Istandwith refugees"—*Human Flow* is not a political film for, as Rancière argues, art is political not when it follows a consciously elaborated and specific political or pedagogical agenda but, on the contrary, when it purposefully withdraws from the "duty" to be political: "Art is not political because of the messages and sentiments it conveys concerning the state of the world. Neither is it political because of the manner in which it might choose to represent society's structures, or social groups, their conflicts or identities. It is political because of the very distance it takes with respect to these functions."[59]

If *Human Flow* suffers from *affective overinvestment*, Gianfranco Rossi's critically acclaimed *Fire at Sea* (2016) deliberately refuses to build any affective relationship between the viewer and the refugees who make it, dead or alive, to Lampedusa. The film depicts the refugee crisis as a thoroughly *mediated* experience, something both the inhabitants of Lampedusa and the film viewers learn about or hear about but do not experience directly. *Fire at Sea* alternates between the storylines of Samuele, a young boy living on the island with his father and grandmother, an old widow, a radio host, a doctor, and the nameless refugees whose arrival on Lampedusa is not represented as a specific event taking place at a particular place and time but rather as a recurring phenomenon to which the locals have become as habituated as they are to natural phenomena like sea winds and tides. The film opens with a shot of enormous radio satellites turning against the night sky—a beautiful, poetic image, if it were not for the conversation we hear, off screen, between a boat full of refugees lost at sea, desperately asking for help, and the Italian Coast Guard trying to locate their position—and then cuts to a shot of the rescue boat, which, without a single human visible on board, looks like a ghost ship, as abandoned in the middle of the Mediterranean as the refugee boat we don't see. The opening sequence, glaringly devoid of human life, sets up the tone for the rest of the film, which represents the refugee crisis as a phenomenon that exists in the "reporting mode" only, with no single sequence privileged visually, narratively, or in terms of emotional appeal or affective resonance. All sequences following the search and rescue mission privilege the reporting mode, further distancing us from the refugees' experience: for example, we only see the representation of the search on computer screens in the helicopter and on the boat—we never see a human being looking at the computer, as if the technology of "care and control" operates on its own, on autopilot, as if the refugee crisis is like one of those automatically recorded images we get back from sending a probe out in space. Later, as the members of the Coast Guard help the refugees off the boat, the dialogue remains in the reporting mode as disembodied voices exchange factual information about the refugees' medical condition without registering any emotional response to the situation. The absence of shot-reverse shots reinforces the sense of absolute, unbridgeable distance between refugees and Italians, and by extension between refugees and viewers.

The two parallel realities depicted in the film—the daily life of the locals of Lampedusa and the refugees' tragedy—never touch even though they take place in the same space and time. At the same time Rosi, somewhat disturbingly, suggests an oblique analogy between the dangerous life of sailors on Lampedusa and the refugees' dangerous sea journey. In one scene Samuele asks his father to tell him what the life of a sailor is like and listens with incredulity as his father tells him of the many occasions when he had to remain on the boat for six or seven months, always at sea, seeing only the sky and the sea, far from home, sleeping in uncomfortable bunk beds and sharing the small room with other sailors. In another scene, Samuele spends a rainy day with his grandmother, listening to her stories of how she used to bring bread to his grandfather when he had gone out fishing all day because the sailors were afraid to go out fishing at night on account of the navy ships passing by, as it was wartime. The navy ships would fire rockets at night and "it was as if there was fire at sea." Later, Samuele goes out fishing with his father but feels sick and throws up (as many refugees making the sea journey do). His father advises him to stand on a ponton bridge to build up his stomach so that being at land and at sea would be the same to him. In yet another scene the old widow calls the radio to request a song, "Fire at Sea," for her son, a fisherman stranded upon the shore, unable to go out fishing on account of the bad weather. The radio host dedicates "Fire at Sea"—a wartime song—to all fishermen prevented from going out fishing, that is, from earning their livelihood. One gets the uncomfortable impression that such scenes are supposed to draw an analogy between the sailors' feeling of homesickness when they find themselves stranded at sea, far from home, and the experience of being forcibly removed from their homeland, unable to ever return, experienced by refugees, or between the dangers of fishing at night during war time and the dangers of refugees crossing the sea at night in peacetime.

Once the refugees have disembarked, members of the Coast Guard, wearing protective facial masks, begin the long process of registering them. The camera remains static as men and women of different ages take their place in front of it. "Blank" and "expressionless," these "portraits" are both informationally and affectively empty. Unlike *Mediterranea* (Jonas Carpignano, 2015) (see Chapter 4), which makes use of the liberated, handheld camera and employs deliberately imperfect, imprecise framing to intensify the viewer's identification with the migrants in the film, Rosi's static shots and long takes, though often startling in their surreal beauty or horror, put the spectator in an affectively catatonic state, essentially depriving her of the ability or desire for a human response to the refugee crisis by denying agency to both Italians and refugees and presenting both as passively enduring the crisis as something that simply happens to them, like a storm at sea. The only time the refugees are given—literally—a voice is in a scene when, gathered in a room, praying, one of them sings, in recitative, what he calls their "testimony," a "testimony" that remains abstract and symbolic rather than familiarizing us with the particular circumstances of individual refugees, who are depicted as a homogenous mass. Instead, the film invites us to identify with the Italian doctor, who functions as the film's moral conscience, as he recounts how difficult it has been for him—the enlightened white European—to do his job.

A similar *dis/misplacement of affect* takes place in Alexander Sokurov's *Francofonia* (2015), subtitled *An Elegy for Europe*, which mournfully reflects on the often tragic fate awaiting works of art as they "migrate" from one country or continent to another as the spoils of war, considering this tragedy—rather than the human tragedy of the refugee crisis, which remains in the background—as nothing less than the twilight of humanism and universalism. Blending documentary with dramatic reconstruction, *Francofonia* tells the story of how an ingenious conspiracy hatched by a French civil servant and a German count managed to save the collections of the Louvre from the Nazis. Sokurov laments the fragmentation of Europe both during and in the aftermath of the Second World War, but also in the wake of the refugee crisis, an event that is only briefly glimpsed, overshadowed by the filmmaker's self-consciously profound, mournful meditation on the timeless value of art. Throughout the film we periodically see the director, sitting in his office, skyping with a Dutch skipper, who is having such difficulties in the mid-Atlantic that he is thinking of throwing out his precious cargo of artworks due for restoration. Even as Sokurov laments the refugee crisis and the fragmentation of the continent, the viewer cannot but feel that the real object of his lament are the masterpieces lying at the bottom of the ocean rather than the dead bodies littering the ocean floor, of which nothing is said in the film in spite of the appeal to French universalism and to "noble" ideals such as Liberté, Égalité, Fraternité.

3 The Ethical Potential of "Co-presence"

With "co-presence" emerging as the dominant theoretical paradigm to describe the migrant's/refugee's deregulated experience of time and space (see Chapter 1), over the last decade "co-presence" has also come to dramatize a *heightened historical consciousness,* as evidenced by European films' growing tendency to frame the ethical questions raised by migrants and refugees in terms of past forms of oppression and marginalization, with the Holocaust serving as the ultimate ground for legitimization.[60] Films like *Transit* (Christian Petzold, 2018), *Happy as Lazzaro* (Alice Rohrwacher, 2018)

and *Dead Europe* (Tony Krawitz, 2012)—in which the past is *literally* made present—can be read as responding to a long-standing debate about the relationship between representation and the "unrepresentable," for which the Shoah serves as the ultimate model. Jean-Michel Frodon's edited volume *Cinema and the Shoah* (2007) is the most comprehensive study of the multiple voices in this debate, from those who, like Frodon himself, posit the Shoah as "the crisis of the visible" and a question of/for cinema, and argue that its unrepresentability constitutes both the aesthetic and ethical criterion according to which films about the Shoah ought to be judged,[61] to those who, like Marie-Jose Mondzain, believe that thinking of the Shoah as unrepresentable, as "Radical Evil," precludes the possibility of expressing the past in the present, of allowing the Shoah to enter history not in order to forget it but precisely to *make it live in the present.*[62]

Ironically, both Rohrwacher and Petzold have stated that they wrote their scripts abroad—in New York and California/Nevada, respectively—

because Italy's and Germany's past was "too much in the present." One way to approach the time warping in these films is by situating their experimentation with time in the context of the larger question about the time–space paradigm specific to neoliberalism. As Mitsuhiro Yoshimoto has argued, specific conceptions of filmic time and space, and the notions of time and space prevalent in a particular historical period, are mutually imbricated.[63] Although Yoshimoto is mainly concerned with accounting for Hollywood films' conception of time and space as infinitely malleable, European films can be productively approached through the same lens, with the understanding that the time–space paradigm undergirding *Transit*, *Lazzaro*, and *Dead Europe* is that of unresolvable copresence (of the past in the present) rather than that of the malleability/multiplicity of time and space, which, as I have argued elsewhere, Hollywood usually treats as confusing but ultimately empowering.[64]

Lazzaro and *Transit* are not the first films to approach the subject of migration, violence, and globalization through temporal and spatial displacement: films like Otar Iosseliani's *La chasse aux papillons* (1992) and Gianni Amelio's *Lamerica* (1994) could be seen as their predecessors. Like *Lazzaro*, Iosseliani's film traces the arrival of neoliberal globalization in a picturesque French village, where time seems to have stopped, focusing on two aging representatives of the former French aristocracy, Marie-Agnès de Bayonette and her cousin Solange, living in a magnificent villa in the hills over a nearby village, lost in their own world of memories, old photographs, and old wealth and oblivious to the rapid social changes around them represented by real estate development interests from the nearby town (whose local magistrate tries to persuade the cousins to sell their family home to a Japanese investment group) and by the arrival of nonwhite, non-European immigrants from Asia and from France's former colonies. When Marie-Agnès dies unexpectedly she leaves the estate to some poor relatives in the Soviet Union, who eventually sell it to the Japanese. Although Iosseliani depicts the decline of one social class and the rise of the nouveau riche in post-Soviet Russia (the film ends with yet another historical turning point as the aging Russian heir watches, through her window, the anti-communist parades in the streets of Moscow) with the apparent objectivity of a historian or an anthropologist studying the vanishing of one species and the appearance of a new one, a latent nostalgia suffuses not only the shots of quaint village life against which the arrival of Japanese investors and their attempt to inscribe themselves in the French way of life appear absurd and "inauthentic," but also the film's title—*Chasing Butterflies*—which positions the old (French) way of life as something fragile and beautiful (like a butterfly), whose chase and eventual capture (neoliberal globalization) destroys it.

Anticipating *Good Bye Lenin!* (Becker, 2003) the neorealist-like *Lamerica* explores the overlapping/haunting of two supposedly different historical periods—in order to expose the continuities between them—through an amnesiac protagonist. In the opening sequence a newsreel bombastically recounts Albania's colonization by Mussolini's army in 1939, presenting it as an act of "civilizing" the backward Balkan country. The story proper begins fifty years later as fascism and communism have both (supposedly) become a thing of the past and Albania is about to be "civilized" again, this time by Western capitalism. Although Albania is no longer Italy's puppet fascist state, it has now entered, predictably enough, the next, neocolonial phase of its national history, with desperate Albanians welcoming their former Italian colonizers, who present themselves as Albania's benefactors, while the Italians themselves (notably Fiore) continue the colonialists' infantilization of colonized subjects, dismiss Albanians as "children," gullible and deprived of rational thought. In 1991, following the fall of communism, Italian con artists Gino and Fiore travel to a lawless Albania to set up a phony shoe factory in order to get their hands on Italian state subsidies to Albania's postcommunist economy. Looking for a front for their fake company they stumble upon a traumatized seventy-year-old anti-communist political prisoner, Spiro, who has been driven mad and amnesiac by twenty years of hard labor in communist labor camps and who looks indistinguishable from a concentration camp victim, blurring the distinction between communist and fascist labor camps and thus between two opposed political ideologies.

Later we find out that Spiro is not an anti-communist hero but an Italian, Michele, who deserted Mussolini's army in 1939 and went into hiding under an Albanian name but was never told that the Second World War had ended and thus still expects to return home to his wife and baby in Sicily (the film thus relies on the trope of impersonation/disguise discussed in Chapter 2). When Spiro/Michele runs off, Gino travels through the poverty-stricken Albania to find him. As Gino sets on the road to look for Spiro he meets roving bands of poor, barefoot Albanians (played by non-professionals) coming down from the mountains and villages and traveling on overcrowded dusty buses and trains to port towns, where they hope to board ships to Italy (many of these images foreshadow more recent media images of refugees trying to get to Europe), and is himself dispossessed of everything he owns, that is, everything that sets him apart as "Italian" (his Suzuki jeep, his chic sunglasses, his clothes, and finally his passport) and imprisoned (after the Albanians discover his ruse). Indistinguishable from the desperate Albanians, Gino is last seen boarding an old ship (significantly bearing the name "Partizani") bound for Italy, the Albanians' idea of "paradise." A series of documentary-like close-ups of the faces of anonymous undocumented immigrants, including Gino and Spiro/Michele (who believes the boat is headed to "L'America" where he will start a new life as an Italian émigré), on the ship recall/overlap with the faces of over four million impoverished immigrants that immigrated to America in the beginning of the twentieth century (fleeing rural poverty in Southern Italy and, later, fascism) thus hinting at one possible meaning of the film's title:

what Italy represents for postcommunist Albanians—the dream of a better life—America represented for Italians a hundred years earlier.⁶⁵

In *Lamerica*, as in *La chasse aux papillons* and *Lazzaro*, allegedly different sociopolitical regimes—in the case of *Lamerica,* fascism, communism, and global capitalism (a memorable scene features a starving, barefoot Albanian girl's perversely bizarre dance mimicking Michael Jackson's dance moves she has seen on Italian television)—become indistinguishable, each one merely reproducing the economic and political structures exploiting the proletariat/precariat. Insofar as it follows the "fall" of a cynical, self-righteous Western European citizen (on numerous occasions Gino invokes, in vain, his Italian citizenship as "grounds" for special treatment) from a "somebody" (a European citizen) to a "nobody" (an 'illegal' migrant forced to return to his own country as a refugee, having been deprived of his Italian nationality and of his privileged membership in the EEC), the film speaks to contemporary debates around "European identity" and "European citizenship," underscoring their formal rather than primordial nature and thus their precariousness/fragility as markers of belonging, for they can be taken away just as easily as they have been granted, as Gino learns when the Albanian police confiscate his passport, informing him that in Albania no one has documents and thus, by a perverse logic, Gino's legal presence in Albania *demands* that he be as illegal as all Albanians.⁶⁶

3.1 *Happy as Lazzaro*

In a book that remains as relevant today as it was at the time of its publication in 2002, Mike Wayne identifies two important sources of Europe's shared past (apart from Roman law, Renaissance humanism, and Enlightenment rationalism): (1) Europe's colonial and postcolonial legacy, and (2) various revivals of collectivism and solidarity, notably the Spanish Civil War, which raised the question of whether the fight against fascism can be separated from the fight for a revolution, a question central to Ken Loach's *Land and Freedom* (1995) and, though less explicitly, to *Happy as Lazzaro*. Significantly, both films draw on the same Biblical figure, Lazarus of Bethany, the subject of a prominent miracle of Jesus in the Gospel of John, in which Jesus restores Lazarus to life four days after his death. Figuring prominently in literature, popular culture, and science, "Lazarus" denotes the apparent restoration to life: for instance, the scientific term *Lazarus taxon* refers to certain organisms that reappear in the fossil record after a period of apparent extinction, a terminological meaning that is very much a part of Rohrwacher's political-allegorical frame of reference. Translated into present day terms, the question raised by the Spanish Civil War—whether the fight against fascism can be separated from the fight for a revolution—becomes the question of whether the struggle against the far right, that is, the struggle for the rights of migrants and refugees—regularly framed as the contemporary "reincarnation" of the Jews, with the extreme right seen as a "reincarnation" of fascism—can be separated from the struggle against neoliberalism (see Chapter 4).

Land and Freedom tells the story of David Carr, a young worker and member of the Communist Party who leaves Liverpool and travels (illegally) to Spain to join the International Brigades but coincidentally ends up being recruited by a POUM (The Workers' Party of Marxist Unification) militia, fighting alongside other foreign volunteers. After being wounded, and following his recovery in a Barcelona hospital, he finally does join the International Brigades, but after witnessing Stalinist propaganda and repression against POUM members and anarchists he returns to his militia group. The film clearly spells out the terms of David's choice: fight with POUM and the anarchists against Franco and for a revolution *now*, or join the International Brigades and accept to "postpone" the revolution or, in terms of present day Europe, fight against the extreme Right or fight *both* against the extreme Right *and* against neoliberalism, with the struggle against neoliberalism now cutting through the traditional right-left divide.

It is precisely at the point in the narrative when David makes his choice that Loach's film—arguably, far less experimental narratively or stylistically than *Lazzaro*—makes a reference to the figure of Lazarus: when David returns to his militia group he is greeted enthusiastically with the words, "Oh, Lazarus has come back from the dead!" Although both films resort to the figure of Lazarus in their realistic (Loach) and magical realistic (Rohrwacher) political allegories of Europe, the symbolic meaning with which the films invest this figure could not be more different. Rohrwacher's Lazzaro is a pure (or naïve, depending on the point of view), Christ-like figure unaware of his own political and economic condition, whereas Loach's David-as-Lazarus is a man who momentarily makes the wrong political decision—abandoning his fellow fighters and friends to join the government-backed International Brigades—but, after "seeing with his own eyes" (as David himself puts it) the workings of Soviet propaganda, returns to his militia group to fight against *both* fascism and capitalism, *against* Franco and *for* a revolution *now*. Thus, while Loach draws upon the figure of Lazarus to represent symbolically David's attainment of class consciousness and his transformation into a "political subject" in Rancière's sense of the term, Lazzaro's main symbolic function is to represent the reproduction of class relations rather than the attainment of class consciousness; in fact, as we shall see, Lazzaro could be seen as the embodiment of *false consciousness*.

Lazzaro tells the unusual story (based on a true story) of a group of villagers exploited by a woman ("the Marchessa") as unpaid labor to harvest tobacco for her, despite the outlawing of sharecropping as a practice in Italy in the early 1980s. In his review of the film Jonathan Romney approaches *Lazzaro*, with its elements of fable, folk, tale and hallucination and its references to the historical rural realism of Ermanno Olmi or the Taviani brothers, as an instance of "magic Neo-Realism."[67] While the first part of the film is set somewhere in rural Italy, in a secluded village named Inviolata ("unspoiled"), the second part, in which the film's protagonist, the holy fool/saint Lazzaro, literally "comes back from the dead," moves to the outskirts of an unnamed bleak Italian city (this part was shot in Turin) where Inviolata's former inhabitants now live—or rather survive—in a roadside silo.

The purposeful withholding of any temporal and spatial coordinates establishes the film's allegorical nature early on. The film begins in the dark, literally keeping us in the dark as to where (and when) we are.[68] As Inviolata's inhabitants argue over who should have the single light bulb they all share, we assume the action takes place in the beginning of the twentieth century, a suspicion seemingly confirmed by the strange marriage ritual we see unfolding in the dim light. Lazzaro's marginal status in Inviolata is established in the very first shot, which finds him outside the house, staring into the void, as he is apparently wont to do. He is summoned inside and ordered to join the other musicians and carry *nonna* to the table so she can partake in the food and wine passed around to celebrate the newly married—Lazzaro himself is not treated to any food or wine but he doesn't seem to mind (the only person who seems to show some kindness to him is a young mother, Antonia), for he is a combination of a saint and holy fool, a Forrest Gump-like boy-man, "a good man." His incorruptibility is signaled throughout the narrative, for instance through his association with nature—in one enchanting scene the villagers, out harvesting tobacco leaves, call out to Lazzaro and as the camera pulls back to reveal the big field of tobacco leaves gently swaying in the wind it seems as though the whole field is calling out to Lazzaro.

Once we have been introduced to the farmhands of Inviolata, their "owner," the Marchessa, and her son, Tancredi, come for a visit, in the course of which Tancredi strikes an unlikely friendship with Lazzaro. Tancredi exiles himself up on the hill, in Lazzaro's hideout, from where he tries to blackmail his mother by pretending he has been kidnapped and demanding that she pay the "ransom." Later, Tancredi disappears mysteriously during a big rainstorm and even after falling ill Lazzaro continues looking for him until he falls down a cliff, only to be "resurrected" and magically transported through time, waking up a couple of decades later, without having aged at all. The "resurrected" Lazzaro finds his way back to the Marchessa's house, now in ruins, where he interrupts a robbery by the grown up Pippo and Ultimo, Antonia's son and husband. The two manage to get rid of Lazzaro for a while and as he continues walking to the city he merges with a flow of unemployed, illegal immigrants of different ethnic and racial backgrounds, a potent image encapsulating the reproduction of the system of inequalities, the peasants and workers of the past now replaced by the refugees and illegal migrants of the present. Eventually Lazzaro runs into Pippo and Ultimo again and they drive him to the drab outskirts of a nearby city, where Lazzaro is reunited with his Inviolata family. He is not particularly welcome: while Antonia kneels in front of Lazzaro, convinced this is a miracle, the others are more interested in gauging Lazzaro's potential usefulness to their household. Antonia tries to "recruit" Lazzaro to "sell" some of the antiques they have stolen from the Marchessa's house, but although she is successful she decides not to use Lazzaro any more, presumably for fear of corrupting him. Soon Lazzaro runs into Tancredi, an unexpected reunion that seems to give the aged Tancredi some hope for the future. He takes Lazzaro, his "good luck charm," to see a German banker, hoping to convince him to invest in Tancredi's family's lost property. Realizing too late that Tancredi actually doesn't own any property, the German banker, beside himself with anger, calls Tancredi and Lazzaro "a parody," commenting on their anachronistic position within the new neoliberal system of classes and values symbolized by the European Central Bank (whose headquarters are in Germany).

In an allegorical film meant as a critique of class relations and of the reproduction of injustice, the choice of a "good man" as a protagonist seems obvious, just as it is inevitable that this kind of essentially melodramatic narrative will figure the protagonist as a victim constantly exploited/made to suffer undeservedly. In this respect *Lazzaro* appears like a perfect illustration of what historians Rene Sigrist and Stella Ghervas have called "the victim paradigm." Throughout the twentieth century, Sigrist and Ghervas argue, Europe was a victim of two totalitarian systems, fascism and communism. The contemporary multicultural "European cocktail" of common values and bricolage of identities is a product of the attempts of various groups to reclaim their identity by positioning themselves as victims of one or both of these systems, often relating their own oppression to previous forms of oppression in their own country or in other European countries: for example, homosexuals frame their claims through an analogy with the extermination of the Jews. Other marginalized and oppressed groups, from feminists, through ethnic minorities, and more recently refugees and stateless people, have followed suit. History has thus become a source of legitimation for these groups, leading to an unprecedented recalibration of values in European societies, which now tend to valorize victims, granting them a special symbolic status. Being a victim has become a durable state, justified and protected by the law, that reproduces itself in a quasi-hereditary fashion, granting the descendants of victims certain rights not accorded to other citizens.[69]

While at first Sigrist and Ghervas appear to be critical of the victim paradigm—drawing attention to its various abuses by different groups—ultimately they suggest that precisely this victim paradigm could serve as the ground for a shared European identity inasmuch as by challenging "les lieux de memoire national" with their transnational claims victim-based groups—

for example, second- and third-generation immigrants, refugees, and asylum seekers—could offer a way to transcend the classical inter-European schisms that have so far defined European history and reform European values along the lines of compassion and solidarity (to/with victims). From this point of view, the parallel emergence of victim groups with similar claims in different European countries—syndicalists, feminists, ecologists, homosexuals, refugees and their defendants—could be seen as evidence of the birth of a civil European society. Thus, if the Jews "served" Europe by offering it a way to define itself as "a lieu de memoire" (the Holocaust as a source of a shared European memory/identity), these new victims—especially immigrants/refugees—offer the newest transnational/European version of "lieu de memoire." Notwithstanding this optimistic conclusion, Sigrist and Ghervas recognize the danger that, rather than being only a transitory stage in the rebirth of European identity, the affirmation of these victim identities and the reparation of their claims could actually lead to the eventual social decomposition of Europe.

Sigrist's and Ghervas's analysis is particularly illuminating in the context of *Lazzaro*. For one thing, Lazzaro is a figure with whom Europeans who perceive themselves as disenfranchised in some way can easily identify, a figure onto which different social groups can project their own claims phrased in terms of victimhood. Although the film invites comparisons with Bresson's 1966 *Au Hasard Balthazar* (itself inspired by a passage in Dostoevsky's *The Idiot*), which follows a donkey as he is given to and mistreated by different owners, such obvious similarities are complicated by the important question—which the film leaves unresolved—whether Lazzaro himself realizes he is exploited (it is clear that, objectively speaking, he is), that is, whether he is aware of his own victimhood. When Tancredi, the Marchessa's rebellious son, asks his mother if she feels guilty that she is exploiting the farmhands, she responds cynically: "Human beings are like animals. Set them free and they realize they are slaves and locked in their own misery.[70] Right now they suffer but they don't know it. Look at him [Lazzaro]. I exploit them and they exploit him. It's a chain reaction that cannot be stopped." "But maybe he doesn't exploit anyone," Tancredi muses, a hypothesis the Marchessa dismisses bluntly as unthinkable. Although the film leaves no doubt as to whether or not Lazzaro exploits anyone (he doesn't) it is less clear how we are supposed to read Lazzaro's attitude toward his own predicament. Consider, for instance, the part in which Tancredi distracts Lazzaro from his regular work duties and asks him to make him coffee. However, when Lazzaro takes Tancredi to his secret hiding place up on the hill and makes him coffee, Tancredi castigates Lazzaro for not working with the other farmhands. Genuinely surprised, Lazzaro responds that he is not working because Tancredi ordered him not to. What this scene makes clear is that Lazzaro never acts out of his own free will, to satisfy his own needs or desires; whatever he does he does because he has been ordered to do it. The idea that he could disobey an order has never even occurred to him. When he says, "I am a good worker," what he means is "I am a good slave," that is, one who has fully internalized the idea that he should be, at all times, at the service of others. At the same time, however, because Lazzaro also belongs to a long tradition of holy fools, the film also invites us to read his willingness to serve as generosity or altruism, a voluntary (Christ-like) submission to the Other's wants and needs that liberates him from the master-slave dialectic into which he would have otherwise been trapped. In short, Lazzaro is either a slave or a saint. But which one is he? Whether or not Lazzaro is a victim, and whether or not he is a slave or a saint, depends on whether he is a "subject" (in Rancière's sense of the term) and thus conscious of his position in the social, political, and economic order, that is, whether he is class-conscious. It is here that the film, which attempts to combine politics with fable/allegory/magic realism, begins to flounder or, alternatively, reveals the subtlety and complexity of its apparently straightforward symbolism. On one hand, Lazzaro, as we see on numerous occasions and as we are told in voice-over, is "a good man," a description that puts him immediately outside the sphere of politics, in the realm of the fable where "good" and "evil" are "natural," that is, given qualities with which certain characters are endowed solely for the purpose of moralistic storytelling. The fact that Lazzaro does not know his parents and cannot remember—does not care to remember—his own origins (like the protagonist of *Problemski Hotel*) adds to our perception of him as a merely allegorical figure endowed with certain properties (such as "goodness"), which cannot be expected to change in the course of the story—in short, a *figure* rather than a *character* (a "figure" has no character arc). On the other hand, the film's ending suggests that Lazzaro undergoes a radical change, one signaled by the poignant moment when, for the first and only time, he cries—the only time the film grants Lazzaro an interior life. This intimate moment, in which Lazzaro becomes conscious of, and reacts personally to, the suffering and injustice he witnesses—a moment in which, we might say, he becomes class-conscious—is followed by a radical decision to act on this realization.

But of what exactly does Lazzaro become conscious? What injustice does he seek to "correct" by going to the bank? Has he finally become aware of the injustices perpetrated against Inviolata's inhabitants who, even after they have seemingly been "emancipated" from their feudal position, continue to be exploited and abandoned by the same system that claimed to have emancipated them? Not really. Soon after Antonia brings him to the roadside silo where she lives with the other villagers, Lazzaro is informed of "the Great Swindle" and shown the newspaper article that led to the villagers' "emancipation" and to the Marchessa's arrest. Surprisingly (or not, as we shall see shortly), Lazzaro does not respond indignantly to this piece of news, for he does not see his (and their) past life in Inviolata as an instance of oppression or exploitation but quite simply as "the order of things." In a later scene, after Lazzaro runs into the now older Tancredi, Tancredi invites him and all the villagers to lunch at his house. When they arrive, however, the villagers are turned away by Tancredi's wife, who explains to them that the bank has ruined the Marchessa's family and confiscated all her properties. Hearing about Tancredi's ruination Lazzaro exclaims, "The Great Swindle!" Although Antonia and the others remind him that "the great swindle" refers to their own victimization and oppression at the hands of the Marchessa, Lazzaro ignores the explanation and is deeply moved by what he perceives as a great injustice done to the Marchessa's family. When, several scenes later, he cries softly under a decorative tree lit by artificial light we are to understand that he has finally become class-conscious, only—ironically—conscious of the injustices suffered by the wrong class, not the class he, and the other villagers, belong to. This is confirmed by the film's last scene, in which Lazzaro goes to the bank to demand that Marchessa's properties be returned to her and her family. Since the villagers, including himself, used to belong to the Marchessa as well, what Lazzaro actually demands is his (and the others') reenslavement and the restoration of the "utopia" that "Inviolata" represents for him, but which the spectator is clearly meant to see as a "dystopia." Lazzaro's demand thus confirms the Marchessa's earlier words to Tancredi that all men (what she really means are the lower classes) are slaves who would rather stay slaves than be emancipated. Arguably, at this point in the story Lazzaro transforms from the saintly, pure figure he was in the beginning of the film into a reactionary figure, an obstacle to class struggle. Nostalgic for the old, pre-neoliberal form of oppression, which for him does not represent oppression but simply the "natural state of things" in which both sides, the peasants and the ruling class, know and accept their places, Lazzaro wants to restore the status quo. It is *not* Lazzaro but the former farmhands—now the lumpenproletariat—who, at the end of the film, begin to show signs of class consciousness as they consider, for the first time, the possibility of resistance (Pippo proposes, half-jokingly, to return to Inviolata and squat in the Marchessa's house "without bosses").

The ambivalence of Lazzaro's character is also foregrounded through the contradictory ways in which religion is used in the film. Clearly, Lazzaro is a Christ-like figure of unquestionable moral and ethical integrity and humility. In one beautiful scene he and the farmhands enter a church to listen to someone playing the organ only to be kicked out because the concert is "a private function." Lazzaro leaves the church but the organ music follows him outside, underscoring the difference between the fake religiosity of the church and the genuine Christian values Lazzaro embodies. However, other scenes unambiguously depict religion as "opium for the masses." In the beginning of the film, when the cunning, hypocritical Nicola, the Marchessa's "representative" in charge of managing her property, arrives in Inviolata to settle accounts—that is, calculate the "inevitable" increase in the peasants' debt—he summons the village kids with "Let the little children come to me" only to offer them cheap candy as a way of ingratiating himself with the villagers and making them see him as "one of them" (something he does again in a later scene when he mocks the Marchessa to show that "he is on their side"). In another scene we hear the Marchessa, reading from the Bible, lecture the farmhands' children about the importance of faith over knowledge: "One should go beyond the thirst for knowledge, which is the source of great disappointment and distraction. What good is knowledge without the fear of God? A humble servant is better at serving God than an erudite scholar who neglects himself." The mobilization of Christianity as a strategy for maintaining class differences and guaranteeing the reproduction of capitalist exploitation also underlies Nicola's praise of Lazzaro as a "model worker" aka model slave, one who works fast and follows orders, no questions asked. In yet another scene exposing the perversion of Christianity into a strategy for keeping oppressed people blind to their oppression, Nicola praises the wine and bread the villagers serve him, reassuring them that their "wine and bread" are authentic while those consumed by rich people in the city are "contaminated" and flavorless. Nicola invites the villagers to embrace their own oppression under the guise of authenticity that their forced, unpaid labor and their connection to the land—a reference to the perennialist notion of national identity which invests the land, and those working it, with the nation's "essence"—supposedly grants them. And yet, despite these jabs at religion as opium for the masses, the film insists on the importance of faith (through Lazzaro's Biblical figure) in sustaining people as a sort of "passive resistance" to capitalist exploitation.

Perhaps the best example of the complex intermingling of equally ambivalent religious and political meanings in the film is the supposedly brotherly relationship between Lazzaro and Tancredi, the Marchessa's spoiled son who feels bored in the countryside until he convinces Lazzaro to help him blackmail the Marchessa, an act Tancredi sees as a "revolt" against his mother's feudal beliefs. One might read Tancredi's name as a reference to Tancredi's character in Visconti's *The Leopard* (1963), an adaptation of Giuseppe di Lampedusa's eponymous novel chronicling the changes in Sicilian life and society during the *Risorgimento*. The novel tells the story of Don Fabrizio Corbera, a nineteenth-century Sicilian prince who, as a result of political upheaval, finds his position in the class system eroded by newly moneyed peasants and minor gentry, and is forced to choose between upholding the continuity of upper-class values and accepting the inevitable death of his class to secure the fortune of his family, in particular his nephew Tancredi. In the novel the corrupted Don Calogero Sedara, eager to upgrade his social status, "pimps" his beautiful daughter Angelica to Tancredi. The engagement of Tancredi to Angelica effectively dramatizes the displacement of the hereditary ruling class by the middle class, and the replacement of monarchy by democracy, while on the surface everything remains the same. Something similar happens in *Lazzaro*, in which middle-class Nicola orchestrates the marriage of his daughter Angelica to the aristocratic Tancredi, while a few decades later we witness their ruination at the hands of "the bank" (presumably as a result of the EU's austerity measures). Michael Wood has argued that while Visconti's film seems to center on Don Corbera, the central character in the sweeping historical changes Italy goes through is actually Tancredi who embodies a new kind of ruthless political and social opportunism evidenced by his shifting allegiances from Garibaldi's insurgent army, which he joins for a while, to the king's army.[71]

In *Lazzaro* Tancredi wears what looks like a worn-out, red, Garibaldi-soldier military jacket, while his conversations, or rather monologues, with Lazzaro present him as a Garibaldi-like figure, whose rhetoric seeks to destroy the class divide between the aristocracy and the peasants in some utopian vision of Italian unity. *Lazzaro*'s Tancredi is as charming as Alain Delon's Tancredi in Visconti's film, his romantic rhetoric of brotherhood enticing Lazzaro into believing that they are "half-brothers." Tancredi paints their joint rebellion—and his own position within it as Lazzaro's "emancipator"—in noble colors, telling Lazzaro that they have to fight the Marchessa "like two cavaliers of old." To "seal" their class-defying brotherhood, Tancredi makes a sling (which immediately malfunctions) and demands that Lazzaro kneel (as if to be knighted) so he can offer him, with a highly ritualized gesture, "the weapon" with which "they will fight all the Marquises of the world." Like Visconti's Tancredi, *Lazzaro*'s Tancredi remains an ambivalent character. Just as Visconti's two-faced Tancredi famously declares, "For everything to stay the same, everything must change," *Lazzaro*'s Tancredi may passionately appeal to Lazzaro as his "brother" and seek to "emancipate" him so he can join Tancredi in his revolt against class privileges, but he still exploits Lazzaro for his own purposes: for example, he asks Lazzaro to sign the blackmail letter with his blood because Tancredi is too weak to do it himself. Like the novel's and Visconti's Tancredi, who initially joins Garibaldi's insurgent army, *Lazzaro*'s Tancredi thinks of himself as rebelling against the class system, which privileges the aristocracy and enslaves the peasants, but he is also an opportunist: he plans to "fund" his rebellion—in the form of a relaxing self-exile up on the hill—by pretending he has been kidnapped for ransom (a trick that, as we learn from the Marchessa who refuses to play along, he has pulled on her before). In several scenes the high-minded Tancredi asks Lazzaro to describe what he sees around him only to rebuff him and offer another way of looking at reality, a gesture that could be read either as emancipatory ("teaching" Lazzaro not to accept things as they are) or as escapist (fictionalizing, instead of facing, reality).

Lazzaro shows the perpetuation of class inequalities by tracing the historical continuity between the aristocracy and the petit bourgeoisie of the past (the Marchessa, Nicola) and the exploiters of the present, the European

Central Bank and the traffickers of illegal labor like the older Nicola, who is seen recruiting dozens of multiethnic, multiracial illegal workers by "auctioning" available jobs to those who offer to do them for the least amount of money. However, the most important class (for Marx)—the working class—is missing from the film: instead, there is Lazzaro, blissfully unaware of being exploited, and the farmhands, who are vaguely aware of some injustice being done to them but whose "revolt" is limited to absurd little pranks and side comments. Di Lampedusa's novel was criticized by both conservative and leftist critics, the former objecting to its depiction of the aristocracy's decadence, the latter attacking it for its criticism of Italian unification and the destruction of the nobility and for its non-Marxist depiction of the Sicilian working class. *Lazzaro* could be criticized, along similar lines, for its ambivalent political stance, which alternates between a critique of the class system and a certain melancholy "for the old times"—for all its social injustices life in the little village of Inviolata, the film suggests, seems like a veritable heaven compared to the struggle for survival in the scavenging urban present.

3.2 *Transit*

Like *Lazzaro*, *Transit*, an adaptation of Anna Seghers's 1944 novel *Transit*, is an allegory explicitly engaged with Europe's current political and humanitarian crisis. Like Rohrwacher, Petzold intentionally keeps the temporal coordinates vague so as to allow the echoes of the past, specifically the Second World War and the Holocaust,[72] reverberate in the present and vice versa,[73] making the viewers feel as though they have fallen into a black hole.[74] The story follows Georg, a man about whom we know practically nothing, except that he is, like many others, on the run in Paris occupied by the Germans, who are already pushing south toward Marseille, a port city providing the only escape route to the Unites States, Mexico, and other safe countries. When we first meet Georg he is sitting despondently in a bar as police cars speed down the street outside, talking to a journalist friend who confides in him that he has obtained a "danger visa" for the United States, a visa given to "especially vulnerable people," a large category of "undesirables" threatened with extermination because of their race (Georg is Jewish) or political beliefs (the journalist friend is a communist). The journalist, whom we see rounded up as soon as he leaves the bar, entrusts Georg with documents belonging to a famous writer (Weidl), including a letter to Weidl from his wife Marie, and asks Georg to deliver them to Weidl in his Paris hotel. However, when Georg goes to the hotel he finds out that Weidl has committed suicide. Georg collects Weidl's documents, including his latest book manuscript, which, it turns out, tells the story we are currently watching, with the intention of delivering them to the Mexican consulate in

Marseille, from where they would be eventually passed on to Weidl's wife. Having crossed paths with Marie several times, each time Marie mistaking him for her husband, Georg finally meets her while looking for a doctor for Driss, the son of a friend, Heinz, with whom Georg travels from Paris to Marseille and who dies on the way. The doctor, Richard, turns out to be living with Marie, with whom he is having an affair. After examining Driss Richard advises Georg to accompany the boy and his mother, Melissa, who are planning to cross the border on foot through the mountains, suggesting that now that Driss's father is dead Georg could be a father figure for the boy. Georg responds that he is leaving for Mexico and, besides, he is not Driss's real father. Richard then tells Georg that he, too, has a chance to leave but that would mean leaving behind a woman (Marie), who is not his real wife.

This short exchange sums up the ethical question with which *Transit* is concerned: To what extent are we ethically bound by "fake" relationships (Georg is neither Driss's father nor Marie's husband, just as Richard is not Marie's husband and she is not his wife)? What are the limits of love and hospitality—are they familial, genetic, territorial, or universal? On the level of plot, this question finds expression in a series of substitutions as one character who was supposed to leave is replaced by another who is, in turn, replaced by another (e.g., Richard and Marie are supposed to leave, but Marie returns; then Richard, who seems to have left, returns; then Georg and Marie are supposed to leave but Georg returns and gives his ticket to Richard; indeed, as in other films examined earlier, Georg's character functions very much like Charon, the ferryman of Hades, taking passengers back and forth). Every time a character speaks of "leaving,"' they are speaking, at the same time, of "abandonment," that is, leaving a place is always figured in terms of abandoning someone. Although Marie has *left* her husband (which, presumably, drove him to suicide, of which she remains unaware), she refuses to *abandon* him—the end of their marriage does not invalidate the deeper, ethical relationship by which they are bound (which is also why despite having an affair, Marie remains loyal to Weidl).

Throughout the film echoes of the past reverberate in the present and vice versa. When Georg arrives in Marseille and tries to check into a hotel, the hotel manager demands that he pay in advance for a week (in case of a raid) and present her with proof of his intention to leave (she advises him to go to the Prefecture with his transatlantic ticket). The absurdity of her request—he is allowed to stay at the hotel only if he proves that he does not intend to stay—and the absurdity of waiting for a visa only to have it expire by the time one can get a transatlantic ticket—sums up the Catch-22 situation in which most refugees and illegal migrants find themselves as they are allowed into a country only on the understanding that they are passing through on their way to another. The time warping through which the film's political allegory functions produces some interesting effects, which are especially noticeable in the sequence showing Georg's night escape from Paris to Marseille accompanied by his wounded friend Heinz, whose wife, Melissa, and son, Driss, are waiting for him in Marseille. While the shots of the trains cannot fail to recall the trains transporting millions of Jews to the death camps, this reference to the past is deliberately conflated with the more recent visual memory of thousands of illegal migrants and refugees trying to enter Europe locked up in the back of TIR trucks, many of them suffocating to death—for example, before Georg and Heinz get on the train, another friend gives Georg instructions on how to get fresh air in the train compartment without attracting the Germans' attention. Here the political allegory flattens all temporal distinctions: the current refugee crisis is figured metaphorically through a reference to the Holocaust while, at the same time, the dystopian present/future day Holocaust, depicted by the film literally/realistically rather than metaphorically, is figured through a reference "back" to the current refugee crisis.

With the introduction of the characters of Melissa and Driss, both of Maghrebi origin and both illegal immigrants—presumably, in the film's dystopian present/future French citizens of Maghrebi origins are stripped of their citizenship and treated as illegal in their own country—France's colonial past adds a third temporal layer to that of the 1930s and the 2000s, with France's beur population becoming the third victimized group in the series of transnational and transhistorical cases of victimhood explored in the film (Second World War Jews and twenty-first-century refugees and illegal migrants). France's colonial legacy, the Holocaust, and the refugee crisis—the first decidedly French, the other two European phenomena—enter into a symbolic chain of mutually exchangeable identities: a beur is a Jew is a refugee/illegal migrant. Each time period, each political order, has its own specific set of "Others"—for example, at the Mexican consulate Georg is asked whether his decision not to apply for a US visa but for a Mexican one was not motivated by the fear that his application would be rejected because of his publications in a communist paper, the United States' principal "other" being communists, rather than Jews—but in the end they are all the same, for they are all products of the same process of exclusion through which identity (national or supranational) is constructed.

On the other hand, although the narrative's temporal complexity and its allegorical function are central to the film, *Transit*, as the title implies, is not so much *about* the refugee crisis or the Holocaust, or even about the continuity or equivalence between the two. Petzold is mostly interested in exploring the existential/phenomenological experience of "passing through," focusing not on the past (what the refugees leave behind) or the future (what they hope to attain in their new "home") but on the temporal and spatial disruption of an existence suspended between the past and the future, there and here, then and now, in the limbo of "co-presence." *Transit* is thus haunted by a figure we are already familiar with from Petzold's previous films (*Ghosts, The State*

I Am In, Yella), that of the ghost, here Marie's ghost, which returns to haunt Georg after he has already learned of her death (*the Montrealer*, the ship that was supposed to take Marie to Mexico, sinks). In a sense all refugees wandering about Marseille, waiting in various consulates for their visas, have become ghosts.[75] In an interview, Franz Rogowski, the actor who plays Georg, comments on the difficulty of playing a character who is supposed to inhabit two temporal frames at the same time: "Georg is a refugee, therefore he has lost his home, but he is also a ghost that starts his journey in Germany's 1940s. He's actually born in the novel, in the book of a German writer, and he finds himself in today's Marseille. But also, Georg is a drifter. There's not much he could lose. He has no family, there's no apartment or work."[76] When Rogowski describes Georg as a drifter and explicitly states, later in the interview, that he was *not* trying to represent a refugee, he urges us to see Georg not as a specific historical figure but as an allegorical figure representing any kind of existential sense of displacement, homelessness, or exile (indeed, at one point in the story Georg tells an allegorical, Kafkaesque story about a man who had to report to Hell and waited for years in front of a door only to be informed that this *is* Hell).

When Richard fails to leave and returns to the apartment he shares with Marie, Marie leaves him and looks for Georg all over Marseille, eventually finding him in the same restaurant he has been going to every day. "I finally found you," she says to him. After a series of misrecognitions—the three times she mistakes Georg for her "real" husband—she finally "recognizes" him. Their "fake" relationship based on lack of knowledge, mistaken identity, and lies has finally become "real." Here *Transit* comes close to other films discussed earlier (*Eastern Boys, Diamantino, The House by the Sea*) in which a "fake" or nonexistent relationship becomes "real"/"legitimate" (lovers become parent/son, or foreign refugee children become one's adopted children). In these types of stories, which could be seen as a European take on the Hollywood rom-com subgenre exemplified by *The Wedding Date, While You Were Sleeping*, etc., a fake/pretend or nonexistent relationship is used as a sort of "test case" (or, to use Elsaesser's term, "a thought experiment") to raise an ethical question, which is then "resolved" by making the fake or nonexistent relationship real. The ending, however, complicates this analysis by having Georg decide, at the last moment, to leave Marie, sensing that she might still be in love with her husband. By having Georg realize that he can never "replace" Marie's "real" husband, that he will always remain merely her "transit lover" (her rebound crush), the film disrupts the hypothetical equation it had suggested between "fake" and "real" relationship, suggesting instead that while ethics demands we treat others *as if they were our real husbands, wives, or sons* (the Kantian categorical imperative), personal relationships (love) cannot attain this equation between fake and real (in this respect the film differs from the happy-ending Hollywood scenarios invoked earlier). Just as Marie left her husband, without abandoning him, Georg must leave Marie (as her lover) while affirming his ethical relationship to her, that is, treating her *as if* she was his wife. The (double) tragedy in the film is that the irreconcilability of the ethical with the amorous results in Marie's death, sentencing Georg to a life-in-transit—a haunted life, in which he is haunted by ghosts until he himself becomes one—with no end in sight (in the film's last shot Georg is sitting at his usual table in the restaurant, he hears the door bell and turns around, expecting, in vain, to see Marie). Here "co-presence" reveals the obverse side of its ethical potential—eternal damnation.

The collapsing of temporal and spatial markers in films like *Transit* and *Lazzaro*, which realigns ethnic, racial, and political differences into a symbolic chain of mutually exchangeable identities ("a beur is a Jew is a refugee") is becoming something of a genre trope in films exploring Europe's current predicament. Filmed in close quarters—in an allotment area in the center of Vienna that recalls the self-enclosed, artificial space of a refugee camp—*Nobadi* (Karl Markovics, 2019) tells the story of the aging, taciturn Robert who, following the death of his dog, needs help to bury him. Adib, a young Afghani refugee desperately looking for work, offers his services, despite his injured foot (injured during his journey to Europe). The film stages the conflict between the two men across political, racial, and generational lines, referencing, *in the same gesture*, The Odyssey—one of the core texts making up Europe's cultural heritage—*and* the absolute negation of that legacy, the Nazi past: the title, "Nobadi," invokes the violation of refugees' human rights *and* the Nazi extermination of the Jews. The collapsing of temporal/historical difference also manifests itself in the film's conflation of the figures of victim and victimizer through that of "nobadi," a figure clearly intended to mediate between them: just as Adib's tattoo "nobadi" brands him as another anonymous victim, Robert's tattoo, which, like the tattoos of all SS members, identifies his blood group, "brands" him as "nobadi": his blood type, "0," references both the erasure of identity (the extermination of the Jews) *and* the erasure of responsibility (on the part of the Nazis) for the erasure of identity. "Nobadi" invokes, in the same breath, "bare life," suppressed guilt, and nomadism/exile ("nobadi" is also the pseudonym used by Odysseus, the ur-nomad).

Like *Nobadi*, *The Barefoot Emperor* (Peter Brosens and Jessica Woodwoth, 2019) mines the trope of spectrality to underscore the copresence of past and present, though in a more surrealist vein. In this toothless political satire, the Belgian king, returning home from Istanbul after learning that during his absence Wallonia has seceded and Belgium no longer exists, is mistakenly shot in Sarajevo during a theatrical reenactment of Franz Ferdinand's 1914 assassination, and later finds himself in an exclusive sanatorium housed in Tito's former summer home, where he is informed that his shooting has sparked the end of the EU and the rise of "Nova Europa" to be ruled by a new emperor, who turns out to be none other than the Belgian king himself. The film's scrambled historical references (from the disintegration of Yugoslavia, seen here as a precedent for the EU's collapse, to Hitler, Mussolini, Che

Guevara, and Ceausescu) turn European history into a hall of mirrors, in which the lines between past and present, politics and popular culture, and between different political ideals, are rendered meaningless (each patient in the sanatorium is named after the room in which various "stars" from the world of politics and entertainment resided back in Tito's time: the Belgian king is now "Brezhnev" and he is surrounded by "Indira Gandhi," "Castro," "Arafat," "Elizabeth Taylor"). Recalling Giordana's *Once You Are Born You Can No Longer Hide* (Chapter 2), *Emperor* imagines the potential "rebirth" of Europe from the ashes of nationalism and fascism in literal terms: the future of Europe is contingent upon Europeans' ability to literally put themselves in refugees' shoes, and so the king and his entourage are able to return to Brussels (Europe) only by being smuggled back illegally by a group of Indian "climate refugees."

Although less formally experimental than *Transit* and *Lazzaro*, *Dead Europe* relies on the same theoretical paradigm of "co-presence" (of past and present) figured here through the familiar trope of the family curse. The film traces a young Greek-Australian man's return journey to his ancestral homeland, where he uncovers his family's secret past. When Isaac, a gay art photographer tells his father, Vassili, that he is going to Athens for a gallery exhibition of his work, his father reacts violently to the news—he drives off in his car at a suicidal speed, eventually dying in a car crash. Isaac takes his father's ashes back to his Greek birthplace, where he gradually learns of a family curse. The story moves from Athens, where Isaac meets his father's brother and his family, to Paris (where he meets a man claiming to be an old friend of his father's) before finally ending in Budapest (where Isaac meets his estranged brother Nico, a junkie working in the porn industry, who finally tells him the truth about their family's wretched past). In Athens Isaac meets teenaged Josef, who takes him back to a slum, where he lives with Natalia, a heroin-addicted prostitute. Isaac starts taking photographs of both of them but he runs out of film; however, when he returns later with his camera recharged the boy and Natalia are gone, having "left long ago" as the neighbors tell Isaac. Throughout the rest of his European journey Isaac keeps seeing the haunting face of Josef everywhere, a metaphor for a past wrong that Isaac and his family can never make right.

3.3 *Dead Europe*

Dead Europe draws on several genres—supernatural horror, historical drama, Holocaust film, refugee film, ghost story, and road movie—to tell an allegorical story about contemporary Europe imagined here as an underground network of illegality, exploitation, racial prejudice, and anti-Semitism and, visually, as a series of camp-like neighborhoods and migrant/refugee-populated apartment buildings whose homogeneity makes the different cities where the action takes place (Athens, Paris, and Budapest) indistinguishable (necessitating the city names to be written on the screen).

The film's ambition is to paint a representative picture of the current state of Europe, which inevitably means that specificity and subtlety (narrative and visual) are sacrificed in the name of making a general statement—or rather judgment—about Europe. By lumping together all problems plaguing Europe, from racial prejudice and anti-Semitism through drug problems and the porno industry to the refugee crisis and religious conflicts, the film feeds into the familiar "migrancy problematic," which blames migrants and refugees for *all* of Europe's social, political, and economic problems.

Given that Isaac is Greek-Australian, he is positioned from the outset as an outsider, a tourist in Europe. There is something more, however, to this apparently simple positioning. Soon after Isaac meets Josef, the boy takes him back to his home in the slums. They make their way through the dirty winding streets of a ghetto-like neighborhood entirely populated by what appear to be migrants and refugees, although there is no way of knowing whether these are migrants, refugees, poor and homeless Greeks, or racialized Others who are legally residing in Greece: the sequence presents them all as variations of "the Other." The neighborhood's inhabitants glance or stare at Isaac with suspicion, a network of looks that position Isaac as not just (or not so much) a tourist but a non-migrant/non-refugee, presumably an exception in the city "overrun" by refugees (indeed, Isaac's uncle tells him that he was forced to leave the city for that very reason). His profession further sets him apart from those around him, even as his choice of subjects to photograph positions him disturbingly close to the porn photography in which his nefarious older brother, Nico, is involved. Witnessing his brother's "work"—hundreds of porn photographs of young boys—Isaac is repulsed and horrified, yet his own attraction to "subjects" (as in "subjects of photography" rather than "political subjects") like Josef and Natalia has something pornographic about it.

Like *Transit*, *Dead Europe* posits anti-Semitism and anti-immigrant attitudes as two faces of the same coin. The dark secret Isaac eventually uncovers concerns a Jewish boy, Elias, whom Isaac's father and his family had offered to protect during the war (in exchange for money) but eventually betrayed: Isaac's grandmother raped the boy and Isaac's father did nothing to prevent it, instead waiting until the boy was almost dead and killing him. Figuring the family sin primarily as one of sexual assault (rape) and only secondarily as murder sets the tone for the whole film, which frames the gay cause (Isaac is gay, Nico services the gay porn industry, and Isaac's grandmother rapes a young boy) through a reference to the Holocaust. When Josef asks Isaac to help him it's not clear what he needs help with. He asks Isaac to take a photo of him, presumably for a fake ID, but before Isaac leaves to recharge his camera Josef whispers to him that Natalia is not his mother, reiterating again that he needs Isaac's help. The later revelation about Isaac's grandmother molesting the young Elias suggests that Natalia might have been doing the same to Josef, that is, acting as the boy's pimp.

Thus, when Isaac fails to help Josef, he repeats the sin of his father who also failed to prevent his own mother from molesting Elias. Also like in *Transit*, the Jewish boy of the past (Elias) returns as a ghost haunting Isaac's family in the present but this time in the form of a young refugee of unknown origins—Josef lives with a Russian, Natalia, but she is not his real mother. The parallel between the Jews of the past and the refugees of the present is made literal when, in response to his uncle's complaints that refugees have taken over Athens and that the government must get rid of them, Isaac replies, "Isn't this what they used to say about Jews?"

Dead Europe depicts the claims of three different groups—Jews, gays, and refugees—as mutually exchangeable, grounding them all in the Holocaust. As if this were not enough, the director adds Muslims and the precariat to the heady mix by having Amina, an Arab refugee, condemn Jews (in a conversation with Isaac) for using the Holocaust to excuse whatever violence they may have inflicted on other people, notably Palestinians, and including footage of the anti-austerity protests in Athens. Curiously, Amina's angry outburst undercuts the premise of the film, which uses precisely the Holocaust to validate the claims of the three groups listed earlier. This self-negating move is mirrored in the no-exit premise of the film inasmuch as the idea of a curse rests precisely on a circular notion of time, in which the curse can never be broken and the sins of the fathers will forever be revisited upon their sons: Isaac will never be able—will have never been able (!)—to help Josef. Furthermore, inasmuch as the film flirts with the idea of Isaac, who has just lost his own father, as a potential father figure for Josef, Isaac's ultimate failure to help Josef makes the film appear as a failed adoption story in line with the trope of adoption discussed earlier. Right after Nico tells Isaac the truth about their family he adds: "Don't you sometimes wish there were no more Jews walking this earth?" which could be read as an anti-Semitic statement but also as a wish to stop referring any and all forms of present injustice and exploitation back to the Holocaust, to stop reducing all instances of evil to one "Radical Evil." Isaac repeats Nico's words almost verbatim seconds before Josef stabs him (in self-defense) voicing, again, an angry wish to free himself from the past even as he realizes that's impossible. Isaac's death does not put an end to the curse: Josef is last seen walking out of a train station, no doubt on his way to meet another guilt-ridden white European.

Happy as Lazzaro, *Transit*, and *Dead Europe* play with narrative and story time in ways that, although reminiscent of high modernist films like *Last Year at Marienbad* (Alain Resnais, 1961), invest such formal experimentation with a political meaning while, at the same time, revealing certain similarities with a subgenre of Hollywood films I have called "the multiple film"—also known as "the Hollywood puzzle film"[77]—which also explores the multiplicity of temporality and identity but in less explicitly political ways. By blurring the boundaries between past, present, and future, and approaching contemporary problems through a magical/fabulist/ farcical/absurdist lens, Rorhwacher and Petzold foreground the historical continuity between various forms of injustice and exploitation, ultimately revealing the relentless reproduction of violence as a cycle seemingly without end.

Notes

1. Paul Bloom, "It's Ridiculous to Use Virtual Reality to Empathize with Refugees," *The Atlantic*, February 3, 2017, https://www.theatlantic.com/technology/archive/2017/02/virtual-reality-won't-make-you-more-empathetic/515511/, accessed August 6, 2019. In *Against Empathy: The Case for Rational Compassion* (New York: Ecco, 2016) Bloom argues that empathy is an irrational emotion that actually contributes to inequality and immorality.
2. qtd in Adi Robertson, "VR Was Sold as an 'Empathy Machine'—But Some Artists Are Getting Sick of It," https://www.theverge.com/2017/5/3/15524404/tribeca-film-festival-2017-vr-empathy-machine-backlash, accessed August 6, 2019.
3. Carl Platinga, *Screen Stories: Emotions and the Ethics of Engagement* (Oxford: Oxford UP, 2018); Asbjorn Gronstad, *Film and the Ethical Imagination* (London: Palgrave Macmillan, 2016); Catherine Wheatley, *Stanley Cavell and Film: Skepticism and Self-Reliance at the Cinema* (London: Bloomsbury, 2019); Miguel Valenti, *More Than a Movie: Ethics in Entertainment* (London: Routledge, 2018), and others.
4. Downing and Saxton, *Film and Ethics*, 2.
5. Ibid., 3.
6. Ibid., 4.
7. Levinas quoted in Downing and Saxton, *Film and Ethics*, 4.
8. Levinas quoted in Downing and Saxton, *Film and Ethics*, 3.
9. Downing and Saxton, *Film and Ethics*, 92.
10. Ibid., 11.
11. Ibid.
12. Ibid.
13. Ibid., 18.
14. Ibid., 57.
15. Ibid., 61.
16. Ibid., 65.
17. Ballesteros, *Immigration Cinema*, 19.
18. Ibid., 17.
19. Ibid.
20. Ibid., 148.

21 In the four films she discusses, *Children of Men* (2006), *Cache* (2005), *Head-On* (2004) and *Hostage* (2005), ethnic and racial others figure as "Objects rather than subjects of their tragic fate" (75).
22 qtd in Berghahn and Sternberg, "Locating Migrant and Diasporic Cinema," 32.
23 Jacques Derrida, *Of Hospitality: Anne Dufourmantelle Invites Jacques Derrida to Respond*, trans. Rachel Bowlby (Stanford, CA: Stanford UP, 2000), 15.
24 Jacques Derrida, *Acts of Religion* (New York: Routledge, 2002), 363.
25 See Kenneth Reinhard, Eric Santner, and Slavoj Žižek, *The Neighbor: Three Inquiries in Political Theology* (Chicago: U of Chicago Press, 2013).
26 The article will appear in the special issue of *Northern Lights: Film and Media Studies Yearbook*, edited by Temenuga Trifonova, forthcoming in winter 2020.
27 See Jacques Derrida, *The Other Heading* (1992) and Rodolphe Gasché, *Europe, or The Infinite Task: A Study of a Philosophical Concept* (Stanford, CA: Stanford UP, 2008). Similar to Elsaesser, who believes the idea of "Europe" has preserved its progressive potential, Gasché affirms that the idea of "Europe" still retains its meaning for philosophy as "the infinite task" of enlightened resistance, most recently a resistance to the forces of neoliberalism.
28 "Atlantis," with its dystopian connotations, has become a frequent symbolic reference in recent European films, for example, *Atlantis* (Valentin Vasyanovych, 2019), set in Eastern Ukraine in the near future, and *Atlantics* (Mati Diop, 2019), another film addressing the refugee crisis not directly but as a background for a love story between two Senegalese youths.
29 Hans-Christian Schmid's *Lichter* (2003), set on the border between Poland and Germany, also focuses on the attempts of Ukrainian migrants to cross the border illegally into Germany.
30 Shakespeare, *The Merchant of Venice*, Act 3, Scene 1.
31 On biopolitical cinema, see Nitzan Lebovic, "The Biopolitical Film (A Nietzschean Paradigm)," *Postmodern Culture* 23, no. 1 (September 2012).
32 Another film approaching the refugee crisis from the point of view of the traffickers rather than the refugees, and focusing on the psychological impact of the crisis on ordinary Europeans, is *Ohthes/Riverbanks* (Panos Karkanevatos, 2015), which follows the tragic love story between a Greek soldier and volunteer minesweeper identifying unexploded land mines planted by the Greek military in 1974 during a conflict with Turkey over Cyprus, and a single mother trafficking refugee children across the river.
33 James McTeigue's *V for Vendetta* (2005) and Michael Winterbottom's *Code 46* (2003) are equally prophetic.
34 The adoption motif and the trope of performativity figure as well in films featuring "legal" immigrants (EU citizens): for example, in *Sole* (Carlo Sironi, 2019) an Italian youth and a pregnant Polish immigrant pretend to be parents living together while they wait for a fake adoption to be finalized.
35 *Color of the Ocean* (Maggie Peren, 2011) reveals the "dirty" underside of hospitality-as-adoption: it is only on the condition that the young Mamadou

becomes an *orphan* (after his father is killed for the money a well-intentioned German tourist gives him to help him and Mamadou travel to France) that his *legal* entry into Europe (conceived metaphorically in terms of adoption) becomes possible.

36 Presumably the idea of calling the refugee "Aryan" was meant as a critique of the racist underside of nationalism; instead, it merely inverts the ideology of Nazism by erecting a new "superior," "more spiritual race" represented by the refugee.

37 The documentary *Those Who Feel the Fire Burning* (Morgan Knibbe, 2014) adopts a similar point of view, that of the wandering ghost of a dead refugee reflecting on the plight of refugees in Europe.

38 Following an explosion at the train station, which leads the police to declare Aryan and his father terrorists and attribute the attack to them, Stern, convinced of Aryan's innocence, miraculously transforms into Aryan's most passionate "disciple" and asks him for forgiveness.

39 Bruckner, *The Tears of the White Man*, 143–44.

40 LUX prize winners include films like *The Edge of Heaven*; *3 Months, 3 Weeks and 2 Days*; *Lorna's Silence*; *Welcome*; *When We Leave*; *Illegal*; *Shun Li and the Poet*; and *Mediterranea*.

41 Neil Archer, "Paris Je t'aime (plus): Europhobia as Europeanness in Luc Besson's and Pierre Morel's Dystopia Trilogy," *The Europeanness of European Cinema: Identity, Meaning and Globalization*, ed. Mary Harrod, Mariana Liz, and Alissa Timoshkina (London: I.B. Tauris, 2015), 187.

42 Ibid., 187.

43 qtd in Archer, "Paris Je t'aime (plus)," 190.

44 Ibid., 196.

45 Ibid.

46 Ibid.

47 Harrod, Liz, and Timoshkina, "The Europeanness of European Cinema," 2.

48 Ibid., 11.

49 Ibid.

50 See Jeff Johnson, *Pervert in the Pulpit: Morality in the Works of David Lynch* (Jefferson, NC: McFarland & Company, 2004).

51 The film's pedagogical agenda recalls the many "denazification" films made after the Second World War, especially *Murderers Among Us* (Wolfgang Staudte, 1948).

52 https://www.sfgate.com/movies/article/Review-The-White-Ribbon-3275853.php, accessed August 6, 2019.

53 See A.O. Scott's review in *The New York Times*, https://www.nytimes.com/2009/12/30/movies/30white.html, accessed August 6, 2019.

54 Segre's documentary *Closed Sea* (2012) tells the story of Somalian and Eritrean refugees who attempted to flee to Italy only to be returned to the hands of Gaddafi as a result of the Friendship Treaty signed by Italy and Libya.

55 qtd in Ballesteros, *Immigration Cinema*, 148.
56 In Greek mythology the ferryman Charon transported the souls of the newly dead across the river Styx into the underworld. In some versions Styx had miraculous powers and could make someone invulnerable (hence the story of Achilles' heel).
57 Ascension Island is the site of Darwin's experiment that transformed a barren volcanic island into a lush tropical cloud forest, an artificial "Garden of Eden."
58 In the story of Rike and Kingsley one hears faint echoes of Robinson Crusoe and *his* man "Friday."
59 Jacques Rancière, *Aesthetics and Its Discontents* (Cambridge: Polity Press, 2009), 23.
60 The naming of the Holocaust as the most important collective European trauma, at the expense of the Gulag, privileges Western European historical experience as a foundation for a shared European identity, placing Eastern Europeans in a condition of "denial of coevalness" they share with former Third World colonies.
61 See Jean-Michel Frodon, "Intersecting Paths," *Cinema and the Shoah*, ed. Jean-Michel Frodon (Paris: Cahiers di cinéma, 2007), 1–14.
62 See Marie-Jose Mondzain, "The Shoah as a Question of Cinema," *Cinema and the Shoah*, 17–25.
63 See Mitsuhiro Yoshimoto, "Cinematic Space and Time in the Age of Neoliberalism," *Transcommunication* 2 (2014).
64 Temenuga Trifonova, "Multiple Personality and the Discourse of the Multiple in Hollywood Cinema," *The European Journal of American Culture* 29, no. 2 (2010): 145–71.
65 Fatmir Koci's *Tirana, Year Zero* (2001), referencing Rossellini's *Germany Year Zero* (1948) and exploring Albanians' attempts to emigrate during the tumultuous days of the Albanian Civil War (1997), could be seen as a "sequel" to *Lamerica*.
66 Albania, as depicted in *Lamerica*, is no longer a nation-state but a camp, entering which makes anyone a refugee.
67 See Jonathan Romney's review, https://www.filmcomment.com/blog/film-week-happy-lazzaro/, accessed August 6, 2019.
68 Christian Mingiu's *Beyond the Hills* (2012) challenges the hypocrisy and moral apathy in postcommunist Romania by introducing a similar temporal and spatial *décalage* between the self-enclosed world of the convent, where time seems to have stopped, and the outside world represented by the symbols of reason and logic, the hospital, and the police.
69 Sigrist and Ghervas, "La memoire européene," 239–40.
70 One cannot but recall Morpheus's words to Neo in *The Matrix* (1999): "The Matrix is everywhere. . . . Like everyone else you were born into bondage, into a prison that you cannot taste or see or touch, a prison for your mind."
71 Wood quoted in Garrett.

72 Markus Imhoof's *Eldorado* (2018) also draws a parallel between the plight of refugees today and the Second World War refugees, while Matthias Kossmehl's documentary *Café Waldluft* (2015) about a Bavarian rustic hotel housing refugees establishes a connection between non-European asylum seekers trying to enter Europe and "refugees from East Germany" arriving in West Germany after the fall of the Berlin Wall.

73 Mahamat Saleh Haroun's *A Season in France* (2017) also imagines refugees as the "new Jews" of fortress Europe. The film tells the story of two brothers (Abbas and Etienne) fleeing the war-torn Central African Republic and settling down in Paris. When Abbas's asylum application is rejected, he leaves his French lover (Carole), taking his two children with him. In his farewell letter to Carole he expresses his hope that history will not repeat what happened in July 1938 at the Evian conference, at which Western democracies failed to reach an agreement about opening their borders to the thousands of Jewish refugees fleeing persecution by the Nazis. Before Abbas leaves her, Carole, a Polish Jew, confides in him that in the past she, too, was *sans-papiers*—the French authorities refused to renew her passport, demanding copies of her parents' birth certificates as proof of her nationality.

74 Petzold admits the idea of conflating the past and the present came from Robert Altman's *The Long Goodbye* (1973), which embeds the past in the present. For a discussion of *Transit* and *Le Havre* (2011) in the context of "post-mortem" films (films conveying a sense of haunting and raise issues of memory, history, and identity), see Alice Bardan's article forthcoming in the special issue of *Northern Lights: Film and Media Studies Yearbook* edited by Temenuga Trifonova (Winter 2020).

75 The trope of "ghosting" or "haunting" recurs regularly in films about migrants/refugees. In Nick Broomfield's drama *Ghosts* (2006), based on the true story of the 2004 Morecambe Bay disaster in which twenty-one Chinese illegal immigrants drowned, "ghosts" refers both to the spectral presence of undocumented migrants, on whose invisible labor the EU economy depends, and to white British people (*gwailou* is a Cantonese expression for "white westerners"). Esther Peeren has explored "spectrality," with which Derrida's "hauntology" shares obvious similarities, as a metaphor of both dispossession and empowerment of certain subjects, including migrants, perceived as living ghosts in contemporary British and American cinema and literature. See Esther Peeren, *The Spectral Metaphor: Living Ghosts and the Agency of Invisibility* (London: Palgrave Macmillan, 2014).

76 https://www.eyeforfilm.co.uk/feature/2018-11-11-franz-rogowski-in-conversation-on-christian-petzolds-transit-and-the-state-we-are-in-feature-story-by-anne-katrin-titze, accessed August 6, 2019.

77 See Warren Buckland, *Hollywood Puzzle Films* (London: Routledge, 2014).

4

Crossovers Between the Cinema of Migration and the Cinema of Precarity

The recent proliferation of studies of nationalism and European cinema has not yet been matched by analyses of the importance of class, a gap that Laurent Berlant's *Cruel Optimism* (2011), Ewa Mazierska and Lars Kristensen's *Contemporary Cinema and Neoliberal Ideology* (2018), and Betty Kaklamanidou and Ana Corbalan's *Contemporary European Cinema: Crisis Narratives and Narratives in Crisis* (2018) seek to address by examining the ways in which contemporary cinema depicts class relations and class struggle in an attempt to imagine alternatives to neoliberalism. While "migrant and diasporic cinema" used to focus on the examination of personal and family bonds, which, as Daniela Berghahn has shown, crystallize different affective responses to growing ethnic, racial, cultural, and religious diversity in Europe,[1] in recent European films, largely in response to the economic crisis and the migrant and refugee crisis, the family is no longer the only—or the most—central, binding, and representative social structure; rather, this function has been taken over by the workplace and work relations, as evidenced by a growing number of films exploring the ties that bind and/or separate coworkers and the erosion of the public/private divide (one need only think of the opening scene of Pedro Pinho's *The Nothing Factory* (2017), in which a worker's intimate moment with his wife is rudely interrupted by a phone call informing him of the possible closure of the factory where he is employed). Michele Placido's *7 Minutes* (2016), in which the workers' council representatives in an Italian textile factory undergoing a takeover by a French company must vote on the new owner's proposal to cut down their lunch break by seven minutes, dramatizes the subtle but far-reaching stakes of the workers' struggle against the erosion of their rights, bargaining power, and solidarity. The council's members, including Italians and immigrants (Romanian, Albanian, and African), spanning several generations and united by their desperate determination to keep their jobs, are a veritable microcosm of contemporary Europe, as well as of recent European cinema, in which precarity, legal and "illegal" migration, and the refugee crisis (briefly glimpsed in the film on a TV screen in the background) have become part of Europe's general "mise en scène," with the conflict of Labor versus Capital attaining the suspenseful (almost epic) dimensions of a classical western or a thriller.

In *Cruel Optimism* (2011), a study of "post-Fordist affect"—the affective language of anxiety, contingency, and precarity—Laurent Berlant asserts that the sense of unbelonging experienced by both the precariat and noncitizens has been responsible for the appearance, starting in the 1990s, of a perverse new affective strategy of adjustment she calls "cruel optimism"—embodied in new genres like the situation tragedy (a combination of melodrama and situation comedy)—and of an emergent aesthetics, the cinema of precarity,[2] which she sees as continuing the legacy of neorealism. What is new about cruel optimism as an adjustment strategy is that it does not develop within the familiar model of trauma since trauma has now lost its extraordinary character. With trauma and crisis becoming mundane, adjustment strategies, too, have changed: they are better seen as responses to the ordinariness of crisis. "Cruel optimism" is, thus, a form of masochism which, however, differs from the special brand of masochism permeating Haneke's guilt-ridden anti-European European cinema (Chapter 3): optimism is "cruel," Berlant explains, "insofar as the very pleasures of being inside a relation have become sustaining regardless of the content of the relation, such that a person or a world finds itself bound to a situation of profound threat that is, at the same time, profoundly confirming."[3] Berlant singles out the Dardenne brothers' *Rosetta* (1999) and *The Promise* (1996), along with Laurent Cantet's *Human Resources* (1999) and *L'emploi du temps/Time Out* (2001), as dramatizing most clearly "cruel optimism" as an affective strategy of adjustment and survival in response to the attrition of social fantasies such as upward mobility, job security, meritocracy, political and social equality, and intimacy. The inherently apolitical or even politically regressive nature of cruel optimism is revealed by its peculiar temporal imaginary:

> What's striking in the temporal imaginary of both the citizen and the migrant workers is the ways they look forward ... to a condition of stasis, of being able to be *somewhere* and to make a life, exercising existence as a fact, not a project. In other words, in this version of transnational class fantasy, mobility is a dream and a nightmare. The end of mobility as a fantasy of endless upwardness, and the shift to the aspiration toward

achieving an impasse and stop-loss, is a subtle redirection of the fantasy bribes transacted to effect the reproduction of life under the present economic conditions. Given these conditions, if one is an informal or unofficial worker, there is little room for imagining revolution or indeed any future beyond the scavenging present.[4]

Significantly, the films Berlant analyzes are *not* centrally organized around migrants but around "citizens who thought that the traditional forms of social reciprocity would provide scenes for life-building, not the attrition of being. [. . .] In the economic life-world of these films, citizens without capital and migrants with fake papers are in proximate, interdependent boats *structurally and affectively*."[5]

Berlant is not the only one to propose reorienting the study of cinema under neoliberalism in terms of the affective language of anxiety, contingency, and precarity. Tim Bergfelder has also made a case for expanding the study of transnational cinema—including European cinema—to a consideration of *affect* and *transnational desire* as a form of "vernacular cosmopolitanism," so as to offer "a more productive access *to the emotional and ethical investment in transnational exchanges* than a blanket equation of transnationalism with issues of globalization or monolithic ideology."[6] Taking his cue from Mica Nava's rereading of Bhabha's "vernacular cosmopolitanism" as "visceral cosmopolitanism," which pays attention to the ways in which "otherness" functions as "an object of attraction and identification at an emotional level,"[7] Bergfelder asserts that reframing debates on transnational cinema around attitudes and emotions would help overcome the risk of essentializing the distinction between migrants and nonmigrants. Enrica Capussotti makes a similar point when she suggests that "the common [affective] experience of displacement [in Spanish and Italian cinema, though we can extend this argument to European cinema in general] may be the basis for new, mobile attachments."[8] Berlant considers cruel optimism as, at one and the same time, a *symptom* of the increasing precarity of life under neoliberalism and a *strategy* of adjustment, whose purpose is to restore, rather than upset, the status quo, what she calls "the soft hierarchies of inequalities." It is my contention, however, that although cruel optimism as a symptom of the precarity of life under neoliberalism continues to inform recent European films structured around the figure of the migrant, these films are no longer concerned with merely dramatizing the effects of cruel optimism as a strategy of adjustment so much as with foregrounding the affective affinities and lines of solidarity between Western and Eastern Europeans, citizens and refugees, Europeans and non-Europeans. These affinities are neatly summed up in Tony Gatlif's otherwise disappointing, heavily didactic *Indignados* (2012)[9]—an activist docudrama inspired by Stephane Hessel's bestselling essay "Time for Outrage!" (2010)—in which Europeans' anti-austerity struggle against high unemployment rates, welfare cuts, and political corruption (core concerns of the cinema of precarity) and the struggle for the rights of non-European migrants and refugees (a core topic in migrant cinema) are posited as two faces of the same struggle.

Before I continue, I should clarify what I mean by "affective affinities." The "affects" have been explored by a range of scholars in the humanities and social sciences as a way of understanding experience that falls outside the representational/semiotic paradigm, giving rise to what has been called "the affective turn."[10] My use of the term "affect," however, is indebted neither to Eugenie Brinkema's theory of the affects as plural and formal,[11] a theory that delinks affectivity from subjectivity and thus remains limited to one specific type of films (experimental films) rather than being applicable to cinema more broadly, nor to the more familiar intellectual legacy of the concept of "affect"—from Deleuze and Guittari back to Spinoza and Bergson—which defines it in terms of pre- or de-subjectivized intensities. Steven Shaviro's analysis of "post-cinematic affect," which seeks to capture the particular *structure of feeling* brought about by digital technologies and neoliberal economic relations, is representative of the Deleuze-inspired strand of affect theory. Following Brian Massumi,[12] Shaviro defines emotion as "affect captured by a subject, or tamed and reduced to the extent that it becomes commensurate with that subject. Subjects are overwhelmed and traversed by affect, but they have or possess their own emotions."[13] While emotion is representable it also "points beyond itself to an affect that works transpersonally and transversally, that is at once singular and common."[14] Both Shaviro and Michael Hardt[15] use "affect" to theorize—and mend—the broken link between the individual and the social in the age of neoliberalism.

Ironically, even as theoreticians of affect *expand* the notion of the subject toward some immaterial, virtual realm beyond subjectivity/representation, a realm imagined as a hidden reserve of freedom and agency but which remains unknowable to us because it is primary, pre-subjective and nonconscious, they also suggest that the subject is *constituted/determined* at an even deeper level by impersonal social and economic flows/forces beyond her control: "It is precisely by means of such affective flows that the subject is *opened to*, and *thereby constituted through* broader social, political and economic processes."[16] Invoking Foucault's notion of neoliberalism's new mutation, *Homo oeconomicus,* as "an entrepreneur of himself,"[17] for whom "emotions are resources to invest,"[18] and reading Massumi and Jameson together, Shaviro draws a parallel between affective flows (transpersonal affect) and financial flows (multinational capital) as equally "unrepresentable" and thus resulting in the failure of "cognitive mapping" (Jameson) and "affective mapping" (Shaviro).

In her intellectual genealogy of "affect," Patricia Clough also fails to resolve the underlying tension between two opposite understandings of "the affects," theorized in terms of "excess" and "agency" and, *at the same time*, as "the site of capital investment for the realization of profit"[19] in "a market-driven circulation of affect and attention,"[20] and thus vulnerable to even more fierce levels of control that go beyond biopolitics, beyond the (mere) internalization of social norms. Elena del Rio, too, sees the turn to affect as contributing to "a reconfiguration of the poststructuralist concept of subjectivity as a more *impersonal*, yet at the same time more expressive, *agency* than is found in the subjugated subject of ideology, psychoanalysis, or semiotics."[21] Once again "affect" is posited as impersonal and, at the same time, said to endow bodies with agency. Del Rio tries to address the irreconcilability of "impersonal" with "agency" by explaining that "it is hardly a question of the performance restoring agency to an individual character or a particular social group; instead, it is a question of the film's mobilization of performance as the catalyst for the dissolution of (narrative, ideological, and generic) meaning in a more abstract, less personalized way."[22] Thus, all the claims del Rio makes on behalf of "affect" are simply another way to describe nothing other than the dissolution of narrative, ideology, and genre, with which we are familiar from postmodern and poststructuralist theory.

In talking about "affect," then, I am generally following Berlant's analysis of post-Fordist affect, as well as historical-political versions of affect theory, as exemplified by Johannes von Moltke's study of the return of a "feeling for history" in German cultural studies and cultural memory in the post-unification era.[23] Indeed, one of my contentions here is that the shift in cultural memory in post-unification Germany articulated by von Moltke—exemplified by the undermining of the strict opposition between victimizers and victims in post-unification German cinema—finds its European equivalent in the increasing tendency of European films to depict Europeans and migrants/refugees as being in the same boat affectively and structurally. Von Moltke's detailed analysis of one particular film, Oliver Hirschbiegel's *Downfall* (2004), offers an alternative to the typically narrow explorations of cinematic affect, which are often "conducted either in universalizing psychological terms or on formal grounds";[24] on the contrary, "only if we locate emotions at the crossroads of cinema's aesthetic devices and of historical [ideological] knowledge," argues von Moltke, "can we begin to talk in any meaningful way of *Geschichtsgefühl*, or a feeling for history."[25] Still, while the erosion of the opposition between "victimizers/ Europeans" and "victims/migrants" in recent European films parallels that between "perpetrators" and "victims" in post-unification German cinema, I should note that von Moltke reads *Downfall* as representative of a wave of "nostalgia films" within the broader cultural history of emotion in postwar Germany, whereas I consider the privileging of the affective and structural affinities between Europeans and non-Europeans, citizens and "illegal" migrants or refugees, as evidence not of nostalgia but, on the contrary, of a socially and politically lucid cinema.

1 The Cinema of Precarity

Originally referring "to lives mired in poverty," the term "précarité" "only became attached to employment in the 1980s when neoliberal restructuring in the guise of flexible labor was becoming a byword in national and transnational corporate politics."[26] Berlant locates this shift in the term's meaning "from limited structure to pervasive life environment" in French "New Realism" of the 1990s and after, marking the emergence of a "cinema of precarity," which builds upon the legacy of 1930s and 1940s Hollywood melodramas and postwar Italian neorealism, whose aesthetic, like that of the cinema of precarity, is based on messy situations, episodes, incidents, and gestures, rather than on dramatic events. The cinema of precarity—for example, Laurent Cantet's *Human Resources* (1999) and *Time Out* (2001), *Mondays in the Sun* (Fernando León de Aranoa, 2002), *The Adversary* (Nicole Garcia, 2002), *Violence des échanges en milieu tempéré* (Jean-Marc Moutot, 2003), *Elle est des nôtres* (Siegrid Alnoy, 2003), *Mi piacce lavorare: Mobbing* (Francesca Comencini, 2004), *Cover Boy . . . The Last Revolution* (Carmine Amoroso, 2006), *La Question Humaine* (Nicolas Klotz, 2007), *Tutta la vita davanti* (Paolo Virzì, 2008), *Choses Secrètes* (Jean-Claude Brisseau, 2011), *Early One Morning* (Jean-Marc Moutot, 2011), *Generazione mille euros* (Massimo Venier, 2009), *Rooftops* (Demian Sabini, 2011), *My Piece of the Pie* (Cedric Klapisch, 2011), *Two Days, One Night* (Jean-Pierre Dardenne and Luc Dardenne, 2014), and *Sorry We Missed You* (Ken Loach, 2019)—focuses on lives in a state of animated suspension "to investigate new potential conditions of solidarity emerging from subjects not with similar historical identities or social locations but with similar adjustment styles to the pressures of the emergent new ordinariness."[27]

In a study of transnational mobility and precarious labor in post–Cold War Europe, Alice Bardan and Aine O'Healy draw on Berlant's "cruel optimism" to analyze the vulnerability shared by migrants, specifically survivors of the collapse of communist ideology, and disenfranchised European citizens. Their main case study is *Cover Boy . . . The Last Revolution* (Carmine Amoroso, 2006), which, unlike other films about internal migration, does not explore cultural, ethnic, or national differences but the precarious labor conditions experienced by *both* illegal migrants and Europeans. Rather than framing the film as an instance of "migrant cinema," however, Bardan and O'Healy situate *Cover Boy* within the legacy of Italian cinema's portrayal of the Italian South as an "Africa a casa" (Mary Wood), drawing attention to the parallel processes of Othering happening outside and inside the EU. *Cover Boy* follows the burgeoning friendship between two disenfranchised men living on the fringes of society, a Romanian youth (Ioan) without prospects traveling to Italy on a tourist visa and remaining there to work illegally as a car mechanic, and a middle-aged Italian (Michele) scraping by as a train station janitor in Rome. The montage sequence that opens the film, another instance of the heightened historical consciousness discussed in Chapter 3—archival footage ranging from the Second World War and the Holocaust to the fall of the Berlin Wall and of the Ceausescu regime—not only reminds Europeans of their shared history but also points to their shared precarious present, in which the fate of Western and Eastern Europeans alike is defined by the *structural violence* of neoliberalism—which, as the title suggests, no revolution has yet tried to overturn—a mirror image of the *physical violence* captured in the opening archival footage sequence. *Cover Boy* depicts neoliberalism as simply the latest incarnation of previous forms of totalitarianism—specifically, fascism and communism—perhaps even more obscene than them, as is suggested by a subplot in which a female photographer, who used to photograph revolutions but eventually abandoned that line of work for the more lucrative world of fashion photography, exploits Ioan's tragic personal history (his father was brutally killed during the 1989 revolution) of forced displacement and precarious existence to advertise a new high-fashion line called, appropriately, "Exile."

Like *Cover Boy*, Ulrich Seidl's *Import/Export* (2007)—in which a Ukrainian nurse (Olga) searches for a better life in the West and an unemployed security guard from Austria (Paulie) heads East for the same reason—explores the continuities between life in the broken Western welfare state and in the forever "in-transition" postcommunist Eastern European state. Olga is a nurse in the neonatal ward of a provincial town's impoverished hospital, where she gets paid only 30 percent of her salary, while Paulie is training to be a security guard but is not physically fit and violent enough for the job. Having tried, in vain, to earn a living through internet phone sex Olga travels to Vienna illegally to look for work. After going through several low-paying jobs, from cleaning lady to a maid in a private home, and being fired from both, she ends up working as a cleaning lady in an old people's nursing home for patients suffering from degenerative diseases. She strikes up a friendship with one of the elderly patients who generously offers to marry her so she can obtain Austrian citizenship but dies of a heart attack before they can get married. Meanwhile, Paulie lives with his mother and stepfather on the outskirts of Vienna. After he is fired from his job as a security guard and his girlfriend breaks up with him he travels with his stepfather to Ukraine hoping to make money setting up video gambling machines. Eventually he parts ways with his stepfather and continues looking for work on his own but his prospects are grim. We last see him walking along a country road, hitchhiking either back to Austria or further into Ukraine.

The isolated communist-style apartment buildings in Olga's hometown, located in the middle of a sprawling industrial landscape, are practically indistinguishable from the equally alienating, despondent-looking apartment building where Paulie lives with his mother and stepfather: were it not for the names of locations flashing on the screen, it would be difficult to tell whether we are in Austria or Ukraine. The film emphasizes the continuities between East and West both in terms of human interactions, presented on both sides as equally regimented and detached, and in terms of the public sphere of work. Olga's sincere attempts to relate to the patients in the old nursing home as human beings are met with reprimands that this is against the rules: after all, she is just a cleaning lady, not a nurse. When she asks the rich Austrian housewife, for whom she has been working as a maid and nanny, why she was fired her employer provides the following explanation: "I just changed my mind. I don't have to give you my reasons. I can hire you and fire you as I wish. This is how it is done in this country." Paulie's inability to "sell" himself or even to understand the unspoken "rules of the market" reveal him to be as maladapted to the world of work under neoliberalism as Olga: the only time he actually manages to get himself hired as a security guard in a mall, he is fired after a group of Turkish immigrants cuff him and humiliate him in the parking lot. Even after attending a job interview training seminar, where the instructor teaches the participants, mostly immigrants, how to "wait respectfully" to be called in for their job interview, how to speak on the phone to potential employers, and how to give oneself a pep talk to feel more competitive on the job market, Paulie remains unable to break the chain of small, low-paying, dead-end jobs and find steady employment.

By following Olga's and Paulie's frustrated attempts to make ends meet the film provides a commentary on the nature and value of "work" in neoliberal Europe, cataloging the kinds of low-paying, temporary, meaningless jobs (Olga's job at a rich family's house in Vienna involves cleaning stuffed animals with a special tiny brush) that make up the lay of the land in the twenty-first century: from an anonymous sex worker and cleaning woman to a mall security guard and purveyor of cheap video games. Cutting back and forth between the two stories, Seidl invites us to see them as mirror images of each other: as the title of the film suggests, in "the new Europe" political identities and conflicts that used to be fundamental to Europe's idea of itself have been leveled out by the logic of neoliberalism—the logic of supply and demand, Import/Export—governing the lives of Eastern and Western Europeans, of legal (Paulie) and illegal (Olga) migrants alike.

Set on the Polish-German border and weaving together several intersecting stories, *Distant Lights* (Hans-Christian Schmid, 2003)—like *Import/Export*—deliberately obscures the differences between the supposedly prosperous West and the impoverished East, presenting both as similarly dominated by a morally and socially bankrupt neoliberal order: on the Eastern side of the border a group of desperate Ukrainians try to cross illegally into Germany while a bankrupt Polish taxi-driver struggles to earn money for his daughter's communion dress; on the Western side a group of orphaned German teens are involved in smuggling cigarettes across the border in exchange for shelter and food while a struggling black-market mattress salesman and an unemployed woman try to survive the economic recession.

As the abovementioned films suggest, the transformation of "work" under neoliberalism and its central role in the construction of personal and collective identity is one of the main preoccupations of the cinema of precarity. It is also one of the reasons for the nostalgia for meaningful employment—more often than not implicitly equated with manual/manufacturing work—that permeates many of these films. With the figure of the worker pushed to the margins, Charity Scribner has argued, contemporary European culture is infused with post-industrial nostalgia in response to the waning of the collective and of labor solidarity, as well as the waning of material history in the age of the virtual, which leaves us "longing for History itself—for the touch of the real that post-industrialist virtualization threatens to subsume."[28] In Robert Guediguian's *The Snows of Kilimanjaro* (2011) the protagonist, Michel, having been laid off from his job at the dockyard, is forced to take a part-time job delivering junk mail from door to door, a humiliating and meaningless occupation strongly contrasted with the "real," "material" labor he used to perform. Similarly, in Jean-Marc Moutot's *Early One Morning* (2011), Paul experiences an existential crisis after being laid off from his soulless office job, a crisis that arguably has less to do with the fact that he is unemployed and more to do with the nature of his office job. In one scene we see him going through old pictures of himself and his wife in Africa, teaching in a school and building houses—meaningful, emotionally gratifying work that is the exact opposite of his present bank job. In another scene, during a job interview, Paul admits he wants to work for a manufacturing company that actually makes useful products rather than merely speculating with money.[29]

Scribner views post-industrial nostalgia as a symptom of the decreasing importance of work as a source of collective European identity: "Multinational unification finds its inverse in the dispersal of laborers; indeed, to a large extent European unification depends upon such dislocation. [. . .] As factories and plants are shut down, the site of culture becomes an important meeting ground for the collective . . . culture's potential [now] exceeds that of the workspace."[30] A growing number of European films set in the workplace—for example, *The Snows of Kilimanjaro*, *Of Snails and Men*, *Two Days, One Night*, *7 Minutes*, *The Nothing Factory*—could be seen as indirectly responding to Scribner's analysis by asking precisely what collective identity means in a post-industrial, neoliberal Europe, and inviting us to rethink "Europe" along Marxist rather than multicultural terms by tracing possible lines of class solidarity rather than looking for a shared cultural identity. Again, it should be noted that these films imagine the possibility of class solidarity only in the context of labor understood in the most Orthodox Marxist sense of the term as material/factory labor posited as the last outpost in the struggle against the neoliberal technocratic order—there have been hardly any films dramatizing white-collar work solidarity.

The fluidity and precariousness of work under neoliberalism represents a threat not only to collective but also to personal identity, a threat that finds expression in neoliberalism's new type of pathologies, for example, "the double life" (a darker version of Elsaesser's "doubly occupied" European identity) explored in films sharing the common premise of a husband losing his job but failing to share the news with his wife and family. Although based on the same (true) story, *Time Out* and *The Adversary* develop this premise in opposite directions: in the first the protagonist discovers a new sense of freedom in his unemployment, in the second he is driven to murder by a combination of shame, guilt, and resentment. While *Days and Clouds* (Silvio Soldini, 2007), which traces the gradual disintegration of a marriage after the husband loses his job and his wife is forced to give up her work as a fine art restorer and look for temporary jobs, brutally shows just how precipitous the fall from a bourgeois to a scavenging existence really is, Jean-Marc Moutot's *Early One Morning* (2011), a sort of French version of *Falling Down* (Joel Schumacher, 1992), reconstructs, through flashbacks, the murderous spree of one of the employees of an investment bank about to be laid off.

As was the case with coming-of-age films exploring the theme of migration from a female versus a male perspective (Chapter 2), there are substantial differences between films about men and women losing their jobs. In films portraying a female protagonist's sudden plunge into socioeconomic hell—*Two Days, One Night*, Birgit Möller's *Valerie* (2006), Cyril Mennegun's *Louise Wimmer* (2011), Francesca Comencini's *Mi piacce lavorare: Mobbing* (2004)—unemployment is depicted as thoroughly demoralizing and anxiety-producing rather than a potential source of freedom (as is the case with films featuring male protagonists). Valerie and Louise are *forced* (by circumstances) to live in their cars rather than *opting* to do so as their male counterparts do. In *Valerie* a washed-up photo model suddenly finds herself homeless in Berlin, forced to live in the parking lot of the Grand Hyatt hotel where she was, until recently, a guest. Unable to pay either for her hotel room or the parking-garage fees that will release her car she finds herself stranded in the parking garage, sleeping in her car while looking for some new gigs, trying (unsuccessfully) to earn some cash as a prostitute, and pretending to be a hotel guest in order to use some of the hotel services. In *Louise Wimmer,* set in the eastern Franche-Comte region of France, the middle-aged Louise is forced to live between her car and a storage unit containing all her belongings, while working part-time as a hotel chambermaid and waiting to obtain public housing. Despite a few references to Louise's recent divorce (her ex-husband has remarried, and their daughter is old enough to live on her own), most questions about her past and the circumstances that led to her current predicament are left unanswered. Instead, the film is mostly interested in exploring what happens to a person when they are suddenly deprived of the sources of material and emotional support that used to sustain them. Like Valerie, whose social life is limited to a few superficial relationships with other fashion models, an ex-photographer, and the Eastern European parking-garage attendants at the Hyatt, Louise finds herself alone, driving around town in her old car with Nina Simone's "Sinnerman" playing like a broken record on the car radio. In the film's dramatic highlight, Louise performs a bizarre dance (to the same song), which figures her "liberation" or, rather, absolute disconnection from any meaningful social bonds as a series of random, meaningless, uncoordinated body movements and tics—the movements of a puppet without a puppet-master, the movements of a woman who has lost control of her life.[31]

Mi piacce lavorare: Mobbing follows the psychological breakdown of Anna, a single mother working in the sales department of a large manufacturing company. After a multinational corporation acquires the company, Anna is moved from her longtime job and assigned a range of random, meaningless jobs as a way of slowly demotivating her so as to eventually fire her. Focusing on the psychological effects of Anna's protracted, exquisite form of torture ("mobbing" is a slang expression referring to harassment in the workplace) the film foregrounds the crucial role work plays in the construction and maintenance of an individual's sense of identity. As Anna's new boss openly denies her any kind of respect, and as her former colleagues abandon her one by one, she loses any sense of who she is, of her place in the social and moral order, sinking deeper and deeper into depression, her relationship with her daughter falling apart as well. Eventually Anna contacts a union representative and sues the company (she wins). Although the film does not explicitly address racial relations—with the exception of a minor subplot about Anna's daughter's African friend—the psychological effects of work harassment it explores through Anna's character uncannily mirror those of "differentialist racism" (see the Introduction) distinguished by its subtlety and invisibility, "a racism without race." Anna is never explicitly criticized or judged by her boss or her colleagues; in fact, her boss makes it a point to present the meaningless jobs he assigns her as "very important" and as "evidence of the great amount of trust the company has in her skills," empty words meant to disguise the company's view of Anna (and of all its employees) as expendable. It is this notion of a human being's expendability, and the grave psychological effects of internalizing it, as Anna does, that the film is most concerned with rather than with the purely economic effects of unemployment.

Paolo Virzi's slightly more upbeat *Tutta la vita davanti* (2008) revolves around Marta who, having just graduated with flying colors with a degree in philosophy (specializing in Heidegger, no less) and finding it impossible to find a job that fits her education and skills, is forced to accept a temporary job in a call center run by a ruthless manager, while also babysitting for one of her telemarketing colleagues. Although successful at her new job, Marta soon becomes aware of the exploitative strategies in her workplace and after meeting and falling for a labor union representative she resolves to make the company's unfair practices known. Still passionate about philosophy, Marta teaches the little girl she is babysitting the famous allegory of Plato's cave, "updating" it as an allegory of workers' self-enslavement in the age of neoliberalism, and yet at the end of the film the allegory remains just that, an allegory: instead of the young female telemarketers uniting and revolting against their manager, the manager is arrested for killing her lover (the telemarketing company's owner) rather than for unfair practices, and the telemarketers, giddy with joy that they can leave work early and unwilling to face the uncertainty of being unemployed yet again, spend the rest of the day in the mall.

By contrast, in *The Adversary* and *Time Out* the male protagonists, having lost their jobs, find refuge in their cars and drive around aimlessly, free for a while from having to face the situation and tell their families the truth. Their unemployment, as anxiety-producing as it might be, gives them a new lease on life, a second life that, though based on lies, shame, and guilt, is also strangely liberating, granting them the freedom (luxury) not to make any decisions just yet but to reflect on what went wrong, or to simply be alone. The title of Fernando León de Aranoa's *Mondays in the Sun* (2002), which centers on the lives of a group of laid-off shipyard workers in northern Spain, imagines precarity as a sort of vacation or "time off." Although the men clearly experience unemployment as a loss of manhood and dignity, sinking further into a state of anxious idleness, that does not preclude them from having some fun times too. *Rooftops* (Demian Sabini, 2011) could be seen as a sequel to *Mondays in the Sun*, although Sabini focuses on the precarious lives of the younger generation, a group of unemployed college-educated friends in their early thirties who spend their long, work-free days on the best rooftops in Barcelona. The film opens with a voice-over—a radio podcast consisting of interviews with government officials—which serves as the film's exposition: Spain is experiencing a severe economic crisis, with unemployment rising to 15–20 percent and social subsidies and extensions on various forms of aid coming to an end, leaving whole families without jobs. The language of crisis and urgency is, however, undercut by the very next shot, which shows a group of young people sunbathing on a rooftop. For a while it's not clear whether they are on vacation—that is, they can afford not to work—or they are unemployed. The upbeat music, the relaxing summer atmosphere, and the beautiful cityscape of Barcelona create an impression that contradicts the gravity and urgency of the radio podcast. Through a series of flashbacks we discover that the protagonist, Leo, and his friends were the staff of a small legal firm, which was forced to close down because of the crisis. Leo and friends spend most of the film drinking, taking magic mushrooms, and complaining about the lack of jobs for overqualified college graduates like them, all the while enjoying the relative security of living on unemployment subsidy. Their predicament is presented as a choice between two options, revolting against the neoliberal order or ignoring it: "Being up here (on the roof) makes you feel that you can rearrange the world," "No, we are up here to ignore it," "Yeah, that too. Fuck it" is representative of their half-joking conversations. And "ignore it" they do. *Rooftops* depicts Spain's economic crisis as a nice break for a privileged set of college graduates, a break that allows Leo to question what he really wants in life—to follow what is expected of him (go to college, get a job, find a girlfriend), or pursue his own passion, which is left unclear, although the end of the film implies it involves leaving his previous "soulless" office job to devote himself to organic farming in his friend's start-up eco co-op. In short, the economic crisis is depicted not as a hardship Leo is forced to undergo but as a chance for self-discovery and reinvention.[32]

If *Mondays in the Sun* and *Rooftops* already make clear that the cinema of Ppecarity is cross-generational, a pair of recent Italian films drive the point home. In Massimo Venier's *Generazione mille euro* (2009), Matteo, a math graduate in his late twenties, is forced, like Marta in *Tutta la vita davanti*, to abandon his real passion and accept a job in the marketing office of a telecommunications company, which is about to cut back on personnel, thereby creating a serial killer-type suspense ('who will be next?'). Very quickly Matteo's relatively stable life is turned upside down: his girlfriend leaves him, he has no money to pay the rent, and he could be laid off any moment. After a new, beautiful roommate moves in with Matteo and his best friend, and an equally charming and sophisticated new boss arrives at Matteo's company, Matteo is faced with a difficult choice, which the film frames as a romantic one even though its significance goes far beyond that: the choice between keeping his humanity, dignity, and honesty at the price of accepting his life's precarity, or climbing up the social ladder by accepting a lucrative job in Barcelona, an option the film clearly condemns as "selling out." In short, the choice is an ethical one: between everything of human (emotional) value to Matteo (his best friend, his new roommate-girlfriend, his colleague at work, who is likely to lose his job) and that which is of purely economic or use value (a stable, lucrative job), that is, between human relationships and capitalist profit.

There are unmistakable echoes of *Generazione* in Duccio Chiarini's comedy *The Guest* (2018), another exploration of the mutual imbrication between work and personal life that draws a parallel between precarious employment and the fear/lack of commitment in romantic relationships, in this case for the generation in their early forties. Although one generation separates *The Guest*'s forty-ish protagonist Guido from *Generazione*'s Matteo, Guido finds his relatively stable life threatened in much the same way as Matteo: his girlfriend leaves him (to pursue a job in Canada), while his lifelong research on Italo Calvino is constantly jeopardized by lack of funding, forcing him to accept temp jobs as a substitute teacher. Guido suddenly finds himself homeless, forced to live between his parents' sofa and the sofas of his two male friends, who have relationship problems of their own. Although there are no references to the refugee crisis, the film's use of the trope of "the guest," with its explicit invocation of hospitality, reveals some deep structural affinities with films exploring the encounter (in terms of the extension or refusal of hospitality) between Europeans and migrants/refugees: while Guido is the only one to find himself homeless for a while, his primary function as a guest in other people's houses (including his parents' house) is to reveal the deep cracks within what appeared to be stable romantic relationships, just as in many migrant films the foreigner/immigrant/refugee exposes the presumed immutability and homogeneity of the nation as a mere façade.

Although *Mi piacce lavorare, Tutta la vita davanti, Time Out, Early One Morning, The Snows of Kilimanjaro, Two Days, One Night*, and *My Piece of the Pie* (Cedric Klapisch, 2011) (the last three discussed next) explore solidarity, class struggle, and ethics in the context of neoliberalism, without however featuring migrants or refugees, they share important structural and narrative similarities with migrant films, allowing us to see a clear parallel between the disintegration of the working class and the question of the ethical limits of one's responsibility to other members of one's class and, on the other hand, between the weakening of the nation-state as a source of identity and the ethical limits of one's responsibility to non-national and/or non-European "others."

2 The Cinema of Migration Meets the Cinema of Precarity

Arguably, *La faute à Voltaire/Poetical Refugee* (Abdellatif Kechiche, 2000), which follows a North African man who immigrates illegally to France (claiming to be a refugee from war-torn Algeria in order to get residency), where he keeps moving between various illegal jobs and homeless shelters, anticipates the recent spate of films exploring the affective and structural affinities between disenfranchised Europeans and migrants and/or refugees. Before turning to specific films, however, I would like to consider briefly an older film, which can also be seen as an exploration of the parallel destinies of "migrant Others" and socially disenfranchised Europeans. Agnes Varda's 1985 *Vagabond* (*Sans toit ni loi*) has been primarily discussed as a feminist film about a young drifter, Mona, a wanderer living outside society's expectations and outside the structures of the law. In the DVD commentary, made eighteen years after the initial release of the film, Varda returns to some of the places and people involved in the production of the film, and even analyzes several key sequences of the film, suggesting that one possible way to read the film is as the fall of an initially "pure," autonomous woman (the first time we see Mona she emerges naked, Venus-like, from the sea) who becomes gradually "sullied" through her interactions with others, who project their own needs, fears, and anxieties onto her. None of the film's reviewers, however, has ever approached the film as a quasi-neorealist docudrama about 1980s France. With a few exceptions (a university professor, a rich old woman and her nephew waiting for her to die so he can inherit her house), the image of rural Southern France that emerges from the film is one of poverty, bordering on squalor, and a general sense of social disenfranchisement, though Varda refuses to make any explicit political commentary. Although it is true that, as most reviewers have observed, Mona's interactions with the people she meets on the road reveal less about her than about them, one could also argue that the figure of the drifter offers a great vantage point from which to observe the social structures and hierarchies Mona has purposefully extracted herself from.

Consider, for instance, one of the rarely examined relationships in the film, that between Mona and an older Tunisian immigrant worker, who invites her to stay with him in the special residence for African immigrant workers. Unlike the other men and women Mona meets on the road, the Tunisian offers to take care of her and provide her with a home. However, when the other North African immigrants return to work (they have been away, in Africa, to visit their families) they refuse to take Mona in, and she is thus forced to leave. This is the only time Mona is rejected by someone (usually she is the one rejecting or abandoning others) and the only time we see her cry. By singling out Mona's relationship with the Tunisian, the only one to show her unconditional hospitality (he is also the only one who, when interviewed about her after her death, remains silent), the film draws a parallel between the precariousness of the European's existence, outside social and legal norms, *sans toit ni loi* (Mona) and the precarious status of North African immigrant workers on the periphery of French society.

Twenty years later the structural and affective affinities between disenfranchised Europeans and migrants glimpsed briefly in Varda's film have become European cinema's general mise en scène, as evidenced by films like *Princesas* (Fernando León de Aranoa, 2005), *It's a Free World* (Ken Loach, 2007), *Amador* (Fernando León de Aranoa, 2010), *La Nostra Vita* (Daniele Luchetti, 2010), *Biutiful* (Alejandro Iñárritu, 2010), *Shun Li and the Poet* (Andrea Segre, 2011), *Terraferma* (Emanuele Crialese, 2011), *My Piece of the Pie* (Cedric Klapisch, 2011), *Three Worlds* (Catherine Corsini, 2012), *Eat Sleep Die* (Gabriela Pichler, 2012), *Two Days, One Night* (Jean-Pierre Dardenne and Luc Dardenne, 2014), *Mediterranea* (Jonas Carpignano, 2015), *A Ciambra* (Jonas Carpignano, 2017), *Twin Flower* (Laura Luchetti, 2018), and others.

The quasi-neorealist *Princesas* explores the transnational reciprocity and female solidarity between Spanish working girls, on the fringes of Spanish society, and Dominican illegal immigrants, both occupying the same socioeconomic strata. The film focuses on the relationship between the middle-class Spanish girl Caye, prostituting herself for cash in the streets of Madrid, and Zulema, part of a new breed of Dominican prostitutes perceived by Spanish working girls as a threat. Caye is saving money for a breast augmentation operation and waiting for "true love" while Zulema is working hard and suffering endless humiliation and abuse by her clients (particularly one client whom she is "servicing" for free in exchange for a work permit he has promised to her, which he never delivers), trying to save money so she can return to the son she has left behind. In the first part of the film we observe Zulema and the other Dominican prostitutes through the eyes of the Spanish working girls, who gather at one of their friends' hair salon to gossip, share secrets of the trade, and observe with resentment the Dominicans "stealing their jobs." In the second part, however, the film renders explicit, in order to critique, the economic foundations of racism: as one of the Spanish girls observes, "It's not racism. The problem is the law of the market."

In Aranoa's next film, *Amador*, poor Bolivian illegal immigrant Marcela lives on the outskirts of Madrid with her boyfriend, Nelson, eking out a precarious living by stealing and reselling flowers. When the refrigerator where they store the flowers breaks down, Marcela, anxious about their financial situation, accepts a job taking care of Amador, a rich woman's (Yolanda) bedridden father. When Amador dies suddenly, Marcela, afraid of losing her income, decides to make it look as though he is still alive. In one of the story's subplots Aranoa depicts the relationship between Marcela and Puri, Amador's middle-aged Andalusian neighbor and prostitute. At one point, Marcela provokes Puri when she says, "Next thing you will tell me that we (Bolivian immigrants) are stealing your jobs." Puri confirms that this is, indeed, what she thinks but surprisingly this confession cements the two women's growing friendship instead of driving them apart. Aranoa thus positions illegal immigrants, like Marcela, and people living on the periphery of Spanish society, like the aging Andalusian prostitute Puri displaced in Madrid, as equally victims of precarity, thus suggesting a possible solidarity between them.

It's a Free World focuses on Angie, a young woman who, frustrated after being fired from her job as a recruiter, decides to set up a recruitment agency of her own, running it from home together with her friend and roommate Rose. At first they hire only immigrants with working papers but as the story unfolds Angie becomes increasingly willing to do whatever it takes to succeed in her business venture, even if it involves hiring illegal immigrants and informing Immigration Services about a camp of illegals, hoping to use the camp, once those living there have been evicted, for newly arriving illegal immigrants that she has hired. As time goes by, her relationship with the illegals she hires gets increasingly strained and she drops all pretenses to be "helping" them find a job, treating them, instead, as cheap labor, and disposing of them matter-of-factly. In a scene that marks her complete transformation from exploited to exploiter, she calls two of the illegal workers she has recruited to have sex with—once a victim of sexual harassment herself, she now expects sexual favors from her employees. When one employer that Angie has been providing with illegal workers refuses to pay them, the workers blame Angie and kidnap her son. Later they release him but demand the rest of the money they are owed from Angie, or she will never see her son again. Abandoning her scruples completely, Angie flies to Ukraine to recruit more illegal workers, offering to obtain forged papers for them.

Although we are supposed to be appalled at Angie's moral degradation, Loach also invites us to see things from Angie's point of view. Angie's father, an old union man, disapproves of his daughter's business but when she dismisses his criticisms as nationalist, anti-immigrant talk, he points out the hypocrisy of her stance: she claims to be helping illegal immigrants but she is paying them far less than the minimum wage. Angie reminds him how out of step with the times he is: he has had one stable job all his life, whereas she lives in a world of precarious labor, a lawless world in which the only law is the survival of the fittest. Ultimately, even as the film traces Angie's transformation from a victim of the neoliberal order to a "winner" exploiting and profiting herself from that order, her survival is revealed to be predicated on crossing over to the other side of the law: to the extent that the free flow of capital remains indifferent to limits like national borders, passports, and labor laws, Angie becomes an illegal herself, as illegal as those she continues to exploit.

La Nostra Vita follows Claudio, a young construction worker living happily with his pregnant wife, two children and a third on the way, on the outskirts of Rome. When his wife dies during childbirth Claudio dedicates himself to making money to make up for his sons' loss by making their lives as materially comfortable as possible. He negotiates a deal with his boss to give him his own construction site to supervise, in exchange for which Claudio promises not to report the death of an illegal Romanian worker that his boss is covering up. After quickly spending the money he borrows from his drug-dealing neighbor, Claudio runs into problems with his site workers (mostly illegal migrants) after he is unable to pay them. They quit stealing most of his equipment. Meanwhile, ridden by guilt, Claudio also has to deal with the dead Romanian's ex-lover and son who come looking for him. Eventually Claudio borrows more money from his brother and sister, hires more expensive workers—part-time Italian workers whom he hires on the condition that he pay them cash—and manages to finish the construction work and repay his debts.

Like *It's a Free World*, Luchetti's film depicts the Italian working class, embodied here by Claudio, as sharing the same precarious existence as that of immigrants, legal or illegal. As Natasha Senjanovic points out in her review of the film, in *La Nostra Vita* "there are no more ideals, only the frenetic, vicious cycle that is 'arrangiarsi.' The word has no direct equivalent in English but signifies something between getting by and hustling."[33] Arguably, the title of the film—"our life"—reflects precisely this sense of a life shared by people that until recently used to see each other as occupying different spaces, Europeans and "Europeans without euros." Like many of the other films considered here *La Nostra Vita* suggests the possibility for solidarity along socioeconomic lines but not along racial ones. Here it is instructive to compare the Italians' perception of Romanians (the ex-lover of the dead Romanian and her son) and their perception of the Senegalese woman, Celeste, whom Claudio wants to hire to take care of his baby. While Celeste lives with Claudio's drug-dealing friend, with whom she has a child, Claudio's sister objects to her being her brother's nanny but refuses to admit that the reason for her objection has to do with Celeste being black. Claudio's sister is equally suspicious of her other brother's budding romance with Gabriela, the dead Romanian's ex-lover, but for different reasons—she suspects Gabriela of being a gold-digger, playing into the familiar stereotype of Eastern Europeans (especially Eastern European women) as "predators" looking to exploit financially "naïve" Western Europeans. In this respect, then, the film reproduces, even while criticizing, the familiar image of the racial Other as the ultimate "Other" and the image of the Eastern European Other as "like us but not quite us." At the same time, however, *La Nostra Vita* also suggests a possible new relationship between East and West, one based on a more open notion of hospitality and reciprocity and embodied by the "unconventional family" of Claudio, his brother, his brother's Romanian girlfriend Gabriela, and Gabriela's son Andrei (Romanian but born in Italy) who by the end of the film has become a kind of surrogate brother to Claudio's sons.

In Loach's film the illegal white Eastern European immigrants are not positioned as completely Other to the "First World" British citizen (Angie). By contrast, *Mediterranea*, *Terraferma*, and *Shun Li and the Poet* complicate the parallels drawn between migrants and disenfranchised Europeans by featuring non-European migrants (African and Chinese). *Mediterranea* tells the story of Ayiva, a man from Burkina Faso who makes the difficult journey from his country, through Algeria and Libya, to Southern Italy, where he is forced to live in a squatted property with other African illegal migrants while working as an orange picker and sending money back to his sister and daughter for their future journey to Italy. Carpignano is especially attentive to capturing the indistinctive, anonymous cartography of migration as Ayiva travels from one nameless place (a refugee camp in Algeria) to another nameless town in Libya, to a small, nondescript provincial town in Italy, looking half-abandoned, which, despite being named, has no distinguishable Italian markers and looks like any-town-whatever in Europe. From the moment the migrants arrive in Rosarno it is made clear that they are not welcome, as some of the locals drive their scooters menacingly around them, break their parties looking for prostitutes, and stare them down threateningly at the dance club. Ayiva is soon introduced to Pio, a charismatic, no-nonsense Italian Romani boy of lower-class origins running his own version of the black market directly from his parents' house, where he sells and buys stolen goods from illegal migrants and Italians alike. Pio smokes, knows how to bargain, and boasts excellent entrepreneurial skills. The film emphasizes Ayiva's and Pio's shared socioeconomic disenfranchisement, once again drawing a parallel between the experience of migrants and nonmigrants, specifically Italians living in a small Southern town far from the industrial, prosperous North. In one scene a female friend of Ayiva makes fun of his clothes, telling him that he looks "like one of those guys hanging out at the train station," referring to unemployed Italians. Ultimately, however, race proves an insurmountable difference (see Chapter 2). The gradually escalating tension between locals and migrants finally erupts in a series of violent outbursts as the migrants are evicted from their house and the house burned. The hostilities quickly escalate into a riot, which Ayiva is initially reluctant to join; however, when the police fire tear gas and start beating up the protesters, Ayiva joins the protesters as they march through the streets yelling "Stop shooting blacks!" (rather than "Stop shooting migrants!"), recalling a very similar sequence from another film exploring racial conflict in America, Spike Lee's *Do the Right Thing* (1989).

A Ciambra, set in the Romani community in Calabria, is a sort of a sequel to *Mediterranea*, in which the protagonist, the adolescent Pio, was already introduced. Carpignano's ambition—to tell a story that is representative of a particular place and time—are clear from the titles of both films, which reference an expansive geographical area (in the first film) and an entire ethnic group (in the second). While *Mediterranea* focused on Italians' racism against black illegal immigrants, *A Ciambra* zooms in on the inter-perceptions of two equally disenfranchised and marginalized communities, the Romani and African illegal immigrants (the tented migrant communities from Burkina Faso and Ghana). An early scene, in which we are introduced to the various members of Pio's extended family, reveals the Roma to be as racist as the Italian inhabitants of Rosarno in *Mediterranea*: Pio's mother scolds her daughter and children for drinking, warning them that they will become "like the Africans," who "drink and fight each other all the time," while the demented grandfather complains that the Africans robbed him, utterly oblivious to his own family's various thieving exploits. At the same time, the film suggests continuities between the Roma's precarious, marginal, criminalized existence and the everyday life of mafia-driven communities on the outskirts of big Italian cities, as seen in Matteo Garrone's *Gomorrah* (2008), especially through establishing shots that show the rooftops of both communities full of "guards" warning the residents of any surprise visits by the police. In addition to the African illegal immigrants and the Roma, a third group of characters, the "Italians" or Ndràngheta mobsters (the Calabria mafia), with whom the Roma are in an open-ended turf war, complete the picture of Italy's "underbelly." The hermetic nature of this self-enclosed criminal underworld dawns on the viewer only when we meet the single character coming from outside it, a confused white, middle-class man from Turin (he keeps repeating that "he is not from here") to whom Pio delivers a stolen car.

The "pecking order" is clear and set in place: the African illegals are at the bottom, scorned by the Roma (with the exception of Pio), while the Roma do various illegal jobs for their "patrons," the Calabrian mobsters, who don't seem to be interested in "hiring" blacks. Within this clearly demarcated, stratified world, an unexpected, quasi-brotherly relationship of loyalty and trust develops (already hinted at in *Mediterranea*) between Pio and Ayiva. In an early scene Pio shows up at the local discotheque, looking for his brother; the next shot shows Pio surprising Ayiva by jumping on his back. Indeed, throughout the film Ayiva is depicted as more of a brother to Pio than Pio's own brother, who refuses to do any "jobs" with him because he considers Pio still a child. Whenever Pio has any problems or needs help, it is Ayiva that he seeks, and that seeks him back, their bond emerging as a variation on the adoption motif I identified earlier, though here the metaphor of adoption—and thus of solidarity and hospitality—links two marginalized ethnic and racial "Others" rather than a white European citizen and a racialized Other. By the end of the film, however, any possible lines of solidarity are compromised by demands for in-group loyalty. Pio inadvertently sabotages a theft mission and, with his brother arrested, he enjoys, for a while, his newly found freedom and the implicit permission to continue his brother's "work." However, when his brother is eventually released from prison, Pio is forced to "atone for his sins" by doing a job that involves betraying Ayiva (he has to distract Ayiva while his brother and his gang steal a truck full of goods stolen by the Africans).

The implicit connection *Mediterranea* draws between the plight of socially and economically disenfranchised Europeans and the plight of refugees becomes even more explicit in *Terraferma*, which examines the encounter between an old Sicilian family of fishermen on the island of Linosa, part of the commune of Lampedusa, and a group of African immigrants, specifically a mother and her two young children. The story centers on the young Filippo, who lives with his mother (Donatella) and grandfather, his father, a fisherman, having disappeared at sea three years earlier. The film paints a detailed picture of the precarious life of fishermen on Linosa, with most of the remaining fishermen getting old and selling their boats, their children having already left the island for better opportunities elsewhere. Tellingly, the Sicilians' backstory in *Terraferma* is the same as that of Baye Laye in *La Pirogue* (2012) (Chapter 1): the fish that once supplied the Senegalese Baye Laye's livelihood has grown scarce, forcing him to accept the dangerous journey to Europe; similarly, the primary source of income on the island, fishing, has become a bankrupt endeavor, forcing many of the island's inhabitants to look for better opportunities on the mainland. When the African refugee shares with Donatella—who also dreams of leaving the island—her plan to join her husband in Torino, Donatella dismisses it as impractical on account of the great distance she has to travel: for Donatella, like for many southerners, Northern Italy is so far away that it might as well be another country. In the film both the Italians living on this small, isolated island and the African refugees trying to enter Europe are desperately looking for "terraferma," not just in the sense of mainland but also in the sense of socioeconomic stability.[34] This portrayal of the Italian South as a poor and archaic region, "an Africa a casa," is in line with a long tradition of representing the migration of Italians from the poor South (the Mezzogiorno) to the affluent North. Matteo Garrone's *Ospiti/Guests* (1998) draws a similar connection between an Albanian illegal immigrant to Italy (supposedly a guest) and a poor, unemployed Italian who migrated thirty years ago from Sardinia to Rome. And yet, even as *Terraferma* invokes the continuities between the plight of African refugees and that of the inhabitants of "Africa a casa," in the most visually striking scene in the film, the "arrival" of the African refugees on the island is depicted as a violent and horrific event. Filippo and a girl are enjoying a date on a boat when dozens of black bodies rise up menacingly from the dark water and swim furiously toward them in a shot strikingly reminiscent of the shark attack in Spielberg's *Jaws* (1975); the girl screams in horror while Filippo fends off the refugees with a stick as they try to climb on board, eventually managing to turn on the motor and speed away, leaving the black bodies behind. In a later scene, those same black bodies, some of them dead, others barely alive, are washed ashore in the middle of a beach resort run by Filippo's uncle.

Shun Li and the Poet tells the story of a Chinese immigrant, Shun Li, working in a café in Venice to pay off for her move to Italy and to bring her son over from China. She befriends Bepi, an older Serbian immigrant who came to Italy thirty years ago and is now perceived by the locals as Italian. The first part of the film emphasizes the widening gap between the older, traditional working-class Italian culture of the fishermen and the younger generation who have grown up under the neoliberal order. Conversations about family, work, and fishing reveal that all characters in the film, regardless of their racial or national background, share the same history of traditional work (related to the sea) passed down from one generation to the next, but this kind of traditional lifestyle, and the worldview that it comes with, is now declining: Shun Li works in a factory (like many other immigrants), Bepi and his old Italian fishermen friends are now retiring, and the younger generation of Italians have none of the work ethic and respect for family and tradition of the older generation. In the second part of the film, as Italians observe with growing suspicion the blossoming friendship between Shun Li and Bepi, class conflicts are gradually overshadowed by racial ones. Significantly, throughout the film Shun Li refers to Bepi as "Italian," that is, she sees him first and foremost as a white European man rather than an immigrant like her. When Bepi tells his Italian friend, Coppe, that if he had become friends with the café's previous owner, Maria, the Italians would not have seen it as a problem, Coppe points out that Maria was neither young nor Chinese. As the Italians become increasingly hostile to Shun Li, they rationalize their racial prejudice through recourse to economics: in one scene Avvocato explains the economic threat Shun Li represents to Italy as Chinese immigrants continue to steal jobs from Italians: "It's an invasion! The New Empire!" With the animosity directed at Shun Li and the Chinese in general escalating, the older and younger generations of Italians that were previously at odds with each other reunite against the common threat of the racialized Other.

In *Biutiful* a divorced Spanish man (Uxbal) struggles with feelings of guilt over inadvertently causing the death of a group of Chinese illegal immigrants. Uxbal lives in a shabby apartment in Barcelona with his two children, whose mother, a prostitute, suffers from alcoholism and bipolar disorder. Uxbal's only family is his wealthier brother Tito, who works in the construction business. Uxbal earns a living by procuring work for illegal Chinese immigrants who make forged designer goods in a basement sweatshop, which a group of African street vendors then sell in the street. Hai, in charge of the Chinese, makes regular payments to Uxbal, who then pays off the police to keep quiet about the whole thing. Uxbal is also a psychic medium to the dead, earning some extra money by passing on messages from the recently deceased at wakes and funerals (Uxbal thus functions symbolically as Charon, the mythic ferryman of Hades who carries the souls of the newly deceased across the river Styx). Diagnosed with terminal prostate cancer, and having only a few months left to live, his world begins to fall apart. When the Africans (who also deal in drugs) get arrested, and one of them is deported to Senegal, Uxbal offers his wife Ige and his baby son a room in his apartment. With the Chinese now out of work, Tito strikes a deal to get them employed at a construction site. However, almost all of them die during the night from carbon monoxide poisoning, because Uxbal has bought them cheap gas heaters that do not meet safety standards. When a human trafficker tries to dump the bodies into the sea they are washed up on the shore, causing a media scandal. With his health deteriorating, Uxbal is plagued with guilt over the death of the Chinese illegal workers and the expulsion of the Senegalese street vendor. He tries to atone for his sins by offering Ige the remainder of his savings and asking her to take care of his children after his death.

Uxbal's humanity is constantly tested by the precarious circumstances he lives in. On one hand, his relations with the Africans and the Chinese are strictly business ones, and he is actually exploiting them (while lying to himself that he is not) by taking a share of their earnings, which are already negligible (although, he reassures himself, back in China they would have made even less). On the other hand, he has a good heart—he buys them gas heaters (although the cheapest ones). He appears to genuinely care about the Senegalese man deported back to Africa—he offers his wife and son all his money and free accommodation, although only after he realizes his death is imminent and he needs to find a caregiver for his children. Ironically, it is Uxbal's "friend" in the police, whom Uxbal has been bribing all along to ensure the police don't threaten his illegal business with the Chinese and the Africans, who ultimately "diagnoses" Uxbal's bad faith. When, in a scene that recalls the conversation between Angie and her father in *It's a Free World*, Uxbal claims he is helping illegal immigrants get work, the policeman reminds him that he is taking a cut of their wage. When Uxbal asks the policeman to help him bring back the Senegalese man who was deported, the policeman reminds him of his own powerlessness: "I am not a government official. I can't keep playing the United Nations. I have a daughter to feed myself." He then goes on to tell Uxbal an anecdote about a man who trained tigers for a circus, which neatly encapsulates life under neoliberalism: "It's dangerous to trust a man who is hungry, and even more so if his children are hungry." Like *Lorna's Silence*, *Biutiful* is full of close-up shots of money—dirty, crumpled banknotes being passed between people, the only currency that matters in the world Uxbal, the policeman, and Chinese and African illegal immigrants all share.

The title of Corsini's *Three Worlds*—a ponderous, self-important film about guilt and atonement, in which three characters are drawn together by a tragic accident—spells out the idea I have been tracing in the films analyzed so far: while Europeans, legal and illegal migrants, and refugees appear to inhabit separate worlds, their destinies are mutually determined in ways that might not be immediately visible. While speeding home from a wild bachelor party Alan hits a pedestrian and drives off. Juliette, a medical student, witnesses the hit-and-run accident from her balcony and calls an ambulance. Later she tracks down the victim, an undocumented Moldovan construction worker and his wife, who is informed by the doctors that if her comatose husband survives at all he will be a quadriplegic. Feeling remorseful, Alan visits the hospital, where Juliette recognizes him from the accident scene.

The son of a cleaning woman, Alan is close to realizing his working-class dream: having climbed up the proverbial ladder within the car dealership owned by the affluent Testard family, he is about to marry Testard's daughter and become a partner in the business. Eventually Juliette confronts Alan and tries to act as a mediator between him and the Moldovan victim's wife, Vera, but complications arise when Juliette and Alan start falling in love. Although there is certainly nothing wrong in structuring a story around an ethical problem—what is Alan's responsibility, how can justice be done, should Alan have to "pay" for what happened—there is something ethically suspect in the unstated assumption that the identity of the victim—a struggling illegal immigrant—has a bearing on the way in which the ethical question is posed. The film suggests that the identity of the victim raises the moral and ethical stakes higher, demanding something like a "super-ethical" resolution to the problem (as distinguished from a "merely" ethical resolution which would have applied if the victim was a French national, for example). Ultimately, Alan, tortured by remorse, surrenders himself to Vera and allows her to take him to the police; however, at the last moment Vera changes her mind and decides not to turn him in, apparently because she believes letting him go free to be a more severe punishment.

Three Worlds draws a parallel between Alan, who comes from a working-class background, and Vera, the illegal Moldovan immigrant. On the surface Alan has "made it": he has worked his way up the hierarchy in Testard's car dealership, is about to marry into an upper-middle-class family, and is in line to take over the family business. Nevertheless, his dream of class mobility remains just that, a dream. When Alan's mother tells him she is ashamed to come to his wedding because she used to wear hand-me-downs from the boss's wife, and Alan reminds her that she does not work for him anymore because now they are "one of them," his mother dismisses his "cruel optimism," convinced that although Alan's circumstances seem to have changed, his (and her) social identity cannot be so easily "upgraded." By insisting on the indestructibility of class barriers—so that a single accidental event, such as a hit-and-run accident, can reinstate the class barriers that Alan appeared to have surmounted—the film underscores the similar status shared by working-class French citizens and undocumented migrants: just as Vera, now a widow, is set to lose everything, her status in France becoming even more precarious, if convicted Alan is set to lose everything he has struggled for all his life (material, professional, and personal success).

Twin Flower, a road movie/migrant film set in Sardinia, follows two teenagers on the run as they gradually form a loving bond that is instinctive and tactile rather than based on verbal communication. Anna is running away from Manfredi, the refugee trafficker for whom her father used to work, and Basim is a refugee from Côte d'Ivoire, hiding from Italian immigration authorities. Both characters are played by nonprofessional actors drawing upon their personal experience: Basim is played by Kallil Kone, a real refugee who came to Italy four months before the film shoot and speaks only French, a few words of Italian, and his native dialect, while Anna is played by a Ukrainian girl who immigrated to Italy as a child. Through several flashbacks we learn that Anna's father's decision to stop working as a human trafficker drove Manfredi to kill him (Anna disapproved of her father's line of work but he was forced to accept it given the difficulties of finding work in Sardinia). Luchetti has stated that the inspiration for the film came from her reading about "the phenomenon of the phantom," referring to the fact that a great number of refugee children arriving on boats in Italy vanish and no one knows what happens to them after their arrival. The film's operative metaphor of "the twin flower"—a flower that Anna comes upon in her work for an old gardener in town—refers not only to the bond of love and trust that gradually forms between Basim and Anna but also to their shared experience of vulnerability, marginalization, and disenfranchisement. The film invites us to see Basim's refugee status and all the dangers and humiliations associated with it as structurally similar to the marginal status of socially disenfranchised Italians like Anna and her father, the lonely cross-dressing male prostitute Basim meets on several occasions, and the prostitutes alongside whom Basim is forced to "work" to make some money (presumably the prostitutes include both Italians and migrants/refugees). The parallel between refugees and other marginal figures (prostitutes, transvestites, beggars) is further underscored by the setting of the film in a small, desolate coastal town consisting of an abandoned salt mine, a little café whose only customers are a few old men, and a lot of abandoned houses, in one of which Anna and Basim seek refuge.

Despite the important affinities between the figure of the refugee and the various marginalized figures on the periphery of Italian society, the story clearly privileges Anna's character. Although both Basim and Anna have been traumatized by their past, it is only Anna's past that the film is interested in, as evidenced by the flashback structure through which Luchetti reconstructs the tragic sequence of events that left Anna speechless. While Anna is thus granted a backstory, an interior life, and a personal trauma that explains her behavior and state of mind in the present, Basim's character remains a blank canvas onto which viewers are invited to project whatever stereotypical images of, and stories about, refugees they are familiar with from the media. The only time the film hints at Basim's backstory is when Anna rummages through his backpack (while Basim is away) and finds a little notebook with a picture of what could be Basim's family in Côte d'Ivoire. Anna is a two-dimensional character; Basim is, and remains, a type ("the refugee").

Having made his directorial debut with *Little Nothings* (1992), a story about the employees of a department store on the verge of bankruptcy, in *My Piece of the Pie* (2011), an English-style social comedy with echoes of *Pretty Woman* (Garry Marshall, 1990) and *Maid in Manhattan* (Wayne Wang, 2002), Cedric Klapisch addresses the European economic crisis, once again on a human scale. After being laid off, along with many others, by the recently bankrupt factory where she has worked for two decades in the port city of Dunkirk, France, mother of three, is forced to commute from Dunkirk to Paris where she finds a temporary job house-cleaning in the luxury penthouse of a suave, greedy banker, Stephane, who turns out to have been responsible for closing down the factory thanks to a successful deal brokered in London, resulting in his transfer to Paris. The film portrays France (whose name conflates the image of a working-class heroine with that of an entire country struggling with an economic crisis) as occupying the same status as that of immigrants (both legal and illegal). Specifically, the film draws two parallel analogies: on one hand, between France's socioeconomic disenfranchisement, which she shares with illegal immigrants and/or refugees in France, and on the other hand, between France's regional identity (she is from Normandy but lives in Dunkirk, in the north of France) and the non-French identity of illegal immigrants and refugees who are, like France, "foreigners" in France (in one scene France explicitly states that as someone living in Dunkirk but originally not from there, she feels like a foreigner, and that in Paris she would feel even more like a foreigner/ immigrant).

France gets the idea of looking for a job in Paris from a former coworker, who offers to ask his father (of Maghrebi origin) in Paris to help her with the job search. The scene in which France meets the father is meant to be doubly ironic: not only does the legal Maghrebi immigrant occupy a position higher on the social ladder than the French woman (he is employed, she is not), but France is also the victim of social déclassement, having fallen down to the rank of legal and illegal immigrants (most house-cleaning-help jobs are performed by illegal immigrants). When the father explains to France that his course is designed "to help the underprivileged" and France admits that "after being laid off I feel pretty underprivileged myself," he agrees with her, observing that, "with all the relocation (outsourcing of jobs to China) you are an immigrant in your own country," indirectly commenting on the persistent view of second- or even third-generation Maghrebi French citizens as still "immigrants in their own country." The man welcomes France into his course on the condition that she speak with an accent for the sake of the immigrant women enrolled in the course, who might find it strange that a French woman is taking the course with them. Predictably, France opts for an Eastern European accent. Later in the film, after she has already been working for Stephane for some time and the two of them have grown closer, he invites her to accompany him to a dull business dinner, presenting her to his colleagues as his Russian escort. On both occasions, France is asked to perform a role—to pretend she is a disenfranchised, legal and/or illegal immigrant, a foreigner in her own country—the irony being that she is pretending to be what she already is. Thus, like other films discussed earlier, *My Piece of the Pie* draws on the trope of performance/ impersonation (Chapter 2) to dramatize the structural affinities between Europeans and (legal and illegal) immigrants, mocking the construction of "French" or "European identity" as a primarily economic type of identity: inasmuch as under neoliberalism Europeans are "reduced" to the status of immigrants/foreigners in their own country, "being European" is defined as a particular socioeconomic status rather than an identity based on blood, territory, and language.

The premise of *Two Days, One Night*, set in Liege, is simple: Sandra is about to be laid off from her job after her coworkers are given the choice between receiving a 1,000-euro bonus or keeping Sandra on the job (the 1,000 euros immediately call to mind the 1,000 euros Lorna gets for "keeping silent" about Claudy's murder in *Lorna's Silence*). Sandra has only a weekend to convince her coworkers to give up their bonuses so that she can keep her job. *Two Days, One Night* foregrounds the dramatic role work plays in the construction of a sense of personal identity and self-worth. Although the financial consequences of losing one's job are, no doubt, important, the story emphasizes much more the effect of unemployment on one's sense of belonging to a community. When she tries to explain to her husband how she feels, Sandra says, "It's as if I don't exist, I am nothing" (words that recall Paul's confession in *Early One Morning* to his therapist that, having invested all of himself in his job the prospect of being laid off makes him feel totally worthless, as well as Anna's nervous breakdown in *Mi piacce lavorare* following her discreet but forceful removal from her job and from the community of coworkers). When Sandra's husband encourages her to talk to her colleagues individually to try to change their minds, he advises her to tell them that "she wants to be with them, not alone on the dole" (rather than telling them, for example, that she needs the job in order to support her family, even though this is also true).

While other films discussed earlier present a European character with the dilemma of evaluating their own life's worth against that of a migrant/refugee, *Two Days, One Night* reframes this dilemma within a national and class context (Sandra and her French coworkers share the same socioeconomic status), emphasizing the structural affinities between the status of illegal immigrants/refugees and that of socially disenfranchised Europeans. The end of the film reframes the dilemma once again, this time within a larger context, as Sandra's boss informs her that he will rehire her and give everyone their bonuses if he does not renew the fixed contract of one of her coworkers (who voted for Sandra to keep her job), an illegal immigrant in a legally precarious situation. Sandra is now faced with the same choice her coworkers were faced with earlier, a choice between her own interests and those of a coworker, whose status is even more precarious than hers. Sandra's rejection of the manager's proposal dismisses the economic premise on which such a choice is predicated—the notion of human beings as expendable commodities defined solely by their exchange value—while her decision to fight her own reduction to a commodity through "face-to-face encounters" with her coworkers restores the human aspect of self-other relationships dismissed by neoliberalism as irrelevant or useless.

In the *Rosetta*-like *Eat Sleep Die*, Rasa, a young woman who was born in Montenegro but moved to Sweden when she was one-year-old, works in a salad-packing factory in rural Sweden. She lives with her father, whom she also supports financially since he has various health problems and cannot work. While her job is boring and repetitive, Rasa is not unhappy, because she has the emotional and moral support of friends and fellow workers, many of whom are immigrants, and the love of her father with whom she has a strong bond. However, the owner of the factory announces that layoffs are necessary to avoid closing the factory. Although Rasa's sudden unemployment clearly threatens her livelihood, the worst part of it is not so much the lack of money but, as in *Two Days, One Night*, the prospect of severing all social ties with the rest of the community (after she has been laid off she continues to visit her former coworkers during the lunch break, not wanting to stay home alone), that is, work is here construed not only, or not mainly, as a source of income but as an important source of personal identity and sense of belonging: *being without work is not being poor but being alone*. The film functions mostly as a coming-of-age story (at the end Rasa has to leave her father and the village to take up a job in another town, a separation that is a lot harder on her than the temporary unemployment she has had to deal with) rather than as a culture-clash narrative exploring differences between Europeans and migrants. On one hand, Rasa and her father are completely integrated: she speaks Swedish like a native, and although her father's Swedish is not that good, he has a lot of Swedish friends and coworkers (with whom he goes to work in Norway for a while). And while Rasa might still be the object of anti-racial and anti-immigrant prejudice—at one point she is not called for a job interview presumably because the employer thought her family name sounded Arabic—her father is equally racist (to Rasa's horror he calls another man a "nigger"). That Rasa and her father are not really perceived as "foreigners" is made clear when some of the older Swedes Rasa hangs out with make a passing comment about Muslims and other foreigners taking their jobs and are genuinely surprised when she tells them she and her father are Muslim too, something apparently they had never thought about.

Rasa is only one among the many Swedish and immigrants workers laid off, that is, she is not laid off *because* she is an immigrant—in fact, as one of the Swedes explains, knowingly, immigrants are usually the last to be laid off because they work for less and are thus more cost-effective from the factory's point of view whereas Swedes have to earn a minimum wage. After Rasa and her coworkers have been laid off, the factory sets up workshops to help them prepare for their next job and to boost their self-confidence. At these workshops we meet some of the Swedes who, like Rasa, have recently lost their jobs, including a young Swedish woman who is clinically depressed and unable to find a new job. The question thus arises: Why does the film focus on Rasa, rather than exploring the equally miserable plight of unemployed Swedes? Given that Rasa's predicament is shared by immigrants and Swedes alike, one could argue that, rather than functioning as the "token" immigrant, whose fate is supposed to represent the fate of all immigrants, the migrant character (Rasa) stands, *metaphorically—rather than metonymically*—for the experience of *everyone* under neoliberalism. Just as France, in Klapisch's film, is "reduced" to the status of an immigrant in her own country, Rasa embodies the status of *all* disenfranchised people in Sweden, both immigrants and nonimmigrants.

I will end this analysis of the crossovers between the cinema of pecarity and the cinema of migration by returning to a film I already mentioned a few times, *The Snows of Kilimanjaro* (2011), inspired by Victor Hugo's poem "How Good Are the Poor." The film follows Michel as he finds himself laid off, along with many others, after working on the docks for thirty years. Forced into early retirement Michel devotes his free time to his lovely family and, thanks to a generous surprise gift for his wedding anniversary (bought by his friends and former coworkers, including those who were laid off like him), is about to go on an African safari with his wife, Marie-Claire. One night when the couple is in the midst of a card game with their best friends Raoul (Michel's coworker) and Denise, two masked men break into his house, hit and tie up the four of them, and steal their credit cards and the money for the trip. Later on Michel, by a sheer stroke of luck, figures out that the robber is young Christophe, another coworker who was laid off and who, we later learn, is the sole provider of his younger brothers, abandoned by their mother (who works on a cruise ship). Michel is initially furious that another unemployed worker would steal from him, but in Christophe's eyes Michel has betrayed working-class ideals for a comfortable, bourgeois life and while he can count on a respectable severance package and a pension, Christophe, who was laid off after being on the job for only six months, has none of that security. Raoul's response to the situation—contrary to Michel, who suffers pangs of conscience as he struggles with the realization that he is living "in bad faith," Raoul freely admits that he is content to see Christophe arrested; in fact, if it was up to Raoul he would have given Christophe a more severe sentence (hard physical work, not just a few years in jail)—points to the cracks within the working class, which, contrary to Michel's idealistic, old-fashioned, and static view of class, turns out to be not necessarily held together by strong bonds of solidarity.

The Snows of Kilimanjaro recalls *It's a Free World* in its attention to the generational conflict between the former working-class-turned-middle-class Michel and Marie-Claire, and the young Christophe, a product of neoliberalism's regime of precarity. When Michel tries to justify himself by pointing out that the workers to be laid off were chosen fairly—with the help of a lottery—and he himself was laid off (although he is a union representative Michel did not remove his name from the lottery as he could have), Christophe responds by showing Michel how out of touch with reality Michel's old-fashioned ideals of justice (distributive justice) are. According to Christophe, what Michel should have done, as a union representative, is examine each case individually so as to lay off those on whom unemployment would have the least negative effect. That the problem is generational is reiterated toward the end of the film, when Michel and his wife inform their children of their plan to "adopt" Christophe's brothers while Christophe is in jail. Michel and Marie-Claire's children, who have kids of their own, are not as enthusiastic about their parents' self-congratulatory "do-goodness." They are unwilling to share with "strangers" (as Michel's daughter calls Christophe's kid brothers) neither the affection of their parents nor their parents' material resources (Flo reminds her parents of the material sacrifices she and her siblings had to accept in order to buy their wedding anniversary gift, the African safari tickets, and even suggests that, now that Michel has returned the tickets for a refund, she and her brother are *entitled* to get back the money they invested in the tickets). Surprised, Michel responds by reminding his son that he can easily charge him for the work Michel has been doing on the pergola, as if to remind his children that whatever is given between family members is given out of love, for free, and that family and personal relationships cannot be treated as business transactions—a way of thinking that sounds increasingly obsolete to the younger generation.

Arguably, the relationship between Michel and Christophe in Guediguian's film mirrors that between the European and the migrant/refugee in the films discussed throughout this chapter. Both *Kilimanjaro*, which doesn't feature any migrants or refugees, and Guediguian's later film *The House by the Sea* (2017), which does, explore white bourgeois guilt, though in the earlier film the middle-class Michel and Marie-Claire atone for their guilt by "adopting" the children of the precariat (Christophe) while in the latter film the white middle-class family "adopts" three Syrian refugee children, thus positing an analogy between the status of the European precariat and the status of non-European refugees. It is precisely because both films are concerned with the problem of "belonging" (rather than "identity") to a community—whether that is a particular social class, the European community or, more generally still, the human community—that the hypothetical "solution" proposed for the common ethical problems raised in both types of films is framed in the same symbolic way, in terms of adoption (Chapter 3).

3 Postscript

In the summer of 2000, German theater director, performance artist, and filmmaker Christoph Schlingensief installed a public "concentration camp"— in the form of three shipping containers—in the middle of Vienna's tourist district. For a week, a dozen real asylum seekers lived in the containers under constant surveillance as in the reality TV show *Big Brother*. Every day Austrians and tourists were invited to "vote" two of the asylum seekers out of the country. Schlingensief's reality television parody, documented in

Paul Poet's film *Foreigners out! Schlingensiefs Container* (*Ausländer raus! Schlingensiefs Container*) (2002), was a response to the formation of a far right, anti-immigration Austrian coalition government and quickly became the subject of international news coverage. *Schlingensief's Container* relies on a Brechtian alienation effect to disrupt stage illusion, that is, prevent the viewer from enjoying the illusion of being an unseen, passive spectator of a self-contained, autonomous artwork. As Schlingensief explains in an interview, exaggeration often reveals more of the truth than any realistic depiction. Paul Poet's comments on the film illuminate further Schlingensief's strategy:

> The main attraction sure was playing out the pig in a safe and cozy environment like your home PC workplace. Sipping up a Coke while pulverizing some blackies out of the beloved borders. [. . .] You don't have to make some humanistic and so-called thought provoking comments on the morally bankrupt multimedia generation. Christoph and I reversed this narrative to a non-escapist spectacle of political value without the hammer of instant moral bludgeoning your brains.[35]

Schlingensief's Container locates the political in the formal aspects of the artwork—the *Big Brother* format and its Brechtian alienation effect. As confrontational and subversive as that art project might be, it still relies on an implicit assumption that the plight of a dozen asylum seekers is separate from that of its spectators, those who have the power to "vote them out" of the country. *Schlingensief's Container* attests to the fact that the figure of the migrant, or what Fran Cetti calls "the global alien,"[36] has been regularly made to serve the rhetorical purpose—both discursively and legally—of endowing the idea of European identity with unity, meaningfulness, and emotional legitimacy in an attempt to obscure the historical nature of the capitalist system by invoking the supposedly organic, timeless nature of the nation-state. Although the migrant remains a key ideological component of the EU's attempt to legitimize its existence among Europeans divided by the unequal effects of neoliberalism,[37] as this study has shown recent European films dramatize the impossibility of separating stories about migration from stories exploring life under neoliberalism in general, that is, separating the plight of "illegal" migrants and refugees from that of Europeans.

Notes

1 Daniela Berghahn's conference talk, http://www.lestudium-ias.com/event/ruins-and-margins-european-identity-cinema-european-identity-era-mass-migration.

2 On the cinema of precarity, see Ewa Mazierska, "Capital Realism in Films about Debt," *Contemporary Cinema and Neoliberal Ideology*, ed. Ewa Mazierska and Lars Kristensen (New York: Routledge, 2018), 105–20.

3   Laurent Berlant, *Cruel Optimism* (Durham, NC: Duke UP, 2011), 2.
4   Ibid., 179.
5   Ibid., 171–72.
6   Bergfelder, "Love beyond the Nation," 61.
7   Ibid., 64.
8   Enrica Capussotti, "Migration, Attachment, Belonging: Filming the Mediterranean in Spain and Italy," *Europe and Love in Cinema*, ed. Luisa Passerini, Jo Labanyi, and Karen Diehl (Bristol: Intellect, 2012), 201.
9   Focusing on French cinema, Nathalie Rachlin and Rosemarie Scullion have come up with the term *le cinéma indigné* to describe films that "condemn globalization . . . by representing in stark cinematic terms the economic and social ills it has spawned" (5). See Nathalie Rachlin and Rosemarie Scullion, "Introduction: From Engagé to Indigné: French Cinema and the Crises of Globalization," *SubStance* 43, no. 1 (2014): 3–12.
10 See *The Affect Theory Reader*, ed. Gregory J. Seigworth and Melissa Gregg (Durham, NC: Duke UP, 2010). For a critique of the affective turn, see Ruth Leys, "The Turn to Affect: A Critique," *Critical Inquiry* 37, no. 3 (2011): 434–72.
11 Eugenie Brinkema, *The Forms of the Affects* (Durham, NC: Duke UP, 2014).
12 See Brian Massumi, *Parables for the Virtual: Movement, Affect, Sensation* (Durham, NC: Duke UP, 2002).
13 Steven Shaviro, *Post Cinematic Affect* (Winchester, UK: Zero Books, 2010), 3.
14 Hardt and Negri qtd in Shaviro, *Post Cinematic Affect*, 4.
15 See Michael Hardt, "Foreword: What Affects Are Good For," *The Affective Turn: Theorizing the Social*, ed. Patricia Clough with Jean Healey (Durham, NC: Duke UP, 2007), ix–xiii.
16 Shaviro, *Post Cinematic Affect*, 4.
17 Michel Foucault, *The Birth of Biopolitics: Lectures at the Collège de France, 1978–1979* (London: Picador, 2010), 226.
18 Shaviro, *Post Cinematic Affect*, 3.
19 Patricia Clough, "Introduction," *The Affective Turn: Theorizing the Social*, ed. Patricia Clough and Jean Healey (Durham, NC: Duke UP, 2007), 21.
20 Ibid., 19.
21 Elena del Rio, *Deleuze and the Cinemas of Performance: Powers of Affection* (Edinburgh: Edinburgh UP, 2008), 16.
22 Ibid., 17.
23 On the discursive shifts in the memorial discourse of the Holocaust in Germany and Europe, see Sven Kramer, "Including and Excluding the Holocaust: Changing Perceptions in German and European Identities," *Europe and Its Others: Essays on Interperception and Identity*, ed. Paul Gifford and Tessa Hauswedell (Bern: Peter Lang, 2010), 153–67.
24 Johannes von Moltke, "Sympathy for the Devil: Cinema, History, and the Politics of Emotion," *New German Critique*, No. 102, *Der Untergang? Nazis, Culture, and Cinema* (Fall 2007), 22.

25 Ibid., 43.
26 Barbier quoted in Berlant, *Cruel Optimism*, 200.
27 Berlant, *Cruel Optimism*, 202.
28 Charity Scribner, *Requiem for Communism* (Cambridge, MA: The MIT Press, 2005), 9.
29 Another sign of post-industrial nostalgia for "material labor" is migrant cinema's preoccupation with unemployment in the working class despite the fact that, according to statistical data, the largest numbers of immigrants to Ireland, for example, come from the middle class and managerial classes (Kakasi 20). See Kakasi, "Transcending the 'Poor Relative' Metaphor," 19–35.
30 Scribner, *Requiem for Communism*, 158.
31 Massimilano Bruno's *Escort in Love* (2011) provides a comic variation on the story of a woman fallen on hard times.
32 Poul-Eric Heilbuth's documentary *The Other Europe* (2006) fills in the gaps missing from the picture of neoliberal Spain we get from *Rooftops* by spelling out the connection between Spain's rising levels of unemployment and the EU's response to it (providing Spain with subsidies, which Spain then uses to build big greenhouses, whose employees are mainly illegal immigrants), showing that illegal immigrant labor is an integral part of Western economies.
33 https://www.reuters.com/article/us-film-life/contemporary-italy-under-spotlight-in-our-life-idUSTRE64J7J120100520, accessed August 6, 2019.
34 Like *Terraferma*, Kaurismaki's *Le Havre* (2011) depicts the French, white citizen (Marcel) as sharing the same status as that of the illegal immigrant (Marcel's Vietnamese friend and fellow worker "Chang").
35 *Ausländer raus! Schlingensiefs Container*. Produzent, Bonus Film GmbH. Monitorpop Entertainment, 2002. Interview with Paul Poet.
36 Fran Cetti, "Asylum and the European 'Security State': The Construction of the 'Global Outsider.'" *Globalization, Migration, and the Future of Europe: Insiders and Outsiders*, ed. Leila Simona Talani (London: Routledge, 2012), 10.
37 Theresa Kuhn's study of Europeans' support for European integration shows a correspondence between socioeconomic status and level of support for integration. In this layer cake model of European integration, affluent, high-skilled, and mobile Europeans, nationals of affluent EU nations form the top, while Europeans of less economically stable EU members, less transnational, and less mobile, form the bottom of the cake. See Theresa Kuhn, *Experiencing European Integration: Transnational Lives and European Identity* (Oxford: Oxford UP, 2015).

BIBLIOGRAPHY

Abderrezak, Hakim. *Ex-Centric Migrations: Europe and the Maghreb in Mediterranean Cinema, Literature, and Music*. Bloomington, IN: Indiana UP, 2016.
Abel, Marco, and Jaimey Fisher. *Berlin School and Its Global Contexts: A Transnational Art Cinema*. Detroit: Wayne State UP, 2019.
Abeles, Marc. "Virtual Europe." In *An Anthropology of the European Union: Building, Imagining, and Experiencing the New Europe*, edited by Irene Belier and Thomas M. Wilson, 31–52. Oxford: Berg, 2000.
Adorno, Theodor. *Aesthetic Theory*. Translated by C. Lenhardt. London: Routledge & Kegan Paul, 1984.
Agamben, Giorgio. *The Coming Community*. Translated by Michael Hardt. Minneapolis: University of Minnesota Press, 1993.
Andersson, Ruben. "Rescued and Caught: The Humanitarian-Security Nexus at Europe's Frontiers." In *The Borders of "Europe": Autonomy of Migration, Tactics of Bordering*, edited by Nicholas de Genova, 64–94. Durham, NC: Duke UP, 2017.
Ang, Ien. "Hegemony-in-Trouble: Nostalgia and the Ideology of the Impossible in European Cinema." In *Screening Europe: Imaging and Identity in Contemporary European Cinema*, edited by Duncan Petrie, 21–32. London: BFI, 1992.
Appadurai, Arjun. *Fear of Small Numbers: An Essay on the Geography of Anger*. Durham, NC: Duke UP, 2006.
Appadurai, Arjun. *Modernity at Large: Cultural Dimensions of Globalization*. Minneapolis: University of Minnesota Press, 1996.
Archer, Neil. "Paris Je t'aime (plus): Europhobia as Europeanness in Luc Besson's and Pierre Morel's Dystopia Trilogy." In *The Europeanness of European Cinema: Identity, Meaning and Globalization*, edited by Mary Harrod, Mariana Liz, and Alissa Timoshkina, 185–97. London: I.B.Tauris, 2015.
Asad, Talal. "Muslims and European Identity: Can Europe Represent Islam?" In *The Idea of Europe: from Antiquity to the European Union*, edited by Anthony Pagden, 209–27. Cambridge: Cambridge UP, 2002.
Aykac, Cagla E. "What Space for Migrant Voices in European Anti-Racism?" In *Identity, Belonging and Migration*, edited by Gerard Delanty, Ruth Wodak and Paul Jones, 120–33. Liverpool: Liverpool UP, 2008.
Badiou, Alain. *Cinema. Textes rassembles et presentes par Antoine de Baccque*. Paris: NOVA Éditions, 2010.
Badiou, Alain. *Ethics: An Essay on the Understanding of Evil*. Translated by Peter Hallward. London: Verso, 2001.

Badiou, Alain, and Marcel Gauchet, *What Is To Be Done? A Dialogue on Communism, Capitalism, and the Future of Democracy.* Cambridge: Polity Press, 2016.

Balibar, Étienne. "Justice and Equality: A Political Dilemma? Pascal, Plato, Marx." In *The Borders of Justice*, edited by Étienne Balibar, Sandro Mezzadra and Ranabir Samaddar, 9-33. Philadelphia: Temple UP, 2012.

Balibar, Étienne, and Immanuel Wallerstein. *Race, nation, classe: les identités ambiguës.* Paris: La decoverte/Poche, 1997.

Balibar, Étienne, Sandro Mezzadra, and Ranabir Samaddar. "Introduction." In *The Borders of Justice*, edited by Étienne Balibar, Sandro Mezzadra, and Ranabir Samaddar, 1-9. Philadelphia: Temple UP, 2012.

Ballesteros, Isolina. *Immigration Cinema in the New Europe.* Bristol: Intellect, 2015.

Bangert, Axel. *The Nazi Past in Contemporary German Film: Viewing Experiences of Intimacy and Immersion.* Rochester, NY: Camden House, 2014.

Bardan, Alice, and Aine O'Healy. "Transnational Mobility and Precarious Labor in Post- Cold War Europe: The Spectral Disruptions of Carmine Amoroso's *Cover Boy.*" In *The Cinemas of Italian Migration: European and Transatlantic Narratives*, edited by Sabine Schrader and Daniel Winkler, 69-90. Newcastle upon Tyne: Cambridge Scholars Publishing, 2013.

Barker, Jesse. *Affect and Belonging in Contemporary Spanish Fiction and Film: Crossroads Visions.* London: Palgrave Macmillan, 2018.

Barnavi, Elie. "Un musée de l'Europe pour les Européens." In *La culture slave et l'Europe: du rêve européen aux réalités*, edited by Antoine Mares, 53-64. Paris: Institut d'etudes slaves, 2005.

Batori, Anna. *Space in Romanian and Hungarian Cinema.* London: Palgrave Macmillan, 2019.

Bauman, Zygmunt. *Globalization: The Human Consequences.* Cambridge: Polity Press, 1998.

Baumbach, Nico. *Cinema/Politics/Philosophy.* New York: Columbia UP, 2019.

Bayraktar, Nilgun. *Mobility and Migration in Film and Moving Image Art: Cinema beyond Europe.* New York: Routledge, 2017.

Beloff, Max. *Europe and the Europeans: An International Discussion. A Report Prepared at the Request of the Council of Europe.* London: Chatto and Windus, 1957.

Berezin, Mabel. "Territory, Emotion and Identity: Spatial Recalibration in a New Europe." In *Europe without Borders: Remapping Territory, Citizenship and Identity in a Transnational Age*, edited by Mabel Berezin and Martin Schain, 1-30. Baltimore, MD: The Johns Hopkins UP, 2003.

Berger, Verena, and Miya Komori. *Polyglot Cinema: Migration and Transcultural Narration in France, Italy, Portugal, and Spain.* Vienna: LIT, 2010.

Bergfelder, Tim. "Love beyond the Nation: Cosmopolitanism and Transnational Desire in Cinema." In *Europe and Love in Cinema*, edited by Luisa Passerini, Jo Labanyi, and Karen Diehl, 61-83. Bristol: Intellect, 2012.

Bergfelder, Tim. "Popular European Cinema in the 2000s: Cinephilia, Genre and Heritage," in *The Europeanness of European Cinema: Identity, Meaning and Globalization*, edited by Mary Harrod, Mariana Liz, and Alissa Timoshkina, 33-57. London: I.B.Tauris, 2015.

Berghahn, Daniela, and Claudia Sternberg. "Introduction." In *European Cinema in Motion: Migrant and Diasporic Film in Contemporary Europe*, edited by Daniela Berghahn and Claudia Sternberg, 1-12. London: Palgrave Macmillan, 2010.

Berghahn, Daniela, and Claudia Sternberg. "Locating Migrant and Diasporic Cinema in Contemporary Europe." In *European Cinema in Motion: Migrant and Diasporic Film in Contemporary Europe*, edited by Daniela Berghahn and Claudia Sternberg, 12-50. London: Palgrave Macmillan, 2010.

Berlant, Laurent. *Cruel Optimism*. Durham, NC: Duke UP, 2011.

Bermant, Laia Soto. "The Mediterranean Question: Europe and Its Predicament in the Southern Peripheries." In *The Borders of "Europe": Autonomy of Migration, Tactics of Bordering*, edited by Nicholas de Genova, 120-141. Durham, NC: Duke UP, 2017.

Bidar, Abdennour. *Libéron-nous! Des chaînes du travail et de la consummation*. Paris: Éditions Les liens qui libèrent, 2018.

Borgolte, Michael. "How Europe Became Diverse: On the Medieval Roots of the Plurality of Values." In *The Cultural Values of Europe*, edited by Hans Joas and Klaus Wiegandt, 77-114. Liverpool: Liverpool UP, 2008.

Bossuat, Gerard. "La quete de l'identité européenne." In *La culture slave et l'Europe: du rêve européen aux réalités*, edited by Antoine Mares, 19-44. Paris: Institut d'etudes slaves, 2005.

Boswell, Christina and Andrew Geddes. *Migration and Mobility in the EU*. London: Palgrave Macmillan, 2011.

Bottici, Chiara, and Benoit Challand, *Imagining Europe: Myth, Memory and Identity*. London: Cambridge UP, 2013.

Boym, Svetlana. *The Future of Nostalgia*. New York: Basic Books, 2001.

Briese, Olaf. "The Camp in the City, the City as Camp." In *Walls, Borders, Boundaries: Spatial and Cultural Practices in Europe*, edited by Marc Silberman, Kren Till, and Janet Ward, 43-59. London: Berghahn Books, 2012.

Broeders, Dennis. "A European 'Border' Surveillance System under Construction." In *Migration and the New Technological Borders*, edited by Huub Dijstelbloem and Albert Meijer, 40-67. London: Palgrave Macmillan, 2011.

Brouwer, Evelien. "Legal Boundaries and the Use of Migration Technology." In *Migration and the New Technological Borders of Europe*, edited by Huub Dijstelbloem and Albert Meijer, 134-69. London: Palgrave Macmillan, 2011.

Brown, William, Dina Iordanova, and Leshu Torchin, *Moving People, Moving Images: Cinema and Trafficking in the New Europe*. London: Wallflower Press, 2010.

Bruckner, Pascal. *The Tears of the White Man: Compassion as Contempt*. Translated by William R. Beer. London: The Free Press, 1986.

Bruter, Michael. *Citizens of Europe? The Emergence of a Mass European Identity*. New York: Palgrave Macmillan, 2005.

Calhoun, Craig. "The Democratic Integration of Europe: Interests, Identity and the Public Sphere." In *Europe without Borders: Remapping Territory, Citizenship and Identity in a Transnational Age*, edited by Mabel Berezin and Martin Schain, 243-74. Baltimore, MD: The Johns Hopkins UP, 2003.

Capussotti, Enrica. "Migration, Attachment, Belonging: Filming the Mediterranean in Spain and Italy." In *Europe and Love in Cinema*, edited by Luisa Passerini, Jo Labanyi, and Karen Diehl, 191-204. Bristol: Intellect, 2012.

Cassin, Barbara. *Nostalgia: When Are We Ever at Home?* Translated by Pascale-Anne Brault. New York: Fordham UP, 2016.
Castoriadis, Cornelius. "Culture in a Democratic Society." In *The Castoriadis Reader*, edited by David Ames Curtis, 338–49. Oxford: Blackwell Publishers Ltd., 1997.
Castoriadis, Cornelius. "The Greek Polis and the Creation of Democracy." In *The Castoriadis Reader*, edited by David Ames Curtis, 267–89. Oxford: Blackwell Publishers Ltd., 1997.
Cattani, Francesco. "New Maps of Europe by Some Contemporary 'Migrant' Artists and Writers." In *Europe in Black and White: Immigration, Race and Identity in the "Old Continent*,*"* edited by Manuela Sanches, Fernando Clara, and João Ferreira Duarte, 55–66. London: Intellect Books, 2011.
Caughie, John. "Becoming European: Art Cinema, Irony and Identity." In *Screening Europe: Imaging and Identity in Contemporary European Cinema*, edited by Duncan Petrie, 32–44. London: BFI, 1992.
Celik, Ipek A. *In Permanent Crisis: Ethnicity in Contemporary European Media and Cinema*. Ann Arbor, MI: University of Michigan Press, 2015.
Cetti, Fran. "Asylum and the European 'Security State': The Construction of the 'Global Outsider.'" In *Globalization, Migration, and the Future of Europe: Insiders and Outsiders*, edited by Leila Simona Talani, 9–21. London: Routledge, 2012.
Chakrabarty, Dipesh. *Provincializing Europe: Postcolonial Thought and Historical Difference*. Princeton: Princeton UP, 2000.
Clough, Patricia. "Introduction." In *The Affective Turn: Theorizing the Social*, edited by Patricia Clough and Jean Healey, 1–33. Durham, NC: Duke UP, 2007.
Compagnon, Antoine. "Appendix 2: Mapping the European Mind." In *Screening Europe: Imaging and Identity in Contemporary European Cinema*, edited by Duncan Petrie, 111–12. London: BFI, 1992.
Davies, William. *The Limits of Neoliberalism: Authority, Sovereignty and the Logic of Competition*. London: SAGE Publications, 2017.
Diminescu, Dana. "Le migrant connecté: pour un manifeste épistémologique." *Migrations Société*, 17.102 (2005): 275–92.
de Cuir, Greg Jr., "The Feather Collectors: Erased Identity and Invisible Representations of the Roma in Yugoslav Cinema." In *The Europeanness of European Cinema: Identity, Meaning and Globalization*, edited by Mary Harrod, Mariana Liz, and Alissa Timoshkina, 101–13. London: I.B.Tauris, 2015.
de Genova, Nicholas. "The Borders of 'Europe.'" In *The Borders of "Europe*,*"* edited by Nicholas de Genova, 1–37. Durham, NC: Duke UP, 2017.
Delanty, Gerard. *Inventing Europe: Idea, Identity, Reality*. London: Palgrave Macmillan, 1995.
Delanty, Gerard, Paul Jones, and Ruth Wodak, "Introduction: Migration, Discrimination and Belonging in Europe." In *Identity, Belonging and Migration*, edited by Gerard Delanty, Ruth Wodak, and Paul Jones, 1–18. Liverpool: Liverpool UP, 2008.
Deleuze, Gilles. *Bergsonism*. Translated by Hugh Tomlinson and Barbara Habberjam. New York: Zone, 1991.

Deliso, Christopher. *Migration, Terrorism, and the Future of a Divided Europe: A Continent Transformed.* Santa Barbara, CA: Praeger Security International, 2017.
del Rio, Elena. *Deleuze and the Cinemas of Performance: Powers of Affection.* Edinburgh: Edinburgh UP, 2008.
de Rougemont, Denis. "Introduction." In Max Beloff. *Europe and the Europeans: An International Discussion. A Report Prepared at the Request of the Council of Europe*, ix–xix. London: Chatto and Windus, 1957.
Derrida, Jacques. *Acts of Religion.* New York: Routledge, 2002.
Derrida, Jacques. *Of Hospitality: Anne Dufourmantelle Invites Jacques Derrida to Respond.* Translated by Rachel Bowlby. Stanford, CA: Stanford UP, 2000.
Derrida, Jacques. *The Other Heading: Reflections on Today's Europe.* Translated by Pascale-Anne Brault and Michael B. Naas. Bloomington, IN: Indiana UP, 1992.
Deveny, Thomas G. *Migration in Contemporary Hispanic Cinema.* Toronto: The Scarecrow Press, 2012.
de Wenden, Catherine Wihtol. *La question migratoire au XXIe siècle: Migrants, refugies et relations internationals.* Paris: Science Po Presses, 2013.
Diez-Medrano, Juan. "Ways of Seeing European Integration: Germany, Great Britain and Spain." In *Europe without Borders: Remapping Territory, Citizenship and Identity in a Transnational Age*, edited by Mabel Berezin and Martin Schain, 169-96. Baltimore, MD: The Johns Hopkins UP, 2003.
Diken, Bulent, and Carsten Bagge Lausten. *The Culture of Exception: Sociology Facing the Camp.* New York: Routledge, 2005.
Downing, Lisa, and Libby Saxton, *Film and Ethics: Foreclosed Encounters.* London: Routledge, 2010.
Dunn, Elizabeth. *No Path Home: Humanitarian Camps and the Grief of Displacement.* Ithaca, NY: Cornell UP, 2017.
Durmelat, Sylvie, and Vinay Swamy, *Screening Integration: Recasting Maghrebi Immigration in Contemporary France.* Lincoln, NE: University of Nebraska Press, 2012.
Ehrkamp, Patricia. "Migrants, Mosques, and Minarets: Reworking the Boundaries of Liberal Democracy in Switzerland and Germany." In *Walls, Borders, Boundaries: Spatial and Cultural Practices in Europe*, edited by Marc Silberman, Kren Till, and Janet Ward, 153-72. London: Berghahn Books, 2012.
Elsaesser, Thomas. *European Cinema and Continental Philosophy: Film as Thought Experiment.* New York: Bloomsbury, 2019.
Elsaesser, Thomas. "European Cinema into the Twenty-First Century: Enlarging the Context." In *The Europeanness of European Cinema: Identity, Meaning and Globalization*, edited by Mary Harrod, Mariana Liz, and Alissa Timoshkina, 17-32. London: I.B.Tauris, 2015.
Engelen, Leen, and Kris van Heuckelom, ed. *European Cinema after the Wall: Screening East-West Mobility.* Lanham, MD: Rowman & Littlefield, 2014.
Engelen, Leen, and Kris Van Heuckelom. "Introduction: From the East to the West and Back: Screening Mobility in Post-1989 European Cinema." In *European Cinema after the Wall: Screening East-West Mobility*, edited by Leen Engelen and Kris van Heuckelom, vii–xxii. Lanham, MD: Rowman & Littlefield, 2014.

Entrikin, J. Nicholas. "Political Community, Identity and Cosmopolitan Place." In *Europe without Borders: Remapping Territory, Citizenship and Identity in a Transnational Age*, edited by Mabel Berezin and Martin Schain, 51-63. Baltimore, MD: The Johns Hopkins UP, 2003.

Everett, Wendy. "Introduction: European Film and the Quest for Identity." In *European Identity in Cinema*, edited by Wendy Everett, 7-15. London: Intellect, 2005.

Everett, Wendy. "Leaving Home: Exile and Displacement in Contemporary European Cinema." In *Cultures of Exile: Images of Displacement*, edited by Wendy Everett and Peter Wagstaff, 18-32. London: Berghahn Books, 2004.

Everett, Wendy, and Peter Wagstaff, ed. *Cultures of Exile: Images of Displacement*. London: Berghahn Books, 2004.

Flasch, Kurt. "The Value of Introspection." In *The Cultural Values of Europe*, edited by Hans Joas and Klaus Wiegandt, 152-65. Liverpool: Liverpool UP, 2008.

Foucault, Michel. *The Birth of Biopolitics: Lectures at the Collège de France, 1978-1979*. London: Picador, 2010.

Garelli, Glenda, and Martina Tazzioli, "Choucha beyond the Camp: Challenging the Border of Migration Studies." In *The Borders of "Europe": Autonomy of Migration, Tactics of Bordering*, edited by Nicholas de Genova, 165-84. Durham, NC: Duke UP, 2017.

Garrett, Daniel. "Luchino Visconti's *The Leopard* and Those Who Are Not Rich in a Country of Arrangements." *Offscreen*, 16.7 (July 2012), https://offscreen.com/view/the_leopard (accessed August 16, 2019).

Gifford, Paul. "Defining 'Others': How Interperceptions Shape Identities." In *Europe and Its Others: Essays on Interperception and Identity*, edited by Paul Gifford and Tessa Hauswedell, 13-38. Bern: Peter Lang, 2010.

Gilroy, Paul. "Foreword: Migrancy, Culture, and a New Map of Europe." In *Blackening Europe: The African American Presence*, edited by Heike Raphael-Hernandez, xi-xxii. London: Routledge, 2004.

Girelli, Elisabetta. "Transnational Orientalism: Ferzan Özpetek's Turkish Dream in Hamam (1997)." *New Cinemas: Journal of Contemporary Film*, 5.1 (2007): 23-38.

Gott, Michael. *French Language Road Cinema: Borders, Diasporas, Migration and "New Europe."* Edinburgh: Edinburgh UP, 2016.

Gott, Michael, and Todd Herzog, ed. *East, West and Centre: Reframing Post-1989 European Cinema*. Edinburgh: Edinburgh UP, 2014.

Gronstad, Asbjorn. *Film and the Ethical Imagination*. London: Palgrave Macmillan, 2016.

Guha, Malini. *From Empire to the World: Migrant London and Paris in the Cinema*. Edinburgh: Edinburgh UP, 2015.

Habermas, Jürgen. The *Postnational Constellation: Political Essays*. Cambridge, MA: MIT Press, 2001.

Hakli, Jouni. "Afterword: Transcending Scale?" In *Scaling Identities: Nationalism and Territoriality*, edited by Guntram H. Herb and David H. Kaplan, 271-82. Lanham, MD: Rowman and Littlefield, 2018.

Hall, Stuart. "Old and New Identities, Old and New Ethnicities." In *Culture, Globalization and the World-system: Contemporary Conditions for the*

Representation of Identity, edited by Anthony D. King, 42–68. Minneapolis: University of Minnesota Press, 1997.

Halle, Randall. *The Europeanization of Cinema: Interzones and Imaginative Communities*. Champaign, IL: University of Illinois Press, 2014.

Hanakova, Petra. "Staying Home and Safe: Czech Cinema and the Refusal to be Transnational." In *European Cinema after the Wall: Screening East-West Mobility*, edited by Leen Engelen and Kris van Heuckelom, 113–25. Lanham, MD: Rowman & Littlefield, 2014.

Harrod, Mary, Mariana Liz, and Alissa Timoshkina. "The Europeanness of European Cinema: An Overview." In *The Europeanness of European Cinema: Identity, Meaning and Globalization*, edited by Mary Harrod, Mariana Liz, and Alissa Timoshkina, 1–13. London: I.B.Tauris, 2015.

Harvey, James. *Nationalism in Contemporary Western European Cinema*. London: Palgrave Macmillan, 2018.

Hauswedell, Tessa. "Introduction." In *Europe and Its Others: Essays on Interperception and Identity*, edited by Paul Gifford and Tessa Hauswedell, 1–13. Bern: Peter Lang, 2010.

Hay, Denys. *Europe: The Emergence of an Idea*. Edinburgh: Edinburgh UP, 1968.

Heffernan, Michael. *The Meaning of Europe: Geography and Geopolitics*. London: Arnold, 1998.

Herzfield, Michael. "The European Self: Rethinking an Attitude." In *The Idea of Europe: from Antiquity to the European Union*, edited by Anthony Pagden, 139–70. Cambridge: Cambridge UP, 2002.

Hoggett, Paul, and Simon Thompson, eds. *Politics and the Emotions: The Affective Turn in Contemporary Political Studies*. London: Bloomsbury, 2012.

Huber, Wolfgang. "The Judeo-Christian Tradition." In *The Cultural Values of Europe*, edited by Hans Joas and Klaus Wiegandt, 43–58. Liverpool: Liverpool UP, 2008.

Iordanova, Dina. "Migration and Cinematic Process in Post-Cold War Europe." In *European Cinema in Motion: Migrant and Diasporic Film in Contemporary Europe*, edited by Daniela Berghahn and Claudia Sternberg, 50–75. London: Palgrave Macmillan, 2010.

Jäckel, Anne. "Changing the Image of Europe? The Role of European Co-Productions, Funds and Film Awards." In *The Europeanness of European Cinema: Identity, Meaning and Globalization*, edited by Mary Harrod, Mariana Liz, and Alissa Timoshkina, 59071. London: I.B.Tauris, 2015.

Joas, Hans. "Introduction." In *The Cultural Values of Europe*, 1–21. Liverpool: Liverpool UP, 2008.

Jones, Paul, and Michal Krzyzanowski, "Identity, Belonging and Migration: Beyond Constructing 'Others.'" In *Identity, Belonging and Migration*, edited by Gerard Delanty, Ruth Wodak, and Paul Jones, 38–53. Liverpool: Liverpool UP, 2008.

Kaelble, Hartmut. *A Social History of Europe, 1945–2000: Recovery and Transformation after Two World Wars*. New York: Berghahn Books, 2013.

Kaklamanidou, Betty, and Ana Corbalan, ed. *Contemporary European Cinema: Crisis Narratives and Narratives in Crisis*. New York: Routledge, 2018.

Karner, Christian. *Negotiating National Identities: Between Globalization, the Past, and the "Other."* Farnham: Ashgate, 2011.

Kastotyano, Riva. "Transnational Networks and Political Participation: The Place of Immigrants in the European Union." In *Europe without Borders: Remapping Territory, Citizenship and Identity in a Transnational Age*, edited by Mabel Berezin and Martin Schain, 64–85. Baltimore, MD: The Johns Hopkins UP, 2003.

Kohn, Steffen. *Mediating Mobility: Visual Anthropology in the Age of Migration*. London: Intellect, 2016.

Kopp, Kristin. "If Your Car Is Stolen, It Will Soon Be in Poland: Criminal Representations of Poland and the Poles in German Fictional Film of the 1990s." In *Postcolonial Approaches to Eastern European Cinema: Portraying Neighbors on Screen*, edited by Ewa Maziersak, Lars Kristensen, and Eva Näripea, 41–66. London: I.B.Tauris, 2014.

Kramer, Gudrun. "The Contest of Values: Notes on Contemporary Islamic Discourse." In *The Cultural Values of Europe*, edited by Hans Joas and Klaus Wiegandt, 338–56. Liverpool: Liverpool UP, 2008.

Kristensen, Lars. "Introduction." In *Postcommunist Film—Russia, Eastern Europe and World Culture: Moving Images of Postcommunism*, edited by Lars Kristensen, 1–11. London: Routledge, 2012.

Kristensen, Lars, ed. *Postcommunist Film - Russia, Eastern Europe and World Culture: Moving Images of Postcommunism*. London: Routledge, 2013.

Kroes, Rob. "Imaginary Americas in Europe's Public Space" in *We Europeans? Media, Representations, Identities*, edited by William Uricchio, 23–41. Bristol: Intellect Books, 2008.

Kumar, Krishan. "The Nation-State, the European Union, and Transnational Identities." In *Muslim Europe or Euro-Islam: Politics, Culture, and Citizenship in the Age of Globalization*, edited by Nezar AlSayyad and Manuel Castells, 51–68. Lanham, MD: Lexington Books, 2002.

Lecadet, Clara. "Europe Confronted by Its Expelled Migrants: The Politics of Expelled Migrants' Associations in Africa." In *The Borders of "Europe": Autonomy of Migration, Tactics of Bordering*, edited by Nicholas de Genova, 141–64. Durham, NC: Duke UP, 2017.

Lentin, Alana. "Racism, Anti-Racism and the Western State." In *Identity, Belonging and Migration*, edited by Gerard Delanty, Ruth Wodak, and Paul Jones, 101–19. Liverpool: Liverpool UP, 2008.

Linke, Uli. "Technologies of Othering: Black Masculinities in the Carceral Zones of European Whiteness." In *Europe in Black and White: Immigration, Race and Identity in the "Old Continent*," edited by Manuela Sanches, Fernando Clara, and João Ferreira Duarte, 121–41. London: Intellect Books, 2011.

Lister, Michael, and Emily Pia, *Citizenship in Contemporary Europe*. Edinburgh: Edinburgh UP, 2008.

Liz, Mariana. "From European Co-Productions to the Euro-Pudding." In *The Europeanness of European Cinema: Identity, Meaning and Globalization*, edited by Mary Harrod, Mariana Liz, and Alissa Timoshkina, 73–85. London: I.B.Tauris, 2015.

Liz, Mariana. *Euro-visions: Europe in Contemporary Cinema*. London: Bloomsbury, 2016.

Locatelli, Massimo, and Francesco Pitassio. "Vesna Run Faster! East European Actresses and Contemporary Italian Cinema." In *European Cinema After the*

Wall: Screening East- West Mobility, edited by Leen Engelen and Kris van Heuckelom, 37-54. Lanham, MD: Rowman & Littlefield, 2014.

Loshitzky, Yosefa. *Screening Strangers: Migration and Diaspora in Contemporary European Cinema*. Bloomington, IN: Indiana UP, 2010.

Lustic, Ian S., and Roy J. Eidelson, "National Identity Repertoires, Territory, and Globalization." In *Europe without Borders: Remapping Territory, Citizenship and Identity in a Transnational Age*, edited by Mabel Berezin and Martin Schain, 89-117. Baltimore, MD: The Johns Hopkins UP, 2003.

Marin, Clara Guillen. *Migrants in Contemporary Spanish Film*. New York: Routledge, 2017.

Marquez, John D. "Nations Re-bound: Race and Biopolitics at EU and US Borders." In *Europe in Black and White: Immigration, Race and Identity in the "Old Continent"*, edited by Manuela Sanches, Fernando Clara, and João Ferreira Duarte, 39-52. London: Intellect Books, 2011.

Mata, Inocencia. "On the Periphery of the Universal and the Splendor of Eurocentrism." In *Europe in Black and White: Immigration, Race and Identity in the "Old Continent"*, edited by Manuela Sanches, Fernando Clara, and João Ferreira Duarte, 91-100. London: Intellect Books, 2011.

Mattar, Daniela Vicherat. "Did Walls Really Come Down? Contemporary B/ordering Walls in Europe." In *Walls, Borders, Boundaries: Spatial and Cultural Practices in Europe*, edited by Marc Silberman, Kren Till, and Janet Ward, 77-93. London: Berghahn Books, 2012.

Mazierska, Ewa. "Neighbors (Almost) Like Us: Representation of Germans, Germanness and Germany in Polish Communist and Postcommunist cinema." In *Postcolonial Approaches to Eastern European Cinema: Portraying Neighbors on Screen*, edited by Ewa Maziersak, Lars Kristensen, and Eva Näripea, 67-89. London: I.B.Tauris, 2014.

Mazierska, Ewa, and Lars Kristensen, ed. *Contemporary Cinema and Neoliberal Ideology*. New York: Routledge, 2018.

Mazierska, Ewa, Lars Kristensen, and Eva Näripea. "Introduction." In *Postcolonial Approaches to Eastern European Cinema: Portraying Neighbors on Screen*, edited by Ewa Maziersak, Lars Kristensen, and Eva Näripea, 1-39. London: I.B.Tauris, 2014.

Mazierska, Ewa, and Laura Rascaroli, ed. *Crossing New Europe: Postmodern Travel and the European Road Movie*. New York: Columbia UP, 2006.

Mazower, Mark. "The Dark Continent – Europe and Totalitarianism." In *The Cultural Values of Europe*, edited by Hans Joas and Klaus Wiegandt, 265-76. Liverpool: Liverpool UP, 2008.

Metermann, Jorg. "'E Giusto vivere cosi?' Contemporary Melodrama and Migration." In *The Cinemas of Italian Migration: European and Transatlantic Narratives*, edited by Sabine Schrader and Daniel Winkler, 247-62. Newcastle upon Tyne: Cambridge Scholars Publishing, 2013.

Mikkeli, Heikki. *Europe as an Idea and an Identity*. New York: St. Martin's Press, Inc., 1998.

Miller, David. *Strangers in Our Midst: The Political Philosophy of Immigration*. Cambridge, MA: Harvard UP, 2016.

McGrance, Bernard. *Beyond Anthropology: Society and the Other*. New York: Columbia UP, 1990.

Millington, Gareth. *Urbanization and the Migrant in British Cinema: Spectres of the City*. London: Palgrave Macmillan, 2016.
Morse, Margaret. "Home: Smell, Taste, Posture, Gleam." In *Home, Exile, Homeland: Film, Media, and the Politics of Place*, edited by Hamid Naficy, 63–74. New York: Routledge, 1999.
Muscio, Giuliana. "Sicilian Film Productions: Between Europe and the Mediterranean Islands." In *We Europeans? Media, Representations, Identities*, edited by William Uricchio, 177–94. Bristol: Intellect Books, 2008.
Naficy, Hamid. *An Accented Cinema: Exilic and Diasporic Filmmaking*. Princeton: Princeton UP, 2001.
Naficy, Hamid. "Framing Exile: From Homeland to Homepage." In *Home, Exile, Homeland: Film, Media, and the Politics of Place*, edited by Hamid Naficy, 1–17. New York: Routledge, 1999.
Nail, Thomas. *The Figure of the Migrant*. Stanford, CA: Stanford UP, 2015.
Naishtat, Francisco. "Global Justice and Politics: On the Transition from the Normative to the Political Level." In *The Borders of Justice*, edited by Étienne Balibar, Sandro Mezzadra, and Ranabir Samaddar, 33–53. Philadelphia: Temple UP, 2012.
Nippel, Wilfried. "Homo Politicus and Homo Oeconomicus: the European Citizen According to Max Weber." In *The Idea of Europe: from Antiquity to the European Union*, edited by Anthony Pagden, 129–38. Cambridge: Cambridge UP, 2002.
Nouss, Alexis. *La condition de l'exilé: Penser les migrations contemporaines*. Paris: Editions de la Maison des sciences de l'homme, 2015.
O'Brien, Peter. *The Muslim Question in Europe: Political Controversies and Public Philosophies*. Philadelphia: Temple UP, 2016.
O'Healy, Aine. *Migrant Anxieties: Italian Cinema in a Transnational Frame*. Bloomington, IN: Indiana UP, 2019.
O'Leary, Alan. *Tragedia all'italiana: Italian Cinema and Italian Terrorisms, 1970–2010*. Frankfurt am Main: Peter Lang, 2011.
Osseiran, Souad. "'Europe' from 'Here': Syrian Migrants/Refugees in Istanbul and Imagined Migrations into and within 'Europe.'" In *The Borders of "Europe": Autonomy of Migration, Tactics of Bordering*, edited by Nicholas de Genova, 185–209. Durham, NC: Duke UP, 2017.
Ostrowska, Elzbieta. "Postcolonial Fantasies: Imagining the Balkans: The Polish Popular Cinema of Wladyslaw Pasikowski." In *Postcolonial Approaches to Eastern European Cinema: Portraying Neighbors on Screen*, edited by Ewa Maziersak, Lars Kristensen, and Eva Näripea, 175–99. London: I.B.Tauris, 2014.
Pagden, Anthony. "Europe: Conceptualizing a Continent." In *The Idea of Europe: From Antiquity to the European Union*, edited by Anthony Pagden, 33–54. Cambridge: Cambridge UP, 2002.
Parvulescu, Anca. *The Traffic in Women's Work: East European Migration and the Making of Europe*. Chicago: University of Chicago Press, 2014.
Passerini, Luisa. "From the Ironies of Identity to the Identities of Irony." In *The Idea of Europe: from Antiquity to the European Union*, edited by Anthony Pagden, 191–208. Cambridge: Cambridge UP, 2002.
Passerini, Luisa, Jo Labanyi, and Karen Diehl, "Introduction." In *Europe and Love in Cinema*, edited by Luisa Passerini, Jo Labanyi, and Karen Diehl, 1–27. Bristol: Intellect, 2012.

Peters, John Durham. "Exile, Nomadism, and Diaspora: The Stakes of Mobility in the Western Canon." In *Home, Exile, Homeland: Film, Media, and the Politics of Place*, edited by Hamid Naficy, 17-41. New York: Routledge, 1999.

Pettegree, Jane. "Writing Christendom in the English Renaissance: A Reappraisal of Denys Hay's View of the Emergence of 'Europe.'" In *Europe and Its Others: Essays on Interperception and Identity*, edited by Paul Gifford and Tessa Hauswedell, 39-55. Bern: Peter Lang, 2010.

Picozza, Fiorenza. "Dubliners: Unthinking Displacement, Illegality, and Refugeeness within Europe's Geographies of Asylum." In *The Borders of "Europe": Autonomy of Migration, Tactics of Bordering*, edited by Nicholas de Genova, 233-54. Durham, NC: Duke UP, 2017.

Platinga, Carl. *Screen Stories: Emotions and the Ethics of Engagement*. Oxford: Oxford UP, 2018.

Ponzanesi, Sandra. "Europe in Motion: Migrant Cinema and the Politics of Encounter." *Social Identities*, 17.1 (2011): 73-92.

Ponzanesi, Sandra, and Bolette B. Blaagaard, ed. *Deconstructing Europe: Postcolonial Perspectives*. London: Routledge, 2011.

Ponzanesi, Sandra, and Marguerite Waller, ed. *Postcolonial Cinema Studies*. London: Routledge, 2012.

Ponzanesi, Sandra, and Verena Berger. "Introduction: Genres and Tropes in Postcolonial Cinemas(s)." *Transnational Cinemas*, 7.2 (2016): 111-17.

Portuges, Catherine. "Memory and Reinvention in Post-Socialist Hungarian Cinema." In *Cinemas in Transition in Central and Eastern Europe after 1989*, edited by Catherine Portuges and Peter Hames, 104-34. Philadelphia: Temple UP, 2013.

Previsic, Boris. "Europe's Blind Spot on Violence: the Fall of Yugoslavia and references to World War II." In *Europe and Its Others: Essays on Interperception and Identity*, edited by Paul Gifford and Tessa Hauswedell, 183-202. Bern: Peter Lang, 2010.

Price, Matthew. *Rethinking Asylum: History, Purpose and Limits*. Cambridge: Cambridge UP, 2009.

Rancière, Jacques. *Aesthetics and Its Discontents*. Cambridge: Polity Press, 2009.

Rancière, Jacques. *Dissensus: On Politics and Aesthetics*. London: Bloomsbury, 2015.

Rancière, Jacques. *The Politics of Aesthetics*. London: Bloomsbury, 2006.

Ravetto-Biagioli, Kriss. *Mythopoetic Cinema: On the Ruins of European Identity*. New York: Columbia UP, 2017.

Ravisco, Maria. "Nation, Boundaries and Otherness in European 'Films of Voyage.'" In *We Europeans? Media, Representations, Identities*, edited by William Uricchio, 141-58. Bristol: Intellect Books, 2008.

Renault, Emmanuel. "Struggles for Justice: Political Discourses, Experiences, and Claims." In *The Borders of "Europe": Autonomy of Migration, Tactics of Bordering*, edited by Nicholas de Genova, 99-122. Durham, NC: Duke UP, 2017.

Rings, Guido. *The Other in Contemporary Migrant Cinema: Imagining a New Europe*. New York: Routledge, 2016.

Risse, Thomas and Daniela Engelmann-Martin, "Identity Politics and European Integration: the Case of Germany." In *The Idea of Europe: from Antiquity to the European Union*, edited by Anthony Pagden, 287–316. Cambridge: Cambridge UP, 2002.

Rivi, Luisa. *European Cinema after 1989*. London: Palgrave Macmillan, 2007.

Robyn, Richard. "Introduction: National versus Supranational Identity in Europe." In *The Changing Face of European Identity*, edited by Richard Robyn, 1–17. London: Routledge, 2005.

Rodono, Aurora E. "Nomadic Narratives: Migration Cinema in Germany and Italy." In *The Cinemas of Italian Migration: European and Transatlantic Narratives*, edited by Sabine Schrader and Daniel Winkler, 171–201. Newcastle upon Tyne: Cambridge Scholars Publishing, 2013.

Rodriguez, Encarnacion Gutierrez. "Transculturation in German and Spanish Migrant and Diasporic Cinema: on Constrained Spaces and Minor Intimacies in *Princesses* and *A Little Bit of Freedom*." In *European Cinema in Motion: Migrant and Diasporic Film in Contemporary Europe*, edited by Daniela Berghahn and Claudia Sternberg, 114–30. London: Palgrave Macmillan, 2010.

Ruttley, Philip. "The Long Road to Unity: The Contribution of Law to the Process of European Integration since 1945." In *The Idea of Europe: From Antiquity to the European Union*, edited by Anthony Pagden, 228–59. Cambridge: Cambridge UP, 2002.

Said, Edward. *Culture and Imperialism*. London: Chatto and Windus, 1993.

Sayad, Abdelmalek. *La Double Absence. Des illusions de l'émigré aux souffrances de l'immigré*. Paris: Seuil, 1999.

Scarlett, Elisabeth. *Religion and Spanish Film: Luis Buñuel, the Franco Era, and Contemporary Directors*. Ann Arbor, MI: University of Michigan Press, 2014.

Scheel, Stephan. "The Secret Is to Look Good on Paper: Appropriating Mobility within and against a Machine of Illegalization." In *The Borders of "Europe": Autonomy of Migration, Tactics of Bordering*, edited by Nicholas de Genova, 37–63. Durham, NC: Duke UP, 2017.

Schrader, Sabine, and Daniel Winkler. "The Cinemas of Italian Migration: from *Il Cammino della Speranza* (1950) to *Into Paradiso* (2010)." In *The Cinemas of Italian Migration: European and Transatlantic Narratives*, edited by Sabine Schrader and Daniel Winkler, 1–18. Newcastle upon Tyne: Cambridge Scholars Publishing, 2013.

Scribner, Charity. *Requiem for Communism*. Cambridge, MA: The MIT Press, 2005.

Shaviro, Steven. *Post Cinematic Affect*. Winchester, UK: Zero Books, 2010.

Shohat, Ella. "By the Bitstream of Babylon: Cyberfrontiers and Diasporic Vistas." In *Home, Exile, Homeland: Film, Media, and the Politics of Place*, edited by Hamid Naficy, 213–32. New York: Routledge, 1999.

Sigrist, Rene, and Stella Ghervas, "La memoire européene a l'heure du 'paradigme victimaire.'" In *Lieux d'Europe: Mythes et limites*, Sous la direction de Stella Ghervas et François Rosset, 215–43. Paris: Editions de la Maison des sciences de l'homme, 2008.

Sloterdijk, Peter. *Rage and Time: A Psychopolitical Investigation*. New York: Columbia UP, 2012.

Skrodzka, Aga. *Magic Realist Cinema in East Central Europe*. Edinburgh: Edinburgh UP, 2012.

Slobodian, Quinn. *Globalists: the End of Empire and the Birth of Neoliberalism.* Cambridge, MA: Harvard University Press, 2018.
Smith, Anthony D. "Towards a Global Culture?" *Theory, Culture and Society*, 7.2-3 (June 1990): 171-91.
Stam, Robert, and Ella Shohat. "The Culture Wars in Translation." In *Europe in Black and White: Immigration, Race, and Identity in the "Old Continent,"* edited by Manuela Sanches, Fernando Clara, and João Ferreira Duarte, 17-36. London: Intellect, 2011.
Stierl, Maurice. "Excessive Migration, Excessive Governance: Border Entanglements in Greek EU-rope." In *The Borders of "Europe": Autonomy of Migration, Tactics of Bordering*, edited by Nicholas de Genova, 210-32. Durham, NC: Duke UP, 2017.
Strath, Bo. "Belonging and European Identity." In *Identity, Belonging and Migration*, edited by Gerard Delanty, Ruth Wodak, and Paul Jones, 21-37. Liverpool: Liverpool UP, 2008.
Szucs, Jeno. *Les Trois Europes.* Paris: Editions L'Hartman, 1985.
Ther, Philipp. *Europe Since 1989: A History.* Princeton: Princeton UP, 2014.
Tibi, Bassam. "The Return of Ethnicity to Europe via Islamic Migration? The Ethnicization of the Islamic Diaspora." In *Ethnic Europe: Mobility, Identity, and Conflict in a Globalized World*, edited by Roland Hus, 127-56. Stanford, CA: Stanford UP, 2010.
Todorova, Maria. *Imagining the Balkans.* London: Oxford UP, 1997.
Trifonova, Temenuga. *The Image in French Philosophy.* Amsterdam: Rodopi, 2007.
Trifonova, Temenuga. "Multiple Personality and the Discourse of the Multiple in Hollywood Cinema." *The European Journal of American Culture*, 29.2 (2010): 145-71.
Tully, James. "The Kantian Idea of Europe: Critical and Cosmopolitan Perspectives." In *The Idea of Europe: From Antiquity to the European Union*, edited by Anthony Pagden, 331-58. Cambridge: Cambridge UP, 2002.
Uricchio, William. "We Europeans? Media, Representations, Identities." In *We Europeans? Media, Representations, Identities*, edited by William Uricchio, 11-23. Bristol: Intellect Books, 2008.
Valenti, Miguel. *More Than a Movie: Ethics in Entertainment.* London: Routledge, 2018. Vattimo, Gianni. *The End of Modernity: Nihilism and Hermeneutics in Postmodern Culture.* Cambridge, UK: Polity Press, 1991.
Verstraette, Ginette. *Tracking Europe: Mobility, Diaspora, and the Politics of Location.* Durham, NC: Duke UP, 2010.
von Moltke, Johannes. "Sympathy for the Devil: Cinema, History, and the Politics of Emotion," *New German Critique*, No. 102, *Der Untergang? Nazis, Culture, and Cinema* (Fall 2007), 17-43.
Wagner, Peter. "Does Europe Have a Cultural Identity?" In *The Cultural Values of Europe*, edited by Hans Joas and Klaus Wiegandt, 357-68. Liverpool: Liverpool UP, 2008.
Wayne, Mike. *The Politics of Contemporary European Cinema: Histories, Borders, Diasporas.* Bristol: Intellect Books, 2002.
Wheatley, Catherine. "Christianity and European Film." in *The Europeanness of European Cinema*, edited by Mary Harrod, Mariana Liz, and Alissa Timoshkina, 87-99. London: I.B.Tauris, 2015.

Wheatley, Catherine. *Stanley Cavell and Film: Skepticism and Self-Reliance at the Cinema*. London: Bloomsbury, 2019.
Williams, John. *The Ethics of Territorial Borders: Drawing Lines in the Shifting Sand*. London: Palgrave Macmillan, 2006.
Wright, Will. *Sixguns and Society: A Structural Study of the Western*. Berkeley, CA: U of California Press, 1977.
Yegenoglu, Meyda. *Islam, Migrancy and Hospitality in Europe*. New York: Palgrave Macmillan, 2012.
Zambenedetti, Alberto. "Multiculturalism in New Italian Cinema: The Impact of Migration, Diaspora, and the Post-Colonial on Italy's Self-Representation." In *Beyond Monopoly: Globalization and Contemporary Italian Media*, edited by Michela Ardizzoni and Chiara Ferrari, 245–68. Washington DC: Lexington Books, 2009.

INDEX

abjection 84, 96, 101, 115–31, 180
'accented cinema' 29, 80, 135
adoption, trope of 150, 167, 187–91, 225, 250, 260
affect
   and the 'affective turn' 19, 41, 234
   and identity 2, 17–19, 25, 31–2, 45–6, 78, 81, 98, 129, 130, 175, 179, 183, 202–6, 231–5, 244–5
Agamben, Giorgio 38–40, 71–3, 120, 123–4, 167
Amador (film) 245–6
Appadurai, Arjun 22, 25, 31–2, 62, 65

Badiou, Alain 23, 38–40, 70–1, 120–1, 175–6
Balibar, Étienne 14, 17, 23, 25–6, 40, 161
The Barefoot Emperor (film) 222–3
Bauman, Zygmunt 21–2, 64, 69
'belonging' 13, 19, 29, 46, 62–3, 68, 75–8, 84–9, 94–103, 139, 164, 180–1, 209, 232, 257–60
Berlant, Laurent 19, 64, 123, 231–6
biopolitics 118, 235
Biutiful (film) 131, 245–6
borders 3–5, 10, 13, 17, 21–30, 32–4, 42–4, 66, 73–6, 81–2, 92, 98, 134–5, 147, 153, 152–8, 174, 193, 202, 247, 261
Bruckner, Pascal 38–9, 192–3

'camp, the' 38, 61, 71–3, 95, 203, 246
Castoriadis, Cornelius 7–8
'cinema of duty' 69, 178, 202
cinephilia 81–3, 141
class 31, 45, 215, 231–60

colonialism 2, 22, 28, 76–80, 90, 117, 157, 178
communitarianism 41–2
cosmopolitanism 5, 16, 29, 41–3, 72, 76, 177–8, 233
'cruel optimism' 19, 64, 123, 231–6, 254
cultural identity 6, 16, 18, 46, 87, 151, 153, 239

Days and Clouds (film) 240
Dead Europe (film) 206, 207, 223–5
De bon matin (film) 236, 239–40, 244, 257
Deleuze, Gilles 64, 118, 120, 128–30, 203, 234
Derrida, Jacques 23, 37, 40, 175, 177, 179, 180
Diamantino (film) 135, 142–50, 160, 174, 187, 189, 191, 221
diaspora 8, 30, 77, 81, 85
'dissensus' 39, 70–1
Djam (film) 93, 97, 136, 189
'double occupancy' 80, 118, 143, 145–6, 159, 240

Eastern Boys (film) 143, 187, 189, 221
Eat Sleep Die (film) 245, 257–9
Elsaesser, Thomas 31, 45, 71, 80, 83–4, 90, 96, 113, 115–32, 145–6, 153, 159, 173, 194–6, 221, 240
Eternity and a Day (film) 73–5
ethics
   and affect 202–6
   of co-presence 206–26
   and 'the ethical turn' 23, 36–41, 115, 175–80, 193

and the figure of the migrant 173–202
as ideology 38–40, 175–7
Eurimages 82–3
Eurocentrism 9, 38–9, 130, 178, 192–3
'Europe'
and borders 3–5, 13, 17–21, 27–30, 34, 39–40, 43–4, 66, 73–7, 81–2, 92, 98, 116, 147, 153, 157–8, 193, 247, 261
and its Enlightenment legacy 2–7, 13–17, 20, 23, 33–4, 115, 118–29, 175, 194, 209
and migration 3–5, 9, 12, 14, 21–7, 33–4, 36–7, 46, 63, 72–4, 77–84, 91, 96, 179, 193
and trauma 67, 82, 96, 118, 123, 176, 193, 232the idea of 1–2, 9–10, 15–18, 34, 46, 72, 82, 125, 132, 179, 201, 261
European cinema
as post-colonial 77–85, 88
as post-communist 77–9, 83–4
as 'thought experiment' 83, 115–55
as trans-national 76–85, 135, 233
European identity
historical and philosophical foundations 5–10
and memory 2, 9, 44–6, 74, 80, 90, 213, 235
racial foundations 13–15
religious foundations 10–13
political foundations 15–21
European Union 3–4, 6–7, 13–18, 25–6, 28–30, 33, 63, 82, 88, 99, 102–3, 120, 137, 146–8, 151, 163, 182, 184, 198, 217, 222–3, 236, 261
Europhobia 193–4
Evaporating Borders (film) 75–6
exile 8, 30, 66–9, 73, 81, 92–4, 96, 102, 221–2, 237

far right, the 3, 20, 30, 146, 153, 156, 209–10, 261
fascism 24, 119, 196, 208–10, 212, 223, 237

Fire at Sea (film) 174, 199, 203–5
flâneur 29, 65–6, 72–3
'fuzzy concepts' 44, 76, 116

Generazione mille euros (film) 236, 243–4
globalization 11, 21–7, 32, 63, 65, 72–3, 79–80, 84, 90–1, 103, 139, 141, 153, 178, 184, 207, 233

Happy as Lazzaro (film)
Happy End (film) 94, 135, 174, 196–7
Holocaust 14, 38, 84, 118, 173, 176, 189, 206, 213, 218–20, 223–5
home/homeland 29–30
'homo sacer' 37, 72
'hospitality' 36–7, 75, 99, 103–4, 115, 133, 147–9, 157, 166, 177–206, 219, 244–50
The House by the Sea (film) 94, 174, 187–9, 221, 260
Human Flow (film) 202–3
humanitarianism 26–8, 36–40, 83, 93, 115, 173, 179, 194, 203, 218
human rights 4, 8, 27–30, 37, 44, 63, 66, 68, 73–6, 84–7, 90–103, 123, 136, 139–46, 205, 220–4

Illegal (film) 161–2
'imagined community' 29, 32
impersonation, trope of 3, 104, 115, 132–66, 191, 208, 256
In This World (film) 92, 95, 97, 132
The Invader (film) 162–4
Islam 11–14, 36, 118
It's a Free World (film) 151, 181, 245–8, 253, 259

Journey of Hope (film) 91–2
Jupiter's Moon (film) 148, 160, 174, 187, 189–91
justice 1–2, 23, 25–6, 30, 34–41, 43–4, 67, 102–3, 115, 120, 133, 178, 214–15, 218, 226, 254, 259

Kant, Immanuel 1, 16, 37–9, 43, 123, 177, 203, 221
Kristeva, Julia 124, 130

La Nostra Vita (film)   245, 247–8
La Pirogue (film)   92–3, 97, 251
La promesse (film)   180, 184
L'emploi du temp (film)   232, 236, 240, 242, 244
Levinas, Emmanuel   1, 36–7, 39, 67, 120, 124, 130, 175–80
'lieu de memoire'   44, 213
Lorna's Silence (film)   180–1, 186, 253, 257
Louise Wimmer (film)   240–1
Lyotard, Jean-François   38, 40

Mediterranea (film)   174, 205, 245, 248–50
migrant and diasporic cinema   2, 80, 136, 231
migration
  autonomy of   63–9, 123
  and gender   86–90, 115, 132, 135–47, 157, 187
  and genre   77–81, 97–103, 115–16, 132–44, 156, 160, 176, 180, 189, 221–5, 232, 235
  globalization of   5, 23–4, 31, 34, 46, 77, 91, 141
  phenomenological approaches to   61–3, 91, 220
  terminology   26–7
Mi piacce lavorare: mobbing (film)   236, 240, 244, 257
mobility   27–9, 42, 46, 63–5, 71–2, 76–81, 85, 97, 101, 150, 232
Mondays in the Sun (film)   236, 242–3
Morgen (film)   147–9, 160, 191
multiculturalism   14, 21, 42, 66, 85–6, 91, 149, 143–54
My Piece of the Pie (film)   236, 244, 255–7
mythopoetics   2, 77, 114–17, 132, 193

national identity   16, 18, 30–5, 74–6, 78, 83, 85, 90, 98–102, 114, 119, 133, 140, 143, 145–6, 216
nationalism   2, 17, 31–4, 66, 76–9, 82–3, 88, 99–103, 147–56, 223, 231

neoliberalism   1, 22–3, 31–4, 64, 102–3, 116, 132, 151–2, 181–3, 207–10, 231–61
neo-racism   14–15, 131, 161, 241
Nobadi (film)   222
'nomadism'   8, 17, 21, 42, 64–9, 78, 95–8, 103, 136, 178, 186, 222
nostalgia   2, 7–8, 19, 66–8, 74–9, 81–2, 139–41, 207, 235, 239

Once You Are Born You Can No Longer Hide (film)   166–7
The Order of Things (film)   174, 197–9
Orientalism   35, 142
'Other, the'   9–13, 34–41, 62, 75–6, 83, 91, 115, 122–4, 127, 130, 143, 146–9, 159, 166, 175–86, 191–6, 214, 224

'passing' (for white/European)   159–65
'pensiero debole'   113–15
Plato's Academy (film)   144–5
political philosophy   25, 37, 43–4, 65, 71, 76, 179
'politics' versus 'police'   23–6, 40, 69–70
postcolonial guilt   38, 190–3, 200
post-communism   25, 77–9, 83–8, 208–9, 237
post-national
  citizenship   2, 17, 41–3, 66
  Europe   17, 22, 29–33, 77, 79–80, 146
  European cinema   80, 114
precarity   132, 154, 179, 231–60
Princesas (film)   245–6

race
  in European cinema   46, 86–7, 90, 115, 147, 152, 157–67, 241, 249
  and European identity   13–15, 24, 33, 46, 90, 115, 241
Ranciere, Jacques   22–6, 38–40, 69–71, 120–1, 128–9, 164, 175, 203, 210, 214
Ravetto-Biagioli, Kris   77, 114–17, 132, 193

're-bordering' 63
refugee 4–5, 17, 23–7, 31–2, 38, 41–3, 61–5, 69–71, 76–7, 89, 92–5, 101–2, 115, 123, 132–5, 143–67, 173–226, 231–61
refugee crisis 3, 26–7, 93–4, 135, 148–9, 153, 156–8, 163–4, 173, 185, 189, 197–206, 220, 224, 231–2, 244

Samba (film) 164–6
Schlingensiefs Container (film) 260–1
secularism 10–13, 143
Shun Li and the Poet (film) 245, 248–9, 251–2
skepticism 2, 5–10, 37, 39, 42, 115–17, 126–7, 176
The Snows of Kilimanjaro (film) 239, 244, 259–60
spectrality 77, 222
Stranger in Paradise (film) 156–9
Styx (film) 174, 197, 199–201

Terrados (film) 236, 242–3
Terraferma (film) 250–2
Toni Erdmann (film) 150–2
Transit (film) 90, 174, 206–7, 212, 218–26
transnational cinema 80–4, 233
Tutta la vita davanti (film) 236, 241, 243–4
Twin Flower (film) 245, 254–5
Two Days, One Night (film) 236, 239, 240, 244–45, 257
The Unknown Girl (film) 197, 201–2

Valerie (film) 240–1
victimhood 38–40, 63–5, 123–4, 130–2, 136, 153, 157–8, 179, 197, 212–22, 235

Welcome (film) 94, 187–8
Welcome to Germany (film) 148–50
Western (film) 97–104
The Workshop (film) 152–6

www.ingramcontent.com/pod-product-compliance
Lightning Source LLC
Chambersburg PA
CBHW072128290426
44111CB00012B/1819